ACADEMIC FREEDOM

IN THE AGE OF THE COLLEGE

ACADEMIC FREEDOM

IN THE AGE OF

THE COLLEGE

BY RICHARD HOFSTADTER

COLUMBIA UNIVERSITY PRESS

NEW YORK AND LONDON

Academic Freedom in the Age of the College, by Richard Hofstadter, and *Academic Freedom in the Age of the University,* by Walter P. Metzger, were originally published in one volume entitled *The Development of Academic Freedom in the United States,* by Richard Hofstadter and Walter P. Metzger.

PREFACE

ACADEMIC FREEDOM has become one of the central issues of our time. It has been our aim in this volume to write an account of the problem of academic freedom in American colleges and universities from the founding of the first college to the recent past. While we have tried to provide historical perspective on the current struggle over intellectual freedom in higher education, we have tried also to avoid the pitfall of interpreting the past solely from the standpoint of present issues and current anxieties. Ours is an analytical history, not a full-throated polemic for academic freedom. We have no desire to conceal an ineluctable prejudice on behalf of freedom of thought, and we hope and expect that this inquiry will be a history, not an autopsy. Our commitment to freedom has no doubt affected in many ways our treatment of the problem, but our foremost intention has been to shed new light on the history of the academic man and the complex circumstances under which he has done his work, in the faith that an enlargement of understanding will in the end be an enlargement of freedom.

One of our earliest decisions in planning this work was to make it more than a running account of "cases." To write only about the outstanding violations of freedom would be to treat the story of academic freedom as though it were nothing but the story of academic suppression. The cases are, in a sense, the pathology of the problem. The distortions that would arise from dealing with them alone are comparable to those that would be found in a history of the labor movement telling only of strikes, a history of science telling only of the encroachments of theology, or a history of political democracy devoted only to its defeats. It is, of course, an important part of our concern to learn what forces in society have ranged themselves against the freedom of teaching and research and what successes they have scored; but we have also been interested to know what freedom has meant to successive generations of academic men, to what extent they have achieved it, and what factors in academic life itself, as well as in American culture at large, have created and sustained it.

We consider it as much a part of our task to explain why freedom exists as to explain why it has been limited.

Cases, moreover, serve only as guides to the nature of the problem; they do not exhaust its meaning. To ask what it was that men wanted to be free about, why the freedoms they claimed were considered by other men to be improper or dangerous, what arguments were employed on both sides, and where the power lay to settle the issues is to pass from the academic institutions to the community that supported them, set their goals, and (in America at least) governed them. Such questions have led us to try to tell our story against the background of the religious, intellectual, and political issues that gave to academic controversies their special urgency and broad social significance. They have taken us not only into the discussion of such matters as the development of the American form of academic government and the professional organization of academic men, but also into the educational policies of religious denominations, the history of theological controversies, the rise of Darwinism in American thought, and the relations between men of business and men of learning.

Broad as our scope has been, we have not dealt with every aspect of the theme. We have discussed primarily the freedom of faculty members and have dealt with the issue of freedom for students only at those points where the two have converged. In our minds the history of student freedoms and student discipline is a matter of comparable importance, but it is a large and in many respects a separate question that deserves a treatise of its own. We have also confined ourselves to college and university education. Those who are interested in the history of freedom of teaching in schools below college grade will be enlightened by Howard K. Beale's two earlier volumes, *A History of Freedom of Teaching in American Schools* (1941) and *Are American Teachers Free?* (1936). Finally, we have brought our story to a close without treating, except by occasional reference, the current crisis in academic freedom; but this is analyzed in the companion volume sponsored by the American Academic Freedom Project, Professor Robert M. MacIver's *Academic Freedom in Our Time*.

There is a sharp difference between the main concern of Part One, which deals with the American college down to the period just after the Civil War, and that of Part Two, which deals with the modern American university. Part One deals with an age overshadowed by religious and theological questions, Part Two with an age preoccupied with science and social problems. Part One begins with an introductory chapter touching upon some phases of the history of intellectual freedom in the universities of Western Europe up to the time of the Reformation. No reader should imagine that this chapter presumes to be even an abbreviated history of intellectual freedom in the universities of Europe—several volumes would be necessary to accomplish that task—but it seemed desirable to touch upon this background in order to bring the long history of this issue, and the various forms it has taken, to the attention of readers who might be excessively preoccupied with recent events and American conditions. Moreover, while it was clear that whatever we might write on the subject of academic freedom before the Reformation would be more than ordinarily incomplete and inadequate, we did not want to indulge ourselves in the provincialism of beginning our story as though the problem originated with the founding of Harvard College in 1636.

The rest of Part One deals with what might be called the prehistory of academic freedom in our own country. It treats of a period when colleges were under denominational control and there were hardly any universities worthy of the name. In the denominational colleges the problem of academic freedom as we now understand it was hardly posed, for the sponsors of such colleges, on the whole, did not intend that they should be to any significant degree intellectually free, and the men who taught in them had for the most part only the slenderest aspirations toward intellectual freedom. Our inquiry into the severe limitations upon freedom in the old colleges should not be taken as a total indictment of their services to their students and the community or as a denial of their right to exist. But in the pre-Civil War era the denominational colleges not only accorded an inadequate measure of freedom to those who taught and studied in them, but their friends and sponsors were disposed to choke, sabotage, and destroy such attempts as were made to establish larger and more capacious institutions supporting advanced scholarship and providing the conditions of university freedom. Despite these limitations, collegiate education before the Civil War had its own merits and on occasion its significant controversies and gestures toward academic freedom; the period was also one of educational agitation when most advanced thinkers presaged the coming era of university development.

Since religious commitments and sectarian aspirations did so much to create the restrictive atmosphere of the old college and to cramp the early work of the rising university, religious leaders figure in an exceptionally prominent way among the opponents of intellectual freedom in the first half of our story. We hope that no reader will infer from this a commitment to aggressive secularism on the part of the authors. While there are still circumstances under which religious interests can restrict the free expression to which the secular mind is entitled, we are also aware that there is now some likelihood that here or there the unconsciously secularist bias of our formally "religious" but too often spiritually hollow society will impinge upon the full development of the genuinely religious student or scholar. Nor have we forgotten that some of the same religious denominations that a hundred years ago were culpable for their indifference or opposition to intellectual freedom have in recent years produced some of its most impassioned and powerful spokesmen.

With the coming of the modern university, the theme of Part Two, the entire situation was transformed within the life span of a single generation. The university, not the college, became the model institution. While in the ante-bellum period the very existence of the entrenched denominational colleges limited or checked the emergent universities, in the later period the development of universities reshaped in some measure all but the most backward colleges. The emergence of the university was nothing less than an educational revolution in the United States. Research took a place along with teaching as a major function. The methods and concepts of science displaced the authority of religion. The academic profession took on, for the first time in a full measure, the character, aspirations, and standards of a learned profession. Within the university, the growth of resources, the proliferation of activities, the assemblage of large faculties gave impetus to bureaucratization—to tenure rules, formal procedures of promotion and dismissal, the delegation of authority. A self-conscious and well-formulated rationale for academic freedom appeared, framed in terms to fit the new realities of academic life. Aspirations for intellectual freedom that had been expressed in the denominational era only by pioneers or rebels in the colleges were now understood and endorsed by powerful figures of the educational world. While freedom in the modern university was, as it always has been, only imperfectly realized in practice, those who would oppose and limit freedom were now for the first time in our history put upon the moral and intellectual defensive. It may put some of our current difficulties into perspective to realize that the academic freedom which is now under fire is not an ancient prerogative but an acquisition of relatively recent date.

It is impossible to acknowledge by name all the scholars—almost three score of them—who have given freely of their time by reading drafts, offering criticism, catching errors, and providing us with access to materials, but our sincere gratitude goes out to them. Without their help this study would have been far less adequate. We are indebted above all to Louis M. Rabinowitz, who conceived the American Academic Freedom Project and brought to it not only ample resources but the close interest of a generous heart and mind. We are grateful for our association with Robert M. MacIver, the director of the American Academic Freedom Project, whose advice and criticism have been of value on many occasions, and who has consistently shown a quality that must be recommended to administrators of academic research projects—a wise and cordial regard for individuality and independence. Finally, without the help of our research assistants, Francis Wilson Smith, Joseph Katz, and Juan Linz, this work would have taken far longer and would have rested on a much less sufficient base of information.

A word on the nature of our collaboration. Although each author has assumed full and final responsibility for a part of the text—Hofstadter for Part One, Metzger for Part Two—the interpretive structure of this volume and all the major problems that have arisen have been objects of frequent discussion, as the text has been of mutual criticism. Thus, except for the fact that it contains no collaborative prose, this has been in every sense a collaborative enterprise. On most of the broad issues the authors have found themselves—not always at the beginning but usually at the end of discussion—in substantial agreement on the meaning of the facts. If there are still marginal inconsistencies in interpretation or in tone, they remain in the text not through an oversight but as a consequence of our resolve not to try to submerge individual differences for the sake of an unnecessary uniformity.

RICHARD HOFSTADTER
WALTER P. METZGER

Columbia University
in the City of New York
April, 1955

Note: The Preface of this volume is reproduced here exactly as it appeared in Hofstadter and Metzger, *The Development of Academic Freedom in the United States,* of which "Part One" is now *Academic Freedom in the Age of the College,* by Richard Hofstadter, and "Part Two" is *Academic Freedom in the Age of the University,* by Walter P. Metzger.

CONTENTS

ACADEMIC FREEDOM
IN THE AGE OF THE COLLEGE

I: THE EUROPEAN HERITAGE

CORPORATE POWER IN THE MIDDLE AGES

ACADEMIC FREEDOM is a modern term for an ancient idea. Although the struggle for freedom in teaching can be traced at least as far back as Socrates' eloquent defense of himself against the charge of corrupting the youth of Athens, its continuous history is concurrent with the history of universities since the twelfth century. The university is in its origin a medieval institution. The first universities of the Middle Ages emerged gradually, often at centers of clerical learning like the cathedral schools, when the numbers of students and masters grew large enough to require some formal organization. Five universities—Salerno, Bologna, Montpellier, Paris, and Oxford—may be said to have come into existence and reached varying degrees of distinctness and complexity by the end of the twelfth century; and by the end of the thirteenth, the first great century of university development, seventeen others had been founded in Italy, France, Spain, Portugal, and England. Rashdall, in his classic study *The Universities of Europe in the Middle Ages,* enumerated seventy-eight that had been founded in Europe to the end of 1500; most of them were still in existence in that year.[1]

In constitutional form we may distinguish two great traditions stemming from two archetypal universities, Paris and Bologna. Bologna, which began as a center for the study of civil law and soon became noted for canon law as well, was patronized very largely by wealthy or noble families, whose sons were both laymen and clergymen. The teachers themselves were frequently laymen, comparatively free of ecclesiastical supervision or jurisdiction. As foreigners and strangers in Bologna, the

---

[1] Hastings Rashdall, *The Universities of Europe in the Middle Ages* (3 vols.; 1895, ed. by F. M. Powicke and A. B. Emden, Oxford, 1936). Salerno was always chiefly a medical school, while Montpellier in the twelfth century had faculties of medicine and law; in 1289 Montpellier was formally constituted as a general university, or *studium generale,* although it had long functioned in that capacity. Among the later universities discussed by Rashdall, 23 were founded in the fourteenth century and 33 in the fifteenth.

students needed organization; as mature and usually wealthy scholars, they were capable of managing their own affairs and setting terms to the teachers. At Bologna, therefore, the gilds, which *were* the university, were organizations of the students, and the masters were hardly more than the hired men of the students, by whom they were subjected to a rigid and detailed academic discipline.[2]

Paris, a center of theological studies and arts, was by contrast a gild of the masters. There the masters and students were either clerics or were so regarded, and the masters' organizations were the units of the university structure. The Italian, Spanish, and Portuguese universities were modeled after Bologna, while most of the German universities and the two in England were modeled after the University of Paris. Some French universities were universities of masters, but others, notably in the South, were of a mixed nature, fusions of the Parisian and Bolognese types.

In intellectual concerns and ecclesiastical relations the two traditions also diverged. The universities of Italy and some in France were notable individually for their work in civil law or medicine, some of them later for natural philosophy. Founded at centers of commerce where ancient Roman traditions had not been altogether lost, the Italian universities were somewhat secular in their preoccupations. A separate faculty of theology had no place in the early organization of the Italian universities, for instance, and in later stages of the universities' development the study of theology was given but secondary or slight importance. Ecclesiastical interference was comparatively moderate, and, when exercised, was the instrument of political rather than doctrinal objectives.[3]

In the North, notably at Paris and Oxford, theology and philosophy reigned, although many northern universities also taught law and medicine. In those northern centers that specialized in theology and where the study of law was also carried on, the legal studies tended to emphasize canon law. At Paris canon law was of much significance, but civil law was not encouraged. Some northern *studia,* however, among them Orléans and Bourges, were distinguished in civil law. Thus while the southern institutions were at first greatest as centers for the pragmatic studies

---

[2] *Ibid.,* I, 149–51, 195–97. The doctors at Bologna much later formed their own faculty gilds that controlled the eligibility and some activities of their members.

[3] *Ibid.,* II, 62. In the thirteenth century theology was taught only at Paris, Toulouse, Oxford, and Salamanca. The papacy did not encourage the multiplication of faculties of theology, and young institutions often avoided it until long after their founding. Stephen d'Irsay, *Histoire des universités,* I (Paris, 1933), 161, 177.

of law and medicine and were intimately linked through their personnel with local aristocracies, many northern institutions took their cue chiefly from the University of Paris, which was the center of a pan-European intellectual influence resting above all upon its faculties of theology and arts. The northern institutions were more acutely torn than the southern ones by the doctrinal controversies of the Middle Ages and ultimately by the bitter struggles of the Reformation.

A study concerned with the general intellectual history of Europe might well give equal attention to both these university traditions; but for our purpose, which is to shed some light on the background of American higher education, a somewhat stronger emphasis on the northern tradition is desirable. During the Middle Ages the intellectual relations between Paris and Oxford were always close. Cambridge was modeled in a broad sense on Oxford; and Cambridge, together with the English dissenting academies, was the primary formative influence on Harvard and most of the American colonial colleges.[4] To examine a few of the theological and philosophical quarrels that ruffled the northern universities is also to deal with some of the central issues in the history of intellectual liberty.

The modern lay reader, under the influence of an old rationalist stereotype, often thinks of the Middle Ages only as an age of dogma and suppression. Unless, however, the diversity of the social background of the medieval university is envisaged, unless the full vigor of the clash of interests and doctrines in its intellectual milieu, notably in the thirteenth and fourteenth centuries, is seen, neither the remarkable corporate power of the university nor the independence and boldness of some of its outstanding masters will be appreciated fully.

In the social structure of the Middle Ages the universities were centers of power and prestige, protected and courted, even deferred to, by emperors and popes. They held this position chiefly because great importance was attached to learning, not only as a necessary part of the whole spiritual enterprise, but also for its own sake. Great nobles, powerful clerics, men of wealth and influence, could go into a career of learning with the feeling that it was a fit thing to do with their lives. Such a theo-

[4] Only much later, in the post-Civil War era, was the English influence on American higher education superseded to an important degree by the example of the German universities. For the impact of the German universities see below, Chap. VIII. Among the colonial institutions of America, only one, William and Mary, was more profoundly influenced by Oxford than by Cambridge.

logical center as the University of Paris stood at the heart of the spiritual life of the age; at Paris for a time sat most of the great masters of philosophy and the great refiners of doctrine from all Europe.[5] If the universities were spiritual centers, they were scarcely less important as agencies of practical life, whose work was as relevant to the ecclesiastical and political life of the thirteenth and fourteenth centuries as the modern university is to the scientific and industrial life of our time.[6] They provided vocational training for the clerical functionaries of church and state—for notaries, secretaries, legates, and lawyers. Much of the strength of the universities rested upon the personal loyalty of former students or masters who were in places of power, who had an intimate and respectful knowledge of the services of the universities, and who were formally bound to them by oaths of loyalty, informally (and perhaps more effectively) by ties of sentiment.[7]

In internal matters the universities had the prerogative of self-government. They were autonomous corporations, conceived in the spirit of the gilds; their members elected their own officials and set the rules for the teaching craft.[8] Although the most prized teaching license, the *ius ubique docendi,* which gave the scholar the theoretical right to teach at any university,[9] could be granted only by *studia* so authorized by emperors, popes, or kings, internal matters of institutional government were in the hands of those immediately connected with learning. Each faculty made its own rules. Each faculty elected its own head and held its own assemblies—and it is significant of the internal vitality of the corporate body that assemblies were held very often and in secret—while the university as a whole had its general assembly, the congregation.[10]

[5] For an estimate of "The Medieval University in Church and Society," see F. M. Powicke, *Ways of Medieval Life and Thought* (Boston, 1951), pp. 198–212.

[6] Rashdall conjectured that at the close of the Middle Ages a larger portion of the population received a university education than is the case in modern countries. *Cambridge Medieval History,* VI (Cambridge, 1929), 601. Presumably this comparison would not apply to the United States, which in the twentieth century has come to offer a university education, or a facsimile thereof, to an unprecedented portion of the total population.

[7] For the text of such an oath see Lynn Thorndike, ed., *University Records and Life in the Middle Ages* (New York, 1944), pp. 103–5.

[8] The terms *universitas* and *collegium* meant a collectivity, corporation, or any organic group or gild.

[9] For the limitations on this right see Rashdall, *Universities of Europe,* I, 13–15. Of less general application was another teaching license, the *licentia docendi,* which gave the right to teach in the diocese in which it was granted.

[10] For a discussion of the organization of the University of Paris in relation to

While great feuds could and did develop within the universities—examples are those at Paris between the faculties of arts and theology and between the secular clergy and the members of the mendicant orders—the universities were aware that their prestige and power depended upon their capacity for cohesion.[11] As Sir Maurice Powicke says, they were "intensely self-conscious and self-important."[12] The universities were encouraged in this self-importance by the fact that the faculties of the great institutions—Bologna, Paris, Oxford—were consulted again and again on vital questions of doctrine and law, and were expected to state their findings and intervene in ecclesiastical and social affairs. In the early fourteenth century, for instance, the theologians of the University of Paris, with the support of the French king, humbled the Avignon Pope, John XXII, who in his capacity as a private theologian had espoused a doctrine concerning the beatific vision against which they had pronounced almost a century before. In this case they reaffirmed their earlier judgment and appealed to the king to enforce it, a strategy which wrung from the pope a reply "as humble and apologetic as if he were a young student in Paris in danger of losing the bachelor's degree for heresy."[13] Ultimately the pope rather equivocally retracted. At crucial junctures in the affairs of the Church, like the Council of Constance, the universities played an important part. When Henry VIII turned to the English universities for a judgment on his divorce—one of the most famous instances of university consultation—he was acting in a well-established tradition; but that in this instance the judgment was extracted rather than freely given was a sign that the autonomy of the universities had been considerably diminished.

At the time of their greatest independence the universities lived in the interstices of medieval society, taking advantage of its decentralization and the balance of its conflicting powers to further their own corporate interests. The absence of a monolithic structure of power, the existence of a real plurality and diversity of interests within the frameworks of both

---

its corporate power and intellectual freedom see Mary Martin McLaughlin, "Intellectual Freedom and Its Limitations in the University of Paris in the Thirteenth and Fourteenth Centuries," unpublished Ph.D. dissertation (Columbia University, 1952), pp. 31–32. We are heavily indebted to this study.

[11] "Do not divide, always cohere," preached one of the chancellors of Paris, "as individuals we are nothing." D'Irsay, *Histoire*, I, 148.

[12] Powicke, *Medieval Life and Thought*, p. 183.

[13] Rashdall, *Universities of Europe*, I, 553; cf. McLaughlin, "Intellectual Freedom," pp. 362–69.

the ecclesiastical and secular powers, put the universities in a position in which they were not easily overwhelmed. They appealed to king or council against pope, to pope against king or bishop, and to kings and popes alike against truculent town governments.

Moreover, they had weapons of their own that put them above the level of mere appellants and gave them independent bargaining power. Among these weapons was the cessation or suspension of lectures, the academic equivalents of the modern strike. A still more powerful device arose, oddly enough, from their very poverty. Unhampered in the beginning by physical apparatus, great libraries, worldly goods, and substantial college foundations, they could and on occasion did migrate, taking with them their large numbers of students and profitable trade. Such migrations were one of the means of the early spread of universities, since at times migrations resulted in new foundations.[14]

In quarrels with local authorities the universities defended themselves with such vigor—and success—that Rashdall speaks of them as living off their misfortunes. Students were commonly young and riotous, and they regularly made enemies among the townspeople, who resented their privileges and their licentiousness. A major conflict at the University of Paris occurred in 1228–29 when successive forays by students and townsmen, arising out of a tavern brawl, caused the regent, Blanche of Castile, to send a company of soldiers against the students. When several students were killed, the masters suspended lectures in protest. Dissatisfied with the immediate results, they went further: they resolved that if justice were not done to the university within a month, they would disband it for six years, and even then would not return unless satisfactory redress had meantime been given. Nor was this an idle threat: most of the masters and scholars actually left. Many went to Oxford and Cambridge, which were much strengthened by their arrival, others to the smaller *studia generalia* or the cathedral schools of France. The dispersion lasted almost two years. It resulted in the recall of the papal legate who had advised the fatal attack and the issuance of an order from Gregory IX to the King and the Queen Mother that they punish the offenders. It is unclear what other redress was granted to the masters, but the episode was followed by a series of papal bulls enlarging the privileges of the university, among them the bull *Parens scientiarum* (1231), which gave the university

---

[14] Eleven institutions are known to have originated in this fashion down to 1456; see the table in Rashdall, *Universities of Europe,* I, xxiv.

apostolic sanction for the right to suspend lectures and ratified its authority to make its own statutes and punish violators by expulsion. Serious limitations were imposed upon the power to punish scholars possessed by the bishop and the university's chancellors. Several years later the university was given another important exemption, the *ius non trahi extra,* that made it impossible for students to be cited to ecclesiastical courts at a distance from Paris.[15]

Somewhat comparable was the aftermath of the riot of St. Scholastica's Day at Oxford in 1355. The townsmen made a frightful organized assault on the university in which scholars were beaten, tortured, and killed. After lectures had been suspended by the masters for several months, the Bishop of Lincoln put the town under interdict and the king ordered a commission of inquiry. Scores of townsmen were arrested and the mayor of Oxford was imprisoned. Under a new charter the greater part of the government of the town and the regulation of its trade was now turned over to the university. A large company of specified municipal officers was put under obligation to attend an annual mass on St. Scholastica's Day for the souls of the murdered clerks and to make a token offering of a penny apiece in their memories—a quaint practice that was not abolished until 1825.[16]

The very solidarity of the masters in such instances suggests more than *esprit de corps*—it suggests discipline. If masters were to undertake a cessation of lectures or migration in a body, if an entire university, or at least a faculty of theology or canon law, was to render corporate judgments on vital issues, some internal regime that would encourage if not compel agreement was necessary.[17] The idea of corporate action, corpor-

---

[15] Rashdall, *Universities of Europe,* I, 334–43.

[16] Charles E. Mallet, *A History of the University of Oxford* (Oxford, 1924), pp. 160–63; Rashdall, *Universities of Europe,* III, 96–103. Rashdall observes, concerning the frequency and bitterness of Oxford's town and gown riots: "There is probably not a single yard of ground in any part of the classic high Street that lies between S. Martin's and S. Mary's which has not, at one time or another, been stained with blood. There are historic battlefields on which less has been spilt." *Ibid.,* III, 96.

[17] In this respect the modern university can be contrasted with its medieval forerunner. The modern university emphasizes that it has no corporate judgment on disputed public questions. It expects, at least in the United States, that its professors in the course of such public activities as they choose to engage in will dissociate their own opinions from the university's reputation, and it hopes, often in vain, that the public will understand that the professor speaks only for himself. The recent tendency among some academic men in the United States to propose more rigorous academic self-discipline or self-censorship in return for an anticipated broader respect for university independence from the community shows a disposition, how-

ate judgment, and corporate power implies some sacrifice of individual independence. Thus, far from being an unqualified guarantee of individual freedom, the corporate power of the university was in some important respects at odds with it. Every corporate unit of the University of Paris, for instance—the nations, the colleges, and the separate faculties—adopted statutes and ordinances affecting almost every conceivable facet of academic life, from trivial details of dress to the subjects and methods of lectures and disputations. (In addition the Dominicans and Franciscans within the academic community were subject, under penalty of the loss of their academic privileges, to the regulations of their own orders.) To insure an understanding of and obedience to the regulations, upon their admission to the faculties masters were expected to take oaths in which they promised to obey the statutes, keep university secrets, and observe cessations. Such oaths give evidence of the premium placed by the university upon its code of internal discipline.[18] A recent student of the history of the University of Paris concludes:

More important in the history of freedom in the university than the sporadic intervention of ecclesiastical authorities were the efforts of the masters themselves to regulate and sometimes to restrict the teaching of their colleagues. For the liberties which enabled them to exercise their intellectual functions made possible also the corporate imposition and enforcement of restrictions. Now it was the institution and its parts which not only claimed freedom but exercised control.[19]

From this it should not be inferred either that the solidarity of the universities was complete (for internal feuds were in fact a vital part of university history), or that the corporate power of the universities involved a net loss to the personal freedom of their members. Far more than the modern university the medieval university was a self-contained intellectual community; not only did the daring and the novelties it produced come from within, but the pressure for intellectual conformity also came chiefly from within. But some faculty, some order, some corporate interest was likely to fly to the aid of most unorthodox thinkers, and it

ever unwitting, to move somewhat closer to the medieval equipoise between corporate autonomy and academic freedom. The difference—and the difficulty—is that the modern American university neither shows the militancy nor enjoys the respect of the medieval university.

[18] On oaths see Rashdall, *Universities of Europe,* I, 378–80; the university seems at length to have called for so many oaths that their sanctity and value were seriously deflated.

[19] McLaughlin, "Intellectual Freedom," pp. 28–29.

was rare indeed that anyone stood alone. In return for their loyalty, teachers were surrounded by an institutional framework that supported their pride and security as men of learning and offered them a vigorous defense against interference. Indeed, in great crises the positions even of such notable heretics as Wyclif and Huss were for a time strengthened by powerful support given them within their universities. As in so many of the relations of medieval life, the interplay between corporate power and individual freedom was complex and many-sided.

PERSONAL FREEDOM IN THE MIDDLE AGES

Freedom, if it is to be meaningful, must ultimately be exercised by individuals. When we turn from the corporate position of the medieval universities and their faculties to the role of the individual thinker, we find him working under conditions that cannot simply be described as free or unfree. He existed, if he had something important to say, in a state of tension between submission to authority and self-assertion.

The term authority, of course, is ambiguous. We must distinguish between positive authority and the authority of tradition. Positive authority —that is, external pressure in the form of positive acts brought to bear by academic or ecclesiastical or civil power—leaves its open record in the form of regulations and prohibitions, censures and censorship, and overt acts of persecution. While the intimidating effects of positive authority are not measurable, its rise and decline can at least be traced by the historian with some degree of specificity. But the authority of traditional belief and the power of deferential habits of thought are intangible; they are woven into the whole texture of intellectual life, and their influence can be assessed only in a highly impressionistic way. When Henry Osborn Taylor speaks of deference to authority as "a first general quality of mediaeval thought," [20] what he means is authority in the second of these two senses. The inherited pattern of deference to philosophic authority, as well as the traditional desire for salvation itself—a goal superior to inquiry—were doubtless far more imposing and consistently operating inhibitions on free speculation than were the formal acts of the Church.[21]

[20] Henry Osborn Taylor, *The Mediaeval Mind*, II (Cambridge, 1949), 327–28.
[21] Cf. Taylor, *Mediaeval Mind*, II, 326: "even in the great twelfth and thirteenth centuries, intellectual inquiry was never unlimbered from bands of deference, nor ever quite dispassionately rational or unaffected by the mortal need to attain a salvation which was bestowed or withheld by God according to His plan authorita-

In all ages the weight of tradition presses in varying degrees upon the capacity of the individual to pose new hypotheses and find new truths. In the Middle Ages tradition was, if Taylor is right, particularly formidable; but to say that it suppressed originality and destroyed the power of the scholastics to produce novelty would be to fly in the face of the intellectual resourcefulness of academic men during the twelfth, thirteenth, and fourteenth centuries. As C. R. S. Harris argues:

> It is undeniable that the dogmas of the Church exercised an influence which was paramount. But this influence was psychological rather than authoritative in the sense of external compulsion. . . . At the height of its maturity medieval thought displayed a latitude which is truly surprising; the speculations of the twelfth and thirteenth centuries contain a diversity which quite belies the notion of any orthodoxy rigorously imposed from without.[22]

The intellectual freedom of the medieval scholar existed within the framework of an authoritative system of faith upheld by vigilant positive authority. The fact that a certain kind of freedom existed within that framework is undeniable; the value that is assigned to it will vary in accordance with the religious and philosophic convictions of the observer. If it were one's sole aim to compare the medieval with the modern world one might with justice emphasize the gravity of the restrictions on inquiry in the medieval university as they appear to the modern intelligence. But since it is our purpose to enter sympathetically into the spirit of the medieval academic experience and to understand the function of the medieval university from the point of view of its period, it is necessary to take for the moment a relativistic view, accepting as given the medieval framework of ideas.

---

tively declared." One can only refer the reader to Taylor's brilliant discussion of this theme (II, 323–28), and the critical comments by Maurice De Wulf, *Philosophy and Civilization in the Middle Ages* (Princeton, 1922), pp. 170–72.

[22] C. R. S. Harris, *Duns Scotus,* I (Oxford, 1927), 40; the order of the sentences has been transposed here. The inherent complexities of the problem of freedom in the medieval framework are illustrated by the same writer when he observes a few pages later, apropos the recantation of Roscellinus: "No dialectic, however persuasive, could be tolerated which imperilled the doctrine of the Church. . . . Whenever a conflict arose between faith and reason, the result was a foregone conclusion; the freedom of thought was limited not so much by an external authority . . . as by the psychological convictions of the unanimous consensus of Christendom, which was impervious to argument, however cogent, and totally unaware of any inconsistency in its attitude." *Ibid.,* p. 47. The illustration, however, does not quite fit the point, for Roscellinus' recantation seems to have been impelled more by external authority in the form of the Council of Soissons than by psychological conviction.

While the tension between faith and inquiry, between the individual and traditional authority, involves hardly less than the history of medieval thought, it is possible at least to convey some idea of the extent to which positive authority was brought to bear and the means used to confront or evade it. Here we may take the fields of philosophy and theology as a touchstone—but it should be emphasized that this procedure is somewhat prejudicial to the Middle Ages, for these two were the most difficult and controversial areas, not the freest. In such fields as law and medicine, grammar and logic, mathematics, statics, optics, and meteorology,[23] prescribed limits were far less restricting than they were for philosophers and theologians, and, as the late C. H. Haskins pointed out, "experiment and research were much freer than has been supposed." [24] The scientific subjects were pursued about as freely if not as effectively as they were in antiquity or in early modern times, and in some of them the groundwork was laid for the development of early modern science. The striking antagonism between religion and science that we find in early modern times was not so characteristic of the Middle Ages, when men of science, so often clerics themselves, maintained a deferential view of theology but went on quietly with their work. Lynn Thorndike once dropped the challenging remark that

there seems no adequate proof for a single specific instance of persecution of men of science by the church for purely scientific views in the twelfth and thirteenth centuries. The occasions when such men got into trouble and when we know the reason why, are just those occasions when they left science to dabble in theological or ecclesiastical concerns.[25]

[23] These subjects are designated here in accordance with modern, not medieval, terminology. In the Middle Ages the lines were not so sharply drawn, and these subjects (except for law and medicine) were pursued as secular studies in the faculty of arts.

[24] C. H. Haskins, *The Renaissance of the Twelfth Century* (Cambridge, Mass., 1939), pp. 360–61; see his discussion of freedom of thought, pp. 360–65, and in *The Rise of the Universities* (New York, 1923), pp. 68–78. Other brief discussions of freedom in the medieval university are those of A. J. Carlyle in F. S. Marvin, ed., *Progress and History* (Oxford, 1916), pp. 89–90, De Wulf, *Philosophy and Civilization in the Middle Ages*, pp. 71–72, and Edgar N. Johnson, "The Background of the University Tradition," in *Freedom and the University* (Ithaca, 1950). G. G. Coulton takes a much dimmer view than most writers of medieval freedom in his *Medieval Panorama* (Cambridge, Mass., 1938), Chap. XXII and *passim,* as he does in his other writings.

[25] Lynn Thorndike, "Natural Science in the Middle Ages," *Popular Science Monthly,* LXXXVII (September, 1915), 279. For a single case in the fourteenth century that may possibly be an exception to this generalization, see Thorndike's *A History of Magic and Experimental Science,* Vol. II (New York, 1929), Chap.

Even in theology and philosophy there was a significant margin for the movement of the mind. Confronted as they were by the task of putting together the traditions of classical philosophy with the teachings of Scripture and the symbology of the faith, the Christian thinkers found themselves working in a realm of inquiry that left large, and to them significant, areas of inquiry open to argument and susceptible to the innovative force of great minds. A hierarchy of authorities might be accepted and defined, but the authorities themselves did not agree, and thus their pronouncements had to be construed, reconciled, even on occasion contradicted, by reason. "Authority," said Alain de Lille in the twelfth century, "has a nose of wax that can be turned in any direction." [26] When in his *Sic et non,* which appeared before the opening of the university era, Abelard ranged together the conflicting opinions of authority on point after point, he was quickening a major method of scholastic criticism. The supreme art of the scholastics was dialectic; and while dialectic had limitations of its own it fed the need of the masters for the clash of mind against mind.[27] It was from the Middle Ages that early modern education inherited the disputation as an academic form, whose value as a medium for the cultivation of ordered thought and cogent expression should not be minimized.[28]

LXXI. Not always, of course, was the line between scientific and theological concerns a clear one.

In such a field as medicine the weight of traditional authority seems far more important in impeding progress than the positive intervention of the Church. The Church attempted to keep clerics from practicing medicine, but for reasons of church discipline, not out of hostility to medical knowledge. Possibly this tendency to make medicine more of a laic profession was an aid to its development. Dissection was not, as often asserted, forbidden by the Church, and dissections became fairly common after 1300. Progress in anatomy was chiefly obstructed by a traditional deference to Galen and Avicenna so intense that teachers of anatomy could obstinately see in a corpse what Galen said would be there, even when it was not, or would attribute discrepancies to changes in the text made by translators or copiers.

[26] Maurice De Wulf, *The History of Mediaeval Philosophy* (New York, 1952), I, 222–23.

[27] Late medieval developments in formal logic also helped to lay some of the foundations for early modern science.

[28] See the brief appreciation of the disputation in Meyrick H. Carré, *Phases of Thought in England* (Oxford, 1949), pp. 94–99. The author remarks (p. 99): "The persistent effort to meet objections against a philosophical position was an education in agile and searching thought. . . . An Oxford or Cambridge scholar of the thirteenth century was obliged to penetrate deeply into the principles in which he believed. . . . The universities afforded a more thorough training in strenuous abstract thinking than was afforded in any later period in England." James J. Walsh has pointed to the enduring pedagogical value of the disputation in colonial American colleges in his *Education of the Founding Fathers of the Republic* (New York, 1935), Chap. X and *passim.*

If some social and professional factors made for timidity on the part of the medieval scholars, others encouraged daring and forcefulness. If there were timid masters of the sort Godfrey of Fontaines rebuked when he wrote: "Masters should be diligently aware lest, frightened where there is nothing to be feared, they think they have good reason for being silent when there is none; few are to be found who can be blamed for excess in speaking truth, but many indeed for silence," [29] the very existence of such an exhortation bespeaks the presence of men of a different turn of mind. One is struck by the appearance among the outstanding scholars of figures of enormous independence and self-confidence, even of arrogance—men of the temper of Abelard, Roger Bacon, and William of Ockham. Some scholars, coming from noble families, added the pride of learning to the pride of place.[30] But whether the scholar's origin was high or low, he was given to feeling that the man of knowledge should have an exalted role in the world. Moreover, he might well be ambitious, like men in other high places, and there was no great distinction to be won by those who could only parrot what had been handed down to them. The greatest numbers of students flocked to hear arresting and stimulating minds like Abelard's; the highest honors were won by ambitious constructions like that of Aquinas—among whose propositions, it should be remembered, were several once cited as unorthodox. Mediocrity might be docile, but high aspiration pressed nervously at the outer limits of the received doctrines. The roll of those whose ideas received some measure of unfavorable attention from some ecclesiastical authority from the twelfth to the fourteenth century is impressive—Roscellinus, Abelard, Gilbert de la Porée, Roger Bacon, Siger de Brabant, Peter John Olivi, Arnald of Villanova, Meister Eckhart, William of Ockham, Nicholas of Autrecourt, Pietro d'Abano, Marsilius of Padua—even Peter Lombard and Aquinas.[31]

One must conclude that the medieval period was neither the nightmare of dogmatism, cruelty, and suppression that it was held to be by the rationalist scholars of the nineteenth century nor the magnificently open ground for free expression that some modern medievalists at times seem

[29] McLaughlin, "Intellectual Freedom," p. 2.
[30] Cf. De Wulf's suggestion that the formulation of the conceptualist doctrine may have been related to the proud individualism of the sons of chevaliers (*Philosophy and Civilization in the Middle Ages*, p. 59).
[31] This list leaves out not only many lesser figures but also such men as Joachim of Floris and Ramon Lull, who were not university teachers but had much influence in the universities.

to be portraying. Intellectual freedom has, of course, both its objective and subjective aspects. A man is objectively free insofar as his society will allow him to express novel or critical ideas without the threat of formal or informal punishment of any serious kind. He is subjectively free insofar as he *feels* free to say what he wishes. Subjective freedom may exist without objective freedom wherever men are so completely confined by the common assumptions of their place, time, or class that they are incapable of engendering any novel or critical ideas that they care to express, and where in fact the expression of such ideas would be dangerous. Such men would be conscious of no restraints, but they would not be free. A high degree of intellectual freedom may be said to exist where both subjective and objective freedom prevail in a considerable measure, and where the latter is present in reasonable proportion to the former. Modern scholars agree that there was considerable liberty in the medieval universities. The range of that liberty was much narrower than that which exists in universities reared under the modern democracies and in the spirit of modern scientific inquiry. But to set up the full range of ideas that can be safely professed in the universities of a modern democracy as an absolute standard for other ages would be perhaps marginally illuminating but unhistoric. Grant the limits of the faith, more elastic than we sometimes incline to believe, within which the medieval scholar himself was usually content to work, and one finds that the range of problems that he dealt with, the variety of solutions, the area of choice that confronted him, were still considerable. Subjectively and objectively he enjoyed a measure of freedom—large enough to make possible creative work of great value but limited enough to bring creative thinkers again and again into conflict with authority—most commonly the authority of their own university colleagues. When such conflicts arose it was not always authority that, in the long run, triumphed.

To define clearly either the difference or the similarities between medieval and modern freedom of inquiry is a task for a far larger study than ours. But one difference that will at once strike the inquirer is that between the two conceptual models of intellectual inquiry and between the amount of emotional tension connected with unorthodox ideas in the Middle Ages and the present day. The modern academic community in a democratic state, although often unable fully to realize it, assumes the right of free inquiry. The medieval academic community, although frequently and intentionally breaching it, assumed the right of some authority to exercise censorship and proscription in theology and on such conclusions of philosophy as were deemed to encroach upon theology. While the Middle Ages sought for unity and completeness in these fields,[32] the modern mind generally accepts as not only inevitable but desirable the existence of a plurality of philosophical perspectives. In many fields there is available to modern inquiry an elaborate apparatus of verification for which there was no adequate medieval counterpart; and the process of verification lowers the level of intellectual animus, takes the center of authority out of the realm of the personal and political, and refers it to criteria that are impersonal and detached. The medieval model of inquiry was limited by the presence of a hard core of accepted doctrine, authoritatively established, which was defined and enforced, made obligatory on all thinkers at the risk not only of their worldly position but of their spiritual privileges and possibly even their eternal souls. Each new accretion of knowledge was expected to be consistent with sound doctrine. Assumed was the desirability, indeed the inevitability, of a single system of truth, anchored in God, and elaborated by man in accordance with a rigorous system of inference.[33] (Of course, the unsettled questions relating to that system were admitted by all but the most anti-intellectualist thinkers to be numerous and important.) Medieval scholars seem for the most part not to have desired to challenge this model of truth when considered abstractly; most of them accepted the notion of a system stemming from a central body of authority, and the concept that somewhere the power must be located to define with finality the limits of truth and of inquiry. In the concrete, however, they were never able to agree on the substantive questions of what could be inferred from or what interfered with the central core of the faith, or on the jurisdictional question of who should have the authority to condemn which propositions and under what circumstances. In short, while they submitted themselves to the Church and the broader principles of the faith, both inwardly, it would seem, and outwardly, some of them did not feel obliged to accept the idea that the hierarchy represented the true Church. It was of the

[32] On this theme in medieval culture see De Wulf, *Philosophy and Civilization in the Middle Ages,* Chap. V. Perhaps it should be added that this quest for ideal unity was itself in part a product of the actual diversity of the Middle Ages.

[33] In theory philosophy was to enjoy independence of theology, but the major philosophical issues had a way of being bound up with theological ones. Thus twelfth-century logical and ontological discussions were associated with heresies concerning the Trinity, while the thirteenth-century reception of Aristotle led some thinkers toward allegedly anti-Christian views.

utmost importance that the outline of the Church's authority was never precisely drawn, even though everyone might think it desirable that the matter should somehow be capable of settlement.

From the standpoint of the Church itself, freedom existed not by design but by default. The exercise of daring and initiative in touchy areas of thought went on not because the Church recognized or openly encouraged the individual's right of free inquiry, but because the Church, at various times and in varying degrees, found it unnecessary, undesirable, inexpedient, or impossible to suppress the work of scholars who were often well protected, tenacious, and powerfully motivated. Very often the Church intervened in intellectual life only because the disputes in the university led to insistent charges of heresy by some group of scholars that could not be ignored.

The various condemnations and censures of the thirteenth and fourteenth centuries, it is true, add up to an enormous imposition on inquiry in philosophy and theology. That it was not a fatal imposition is much to the credit of the scholars whose beliefs were questioned; in many cases they showed a hardihood and stubbornness in the pursuit of truth that outlasted and even reversed condemnations. Modern scholarship tends to emphasize the variety, boldness, and ultimate fruitfulness of the academic work of the thirteenth and fourteenth centuries. These qualities were achieved under difficult circumstances; the considerable measure of freedom enjoyed by many distinguished masters in the great days of the medieval university was not handed to them as a generous offering of Church or society, but was laboriously and patiently wrested from meddlesome colleagues, bishops, or papal legates at much sacrifice. One cannot escape the feeling that intellectual life in the medieval university, as compared with that of our own age, was lived at an exceptionally high voltage, that the morale and tenacity of the medieval masters at their best marks a high point in the history of the human spirit.

In justice to the Church it should be said that if its theory did not allow for freedom of thought, its practice was far from consistently repressive. Before the emergence of the university system, indeed, the Church had been rather inefficiently organized for the repression of speculation.[34] For centuries it had of necessity been much more concerned with the defense of its temporal interest than with the detailed definition

[34] Cf. the discussion of the subject by A. J. Macdonald, *Authority and Reason in the Early Middle Ages* (Oxford, 1933).

of points of dogma or with interference with the work of scholars.[35] The cathedral schools had been relatively free from interference by positive authority in their substantive intellectual tasks, although in the matter of their external administration a considerable amount of ecclesiastical exhortation and some regulations were forthcoming.[36] The Church seems to have had, at the beginning of the university era, no regular mechanism for the censorship of scholarly work.[37] However, in the twelfth century, when some individual thinkers seemed to be veering into dangerous ground, the Church began to raise a heavy hand, in the form of the condemnation of books or doctrines deemed heretical; such condemnation usually proceeded from the councils of bishops. Notable in this respect were the condemnations of some of the ideas of Roscellinus, Abelard, and Gilbert de la Porée. These were serious and harmful incursions upon freedom of speculation. They inhibited, but could not altogether quiet, their victims; they checked the growth of, but did not stifle, new ideas. Repeatedly it happened that ideas that were subject to condemnations long afterward continued to receive respectful attention from scholars. The notions of some nominalist writers, for instance, might be condemned and yet survive for generations to excite agitated controversy in the schools. Aristotle was proscribed at one point and yet became the established object of study and source of authority for the next generation.

During the very period in which the university system was taking form, the attitude of the Church was growing much harsher. At the same time it found itself more capable, when it was considered necessary, of carrying out organized repression. In the thirteenth century, an age of increasingly defined doctrine and also of well-organized heresy, the Church reached the zenith of its power, spiritual and temporal. The Waldensian and Albigensian movements had made the Church's officials alert to the danger of its destruction, and about 1230 the existing, relatively informal,

[35] Even J. B. Bury, in his rationalist polemic, *A History of Freedom of Thought* (New York, 1913), concedes that before the end of the twelfth century the Church was far from systematic in its pursuit of heresy, that it was "mainly guided by considerations of its temporal interest, and was roused to severe action only when the spread of false doctrines threatened to reduce its revenues or seemed a menace to society" (pp. 55–56).

[36] See the brief survey by E. P. Pride, "Ecclesiastical Legislation on Education, A.D. 300–1200," *Church History*, XII (December, 1943), 235–54. D'Irsay concludes that this tradition was substantially continued in the early university period. *Histoire*, I, 149–50.

[37] G. B. Flahiff, "The Ecclesiastical Censorship of Books in the Twelfth Century," *Mediaeval Studies*, IV (1942), 1–22.

means for the location and trial of heretics were replaced by the systematic machinery of the Inquisition. But intellectual life had already been enormously quickened by the recovery of the greater part of the works of Aristotle. The philosophical and doctrinal ferment was further complicated by the rise of the mendicant orders and the problems they created by their entrance into the universities, where conflicts arose between regulars and seculars and between Dominicans and Franciscans. Thus the universities arose in a period of ecclesiastical and doctrinal turmoil and considerable repression, and at least one of them (Toulouse, in 1229) was founded for the specific purpose of providing a doctrinal antidote to the heresies of Languedoc.[38]

The Church had always been far more concerned about doctrinal deviations that had a practical bearing upon its safety and power than upon those that were primarily of academic significance and offered it no fundamental challenge. Gregory of Heimburg in the fifteenth century sardonically declared that it was safer to discuss the power of God than the power of the popes.[39] Thus the existence of heretical movements or tendencies among the population at large made certain positions more dangerous for teachers to espouse. A suggestion playfully discussed in the dialectical process was one thing; an idea that corresponded with a popular heresy, a schismatic tendency, an attack on the friars, or the antipapal objectives of some powerful prince was quite another. Heretical scholars who risked their necks over matters of such fundamental importance might survive, but only by the grace of powerful protectors far

[38] Cf. Rashdall, *Universities of Europe,* II, 162: "It was . . . recognized that even among the clerks of Paris the spirit of inquiry and bold speculation had made great advances: at Toulouse the danger was to be avoided by a careful choice of teachers." However, when the masters of Toulouse issued a circular letter in 1229 to invite other teachers to join them, they promised: "Those who wish to scrutinize the bosom of nature to the inmost can hear here the books of Aristotle which were forbidden at Paris. What then will you lack? Scholastic liberty? By no means, since tied to no one's apron strings you will enjoy your own liberty." Thorndike, *University Records and Life in the Middle Ages,* p. 34.

[39] H. C. Lea, *A History of the Inquisition of the Middle Ages* (New York, 1887), III, 569. This principle was more applicable during the days of the secularized Renaissance popes than it had been earlier. Cf. Mandell Creighton, *Persecution and Tolerance* (London, 1895), p. 109: "Leo X was tolerant of the philosophic doubts of Pomponazzi concerning the immortality of the soul, because such speculations were not likely to affect the position of the Papacy; but could not allow Luther to discuss the dubious and complicated question of indulgences, because it might have disastrous effects upon the system of papal finance."

For evidence, however, on the extent to which issues of ecclesiastical politics were discussed at Paris, see McLaughlin, "Intellectual Freedom," Chaps. IV, V.

stronger than the universities themselves. Thus in the early fourteenth century, Marsilius of Padua, at one time a rector of the University of Paris, an opponent of papal power, and one of the most significant political thinkers of the Middle Ages, fled from Paris in the company of John of Jandun, who shared his opposition to papal power, to the court of Louis of Bavaria, where both men placed themselves under the German emperor's protection. William of Ockham, after preaching somewhat similar views, took the same course. Toward the end of the century John Wyclif, an influential theologian at Oxford, was protected by John of Gaunt, the Duke of Lancaster, one of the most powerful men in England. For his political opposition to the Church Wyclif found widespread backing, not only from John but within Oxford; but when he went on to espouse a sweeping range of heresies touching upon the Eucharist, he lost many friends and was expelled from the university along with some of his followers. Further prosecution was probably prevented only by his death, which occurred when the controversy inspired by his teaching was still raging.[40] Not long afterward, John Huss, the rector of the University of Prague, was condemned by the Council of Constance and, despite strong support both in his university and among the Bohemian populace, was brought to the stake.[41] A century later Martin Luther, who was teaching at the University of Wittenberg at the time he posted his ninety-five theses, survived and triumphed only with the protection of powerful lay lords.

But these are all spectacular cases in which men who were playing an important role in political and religious life happened to be doing so as occupants of academic posts. That Wyclif, Huss, and Luther were all academic men, like many other prominent reformers of the age, is testimony to the significance of academic life even after the great age of the medieval universities was over, but the fate of these men belongs more intimately to the broader story of religious liberty than to that of intellectual freedom in the universities. Their histories would be a poor point from which to estimate the situation of the characteristic academic man, or to test the common processes of academic life. What of the more typical university masters whose teaching led them a little off the beaten path?

Presumably Paris, with its great influence and its conspicuous place in

[40] For Wyclif and Lollardry at Oxford see Mallet, *History of Oxford*, I, 221–40, and the more recent study by Joseph H. Dahmus, *The Prosecution of John Wyclyf* (New Haven, 1952), esp. Chap. III.
[41] Rashdall, *Universities of Europe*, II, 225–34.

the Church, supplies a somewhat untypical example of university affairs
It serves, however, to confront us with the most intense realization of th
medieval struggle between freedom and authority. It was the center o
European intellectual life, destined not only to find some of its masters
works under censure or condemnation but to be in the end a center o
settled authority in its own right. During the thirteenth century Paris wa
rocked by a series of crises in whose course the masters waged an inter
mittent struggle against the watchdogs of authority, papal, episcopal, an
academic.

The first and most severe of these crises, which grew out of the increas
ing worries of ecclesiastical authorities over heresies outside and bol
speculative thinking inside the university, was a manifestation of th
generally heightened concern for doctrinal orthodoxy shown in the Fourt
Lateran Council in 1215. From the standpoint of the masters, particularl
those of the arts faculty, this struggle was an attempt to preserve unde
mounting pressure the freedom they already enjoyed.

In 1210 a council of bishops, for the first and only time, treated
speculative movement among the Paris masters very much as it woul
have treated a popular heresy. Amalric de Bène, a master of arts who ha
turned to the study of theology, had developed a system of though
influenced by Neoplatonism and particularly by the work of John Scotu
Erigena, which has been described as pantheistic. Some of his own col
leagues had censured him and he had appealed to the pope, but thei
judgment was upheld and he was compelled to retract his errors. A num
ber of his followers, however, carried on with the implications of his wor
and developed it into an heretical movement that had already spread out
side the university itself. A synod at Paris not only condemned a list o
relevant errors but acted with a severity that was "unique in the histor
of the medieval university of Paris." [42] The same synod (in which,
should be noted, some of the masters of the university took part) con
demned and burned the writings of David of Dinant, a teacher whos
works showed the influence of the rediscovered writings of Aristotle
While the characteristic penalty for masters who were recusant unde
accusation was the loss of ecclesiastical and teaching offices, and perhap
excommunication, the dissenters of 1210 were shown little mercy. Te
of the heretics who followed Amalric, all either masters or former stu

[42] McLaughlin, "Intellectual Freedom," p. 26; cf. pp. 25–26, 57–60 for thi
movement. See also Rashdall, *Universities of Europe*, I, 354–56.

lents at Paris, were degraded from their clerical rank and released to the
ecular authority; four others were degraded and imprisoned for life.
Nine or ten were burned in November, 1210. Thus they were treated not
.s academic men customarily were, but as the Inquisition was later to
reat popular heretics, and probably because their belief was regarded in
he same light as a popular heresy. One might have expected a repressive
.ction of such savagery to quiet for an indefinite period any experimenta-
ion with further novelties or heresies. In fact it was followed by a period
•f remarkable speculative activity,[43] and by a notable expansion in the
vork and interests of the arts faculty.

The outbreak of bold philosophizing that conservative theologians were
omplaining of at Paris from the late twelfth through the early years of
he thirteenth century was now climaxed by an intellectual revolution
entering around the rediscovery of the greater part of the works of Aris-
otle, which had been unknown to Latin Christianity. Now the older and
nore traditional teachers in the theological faculty were challenged by
'ounger men who liked to mix their theology with philosophy; and the
heological faculty found itself disturbed by the tendency of the philoso-
•hers in the arts faculty to address themselves to questions previously
he concern of theologians.[44]

The story of the reception of the new Aristotle is a good example of
low the institutional inconsistencies of the Church and the tenacity of
ome of the masters helped intellectual innovation. In what seems to have

[43] Thirty years after the executions of 1210 Albertus Magnus still found it worth
vhile to refute in detail the ideas of David of Dinant. This seems to have been part
•f a general effort to prevent Aristotle from being compromised by such heterodox
ollowers. See G. Théry, *Autour de décret de 1210* (Paris, 1925).

[44] Two significant mid-century cases seem to have arisen in good part as a
consequence of internal rivalries. In 1247 John of Brescain was cited before the
papal legate, the chancellor, masters of theology, and others on the ground that
1e had repeatedly espoused several errors in teaching logical exercises. With him
vas involved a Master Raymond who had already been imprisoned. It was decided
hat John of Brescain, for introducing theological questions and heretical opinions
nto logical exercises, should be deprived of the right to teach and expelled from
he city and diocese of Paris. McLaughlin, "Intellectual Freedom," pp. 81–83.
Another very bitter constitutional struggle, that between the secular clergy and
he mendicant friars over the place of the latter in the university, resulted in an
mportant case in 1256. William of St. Amour, a leader among the secular masters,
1ad written an apocalyptic tract against the mendicant orders, pointing to the rise
•f these orders as a sign of the coming of the Antichrist and the end of the world.
Despite remarkably bold support among the secular masters, his book was con-
1emned. He refused, unlike some of his fellows, to retract, was banished from
France and suspended forever from preaching or teaching. Rashdall, *Universities
•f Europe*, I, 385–89.

been an original effort to choke off at its source the impending revolution, the synod of 1210 had forbidden the reading or teaching at Paris of some unspecified works of Aristotle on natural philosophy, an act which was ratified in 1215 by the papal legate, who confirmed a body of statutes drawn up by the masters. But the intellectual riches of the new Aristotle were a powerful temptation. Presumably there was at first no public violation of the prohibition, but one of the chancellors complained that the forbidden works were being read secretly, another that the students liked nothing but to read forbidden books. By 1228 Pope Gregory IX was warning the faculty of theology against trying to confirm theological doctrines by resorting to philosophy. In 1231 he opened the door to a retreat by the Church when he authorized the prior of the Dominicans to absolve all masters and students who had violated the prohibition against lecturing on or reading the forbidden books, and the masters of arts were told that they were not to use these books until they were purged of objectionable matter. Such a purgation seems never to have taken place—at any rate it would have been difficult to solve the problem by such a procedure, for Aristotle had to be taken in hand and interpreted more or less whole in order to be Christianized. In the 1240s, for instance, Roger Bacon openly flouted the fading prohibition by lecturing on the proscribed books, and at this time Aristotle seems to have been rapidly gaining in popularity among both the faculties of arts and theology.[45] Gradually the internal opposition to the new Aristotle collapsed. In 1243 the new pope, Innocent IV, repeated Gregory's promise of an expurgation and for the first time extended the prohibition to the University of Toulouse, where the new Aristotle had been freely taught for fourteen years. But by 1255 Aristotle was not only studied but was prescribed reading in the faculty of arts at Paris, even though no expurgation had been made. Thus within a period of thirty years, thanks to the stubbornness of the masters and the laxity of the authorities, his natural philosophy had run the entire range from unqualified proscription to general use.[46]

[45] The literature on the gradual dissolution of the prohibition is briefly reviewed by Stewart Easton, *Roger Bacon and His Search for a Universal Science* (New York, 1952), pp. 35–45; cf. McLaughlin, "Intellectual Freedom," pp. 60 ff.

[46] Oddly enough, the now obsolete and unenforceable prohibition was actually renewed as late as 1263. Mandonnet suggests that the Church saw real value in the study of Aristotle but was inhibited by fear of the heresies he might unleash. It could not without serious inconvenience either lift or enforce its ban, and therefore found an advantage in allowing the situation to remain ambiguous. Pierre Mandonnet, *Siger de Brabant et l'Averroisme latin au XIIIme siècle* (Louvain, 1911), pp. 22–26.

A second major crisis, involving both the implications of the Aristotelian revolution and the struggle of the masters of arts for autonomy, came in the 1270s. Moslem scholars had long been familiar with the natural philosophy of Aristotle, and when this part of his work dawned on the Christian thinkers it was with the guidance of Arab and Greek commentators. Among the great commentators on the Aristotelian texts was Averroës of Córdoba, a doctor by profession, who died in 1198. The commentaries of Averroës became so widely read in the Latin world that he was known as "the commentator" in the same sense that Aristotle was "the philosopher." As a learned commentator on the Peripatetic, Averroës was useful and acceptable, but his own philosophical views were heretical both in the Moslem and the Christian worlds, for he believed that the individual soul expires with the body, that matter is eternal rather than created, and that all possible intellect in the human species is ultimately one.[47] His philosophy was widely professed in Spain and his commentaries caused more than a ripple in the arts faculty at Paris.

The leader of the Parisian "Averroists" was a master of arts, Siger de Brabant. When Bishop Tempier of Paris condemned the doctrines of Averroës in 1270, declaring that all who knowingly taught or asserted them were excommunicated, Siger went on calmly and only a bit more prudently with his teaching. Seven years later, when Pope John XXI complained to Bishop Tempier about the dangerous errors circulating at Paris, the bishop, urged on by a group of zealous masters of theology, responded by condemning indiscriminately 219 propositions of various sorts, including some upheld by Aquinas. The issue was joined as to how far the thought of Aristotle might be carried and how real was the philosophical autonomy of the arts faculty.[48] Siger and one of his associates,

[47] The principal contentions of Averroism that aroused concern in the Christian world were: that God knows nothing outside Himself, and that He does not have knowledge of particulars, and that human actions are not ruled by divine providence; that the world is eternal, and there was no first man; that there is only one intelligence for all men, that the individual soul dies with the body, and that the soul after death could not suffer from a corporeal fire; that the world is governed by necessity and is under the influence of the celestial bodies, and that the human will acts only within the realm of necessity.

[48] On Siger and heterodox Aristotelianism see Fernand van Steenberghen, *Siger de Brabant d'après ses oeuvres inédites*, Vol. II: *Siger dans l'histoire de l'aristotélisme* (Louvain, 1952). The terms "Averroism" and "Averroists" have often been used rather loosely to designate some of the heterodox Aristotelians, who cannot in fact always be assumed to have been followers of Averroës or even to have been profoundly influenced by him. The use of the conventional terms in the text should not be taken as necessarily implying a close affiliation between Latin writers and Averroës.

Bernier of Nivelles, seem to have been summoned before the Inquisitor General of France, although it is uncertain that they ever obeyed. Siger appealed to the protection of the Roman court and was imprisoned in a mild custodial fashion with another of his followers (Bernier was restored to favor), and then apparently spent his remaining years at the papal court at Orvieto, where he was murdered by a demented clerk. To many of his contemporaries Siger appeared not as a heretic but as a great martyr to philosophical independence and freedom of thought. Dante in the *Paradiso* put him in heaven, at the left hand of Thomas Aquinas.[49] The Averroistic strain of rationalism survived not only at Paris, where it can be seen in the work of John of Jandun and others in the fourteenth century, but above all at Padua and Bologna. It seems to have contributed significantly to the primary skeptical currents of the late Middle Ages.[50]

At Paris, despite Siger's incarceration, the continued struggle of the arts faculty for its independence from the theologians was won by the close of the thirteenth century. After 1277 "there was no further effective intervention on the part of the theologians in either the organization or the studies of the arts faculty," [51] and the pride and self-confidence of the masters of arts henceforth increased. Another philosophic crisis, however, took place in the first half of the fourteenth century, partly in connection with the work and influence of William of Ockham. Ockham was cited to the papal curia in 1324 by a commission of Paris and Oxford theologians which, after carefully examining his work for all of three years, censured fifty-one articles, not only in theology but in metaphysics, natural philosophy, psychology, and logic. Yet no official condemnation ever seems to have resulted from this examination, and a quarter-century after the event the Paris masters seem to have been unaware of it.[52] Ockham's doctrines caused so much tumult, particularly among the younger scholars, that the public and private reading of his works was prohibited by the arts faculty at Paris in 1339. Again in the following year the prohibition was renewed, but under circumstances that suggest that the object

[49] Canto X, 136–38. To Averroës himself Dante assigned an easy place in Hell, the limbo of the unbaptized, along with some very distinguished company. *Inferno*, Canto IV, 144.

[50] Cf. Anneliese Maier, *Die Vorläufer Galileis im 14. Jahrhundert* (Rome, 1949), Chaps. IX, X.

[51] McLaughlin, "Intellectual Freedom," p. 133; for the exercise of this autonomy see Chap. III.

[52] *Ibid.*, pp. 354–56. On the examination of Ockham see A. Vacant and E. Mangenot, *Dictionnaire de théologie catholique*, Vol. XI, col. 889 ff.

was now rather to quiet some of the more obstreperous anti-Ockhamists.[53] One of the scholars affected by the action of 1340 was Nicholas of Autrecourt, a leading philosophical skeptic of the fourteenth century. Six years later Nicholas was gravely censured by a papal commission for teachings repudiating the entire framework of the now altogether orthodox Aristotelian thought and for propounding doctrines that were held to be a menace to the faith. But the censure neither erased his influence nor ended his career, for he seems to have been, not long after, still dean of the cathedral at Metz and still in possession of the degrees and benefices of which he was supposed to have been deprived.[54] The outcome of these two cases, like the earlier reception of Aristotle, illustrates the futility of such intervention against important ideas.

FAITH, REASON, AND COMMUNICATION

Something must be said concerning the degree of awareness of the issue of freedom among the medieval masters and the devices they used to challenge or circumvent authority. It would be less true to say that they had an elaborate rationale for freedom of thought than to say simply that they were driven to claim and exercise a measure of freedom by the nature of their task.[55] They were aware of themselves as members of a great fellowship, extending across the ages, as men whose lives were dedicated to the search for truth and whose work was subject to harassment by the ignorant or uncharitable. From Latin sources they knew of Plato's *Apology* and on occasion found some personal meaning for themselves in the persecution of Socrates and his great self-defense.[56] The conditions of their profession as teachers made it urgent for the more original masters to maintain an area in which their minds could move about.

---

[53] See Ernest A. Moody, "Ockham, Buridan, and Nicholas of Autrecourt: The Parisian Statutes of 1339 and 1340," *Franciscan Studies,* VII (June, 1947), 113–46.

[54] McLaughlin, "Intellectual Freedom," pp. 190–220; cf. J. R. Weinberg, *Nicolaus of Autrecourt* (Princeton, 1948), p. 3.

[55] Cf. McLaughlin's conclusion that the typical response of the thirteenth- and fourteenth-century masters to restriction was not to analyze the issue as a problem in freedom and to expound a theory but "simply to claim freedom as a practical necessity in the fulfillment of those intellectual functions which they were ever concerned to define and extend." "Intellectual Freedom," p. 388. Sir Maurice Powicke is content to sidestep the problem with the remark that "they were not so perplexed as we are by the problem of freedom, for they believed that truth is one, and would be seen later. They had quite enough freedom to be contentious, and they liked controversy." *Medieval Life and Thought,* p. 212.

[56] Thorndike, *History of Magic and Experimental Science,* II, 639–40.

Without some philosophical differentiation that stamped them as men with something singular to say, how could they attract students or teach with vigor? [57]

Before the beginning of the university epoch the conflict between authority and individual scholars of distinction had led to a series of actions against speculative freedom. Abelard, despite his own earnest intention to put dialectic in the service of faith,[58] was among those who fell under criticism. It was not uncommon, either in the theological and philosophical revival of the twelfth century or afterwards, for philosophers to hurl at each other the accusation of heresy—Abelard himself was not above using this device as a kind of dialectical *coup de grâce*—and the question was inevitably raised by his critics whether his use of dialectic had not become dangerous to sound doctrine. His enemies, he complained, had argued that it was unlawful for a Christian to treat of things that do not pertain to the faith. He replied with a burst of self-assertion that reveals the extent to which his kind of intellectualism would carry him in his claims to freedom:

It is wonderful if I must not discuss what is permitted them [i.e. his critics] to read. . . . Truth is not opposed to truth . . . as falsehood may be opposed to falsity, or evil to evil . . . but rather all good things are in accord. All knowledge is good, even that which relates to evil, because a righteous man must have it. Since he may guard against evil, it is necessary that he should know it beforehand; otherwise he could not shun it. Though an act be evil, knowledge regarding it is good; though it be evil to sin, it is good to know the sin, which otherwise we could not shun. . . . If therefore it is not wrong to know, but to do, the evil is to be referred to the act and not to the knowledge. Hence we are convinced that all knowledge, which indeed comes from God alone and from his bounty, is good. Wherefore the study of every science should be conceded to be good, because that which is good comes from it; and especially one must insist upon the study of that *doctrina* by which the greater truth is known. This is dialectic, whose function is to distinguish between every truth and falsity: as leader in all knowledge, it holds the primacy and rule of all philosophy. The same also is shown to be needful to the Catholic Faith, which cannot without its aid resist the sophistries of schismatics.[59]

[57] That novel ideas were being advanced in the twelfth century with a considerable awareness of risk is indicated by Adelard of Bath's remark that his generation was so unreceptive to novel ideas that authors commonly published new views by attributing them to others. Thorndike, *History of Magic and Experimental Science*, II, 24–25.

[58] On faith and reason in Abelard see J. G. Sikes, *Peter Abailard* (Cambridge, 1932).

[59] Taylor, *The Mediaeval Mind*, II, 379.

What Abelard had to say was naturally written from the standpoint of a devout man who, even though some of his own theological notions were condemned, considered it the primary business of intellect to defend the faith. This belief in the value of intellect was the outstanding quality in his heritage. It was by the power of reason, not by force or mere preachments, that he hoped to impel heretics to return to the faith.[60] Similarly, in pedagogy he placed a high value upon the cultivation of dialectical skill as opposed to the mere imparting of information. In his *Sic et non,* which was written for the benefit of young students, he counterposed the contradictory statements of great authorities on important theological questions. By encouraging such a method for the teaching of the young, he quickened the tradition of dialectical rigor.[61] It was his objective, he said, by raising issues from the "apparent repugnancy" in the writings of the holy Fathers to excite the students "to search out the truth of the matter, and render them the sharper for the investigation. For the first key to wisdom is called interrogation, diligent and unceasing. . . . By doubting we are led to inquiry; and from inquiry we perceive the truth." [62]

As we have seen, the accepted Christian ideal of the intellectual enterprise was that of a system of knowledge partly stemming from and entirely consistent with the faith. While no one challenged the concept in principle, it had to be qualified repeatedly in practice if there was to be any considerable measure of freedom of thought. Freedom implies choice, and choice implies the existence of diversity of ideas and beliefs. The struggle of the dissident scholars against positive authority therefore consisted chiefly of taking advantage of intellectual or political methods by which a real plurality of intellectual opportunities and perspectives could be maintained within the ideal structure of unified doctrine.

The boldest, probably the most effective, and yet the quietest of all these methods was the simple one of ignoring condemnations and censures without openly challenging them—for masters again and again continued to discuss and even to assert ideas that positive authority had condemned as erroneous. It was by just this kind of stubbornness, as we have seen, that the new books of Aristotle, once under proscription

---

[60] *Ibid.,* II, 380.

[61] Sikes, *Peter Abailard,* Chap. IV.

[62] Taylor, *The Mediaeval Mind,* p. 335. Cf. Adelard of Bath's perspicuous argument for following reason rather than authority. Thorndike, *History of Magic and Experimental Science,* II, 28–29.

at Paris, were opened to general study there. A second method, suited to the pluralistic structure of medieval society and the lacunae in the organization of the Church, was to act upon a geographical plurality of truths—that is, to ignore in one diocese a prohibition that had had its origin in another. Thus one finds a mid-fourteenth-century master like Jean Buridan expressing some doubts as to the validity of the indiscriminate condemnations of 1277, remarking that he had heard a famous doctor of theology say that it would not be improper for someone to uphold outside of the diocese of Paris an opinion that was contrary to the decisions of the Bishop of Paris.[63] Nor was this a mere flippancy. Before the beginning of the Inquisition the Church had left the defense of the faith against heresy in the hands of the bishops. With the development of the Inquisition, the popes and the inquisitors became the guardians of orthodoxy so far as popular heresies were concerned, but in academic matters the officials of the universities and the bishops continued to bear the primary responsibility. This tradition of decentralization worked to the advantage of the academic community. Tempier's condemnations of 1277 had, in fact, no binding force outside the university and diocese of Paris. To put them into effect at Oxford required another separate and somewhat different censure by Archbishop Robert Kilwardby— presumably the result of an understanding between the two men—in which the doctrines of Thomas Aquinas were singled out.[64] This action was, of course, even more freely ignored at Paris than the little-observed condemnation of its own bishop, and at Oxford it was far from effective.

Still another factor that gave protection to the masters was that their primary function was to teach, and in teaching the process of communication was informal.[65] Often the only evidence of the heterodoxy of the teacher would be in the notes of the students. It was also possible for scholars who wished either to communicate ideas of questionable orthodoxy for the consideration of others, or to cross the line that was supposed to separate philosophical from theological inquiry, to express in advance their willingness to submit to the judgment of the theologians

[63] McLaughlin, "Intellectual Freedom," p. 179.

[64] A brief account of the condemnations in relation to intellectual changes is given by Maurice De Wulf, *The History of Mediaeval Philosophy* (London, 1939), II, 224–232. The Parisian condemnation of Aquinas' propositions was retracted by the Bishop of Paris in 1325, two years after St. Thomas' canonization.

[65] Étienne Gilson, *La Philosophie au moyen âge* (Paris, 1947), p. 413.

or the Church.[66] Since it was common to assume that heresy existed only where there was pertinacity in error, this was sometimes helpful.

Attacks on inquiry did not go without frequent direct and open challenge. While some masters might choose simply to circumvent such attacks, open criticism was often made. The lengths to which some masters were prepared to go in making direct challenges on behalf of freedom may be illustrated from the writings of Godfrey of Fontaines, a late-thirteenth-century secular master of the Paris faculty of theology, a regent master for thirteen years, who was elected to the bishopric of Tournai in 1300. A highly respected figure, frequently known after his death as *doctor venerabilis,* Godfrey indulged in discussions both of doctrine and church policy. He was one of a number of masters, regular and secular, who refused to acknowledge the validity of the condemnations of 1277. Not only did he continue to discuss some of the doctrines condemned, like the idea of the eternity of the world, but he scathingly criticized the indiscriminate condemnations themselves. He denied the right of a prelate to condemn doctrines as heretical, asserting that this concerned the whole community of the faithful and could be done only by a council or by the pope. To bind men, he asserted, to an opinion on questions on which there may be a diversity of views without danger to faith would impede the pursuit of truth. Since the conflict of opinion among learned men would stimulate discussion, the truth would be discovered more readily if men were left free to seek through discussion not what is more pleasing but what agrees with right reason.[67]

Godfrey denounced as ignorant and naive the condemnations of 1277 and called upon Bishop Tempier's second successor, Simon de Bucy, to revoke his act:

[66] Cf. Buridan, when he discusses the problem of whether there is an infinite immobile space beyond the visible heavens: "I leave the determination of all that I say in this question to the theologians and I wish to acquiesce in their determination." McLaughlin, "Intellectual Freedom," p. 178. Sometimes the retractions came only after the event. Meister Eckhart, when he got into difficulties just before his death, avowed his willingness to retract anything he had ever written or said that might be deemed erroneous and heretical, just as though it had never been uttered. "Although I may err," he argued, "I cannot be a heretic; for the first pertains to the intellect, the second to the will." *Ibid.,* p. 361.

[67] See the discussion of Godfrey of Fontaines' rationale for freedom in McLaughlin, "Intellectual Freedom," pp. 271–80, 310–11, 314–15 and Maurice De Wulf, "Étude sur la vie, les oeuvres et l'influence de Godefroid de Fontaines," *Mémoires de l'Académie Royale de Belgique,* Ser. 2, Vol. I, Classe des Lettres et des Sciences (Brussels, 1906), Chap. III.

If right reason or an authority demonstrates that that which a prelate condemns as false and erroneous is true; or even, without being absolutely certain, that the condemned thesis is probable . . . ; or again if it is susceptible of being made the basis of contrary opinions, it appears that both excommunication and condemnation are equally erroneous, since they hinder inquiry into and knowledge of the truth. Certainly it is not proper that any individual should take it upon himself alone to resist that measure . . . but one should ask that the prelate himself revoke the condemnation and excommunication. For even if it is true that to maintain them does not entail a danger to salvation, it does involve a blow to perfect understanding, for it would deprive men of freedom of research into truths through which their understanding would be in no small measure improved. And then, what a scandal in the eyes of both many believers and unbelievers that prelates should be so ignorant and naive as to hold as erroneous and contrary to faith that which is irreconcilable neither with faith nor with good morals! [68]

It was by no means unusual that this master should have invoked the criterion of *intellectual competence* in theology as a thing far more relevant than the bishop's formal place in the hierarchy as a warrant for repudiating his authority.[69]

The impact of Aristotelianism itself brought substantive changes in the pursuit of knowledge that proved to be profoundly liberating. By opening up whole unfamiliar realms to inquiry it created a necessity for some workable equipoise between the traditional and universally accepted claims of belief and the desire of scholars to pursue secular studies. Institutionally such an equipoise was found at Paris in the growing autonomy of the faculty of arts. Intellectually it was manifested in the separation of reason from faith, of philosophy from theology, and of logical and epistemological inquiry from ontological considerations.

Broadly speaking, three views prevailed as to the significance of the vast new world of knowledge and speculative activity that was opened

[68] De Wulf, "Étude sur la vie," pp. 40–41.

[69] Godfrey goes on to say of the current bishop that while he is eminent in the literature of canon and civil law, his knowledge of theology is not sufficient to warrant his trying to correct the condemned articles without the advice of masters competent in the subject. *Ibid.*, p. 46. Godfrey could hardly bring himself to excuse the bishop for this. He was aware, however, that the masters would not have been found in complete agreement on some of the articles, a consideration which he felt would have justified the bishop in simply abstaining from action.

For a brief but extraordinarily strong statement in behalf of freedom of thought in physics, logic, and grammar when these do not pertain to theology, see William of Ockham as quoted by Friedrich Ueberweg, *Grundriss der Geschichte der Philosophie*, II, ed. Bernhard Geyer (Berlin, 1928), 582. Ockham's position goes beyond Godfrey's in its forthrightness.

up by the new Aristotle. One school, that of the traditionalists, preferred to eschew it. A second, in which St. Thomas Aquinas was preeminent, set about with great ingenuity to Christianize Aristotle and construct a philosophical synthesis out of Peripateticism and the Christian faith. Still another school, which has been commonly called that of the Latin Averroists but which might more accurately be designated as that of the heterodox Aristotelians, was confronted with a knotty problem arising from its desire to explore as fully as possible the views of Aristotle in the arena of natural reason without being confined by a primary concern with the consequences for Christian faith. This school, whose most notable figure was Siger de Brabant, was confronted with the problem of the relations of faith and reason in an acute form.

A gap had appeared between those ideas that it was safe and proper to profess as true and some ideas about which the philosophy of Aristotle tempted one to speculate—the eternity of the world, the unity of intellect, the immortality of the individual soul, the providential character of God. Some of the conclusions of Aristotle, faithfully pursued, seemed to challenge Christian faith. Siger tried to solve this problem by emphasizing the distinction between the natural order (the object of philosophical attention) and the supernatural order (the sphere of theology and faith). He held that while the operations of man's natural reason might necessarily lead to one conclusion, it was possible by faith to maintain the opposite as true. Like Averroës himself, the Latin Averroists were accused by their opponents of maintaining the theory of the "double truth"—that is, of asserting that what is true in theology can be false in philosophy, and vice versa.[70] Such a self-contradictory position was

---

[70] Averroës, who himself once suffered exile for opinions not altogether congenial to the Moslem world, made a famous attempt to reconcile the claims of philosophy and theology in a work that did not become known in the Latin world until the fourteenth century. In his little treatise *The Agreement of Religion and Philosophy* Averroës delineated three levels of discourse that exist for three different types of men: the first is operative among the great mass of men, who are moved only by rhetoric; the second is for those (the theologians) who like to have their religious views somewhat rationalized by dialectical interpretation; the third is for the philosophers who, like Aristotle, seek for certain demonstration. Averroës believed that social strife over matters of faith might be avoided if these three types of discourse were kept separate—if the populace were never confronted with matters of theology, if theologians never tried to be philosophers, and if philosophers stayed clear of theology. Of course it was the philosophers who strove for the profound, the ultimate, the certain truth, which the theologians apprehended less clearly, and the masses crudely through the means of symbology and simple legend. Averroës believed, moreover, that it was a mistake for the learned to try to communicate their findings to the masses. Although his appeal was rather seriously flawed by the

in fact espoused by no one.[71] Averroës himself had maintained that the real truth was to be found in the full exercise of natural reason; while Siger, although claiming that philosophical truth expressed the utmost capacities of man's natural reason, conceded nonetheless that where it conflicted with revealed faith the claims of faith must be taken as superior. The Latin Averroists in their most radical formulations declared only that philosophical conclusions are "necessary"—that is, inevitable within the framework of natural rationality—even though they might be contrary to the findings of the faith, which are really *true*.[72] It was the business of the philosopher, Siger maintained, to explain the natural order, which is accessible to experience and reason. But by divine intervention a supernatural order may be instituted, concerning which the philosophical conclusions that are true on the hypothesis of a purely natural order will not hold.[73] Through revelation one may have access to truths beyond the reach of natural reason.

Some students have suggested that Siger's abstract willingness to submit to the doctrines of the faith, while toying speculatively with the most heterodox suggestions of natural philosophy, was merely a protective device that was to enable him to teach as a freethinker. One of the earlier students of his work concluded that the religious faith of the Latin Averroists was "at least rather feeble if not altogether fictitious," and considered their work "a disguised form of free thought." [74] The preponderant opinion, however, including the most recent and thorough

tones of condescension with which Averroës referred to theologians, there seems little doubt that he was trying to arrive at a strategy for social peace and intellectual tolerance. He was also trying, however roughly, to make a point in what we would now call the sociology of knowledge. Having inherited the tradition of a lofty and tolerant culture, and having been sustained by two Caliphs and the upper classes and banished by pressure from intolerant theologians and an ignorant populace, it was natural for him to approach the problem from the standpoint of a broadminded elitist. See Ibn Rochd (Averroës), *Traité décisif sur l'accord de la religion et de la philosophie,* trans. and ed. by Léon Gauthier (Algiers, 1942), esp. pp. 25 ff., and the discussion in Étienne Gilson, *Reason and Revelation in the Middle Ages,* pp. 39–66.

[71] Etienne Gilson, "La Doctrine de la double vérité," in *Études de philosophie médiévale* (Strasbourg, 1921), p. 68.

[72] Van Steenberghen, *Siger de Brabant,* p. 688.

[73] *Ibid.,* p. 694; cf. the discussion of this subject, pp. 677–88. This makes it easier to understand why some of the boldest thinkers of the fourteenth century liked to place the greatest emphasis on divine omnipotence.

[74] Mandonnet, *Siger de Brabant et l'Averroisme latin au XIIIme siècle,* pp. 190–95; cf. pp. 149–52.

inquiry,[75] leans to the view that Siger was entirely sincere in his professions of faith. This elusive question of sincerity, which is unlikely ever to be settled with finality, is an issue of some importance to the history of intellectual freedom. But if motives and subjective states cannot be assessed with certainty, results sometimes can; it is at least clear that the duality between faith and reason that found its inception in the problems of the heterodox Aristotelians tended to free the speculative mind from doctrinal limitations by making it possible to follow the play of natural reason while paying full respect to the demands of faith.

A somewhat more challenging problem of historical interpretation is raised by the writings of John of Jandun in the fourteenth century, whose sincerity as a Christian is doubted by some scholars, like Gilson, who readily credit the sincerity of Siger. By John of Jandun's time Aristotelianism had become so securely established and the rights of the arts faculty so generally respected that he can hardly be considered an innovator in the manner of Siger. But he was a notable figure, and his writings show a certain insouciance of tone that has made his meaning suspect. He is disquieting, as Gilson says, not so much for his matter as his manner.[76] In his case it has seemed much more likely than in Siger's that he was using the now conventional obeisance to orthodoxy as a mask behind which to express a fundamental irreverence.[77] "I do believe that that is true," he writes concerning an article of faith, "but I cannot prove it. Good luck to those who can!" He concludes a long

[75] Van Steenberghen, *Siger de Brabant,* pp. 689–700. Gilson also resolves this question in Siger's favor (*Reason and Revelation in the Middle Ages,* pp. 59–60), while De Wulf seems to have it both ways, arguing on one page that Siger "in order to shelter himself . . . adopted a prudential attitude" (*History of Mediaeval Philosophy,* II, 161) and on the next that he was sincere (*ibid.,* pp. 162–63). Whatever the true intentions of the Latin Averroists, the consequences of their approach were feared by some church authorities. Tempier's condemnations of 1277 include those who say that what they are writing is true according to philosophy but not according to the Catholic faith, as if there were two contradictory truths.

[76] Gilson, "La Doctrine de la double vérité," p. 65.

[77] Stuart MacClintock in a recent review of the literature, however, argues forcefully in favor of the ultimate sincerity of the Latin Averroists, and concludes that they can best be understood as trying simply to establish an autonomous area for the play of the mind in accordance with the principles of natural reason without, in their religious profession, really deviating from the tenets of the faith. In effect, nonetheless, their attitude did involve a radical circumscription of the realm of faith. Stuart MacClintock, "John of Jandun and the Problem of Latin Averroism," unpublished doctoral dissertation (Columbia University, 1951), esp. pp. 91 ff. and 103 ff. Cf. the discussion of this school by A. J. Rahilly, *Studies,* II (September, 1913), 301–24; III (March, 1914), 686–713.

argument in which he demonstrates the philosophical impossibility of
the idea of creation by asserting that we ought to believe it anyway.
"Let it be added," he ends, "that creation very seldom happens; there has
never been but one, and that was a very long time ago." [78] When we find
the same writer telling us that belief is simply a habit induced by listening
to certain teachings from childhood,[79] we may well wonder if we are not,
as Gilson suggests, listening to some daring precursor of the Enlightenment who is carrying on with criticism of the faith without unduly en-
dangering himself.[80] John did in the end find it necessary to leave Paris,
but it was not his rationalism but his antipapal politics that drove him
off to the court of Louis of Bavaria.

Unlike John of Jandun, many of the fourteenth-century masters were
trying to free themselves from the trammels of an Aristotelianism that
had hardened into an orthodoxy. In many respects the position of these
men vis-à-vis possible charges of heresy was much simpler than that of
their predecessors of the 1270s. While the Averroists had found themselves ranged against dogmatic religion, the new critical writers were
interested chiefly in attacking dogmatic philosophy and liberating themselves from philosophic authority. It was their goal to question Aristotle
or to raise problems in natural philosophy that he had not considered.
Having more than one authoritative tradition to appeal to, they could
subtly turn upon itself the whole apparatus of authoritative definition.[81]

The method of probable argument, which became a commonplace
among the fourteenth-century masters and was employed to notable
effect by Nicholas of Autrecourt, made possible the development of
philosophical criticism and the exploration of new ideas without pre-
suming to offer a direct challenge to the faith. In employing the method
of hypothetical statement and dealing in probabilities rather than assertions of necessary truths, those who followed the method of probable
argument also found themselves in the possession of an intellectually
liberating technique.[82] They unambiguously denied upholding what had

[78] Gilson, *Reason and Revelation in the Middle Ages,* pp. 61–63.

[79] McLaughlin, "Intellectual Freedom," p. 182.

[80] See MacClintock's reasons, however, for suspecting this judgment, in "John
of Jandun," pp. 112–21 and *passim.*

[81] McLaughlin, "Intellectual Freedom," pp. 188–89.

[82] We have drawn on the explication of "probabilism" in Weinberg, *Nicolaus
of Autrecourt,* Chap. VI. The nub of the difference between Siger's approach to
truth and that of later probable argument, insofar as it bears on the problem of
heresy, is that while Siger maintained that certain philosophical propositions con-

been so unfairly attributed to the earlier Averroists—the idea that truths can be opposed. But they insisted that there is a legitimate arena of speculative and probable argument in which certain undenied truths of the faith can actually be less probable in the light of pure reason than their contradictories.[83] Human information, mental powers, and types of argument, they held, are at any time quite limited. Errors and limited comprehension are inevitable. While some things are absolutely certain from experience or logic and others must be believed certain as articles of faith, there is still a third ground for the proper operation of the mind—the area of probability, which is where man must work when all those factors making for uncertainty are in play. Men arrive through reason at propositions which are probable to them, and which may be in themselves true or false but cannot, at the moment, be *known* as true or false. Thus one can disputatively, and in a sense experimentally, advance a wide range of propositions as the best yield of current information and reason, without being prepared to profess them as true.[84] It is

---

trary to faith are *necessary* in reason, the "probabilists" held that such propositions are merely the most probable that can be achieved by the best human reason at a given time and with a given set of data.

For convenience we have followed Weinberg in using here the term "probabilism," although it did not come into general use until near the end of the sixteenth century, when it denoted a particular theory in moral theology.

[83] Thus one Pierre de Ceffons wrote: "I do not fall into that error that I say that this is true according to Aristotle but not according to faith, because I know that truths are never opposed. . . . Although it is erroneous to say that God is not three and one and that the world had no beginning, it is nevertheless not erroneous to assert that, faith aside, it is more *probable* that God is not three and one or that the world never began than to assert their opposites. For nothing prevents some false propositions from being more probable than some true ones." *Ibid.*, pp. 116–17.

[84] Nicholas avowed at his trial at Avignon that he had done precisely this, and that he was prepared to retract those of his propositions that his judges found heretical and blasphemous. He had, he said, stated them only disputatively, not definitively and did not mean to adhere to them pertinaciously. His defense was dismissed as a "foxy excuse," but it is difficult to say whether or not this was a fair judgment. *Ibid.*, pp. 6, 114–15; McLaughlin, "Intellectual Freedom," pp. 213–15.

As an alternative to the theory that Aristotelians of Siger's caliber and the later "probabilists" were really rationalists who tried to protect themselves through "foxy" and insincere professions of faith, and the opposite theory that they were unable to see any gaps between their philosophical rationalism and their fideism in theology, one can envisage still a third possibility that somewhat reconciles the two—namely, that their minds were sundered by the duality of their social roles and that they had developed completely functional and humanly satisfactory dual mentalities. On one hand they were believing Catholics who accepted revealed truth and had no desire to spread heresies or subvert the faith; on the other they were passionate intellectuals, scholars, teachers, profoundly moved by the quest for knowledge and the desire for achievement.

easy to see that under such criteria of knowledge the rich and significant ground of inquiry for some thinkers might be entirely in the area of probable and hypothetical statement, and that here some very fresh and remarkable things might be said. The work of such a master as Jean Buridan, a great fourteenth-century precursor of modern science, shows how the method of probable argument and hypothetical statement could be identified with honestly tentative ways of thinking, the capacity for suspension of belief, modesty of assertion, tolerance of differences and ambiguities, and the spirit of intellectual play.[85]

Thus scholastic thought from the early fourteenth century onwards was characterized by a radical separation between the sphere of the senses, reason, and natural knowledge on one side and the sphere of faith and revelation on the other. There was a growing tendency to give up the effort to demonstrate the truths of faith by reason and to rely solely on revelation or intuition for their foundation. Central in the philosophy of William of Ockham, this separation of faith and reason became completely familiar in the schools.[86] In the minds of many thinkers one of its chief functions was to protect the faith from new currents of philosophical skepticism and natural inquiry (Ockham, for instance, was a passionately devout Christian), but in time it also had the contrary effect of protecting philosophical skepticism from inquisitive guardians of the faith.[87] And perhaps in the long run of propagating skepticism; for it was not, as De Wulf remarks, a far cry from saying that the ideas of faith are inaccessible to reason to saying that they are

[85] See McLaughlin's discussion of Buridan in relation to the problem of freedom, "Intellectual Freedom," pp. 156–90.

[86] Gilson, *La Philosophie au moyen âge,* pp. 638 ff., 655.

[87] This stratagem had a long subsequent history. Thus even as late as the seventeenth century Francis Bacon is to be found arguing for a twofold theory of truth and asserting that "the more absurd and incredible any divine mystery is, the greater honour we do to God in believing it; and so much the more noble the victory of faith." In commenting on the passage in which this quotation appears, Basil Willey finds his confidence in Bacon's sincerity shaken by "the ceremonial and formal obeisance about many of his salutes to religion." He concludes, however, that "Bacon's desire to separate religious truth and scientific truth was in the interests of science, not of religion. He wished to *keep science pure from religion;* the opposite part of the process—keeping religion pure from science—did not interest him nearly so much. . . . Religious truth, then, must be 'skied', elevated far out of reach, not in order that it may be more devoutly approached, but in order to keep it out of mischief. But having secured his main object, namely, to clear the universe for science, Bacon can afford to be quite orthodox (just as, in another context, he can concede poetry to human weakness)." Basil Willey, *The Seventeenth Century Background* (New York, 1934), pp. 28–29.

contrary to reason. This radical dissociation of faith and reason seems, in any case, to have had a valuable function in the development of late medieval philosophy and science. It can hardly be coincidental that the two schools that are now considered to have mediated the fruitful continuity between medieval and early modern science, the Ockhamists at Paris and the Paduan Averroists,[88] both resorted to philosophical techniques that in some measure freed speculation and inquiry by divorcing their consequences from the tenets of the faith. For a time, as we shall see, such a formula even became within limits acceptable to authority itself. While it grew out of the substantive problems of the thought of the thirteenth century and afterward, this separation of natural reason from faith seems to have become a protective convention among some of the later writers.

What was most commonly referred to in the earlier days as the differentiation between revealed truth and natural reason also became transmuted later into a differentiation between revealed truth and scientific hypothesis as well. Thus in the fourteenth century Nicole Oresme, after summarizing with striking cogency the case for the diurnal rotation of the earth, added a passage deferring on grounds of faith to the movement of the heavens and remarking that this additional instance of the conflict between articles of faith and natural reason could really be useful in the defense of the faith;[89] while Jean Buridan, after suggesting that the celestial orbs were moved by an inherent impetus rather than by intelligences, added that he asserted this only tentatively and sought further

[88] For a brief account see John Herman Randall, Jr., "The Development of Scientific Method in the School of Padua," *Journal of the History of Ideas,* I (April, 1940), 177–206.

[89] "It appears thus that it cannot be shown by any experience that the heavens are moved by a daily movement. . . . It cannot be concluded by reasons that the heavens may be moved. And third, reasons have been offered to the contrary, that it is not so moved. Nevertheless all hold and I believe that it is so moved and that the earth is not: 'God has established the sphere of the earth, which shall not be moved'—the arguments to the contrary notwithstanding, for these are persuasions which do not lead to evident conclusions. But considering all that has been said, it is possible to believe that the earth is so moved and that the heavens are not, and it is not evident to the contrary. And, in any case, it seems on the face of it, as much or more against natural reason, as are either all or some of the articles of our faith. And thus what I have said for fun in this manner could be of value in confuting or reproving those who would attack our faith by rational arguments." From *Le Livre du ciel et du monde* (1377) translated in James Bruce Ross and Mary Martin McLaughlin, *The Renaissance Reader* (New York, 1953), p. 583. Did Oresme, in the face of his own reasoning, really believe that the earth does not move? On this as in other matters we merely seek enlightenment from historians of medieval thought, and humbly submit to their judgments.

judgment on the matter from the theologians.[90] And in 1543, when Copernicus' friends and editors published the dying man's *De revolutionibus orbium coelestium,* one of them, the Lutheran Andreas Osiander, inserted a protective anonymous preface in which it was declared that the work provided only another hypothesis for the use of astronomers, not a new description of the universe: "For it is not necessary that these hypotheses be true, nor even probable, but this alone is sufficient, if they show reasoning fitting the observations." [91]

THE NEW LEARNING AND THE NEW SCIENCE

In the late fourteenth century and in the fifteenth, there was some shift in the center of intellectual gravity as some of the North Italian universities became infused with the scientific teachings that had flourished at Oxford and Paris, and other universities to the east, notably Prague and Heidelberg, rose in eminence. New interests and new areas of inquiry—humanistic scholarship and scientific investigation—were now beginning more and more to be fostered outside the universities as well as within them, and outside Italy the relative importance of universities in the sum total of intellectual life tended to be smaller. In some institutions, moreover, professors and students became negligent, and academic requirements degenerated into empty forms. As late scholasticism became more preoccupied with the details and refinements of intellectual systems that had passed beyond their first great days of formulation and advancement, the intellectual life of the universities lost some of its appeal. One important function, however, the universities did not lose—that of supplying the fundamental education of great men of achievement in all lines of creative work. Even those leading humanist scholars and writers, for instance, whose fate it was to do their work outside university walls, were for the most part educated within them. The great political critics of the papacy were men whose dialectic had been sharpened in the schools. The precursors and early leaders of the Reformation—Wyclif, Huss, and Luther—were university men; and when, in the

[90] The passage from Buridan is quoted in Anneliese Maier, *Die Impetustheorie der Scholastik* (Vienna, 1940), p. 85.

[91] Dorothy Stimson, *The Gradual Acceptance of the Copernican Theory of the Universe* (Hanover, N.H., 1917), pp. 28–30. The text of this preface is in Edward Rosen, *Three Copernican Treatises* (New York, 1939), pp. 24–25, along with a discussion of the philosophical strategy behind it and Copernicus' own rejection of the idea, pp. 22–33.

early days of the Reformation, Luther found himself in combat with Pope Adrian VI, the struggle was led on one side by a theologian of Wittenberg and on the other by a theologian from Louvain.

While the intellectual vitality of the universities varied greatly from place to place, their power and corporate autonomy were quite generally declining, for these depended upon characteristics of medieval organization that were waning—the supremacy of the popes, the universality and integrity of the Church, the extranational and primarily ecclesiastical character of intellectual life. Some of the weapons of the universities had lost their force. Migrations, which had done so much at the beginning to diffuse the university system and strengthen university power, proved in the long run to be self-limiting. Both migrations and cessations had depended for their effect upon the scarcity as well as the effectuality of the services rendered by the university. The result of the migrations, together with the great numbers of new university foundations of the fourteenth and fifteenth centuries, was to overbuild the university system to a point at which the University of Paris begged the pope not to authorize any more foundations. In the last quarter of the fifteenth century new foundations did in fact finally dwindle to nothing. Migrations were now an empty threat, and talk of cessation was more likely under the new conditions to bring university faculties under the retaliatory hand of secular power than it was to win new privileges or safeguard the old. As universities became more heavily endowed with college foundations and other properties, and as their intellectual life became increasingly committed to permanent libraries, they became timid and immobile, and their financial dependence provided princes and municipalities with a pretext for unprecedented intervention in their affairs. But it had been, above all, the pluralism of medieval life that provided these powerful corporations with the source of their autonomy; as national states arose, sovereigns, princes, and parliaments took upon themselves the right to meddle in the internal affairs of universities, appointing and discharging professors at will and mocking at the former pride and autonomy of the masters.[92]

Paris itself remained a center of corporate power long after the creative intellectual life centering upon its famous masters had passed. But this power, once associated with the creativity of its teachers, now seemed to rest primarily upon its role as a center of orthodoxy, its ability to

[92] D'Irsay, *Histoire*, I, 191–222, sketches the decline of the medieval university.

limit the freedom of others. The Paris theological faculty began to intervene regularly in spheres ordinarily belonging to the Inquisition, and by the late fourteenth century had virtually supplanted the Inquisition as the judge of heresy for Paris and northern France.[93] It was this body that drew up the articles convicting Joan of Arc of heresy. The latter-day role of Paris in church affairs reached a peak with its place in the Council of Constance, 1414–18, but its function as a political sounding board seems to have long continued.[94] Like lesser universities, it was ultimately victimized by the growing power of the monarchs and other secular agencies of government. In 1446 the Parlement of Paris became the supreme tribunal of the university by order of a royal edict which was intended to stop the intervention of the university in attempts of the Crown to tax the wealthy academic clergy. The university remained contentious, however, until the reign of Louis XI, when its attempt to check the monarch's demand to control its rector was utterly defeated and its autonomy was completely broken. The university's final act of self-assertion came in 1499, when it called a cessation to protest against new infringements on its privileges. This protest was hastily withdrawn in response to dire threats from Louis XII, who revoked the right of cessation itself.[95] Such independence as the university continued to have now existed only on the sufferance of the kings.

Oxford, which had enjoyed an independence, if not an authority, comparable to that of Paris, remained throughout most of the fourteenth century the arena of vigorous philosophical thought, concerning which Wyclif once complained that a new logical system sprang up every twenty years.[96] The suppression of Wyclif's own school, however, marked the turning point in the history of his university. Since he taught a doctrine of the Eucharist that struck at the heart of Catholic theology and a doctrine of clerical poverty that struck at the prevailing practices of

[93] McLaughlin, "Intellectual Freedom," pp. 381–85.

[94] D'Irsay, *Histoire*, I, 191–95.

[95] Rashdall, *Universities of Europe*, I, 425–32. Louis XI had also interfered with the curricular freedom of the university in 1474, when he promulgated an edict proscribing the nominalist writers in the faculties of arts and theology. Fifteenth-century scholastics divided broadly into the ancients and the moderns, the former of which were the standard realist writers in the tradition of Aquinas and Albertus Magnus and the latter the nominalistic followers of Ockham. In proscribing the moderns Louis XI was binding Paris to a course of action less liberal than that of some institutions that offered alternate courses in both philosophical persuasions. Within less than a decade, however, nominalism was again permitted at Paris.

[96] Carré, *Phases of Thought in England*, p. 144.

the Church itself, it is not surprising that the bishops should have sought to quiet him or that they should have had the authorization of the Crown. What was remarkable was the loyalty Wyclif commanded within the university and the stubbornness with which it, in common with a very large section of public opinion, defended him. Even for some years after the chancellor of the university received a papal bull demanding that Wyclif be turned over to the Primate and Bishop of London, he was supported at Oxford. His followers in the university and the town, who were prepared to resist Wyclif's suppression by force of arms, were at length put down only by the united power of the Crown and the Church; but even after Wyclif's death there was so much Lollardy left at Oxford that new repressive intervention was undertaken in 1408, more than two decades afterward. Wyclif's Bible was then prohibited, university teachers were forbidden to teach heretical doctrines or allow discussion of the sacraments or essential articles of faith, a monthly inquisition into heresy was ordered in all colleges and halls, and a rigid censorship was imposed. When Archbishop Arundel went beyond these measures to demand that the university itself appoint a commission to draw up a formal list of Wyclif's errors, he met with sabotage and rioting before he had his way. In 1411, when he proposed to make a visitation of the university, which was a violation of its traditional papal privileges, the scholars defied him, fortified the church against him, celebrated Mass in the face of the interdict, and poured into the streets with arms to rout his followers. Only the forceful intervention of the Crown established the archbishop's authority in the end, and compelled the scholars to acknowledge his power of visitation. With this the independent spirit of the Oxford scholars was broken at last.[97] The comparable suppression of the Hussites a few years later added to the chill that settled over the northern universities.[98]

In the development of humanistic learning the Italian universities took the leadership, as they had earlier done with medicine and law and were later to do with physical science. Toward the end of the fourteenth century the infiltration of Greek influences and the collection of Greek manuscripts was already well under way, and by the middle of the fifteenth century, when humanistic learning was rapidly spreading in

[97] Mallet, *History of Oxford*, I, 221–40.
[98] Cf. James B. Mullinger, *A History of the University of Cambridge* (London, 1888), p. 60; Mallet, *History of Oxford*, I, 338. See also Clara P. McMahon, *Education in Fifteenth-Century England* (Baltimore, 1947), Chap. II.

the North, the first great generation of Italian Hellenists had already passed from the scene.[99] While it brought new interest and energy to university life throughout Europe, the development of humanist learning took place under new conditions in which the relative position of the universities in the whole of intellectual life was considerably lowered. The universities of the Middle Ages had been well knit into the ecclesiastical system, and university men could be credited with a large proportion of the sum of intellectual work. Humanism grew up within the framework of a well-developed system of patronage in which learning was fostered not so much by the universities as by princes and nobles, the *haute bourgeoisie,* and the Roman court itself. Significantly, the indispensable libraries of the great age of humanist scholarship were gathered almost entirely by princes and private persons, while the universities played a very small part.[100] A secular intellectual life was emerging on a scale hitherto unknown; and for this reason the presence or absence of intellectual freedom in the universities represents a considerably less significant part of the whole story of intellectual liberty in the humanist period than it did at the peak of the Middle Ages.

There existed, nonetheless, a problem of intellectual freedom for the academic humanists, particularly in the northern universities, a problem which posed itself in a far different form from that which had been characteristic of the medieval university. In Italy, to which the northern humanists almost universally turned for their first draughts of classical learning, skepticism was rife, and the measure of latitude permissible to free thought was very broad. The papacy itself became for a time hardly more than a secular institution, served by men like Guicciardini, who disdained it, and Valla, who had struck a scholarly blow at its historical pretensions to temporal power. It was Italian learning primarily, and not that of the North, that Ariosto characterized when he asked, "Why is it that learning and infidelity go hand in hand?" [101] During the age of the Renaissance popes a remarkable degree of latitude was given, albeit inconsistently, to Italian thinkers. The machinery of the Inquisition existed, and might at any time be called into action; and yet widespread freedom of thought must always have acted as a temptation to boldness.

[99] D'Irsay, *Histoire,* Vol. I, Chaps. X, XI.
[100] Myron P. Gilmore, *The World of Humanism* (New York, 1952), pp. 184–86.
[101] Preserved Smith, *The Age of the Reformation* (New York, 1920), p. 628.

The case of Pietro Pomponazzi, the foremost academic philosopher of Italy in the early sixteenth century, suggests how far one might go, if he had the proper connections, under the system of licensed hypocrisy that for a time prevailed in Italy. In 1516 Pomponazzi, who had been for over two decades a professor, first at Padua, then Ferrara, and finally at Bologna, published his famous treatise on the immortality of the soul, a problem which had for the Italians of the period an especially lively speculative interest. For his skepticism Pomponazzi might be considered among the first of the modern philosophers. But for his interest in certain problems inherited from the Aristotelian scholastics, and notably in those raised by Averroës for thinkers of what was loosely called the "school of Padua," he might well be placed among the more tenacious of the latter-day scholastics.[102] It may be enough to say here of Pomponazzi's work that it denied that one could by rational Aristotelian methods prove the immortality of the soul as maintained by the Christian Church, that its conception of ethics was far more naturalistic than Christian, and that it bowed to orthodoxy in the traditional manner of the "double-truth" school by concluding that faith shows that the soul is immortal.[103]

Pomponazzi's book was published in the face of a decree, issued only three years before by a Lateran Council, against philosophical skepticism concerning the immortality of the soul.[104] The thinness of Pom-

[102] On Pomponazzi see the discussion by John Herman Randall, Jr., in Ernst Cassirer, et al., *The Renaissance Philosophy of Man* (Chicago, 1948), pp. 257-79, and the text, pp. 280 ff.

[103] The Averroists denied that the individual soul was immortal because it did not possess the attribute of intelligence, but granted it a kind of collective immortality insofar as it participated in the unity of intellect. Pomponazzi denied the possibility of rationally demonstrating the existence of intelligence independent of corporeal embodiment.

Pomponazzi's formula, which proved acceptable to the papacy, was this: "I do not firmly adhere to anything which I have said in my book, save in so far as the Apostolic See determines. Whatever, therefore, I may have said, whether it be true or false, whether it be in accordance with the faith or contrary to it, I ought not in any way to be held heretical." In reply to one of his critics he declared: "He will not find that in any part of my little treatise I have affirmed that the soul is mortal. I have only said that Aristotle thought so, and that immortality cannot be proved by natural reason, but is to be held by sincere faith." Mandell Creighton, *A History of the Papacy from the Great Schism to the Sack of Rome*, V (London, 1901), 272, 274. Cf. Pomponazzi's careful phrasing in his original treatise, Cassirer, et al., *Renaissance Philosophy of Man*, pp. 302-3, 379, 381.

[104] Creighton, however, points to the apologetic, hortatory, and toothless character of this decree not as evidence of suppression but as "significant testimony to the decay of dogmatic theology." *Ibid.*, p. 222.

ponazzi's use of the "double truth" stratagem did not escape the clergy, who appealed to the Doge of Venice to suppress him. The Doge ordered the book burned, and Pomponazzi seems to have felt it discreet to stay away from Venice; but when Pope Leo X was petitioned to suppress Pomponazzi, he neglected to prosecute the philosopher, partly because of the intercession of Cardinal Gonzaga (to whom Pomponazzi dedicated one of his books) and the humanist Cardinal Bembo. Far from intimidated by the possibility of prosecution, Pomponazzi followed his critique of immortality with an attack on the clergy. Nor did his independence harm his professional career. Other Italian universities clamored for him, and the Bolognese magistrates were eager enough to keep him in their university to confirm his professorship for eight years and raise his salary. At his death Cardinal Gonzaga erected a monument to him in his native town of Mantua. The incident perhaps represents the zenith of the Italian skepticism of the period, which before many years went into eclipse under the combined impact of the Reformation struggle and the decline of Italian political and cultural life.

Despite the immense authority of Italian learning among the humanists of the northern universities, neither the skepticism nor the frequently cynical character of Italian thought was disseminated as readily as the model of Italian scholarship itself. Academic humanism in the North was predominantly pious, moderate, and compromising. Conservative churchmen foresaw that the intellectual concerns of the humanists, as well as their interest in church reform, might have subversive implications, but subversion was far from the intent of the humanists themselves. They were not schismatics, they wanted to lead no movement of revolt against the Church; indeed, they wanted to see no popular movement of any kind. If they wanted to be free to criticize the corruptions that had become so common in the Church or the superstitions that prevailed so widely among the populace, their purpose was not to undermine the Church's moral authority but to purge and strengthen it. The touchstone was the Reformation itself: while some of the humanists had initial sympathies with Luther, the leaders turned overwhelmingly against the Reformation when the break finally came, and most of them died within the bonds of the faith.[105]

---

[105] But concerning the complexities of this relationship and the tie between some humanists and Protestantism, see Paul Kalkoff, "Die Stellung der Deutschen Humanisten zur Reformation," *Zeitschrift für Kirchengeschichte*, XLVI (Gotha, 1928), 161–231.

Indeed, the ideal of such men as Erasmus, Colet, and Lefèvre d'Étaples was to put letters into the service of Christ, for among them the strain of literary and esthetic concern was subordinate to the textual and philological. Unlike the scholastics, the humanists were not so much concerned with dialectics or the subtleties of dogma as they were with getting at the true spirit of Christianity through a proper reading of the sources. Erasmus was revolted at the thought that people read Holy Scripture in the Vulgate when the Greek text was available for a more accurate reading. "I should wish," he once wrote, "that this simple and pure Christ might be deeply impressed upon the mind of men, and that I deem best attainable in this way, that we, supported by our knowledge of the original languages, should philosophize *at the sources* themselves." [106] Similarly Sir Thomas More, when the study of Greek at Oxford was made the object of a demonstration on the part of the traditionalist or "Trojan" faction there, wrote a letter to the authorities in which he defended humanistic education on the primary ground not of its professional usefulness—although for this also high claims could be made—but because it could "train the soul in virtue" and "build a path to Theology through Philosophy and the Liberal Arts." [107]

One sometimes gets the no doubt exaggerated impression that to the northern humanists religion was a combination of sound morals and sound philology that should be taken altogether out of the hands of the vulgar masses who had no Greek. Huizinga comments on Erasmus' failure to see that

[106] J. Huizinga, *Erasmus of Rotterdam* (London, 1952), p. 109; cf. Chaps. XII, XIII, *passim*.

[107] "This fellow declares that only theology should be studied; but if he admits even that, I don't see how he can accomplish his aim without some knowledge of languages, whether Hebrew or Greek or Latin; unless, of course, the elegant gentleman has convinced himself that there is enough theology written in English or that all theology can be squeezed into the limits of those [late scholastic] 'questions' which he likes to pose and answer, for which a modicum of Latin would, I admit, suffice. But really, I cannot admit that Theology, that august Queen of Heaven, can be thus confined. Does she not dwell and abide in Holy Scripture? Does she not pursue her pilgrim way through the cells of the holy Fathers: Augustine and Jerome; Ambrose and Cyprian; Chrysostom, Gregory, Basil and their like? The study of theology has been solidly based on these now despised expositors of fundamental truth during all the Christian centuries until the invention of these petty and meretricious 'questions' which alone are today glibly tossed back and forth. Anyone who boasts that he can understand the works of the Fathers without an uncommon acquaintance with the languages of each and all of them will in his ignorance boast for a long time before the learned trust his judgment." Gilmore, *The World of Humanism*, p. 214.

his conceptions of the Church, the sacraments and the dogmas were no longer purely Catholic because they had become subordinated to his philological insight. He could not be aware of it because, in spite of all his natural piety and his fervent ethical sentiments, he lacked the mystic insight which is the foundation of every creed.[108]

Their aristocratic outlook, their disdain for the grosser forms of popular religious practice and belief, their scholarly niceties, and their lack of interest in doctrine or dialectics kept the humanists of the North free from heresy and prevented them from having broad popular influence, while their insistence on the value of letters to the religion of the civilized man put them in the position of having something positive to bring to the Church. In them the desire for freedom took the form of a desire for complete latitude for scholarship within a limited but significant area of inquiry.

For all their moderation, the humanists found enemies among the conservatives in the Church and the traditional scholastics within the universities. Humanism was a threat to academic vested interests. Good churchmen, moreover, recognizing in the moralistic and rationalistic criticisms of the humanist scholars the first rumblings of what became the Reformation, saw that their concern with philological accuracy might in the end lead to questions about some church practices that hung upon philologically precise interpretations of scriptural texts. With the scholastics the humanists had to wage an open and bitter warfare, in the course of which the humanists expressed unreservedly their disdain for the sterility of scholastic exercises, for the traditional concern with forms and refinement of doctrine, and for the bad Latin and negligible Greek of their opponents. Paradoxically, in their repudiation of scholastic modes of thought they reacted toward a kind of intellectual indifferentism that can almost be called anti-intellectualistic, yet is intimately linked with the development of a spirit of tolerance. "We have defined so much," Erasmus lamented,

that without danger to our salvation might have remained unknown or undecided. . . . The essentials of our religion are peace and unanimity. These can hardly exist unless we make definitions about as few points as possible and leave many questions to individual judgment. Numerous problems are now postponed till the oecumenical Council. It would be much better to put off such questions till the time when the glass shall be removed and the darkness cleared away, and we shall see God face to face.[109]

[108] Huizinga, *Erasmus of Rotterdam*, p. 136.   [109] *Ibid.*, p. 116.

In this frame of mind a man was prepared neither to persecute others nor to espouse ideas with such passion as to risk persecution for them, as scholars had done in the great days of scholasticism.[110]

If the humanists committed many injustices in their estimation of scholasticism, these were matched by the discriminations practiced against them in the universities by a combination of schoolmen and churchmen. Although the humanists, like the early thirteenth-century Aristotelians, had the advantage of being associated with a fresh and powerful impetus to new learning, they made their way in many northern universities slowly and under disadvantages. Through most of Erasmus' life the firmly entrenched upholders of the old systems and ideals succeeded in maintaining their supremacy in the schools.[111] Many humanist careers that might well have graced the universities were sustained by private patronage or within separate academies, and the resistance of the university conservatives to humanism helped to keep much of the most significant intellectual work outside of university walls.

Humanism made its way in the universities with varying degrees of success. At Paris a Catholic humanist like Lefèvre d'Étaples and for a time even an heretical one like Louis Berquin was protected from the reactionary theologians of the Sorbonne by King Francis I, who discriminated sharply between learned men whom he wished to indulge and popular heretics whom he suppressed without hesitation.[112] Although an effort at Louvain to combine the doctrinal orthodoxy of Paris with humanist scholarship met with a measure of success during the years from 1490 to 1520, the place was the despair of Erasmus, who left it because its atmosphere was oppressive.[113] In England the humanists at both uni-

---

[110] Erasmus had much sympathy with some of the practices of an heretical sect, the Bohemian Brethren, but to them he wrote: "You must not think that any words of mine will bring you support; indeed my own influence, such as it is, requires the backing of others. If it is true that my writings are of any value to divine and useful learning, it seems to me unwise to jeopardize their influence by proclaiming publicly the agreement between us: such actions might lead to their being torn from the hands of the public. Forgive me this caution, you will perhaps call it fear. . . ." P. S. Allen, *The Age of Erasmus* (Oxford, 1914), pp. 295–96.

[111] *Ibid.*, p. 257; cf. Henry Osborn Taylor, *Thought and Expression in the Sixteenth Century* (New York, 1930), I, 151–52. Gerhard Ritter, however, has emphasized the superficial character of the conflicts between humanism and scholasticism, "Die geschichtliche Bedeutung des deutschen Humanismus," *Historische Zeitschrift*, CXXVII (1923), 393–453.

[112] See Georg Florian Münzer, *Franz I und die Anfänge der Französischen Reformation* (Freiburg, 1935).

[113] D'Irsay. *Histoire*, I, 255–57; Huizinga, *Erasmus of Rotterdam*, pp. 149–50.

versities, while at first faced with bitter opposition from within, made their way under powerful protectors like Cardinal Wolsey, Archbishop Warham, Bishop Fisher, Sir Thomas More, and Henry VIII himself.[114] In Germany Cologne played a reactionary role like that of the Sorbonne, while Erfurt was most hospitable to humanism.

It was Germany that provided the *cause célèbre* of northern humanism in the case of Pfefferkorn and Reuchlin. The incident began when Johann Pfefferkorn, a converted Jew, proposed that several new disabilities should be imposed upon the Jews, among them that all their books, with the exception of the Old Testament, should be delivered up to be burned. With the support of the Dominicans and the emperor's sister, he succeeded in persuading Emperor Maximilian to authorize the destruction of such books. When Pfefferkorn's procedure was found objectionable by the Archbishop of Mainz, the controversy over the propriety of burning the books was referred in 1510 to the faculties of four universities and to a few private scholars, among whom was Johann Reuchlin. Reuchlin, then in his middle fifties, was probably the outstanding scholar in Germany.[115] Educated at the universities of Freiburg, Basel, Orleans, and Poitiers, he was not only a Greek scholar but a great Hebraist. Having always earned his living under patronage and as a private teacher, he was not, strictly speaking, an academic man, but he was a hero to the entire learned world in Germany, academic and otherwise. One of his enthusiasms, which perhaps dates from his acquaintance with Pico della Mirandola during his Italian travels, was his interest in the cabala, in which he thought might be found the answers to some of the perplexing questions of Neoplatonic and Christian philosophy.

To a man with Reuchlin's Hebraic interests nothing could be more shocking than the proposed destruction of the very means of his intellectual existence. His connections with and indebtedness to some of the more learned Jews of his time had not placed him above the measure of prejudice that was common for his times.[116] He did not object, he said in reply to the inquiry, to the destruction of those few Jewish books which were solely and expressly aimed at Christianity; but the rest of the Jewish

---

[114] Mallet, *History of Oxford,* Vol. I, Chap. X; James Bass Mullinger, *The University of Cambridge from the Earliest Times to the Royal Injunctions of 1535* (Cambridge, 1873), Chap. V.

[115] Francis Griffin Stokes, in the introduction to his translation of the *Epistolae obscurorum virorum* (London, 1909), p. xxvi; this introduction gives a brief account of the controversy.

[116] Ludwig Geiger, *Johann Reuchlin* (Leipzig, 1871), pp. 162–64, 249–51.

literature, including the Talmud, the cabala, commentaries, sermons, and other writings were of use to the Christian religion and to knowledge, and he saw no reason why this ancient literature, long tolerated in Christian law, should be destroyed. The conversion of the Jews themselves—the supposed purpose of Pfefferkorn—could best be served by a careful study of their literature and thought. This opinion inspired an attack on Reuchlin by Pfefferkorn, and a reply by Reuchlin which was alleged by the theologians to be heretical. The Inquisitor-General, Jacob Hochstraten, collected a parcel of condemnations from the faculties of the German universities and the University of Paris and summoned Reuchlin to a trial at Mainz. When Reuchlin appealed to the Holy See, the case went to the bishops of Speyer and Worms; and when the Bishop of Speyer found Reuchlin free of heresy, Hochstraten carried the embarrassing issue once more to Rome.

The Reuchlin case came before Pope Leo X at almost the same time as did that of Pietro Pomponazzi, and one might expect, judging from the sheer merits of the issues, that the pontiff who had dealt so liberally with the controversial speculations of the Italian would have thrown out of court the far less imposing case against the German. But before the issue had ground altogether to its conclusion, new rumblings of discontent had been heard from Wittenberg; and even though a commission of experts advised the papal curia in Reuchlin's favor, Leo decided, in 1520, that the book in question was offensive, ordered it to be suppressed, and enjoined silence on Reuchlin. The pope was not prepared to add to his German troubles an affront to the Dominicans and the universities of both Germany and France.[117] Reuchlin himself, although impoverished by the expenses of the proceeding, carried on with his work, spending the few years remaining to him as professor of Greek and Hebrew at Ingolstadt and then Tübingen. He died in 1522, while the bitter controversy aroused by Luther was raging, firm in the bosom of the faith.

While the Reuchlin case was still under consideration there appeared a scathing document that Herder has called the *Don Quixote* of German theology—*The Letters of Obscure Men,* a product of the humanist circle at Erfurt.[118] This work is something of a landmark in the history of the intellectual class in the sense that for the first time it rallied the public

[117] Creighton, *A History of the Papacy*, VI, 60.
[118] On authorship see Stokes, introduction to *Epistolae obscurorum virorum*. pp. lvi–lxviii.

opinion of the learned world around an issue of interest to scholars. It is, of course, an exercise in pure *ad hominem,* for its sole effect is to pour ridicule on the ignorance and hoggishness of the traditional party. In this it was, according to common report, enormously effective. At a time when the attention of the world of western learning was focused upon the case of the Jewish books it crystallized the sentiments of the liberals and gave expression to the utter disdain with which the humanists regarded their opponents. But this intensely personal attack upon the Colognists (as the Pfefferkorn-Hochstraten party was called) has only a marginal significance for the history of the notions of tolerance and intellectual freedom. It was not a sober defense of free learning. It was a ribald assault on the limitations and foibles of the conservatives. Erasmus, with his characteristic urbanity, saw at once that neither the Colognist accusations of heresy nor the personal ridicule of the Erfurt group dealt with the fundamental issue of how religion and learning could best be served. In a magisterial letter of 1519 he rebuked Hochstraten for his part in the proceedings, especially his effort to obscure the question by pressing the factitious charge of infidelity and heresy. "Separate the person from the issue," he insisted. "A man can err, and then his error is to be condemned, but his honor ought to be saved, the scientific effort esteemed, with which he enlightens and serves theology rather than obscuring or fighting it." [119] To Erasmus the form taken by the controversy seemed to endanger rather than advance learning. And while many modern writers find in its outcome a moral victory for the cause of humanist scholarship, the evidence for such a view is extremely vague; what is perhaps clear is that the conflict showed how unready were both conservatives and reformers in the world of learning to discuss a problem of free inquiry from the standpoint of some criterion of the welfare of either religion or learning. The temper of the controversy presaged not the advancement of learning but the maelstrom of the Reformation.

[119] Geiger, *Johann Reuchlin,* p. 430; for Erasmus' role see pp. 427–35. An interesting opinion that reflects the thoroughgoing elitist position of the humanist scholar was expressed by Mutianus Rufus, the leader of the Erfurt circle and one of the most enlightened of the humanists. Although wholeheartedly on Reuchlin's side, he expressed during the early stages of the dispute his disapproval of anything that would agitate the masses, who must be left with their simple views of religion, lest they be stirred up against the Empire, the Church, and the men of learning. One sees here an anxious anticipation of the Reformation and an accurate reflection of the humanist feeling that church reform must not become a popular affair. See Karl Völker, *Toleranz und Intoleranz im Zeitalter der Reformation* (Leipzig, 1912), pp. 19–20.

Whatever their problems, the early humanists had been fortunate to work in an age when the ecclesiastical unity of Christendom had not yet been profoundly riven by the reformers. The great achievements of early modern science, however, took place within an atmosphere of bitterness, dogmatism, and intimidation. Since the universities after the beginning of the Reformation were under still closer church-state control and surveillance, and more favorable circumstances for innovation were provided under private auspices, early modern science tended more and more to flourish outside the universities. Thus, while the Italian universities carried on the most significant intellectual activity in Christendom, the share of the universities elsewhere in the sum of intellectual work was again substantially reduced.

The history of the Copernican system suggests that the Church had grown somewhat less hospitable to astronomical speculation than it had been during the fourteenth and fifteenth centuries. Nicole Oresme and Albert of Saxony had spoken with impunity of a moving earth. Nicholas of Cusa had toyed with several daring ideas about the universe which were rather similar to those that were to cost Bruno his life; [120] for all this he remained Bishop of Brixen and later became a cardinal. By the time of Copernicus the atmosphere was not so free. Copernicus himself might have brought his ideas forward several years before he did had he not been at odds with his bishop (partly for personal reasons, partly over his friendship for the Protestant scholar Rheticus). When he finally arranged for the publication of his *De revolutionibus orbium coelestium* (1543) after many years of delay, it was done only after carefully discussing the matter with his friends, Cardinal von Schönberg and Bishop Tiedemann Giese, and under the protective cover of a carefully written preface in which the work was dedicated to Pope Paul III, a scholarly man whose intellectual interests and character were such as to promise that there would be no persecution.[121] Even after these precautions, Osiander, as we have seen, felt it discreet to add another safeguard by inserting without Copernicus' consent the anonymous preface in which the device of hypothetical statement was employed.

Launched with all this caution, the Copernican system did not at first

---

[120] On the influence of Nicholas of Cusa on Bruno see Dorothea Waley Singer, *Giordano Bruno* (New York, 1950), pp. 54–59; Nicholas' actual scientific accomplishments are discussed by Lynn Thorndike, *Science and Thought in the Fifteenth Century* (New York, 1929), Chap. VII.

[121] Rosen, *Three Copernican Treatises*, pp. 26–27.

arouse anything like the furor that might have been anticipated. Part of its quiet reception may perhaps be credited to the last-minute precaution of Copernicus' editors. But more surely its failure to draw the fire of officialdom can be attributed to the fact that it was not widely accepted by scientists themselves.[122] This was not entirely due to fear (although there were men like Kepler's teacher, Professor Maestlin of Tübingen, who believed in and who was widely known as a teacher of the Copernican system, but who espoused the Ptolemaic system in his published textbook),[123] but can be traced in substantial measure to the fact that there were many intrinsic unresolved difficulties about the Copernican system that troubled even men of open mind.[124] Tycho Brahe, the leading astronomer of Europe, did not adopt it. The Roman Church was largely indifferent to it, the Protestants with their greater bibliolatry were contemptuously opposed,[125] and civilized minds like Montaigne, Bodin, and Bacon did not accept it. At the close of the sixteenth century the doctrine still had few supporters. It was Giordano Bruno who by elaborating the new theory into a vision of the universe first alerted the Church to its dangers.

In his survey *Science since 1500,* H. T. Pledge makes the suggestive remark that "it is philosophies rather than scientific discoveries which are persecuted."[126] While there are undoubtedly some exceptions to this generalization—Galileo represents not the least of them—it seems that the severe findings of science, under their simple armor of matter-of-fact frequently stood a better chance of escaping the inquisitor's eye than the speculations of grand theorists. So it was in the case of Bruno, who combined with his great imagination and remarkable courage a tremendous capacity for provocation. The story of Bruno's career as a wandering scholar in the university world would in itself provide a lengthy footnote

[122] Stimson, *The Gradual Acceptance of the Copernican Theory of the Universe,* p. 32 and *passim.*

[123] *Ibid.,* p. 48; even Galileo continued out of a spirit of compliance to teach the Ptolemaic cosmology at Padua in the 1590s after being persuaded of the Copernican system. J. J. Fahie, *Galileo* (London, 1903), pp. 39–40.

[124] These are assessed lucidly by Herbert Butterfield, *The Origins of Modern Science, 1300–1800* (London, 1950), Chaps. II and IV. Cf. Francis R. Johnson *Astronomical Thought in Renaissance England* (Baltimore, 1937), Chap. IV.

[125] During Copernicus' lifetime Luther said of him: "The fool wants to overthrow the whole art of astronomy. But as Holy Scripture declares, Joshua bade the sun stand still, and not the earth." Stimson, *The Gradual Acceptance of the Copernican Theory of the Universe,* p. 39n. On Melanchthon, Calvin, Montaigne and Bodin, *ibid.,* pp. 39–48.

[126] H. T. Pledge, *Science since 1500* (London, 1947), p. 54.

to the history of intellectual liberty. The fact that this heretical and immensely difficult man was able to live for many years in the university world offers a morsel of evidence that intellectual liberties were not totally absent from the northern *studia* of the late sixteenth century,[127] but his wanderings and discomforts likewise make it clear that genius and originality were far from sufficient to provide a scholar with a secure career. Bruno was a profoundly unorthodox thinker, seemingly without any real attachment to any of the standard theological positions of his day. His end is perhaps too familiar to require much comment; it forms one of the ugliest passages in the history of the Inquisition. There can be little doubt today that he was persecuted chiefly for his theological ideas, and that his views pertaining to or deriving from science were of only incidental significance. But what is most pertinent here is that by reopening the horrible but by no means novel prospect of an infinity of worlds he caused authority to give full attention to the dangerous implications of Copernicanism, and that his burning in 1600 marks the turning point from official indifference or liberality to persecution.[128] The day was not far distant when a campaign would be inaugurated to prevent Galileo from proclaiming the results of his observations.

Galileo had no sooner published his *Sidereus nuncius* (1610), which reported his telescopic observations, than he was listed as a suspect in the secret books of the Inquisition. Within a few years the jealousy of scientific rivals, the religious scruples of the Dowager Grand Duchess of Tuscany, and the suspicions of the Dominicans and Jesuits had combined to arouse vigilance against him. A professor at Pisa was soon forbidden to discuss the double motion of the earth even within the customary formula of probability. In 1616 Copernicus' *De revolutionibus,* after almost three

[127] See his touching words of gratitude to Wittenberg, quoted in Wilhelm Dilthey, *Weltanschauung und Analyse des Menschen seit Renaissance und Reformation, Gesammelte Schriften* (Leipzig, 1914), II, 509.

[128] One could probably argue that Bruno all but sought persecution by his manner and methods, and that his devotion to his ideas only resulted in a setback to the advance of scientific knowledge. Cf. the remarks by Mark Graubard, "Persecution as the Pathology of Freedom and Authority," in Lyman Bryson, *et al.,* eds., *Freedom and Authority in Our Time* (New York, 1953), especially pp. 399–401. In fact, the ethic of tact, moderation, compromise, and concentration upon the essentials is an altogether defensible one in relation to the problem of freedom. The sole danger is that the entire onus of manifesting these qualities may be thrown upon those standing for innovation, while they ought to be with equal reason demanded of the authorities. Noteworthy in Bruno's case is his somewhat belated appeal to the double truth tradition, which was of course quite fruitless. See Harald Höffding, *A History of Modern Philosophy* (New York, 1950), I, 120–21.

quarters of a century, was put on the Index as subject to correction; [129] and, while the record here is obscure and controversial, Galileo was apparently given some inkling at this time that further discussion of the condemned opinion would have its dangers. Galileo abjured,[130] and went on with his work, much troubled, until his admirer Cardinal Maffeo Barberini became Pope Urban VIII. Imagining that the time was again opportune to assert the truth, Galileo appeared in 1630 before the Grand Master of the Sacred Palace with a new manuscript in dialogue form in which the two great cosmologies were discussed. After much study the pope's representatives gave permission for the publication of the work upon condition that the hypothetical form of statement be used and that some of the pope's own reasoning concerning the question of the tides be incorporated. Accordingly Galileo's *Dialogue on the Two Chief Systems of the World* was published in 1632 under the cover of an introduction in which Galileo asserted that he was "taking up . . . the Copernican side of the question, treating it as a pure mathematical hypothesis . . ." [131] Despite his compliance with the forms, it was obvious that the work was a powerful plea for the truth of the Copernican system, not as a mathematical convenience but as a description of the universe. Also, Galileo's enemies prevailed upon the pope to believe that his own point of view had been subtly ridiculed. Galileo was charged with violating the decree of 1616 and maintaining the heliocentric system contrary to Scripture. An old and ailing man, he was summoned to Rome in 1633, tried, threatened with torture, and subjected to the humiliation of recanting and disavowing what he knew to be true, and sentenced to custodial imprisonment that lasted until his death in 1642.[132]

[129] Copies of the book were allowed to circulate provided all passages dealing with the motion of the earth were altered so as to assert that this idea, although false, was introduced merely as a mathematical hypothesis for simplifying calculations. The works of Copernicus, Galileo, and Kepler were removed from the Index in 1835.

[130] He did, however, send a copy of one of his works to the Archduke Leopold of Austria, under the protective cover of a very touching letter in which he offers his ideas not as true—for to do so has been condemned by the authorities—but as "a poetical conceit or a dream." "But," he adds pathetically, "even poets sometimes attach a value to one or another of their fantasies, and I likewise attach some value to this fancy of mine." Fahie, *Galileo,* p. 180.

The case of Galileo, notably the question of exactly what happened in 1616 is fraught with many complexities that we have had to pass over. See Karl von Gebler, *Galileo Galilei and the Roman Curia* (London, 1879), and Léon Garzend, *L'Inquisition et l'heresie . . . à propos de l'affaire Galilée* (Paris, 1912).

[131] *Ibid.,* p. 247.

[132] The legend that Galileo muttered his defiance of the Inquisitors is not credited

The most important literary document occasioned by Galileo's persecution was Tommaso Campanella's *The Defense of Galileo,* which appeared in 1622 at a time when its author, a Calabrian, was serving his twenty-seven years of imprisonment at the hands of the Spanish government. As a consequence of the discontents in Calabria this remarkable monk had been accused of heresy and of plotting against the state, and had resumed his philosophic and literary labors as soon as the physical circumstances of his imprisonment had been sufficiently lightened to make it possible. An intensely loyal Catholic, for all the novelty of his philosophical and social ideas, Campanella later secured the aid and protection of the pope, which made it possible for him to spend his last years at liberty in France. Although his most famous work is his utopia, *The City of the Sun* (1623), his *Defense of Galileo* has been called "the first reasoned argument to be published in support of the freedom of scientific investigation." [133] The tract was written after Campanella had learned of Galileo's initial encounters with the Church, but before the latter's final trial and sentence, which Campanella, as a loyal Catholic, accepted. The Calabrian was a complex and often seemingly inconsistent thinker, and it is difficult in a brief passage to do justice to the character of his defense. Despite its anticipation of modernity, its argument would probably not have seemed strange to Adelard of Bath, Abelard, St. Thomas Aquinas, or Godfrey of Fontaines. In broad outline the book attempts to establish two things: that there is nothing canonical, so to speak, about the ideas of Aristotle, least of all his cosmology; and that with proper exegesis it is possible to make a consistent harmony between new scientific discoveries and Scripture. The strategy of the book is quite compelling. Campanella seems to be trying to urge the Church out of its growing rigidity and into an intellectual statecraft that he feels is closer to the flexibility and liberality of its earlier policies. Its tone, as well as its argument, is such as to give comfort to those modern scholars who like to emphasize the continuity between the thought of the Middle Ages and early modern times. In true medieval fashion the book shows great deference to authority—

by modern scholarship. He did something more sensible: he continued, despite failing health and eyesight, to carry on his scientific work to the end, doing tremendously important work in dynamics in the face of obstacles to publication imposed by the Church. Fahie, *Galileo,* Chap. XV. The most recent study, Giorgio de Santillana's *The Crime of Galileo* (Chicago, 1955), appeared too late to be drawn upon for these pages.

[133] Robert B. Sutton, "The Phrase *Libertas Philosophandi,*" *Journal of the History of Ideas,* XIV (April, 1953), 311.

the authority of Scripture, of the Church Fathers, of St. Thomas, of the Lateran Councils—but always with the purpose of deposing the authority of Aristotle, and of providing authoritative precedents for the findings of Galileo.[134]

Although his particular application of his views to the case of Galileo was such as could have been made only by a man of considerable learning and ingenuity, Campanella's line of argument was composed upon familiar premises that had long been used to confute obscurantists. Indeed, perhaps the most striking thing about this early modern defense of scientific freedom is its thoroughly medieval tone. God had given man his reason and his senses in order that he make use of them, and to fail to do so is to "transgress the natural law of God." Moreover, truth does not contradict truth. Therefore there can be no contradiction between nature, "the created book of God's wisdom" and Scripture, "the revealed book of His divine wisdom." Wisdom is to be sought in "the whole book of God." What we learn of nature through reason and our senses must therefore be legitimate and consistent with the rest of God's truth, properly understood. But, as to the proper understanding of Scripture, there is a difference between its "mystical meaning for the wise" and its "obvious meaning for the vulgar." (How consistently this distinction runs through the early justifications of free thought!) The learned know that Scripture needs sound interpretation and that this does not always come easily. Since natural knowledge cannot be inconsistent with the true meaning of Scripture, advances in natural knowledge may give us clues to interpretation. The miracle of Joshua, then, is no less a miracle when we know that the sun is at rest—it is merely a miracle the mechanics of which is better understood.[135]

Campanella not only strikes this blow at Biblical literalism, but he keeps the problem of freedom of inquiry uppermost in mind. He quotes St. Thomas Aquinas as having said that "new theories always may be in-

---

[134] "Saint Thomas," Campanella writes characteristically, "teaches that Aristotelianism is not a doctrine of faith. . . . The Fathers and the two masters of the scholastics, Saint Thomas and Peter Lombard, support more than they oppose Galileo, and Scripture favors more than it censures him." Grant McColley, tr. and ed., *The Defense of Galileo* ("Smith College Studies in History," Vol. XXII [April–July, 1937]), pp. 35–49. Campanella stressed the heretical potentialities of Aristotelianism. *Ibid.*, pp. 40–42.

[135] *Ibid.*, pp. 18, 27, 28, 30, 54. The passage on Joshua is obscure, but Campanella seems to be suggesting that a miracle did take place, the mechanical form of which can be interpreted as well by the Copernican as the Ptolemaic system; cf. the reasoning of Oresme in 1377, Ross and McLaughlin, *Renaissance Reader*, p. 582.

troduced under the name of philosophy, and such theories should not be opposed on the grounds that they are contrary to faith . . ." and St. Gregory as having said that "if scandal develops because of truth, it is desirable that we permit scandal to be born, for by it truth will be left standing." [136] "Effective discussion," he declares, "is made sterile by bondage." [137] He expresses the modern confidence that error cannot survive: "If Galileo's theory be unsound it will not endure"; therefore, it is unnecessary to forbid it.[138] Significant too is the appearance in his text, possibly for the first time, of the phrase *libertas philosophandi,* freedom of philosophizing, which was the fruit of the medieval autonomy of philosophy and was the forerunner of more modern terms like *Lehrfreiheit* and "academic freedom." This phrase became fairly common usage in the seventeenth century.[139]

Of course Campanella's argument was ignored by the Church. After Galileo's abjuration and final sentence, copies of both were sent to all inquisitors and papal nuncios that they might notify their clergy and all the professors of mathematics and philosophy at the universities. Special care was taken to see that those at Florence, Padua, and Pisa were notified.[140] It is impossible to measure the extent of the blight that fell on such science as there was in the universities, or upon men of learning in general. Presumably many were like Descartes (of whom it has been said that he had no vocation for martyrdom), who had prepared a physical treatise which he was about to release when he learned of Galileo's trial, and who promptly suppressed his own work.

We think of the seventeenth century as a century of genius, of great

---

[136] McColley, *Defense of Galileo,* pp. 34, 67. St. Thomas is quoted from the preface to his *Tract against the Errors of the Greeks,* where he is arguing for a certain autonomy of philosophy from the faith. St. Gregory is quoted from a commentary on Ezekiel.

[137] *Ibid.,* p. 33.   [138] *Ibid.,* p. 37.

[139] *Ibid.,* p. 33: "I have shown that liberty of thought [or liberty of philosophizing] is more vigorous in Christian than in other nations." Cf. Sutton, "The Phrase *Libertas Philosophandi,*" p. 311 and *passim.* Actually the phrase had been used in a slightly different form by Bruno in 1588, Kepler in 1610, and Galileo in 1612, as Sutton shows. Among those who used it later in the seventeenth century were Descartes and Spinoza. The subtitle of the latter's *Theologico-Political Treatise* (1670) reads: *Containing Certain Discussions Wherein is Set Forth That the Freedom of Philosophizing Not Only May, without Prejudice to Piety and the Public Peace, be Granted; But Also May Not, without Danger to Piety and the Public Peace be Withheld.* The phrase itself was perhaps new, but the idea, as many a medieval master could have testified, was old.

[140] Stimson, *The Gradual Acceptance of the Copernican Theory of the Universe,* pp. 67–68.

advances in all branches of science, of brilliant philosophy and liberal theology. Although work of much importance to science was carried on at Leiden and Cambridge, there was a tendency for such investigation to be fostered more effectively in scientific societies. Most of university life was still substantially bounded by the medieval curriculum, the Latin language, and Greek thought. Its science was the science of Ptolemy, Euclid, Aristotle, Galen, and Hippocrates. Ecclesiasticism and confessional requirements were all but universal, and freedom of thought was neither practiced nor professed. "The teacher," ran one statement of the predominant ideal,

is not to permit any novel opinions or discussions to be mooted; nor to cite or allow others to cite the opinions of an author not of known repute; nor to teach or suffer to be taught anything contrary to prevalent opinions of acknowledged doctors current in the schools. Obsolete and false opinions are not to be mentioned at all even for refutation nor are objections to received teaching to be dwelt on at any length. . . . In philosophy Aristotle is always to be followed and St. Thomas Aquinas generally.[141]

The exceptions to this generally bleak picture existed where universities were sponsored by municipalities and where the hand of ecclesiasticism rested less heavily—at the northern Italian universities, in Holland, where Leiden was notably hospitable to science and where Cartesianism had its warmest reception, and at Halle, Heidelberg, and Altdorf.[142] But even at Padua Vesalius found that he had to conform to Galen and met so much opposition to novel discovery that he lost his temper and left for the court of Spain.

At the University of Paris tradition was everything. The university was still the censor of books, and in 1626 the death penalty was prescribed by civil authority for anyone who published without university authorization, while another rule forbade any teacher to hold or teach anything against the ancient authors. Although Descartes had dedicated his *Discourse on Method* to the Sorbonne, the Paris theologians in 1663 had his works, except as corrected, put on the Index. In 1671, when the Archbishop of Paris warned all four faculties against allowing any opin-

[141] Quoted from Acquaviva, the Jesuit general, by Martha Ornstein, *The Role of Scientific Societies in the Seventeenth Century* (Chicago, 1938), p. 215; the factual material in this paragraph is drawn from that work, Chap. VIII. See also D'Irsay *Histoire,* Vol. II, Chap. XV, and Friedrich Paulsen, *The German Universities* (New York, 1906), pp. 42–44.

[142] Some aspects of the situation in German universities are dealt with in A. Tholuck, *Das Akademische Leben des Siebzehnten Jahrhunderts* (Halle, 1853).

ions that might breed doctrinal confusion, his warnings were accepted without a dissenting voice. Only with modest exceptions was the picture different in England, where the Laudian statutes of 1636 enjoined Aristotle upon the faculties. Oxford, to be sure, had a striking upsurge of scientific interest around the middle of the century, but most of this was attributable to Oxford residents without formal connection with the university, and it petered out when most of these men went to London.[143] At Cambridge something of a turning point occurred in 1663 with the endowment of the Lucasian professorship of mathematics and astronomy, which was to be filled by Newton from 1669 to 1702; but it was the Royal Society, not the university, that showed the more alert interest in Newton's work. Only at the dawning of the eighteenth century, when some universities expressly adopted the principle of *libertas philosophandi* and even Paris (in 1720) set Descartes beside Aristotle, did the more traditionalist institutions show some signs of yielding to the times.

THE IDEA OF TOLERATION

The modern idea of academic freedom has been developed by men who have absorbed analogous ideas from the larger life of society. From modern science they have taken the notion of a continuing search for new truths, fostered by freedom of inquiry, verified by objective processes, and judged by those who are competent. From commerce they have taken the concept of a free competition among ideas—hence the suggestive metaphor of a free market in thought. From the politics of the liberal state they have taken the ideas of free speech and a free press and an appreciation of the multitude of perspectives in a pluralistic society. From religious liberalism and from the long historical development which led to the taming of sectarian animus have come the ideas of toleration and religious liberty [144] by which they have benefited.

While it would be idle to attempt to establish priorities of importance

[143] Ornstein, *Role of Scientific Societies in the Seventeenth Century,* pp. 92 ff., 241–47; on university science at mid-century see James B. Conant, "The Advancement of Learning during the Puritan Commonwealth," *Proceedings of the Massachusetts Historical Society,* LXVI (Boston, 1942), 3–31.

[144] By religious toleration we mean a state policy under which religious groups other than the established church are permitted to carry on worship; by religious liberty a policy under which worship is freely allowed to all groups and no civil disabilities are attached to membership in any church. By tolerance we mean simply an attitude of forbearance and a disposition to extend toleration or religious liberty.

among these forces, it is clear that modern intellectual liberty on any considerable scale was an impossibility until the ferocious dogmatism and intolerance that flourished with the Reformation and Counter Reformation were in some measure quieted. Thus religious tolerance and religious liberty were the historical matrix of intellectual freedom within such traditionally religious institutions as the universities. As modern science and modern liberal politics may be said to have provided the conceptual models for the positive content of academic freedom, tolerance and religious liberty may be said to have cleared the ground for it by eliminating or moderating its most formidable obstacles, notably the union between church and state. Academic freedom and religious freedom have one root in common: both are based upon the freedom of conscience, hence neither can flourish in a community that has no respect for human individuality.

Traditionally Protestantism is quite rightly credited with having led to immense gains in personal freedom by forcing a breach in religious authority, by creating religious diversity, and by asserting the rights of the individual conscience. This, however, was no part of the intention of the major Protestant reformers; it was an outcome of two centuries of laborious historical evolution. The immediate consequences of the Reformation were disastrous to tranquillity and to intellectual freedom. With the Reformation the genial secularization that had been under way within the Roman Church was abruptly ended, and with it disappeared most of that inconsistent but highly valuable indulgence for critical thought that the Church had allowed. Toward science and learning, toward the rights of conscience, the major Protestant groups were no more indulgent than the Roman Church, which now became far more severe than before in its attempts to meet these new challenges to its power.

Toleration and religious liberty made headway not because men were wise enough to anticipate and avoid the consequences of persecution but because they had witnessed and endured those consequences for more than two centuries after Luther's manifesto of 1517. Toleration and religious liberty slowly won acceptance where men of power and authority learned to consider them necessary to civil order and flourishing commerce; [145] where religious minorities and small sects protested with some

[145] A notable case was that of the *politiques* in France, who although chiefly Catholics were driven by the disorder of their country to advocate toleration as

effect against persecution; where secularized thinkers and ethical Christians spoke out in behalf of freedom of thought and conscience or of the softer principles of Christian morality. And yet progress along these lines was so slow in making itself felt in academic life that even in America, where the multitude of religious denominations made mutual accommodation imperative, the application of toleration to academic life had only limited results for many generations. For about two hundred and fifty years after the founding of Harvard in 1636, the very form in which the problem of freedom was posed in American colleges—insofar as there was a formulation of the problem of freedom—was set by the conditions of religious sectarianism; and the ebb and flow of both liberty and achievement in collegiate education could be measured by the rise and fall of tolerance and religious liberalism. Part I of this volume traces that story, but before we can focus upon the American scene itself a final word must be said about the forms in which the rationale for tolerance was inherited.

From the standpoint of one who believed in the doctrine of exclusive salvation—that is, one who felt that heresy damns souls and that there was no salvation outside the bounds of his own confession—there had always been a rigorous logic behind persecution. To do anything less than try to force the heretic to conform seemed an abandonment of his soul; to permit him to infect others with damning ideas would be to compound this sin. There were, moreover, Scriptural admonitions to which appeal could be made, especially the fatal text of Luke: "Compel them to come in." In fact, however, a dual tradition existed within Christianity, and it was possible to find authoritative Scriptural or patristic justification either for persecuting or tolerating—often, as in the case of Augustine, within the writings of a single authority.[146]

In order to persecute, three things, at least, were necessary: the persecutor must be sure that he was right on the point of dogma at issue; he

---

an expedient in the interests of national concord and unity. Close to them was Jean Bodin, who significantly looked to the educational process under the guidance of the state as the means by which that unity of sentiment, once provided by religion, could be instilled in the children. See especially his *Oeuvres philosophiques*, ed. Pierre Mesnard (Paris, 1951), pp. 57 ff.

[146] This discussion of persecution owes much to Roland Bainton's article, "The Struggle for Religious Liberty," *Church History*, X (June, 1941), 96–124, which says a great deal in small compass, and to the same author's introductory essay in his translation of Castellio's *Concerning Heretics* (New York, 1935). An extremely suggestive analysis is that of Johannes Kühn, *Toleranz und Offenbarung* (Leipzig, 1923).

must be sure that the issue was important (i.e., vital to salvation) and not inessential; and he must be convinced that coercion is actually effective. The advance of arguments for toleration or religious liberty is the story of the progressive weakening of one or another of these assumptions in different times and places. While for the firm Catholic it was unthinkable to doubt either of the first two of these assumptions, the development within Catholicism, prior to the Reformation, of mysticism, humanism, and sectarianism had already set in motion currents of thought and feeling that weakened the determination to persecute. Mystics turned attention away from dogma and toward personal and inward religious experience, and introduced an element of subjectivism that made for mutual forbearance. Humanists also disparaged dogma, partly because they wanted freedom of investigation in those areas that to them were of most concern, but partly too because of the emphasis upon Christian ethics in their thinking.[147] Sectarianism, as expressed within the Church by the Spiritual Franciscans, set obedience to God above obedience to the pope (later this principle of mundane resistance was extended by others to other religious authority). The Reformation, by releasing innumerable substreams of religious thought and setting the example of successful resistance to authority, shattered the possibility of common agreement upon enforceable principles and ultimately allowed these three seeds of liberalism to take root and grow. By establishing an open competition of sects, it made inevitable an ultimate appeal to individual conscience and individual choice. Under the impact of generations of increasingly rationalistic criticism men came to doubt their own certainty in matters of faith and to understand more and more widely the import of Montaigne's remark that it is setting a very high value on one's ideas to burn men for them. As the importance of doctrinal differences receded, the importance of conduct as a criterion of true religion rose. The exercise of Christian charity came to be considered far more important than what John Locke called "nice and intricate matters that exceed the capacity of ordinary understandings." [148] There was a tendency to try to cut down on the number of points considered essential to religion, and by the same token

[147] Cf. Erasmus: "You will not be damned if you do not know whether the Spirit proceeding from the Father and the Son has one or two beginnings, but you will not escape damnation if you do not cultivate the fruits of the Spirit which are love, joy, peace, patience, kindness, goodness, long-suffering, mercy, faith, modesty, continence, and chastity." Bainton, introduction to Castellio's *Concerning Heretics*, p. 33.

[148] *A Letter concerning Toleration*, 1689 (New York, 1950), p. 15.

to minimize the number of differences deemed worth persecuting men for.[149]

Finally, while there were, as we have said, powerful reasons for toleration which stemmed from considerations of secular expediency, there were distinctively religious reasons for toleration which stemmed from psychological impulses that had long had their formulation in Christian ethics.[150] As George Lincoln Burr once wrote,

It was not science, not reason, that put an end to inhumanity in so many fields: the pedants were as cruel as the bigots. Reason came in only to sanction here reforms which had been wrought in spite of her. The real antagonist of theology and of rationalism alike was the unreasoning impulse of human kindliness.[151]

Pious men saw that forced acceptance of a faith would not be sincere, that instead of saving souls, it created hypocrites; [152] and many of them found in the acts of persecution a breach of Christian charity far more objectionable than any notions of the alleged heretic.[153]

Some writers came to see the very search for religious truth and the willingness to endure persecution for it as a religious merit, a token of spiritual sincerity that contrasted nobly with the readiness of some men to submit to coercion. It was argued that religious conversion should be sought by humility, devotion, and persuasion, rather than by force, and many liberals expressed their confidence that truth would in the long run

[149] This attempt to strip off inessentials often had a practical urgency when it seemed that by so doing some Protestant groups otherwise close together might be able to unite. This distinction between fundamentals and inessentials, however, could cut both ways, for authority might argue that if some matters were really inessential to the main body of faith the nonconformists were being obstinate and petty for stickling over them. Thus Laud, who was strong on discipline and matters of form but broadminded about doctrine, still grated upon the Puritans. In the end it was realized that what is fundamental to one sect is not to another, and the whole distinction tended to break down. Bainton, "The Struggle for Religious Liberty," pp. 103–5.

[150] Thus even W. E. H. Lecky in his *History of the Rise and Influence of the Spirit of Rationalism in Europe* (1865; London, 1946), part II, p. 30, concedes concerning the rise of toleration in England that "the most illustrious of the advocates of toleration were earnestly attached to positive religion."

[151] Roland H. Bainton and Lois Oliphand Gibbons, *George Lincoln Burr, His Life: Selections from His Writings* (Ithaca, N. Y., 1943), p. 56.

[152] Cf. Erasmus: "That which is forced cannot be sincere, and that which is not voluntary cannot please Christ." Bainton, introduction to Castellio's *Concerning Heretics*, p. 34.

[153] For a beautiful example of the precedents for tolerance in mystical and devotional literature of the waning Middle Ages see Chap. XVI of Thomas à Kempis' *Imitation of Christ*.

command assent. Thus out of centuries of argument for religious tolerance certain perspectives emerged that, in a more secular context, were
readily translated into arguments for intellectual freedom. Fallibilism—
the recognition that man is prone to error and that to this no one can
presume himself an exception—became a leading theme in the rationalist
tradition.[154] With it came the recognition that the truth is not static, but
is progressively unfolded, and that the quest for truth is itself a human
activity deserving of respect as an ultimate value. Some religious writers
understood, before it became a commonplace in the history of science,
the principle that error may have its value, or its indispensable place, in
the search for truth.[155] And finally the humanist idea that personal piety
and morals are more important than doctrinal tenets could easily be translated into the secular principle that it is only misconduct, not opinions,
that should make one liable to prosecution or to disabilities.

The impulse to persecute had, among other things, its psychological
sources, and these were projected into theology in the form of a harsh
conception of the nature of both God and man and of the relation between them. Men who were pre-eminently concerned with justice on
earth were more likely to believe that the decrees of God were also limited by considerations of justice and were not the products of an arbitrary
and inscrutable will. Those theologies that emphasized the charity, mercy,
and justness of God in terms amenable to human reason, that asserted the
ability of man to better his nature and help himself toward salvation, were
most disposed to tolerate; while those theologies that held to a wrathful
and arbitrary God whose decrees were beyond human scrutiny and
preached predestination and the helplessness and wretchedness of man
were more consonant with persecution.

The argument for tolerance entered into modern thought through many
channels, of which we can choose but one illustration. If a single work
must be chosen from early modern history as a repository of the argument
for tolerance to set beside Campanella's later defense of Galileo, it would
probably be Sébastien Castellio's *Concerning Heretics,* which appeared in

---

[154] Actually the roots of this idea can be found in the fourteenth and fifteenth
centuries.

[155] In 1531 the mystical apostate Lutheran, Sebastian Franck, put it in these
terms: "Truth, when set over against error, shines forth only the more clearly and
steadily. That is why God permitted heresies to arise, and it is expedient that there
should be lies for the proving and establishing of the truth, for every proposition
carries with it and demands its contrary." Quoted in Bainton's translation of
Castellio's *Concerning Heretics,* p. 188.

1554 as a protest against the burning of Servetus in Geneva the previous year at the behest of Calvin.[156] Castellio, a Frenchman by birth, who had been called by Calvin to be rector of the college at Geneva but had broken with Calvin over theological questions, was at the time professor of Greek at the University of Basel. A few years earlier he had published a Latin translation of the Bible in whose footnotes and dedicatory preface (to Edward VI of England) he had already made a plea for tolerance. Castellio's *Concerning Heretics* was answered on Calvin's behalf by Theodore Beza. The views it expressed led to Castellio's being hounded almost to the point of leaving Basel and seeking refuge elsewhere, but he hung on until his death in 1563.

The greater part of Castellio's book consisted of excerpts from authoritative writers from patristic times down to such immediate predecessors as Erasmus and Sebastian Franck, who had argued either for liberty or for very mild penalties for heretics. Its dedication to Duke Christoph summarized Castellio's own views, which were profoundly affected by the humanistic emphasis on conduct as opposed to beliefs. Christ had commanded men to "live together in a Christian manner, amicably, without controversy and contention, loving one another." Nothing then could be more repugnant to the nature and will of Christ than to strangle and burn others who differ on matters of faith. Others may be sincere, they may cling to their different ways not out of contumacy or obstinacy but out of a sincere fear of offending Christ (for his servant Paul had enjoined men not to do anything about which they were in doubt).[157] Castellio professed to hate heretics himself, but he was troubled by the thought that men might be held for heresy who were not heretics, and that punishment might be carried far beyond what was demanded by Christian discipline. He saw that there had already come to be so many sects that if each one persisted in regarding the others as heretical, persecution might go on endlessly. He denied that there was an inevitable linkage between doctrine and morals, insisting that good lives could be lived by men of many different opinions.[158]

Castellio's book was widely read on the Continent, but nowhere was it so influential as in Holland. There the liberal-minded Erasmian scholar

[156] On Castellio and Servetus see Earl Morse Wilbur, *A History of Unitarianism: Socinianism and Its Antecedents* (Cambridge, 1947), Chaps. XIII and XIV.

[157] Romans 14:23.

[158] Bainton's translation of Castellio's *Concerning Heretics,* pp. 121–40; cf. Castellio's other remarks on this theme, *ibid.*, pp. 257 ff.

and writer, Dirk Volkertszoon Coornhert, made himself thoroughly familiar with Castellio, translated two of Castellio's pamphlets and tried to popularize his arguments. A layman and a former secretary of state, Coornhert belonged to the liberal and cultivated minority in Holland that found itself out of sympathy with the rigorous orthodox Calvinism of the Reformed Church. His denial of the doctrine of predestination and his advocacy of toleration for all the major religious groups brought him the disapproval of the orthodox ministers, who forbade him to publish his views. They also arranged for a formal answer to his heresies; and at this juncture occurred one of the most interesting episodes in modern intellectual history. Among those summoned to reply to Coornhert was one Jacobus Arminius, a minister of Amsterdam who had studied under Beza at Geneva, and who was thus thought to be eminently equipped to defend predestination and capital punishment for heretics. "The acute and distinct Arminius," as Milton was to call him, set about to restudy the question with care, and in consequence almost completely reversed his position, adopting tenets very close to those of Coornhert himself.[159] Arminius became the founder of a theological movement of wide influence among the Dutch clergy and laity.

The full terms of the theological argument between the Arminians and the Calvinists are endlessly complicated. Suffice it to say that the Calvinists had one of the most impregnable arguments for the validity of persecution, for according to them its purpose was not to persuade or to save —the efficacy of which could always be readily doubted—but simply and purely to punish for the greater glory of God. Its implicit premise was that such punishment was gratifying to God, an assumption that could be doubted but hardly disproved.[160] Arminianism was essentially a criticism of Calvinist theology from an ethical standpoint. The Arminians held that God was limited by his own regard for justice.[161] They objected to

[159] On Arminianism and the split in Dutch Calvinism see A. W. Harrison, *The Beginnings of Arminianism* (London, 1926) and the same author's *Arminianism* (London, 1937); see also Petrus J. Blok, *History of the People of the Netherlands* (New York, 1900), Vol. III, Chaps. XIV, XV.

[160] Some critics pointed out that if the eternal fate of the heretic's soul was predestined, punishments and means of coercion could not in any case save him. Thorough Calvinists were not very much affected by this, for in their view heresy was above all an offense to God, and hence more serious than any offense to man, such as murder or treason, that ordinarily called for capital punishment.

[161] Cf. Arminius: "God can indeed do what He wills with His own; but He cannot will to do with His own what He cannot rightfully do, for His will is circumscribed within the bounds of justice." Harrison, *Arminianism*, p. 21.

the idea that God had found it necessary to decree damnation in order then to effect salvation. This, they asserted, made God Himself the author of sin. Moreover, they objected that the Calvinists' doctrines left the great multitude of men without hope of salvation, while providing a few with an arrogant sense of election contingent upon no ethical qualities. They insisted that Christ had died not only for the elect, as the Calvinists would have it, but for "the world"—that is, for all men. They held that the grace of God is indispensable to man, but not irresistible, and that it would be possible to fall from grace—a notion that was meant to induce a necessary moral discipline into the behavior of the elect. All this tended to soften the image of God's arbitrary judgment, to make ethics more important at the expense of dogmatics, and to suggest doubts to the persecuting mind. Thus while the Arminians preached toleration for the compelling reason that they were a minority subject to persecution, they also developed a theology that was in consonance with toleration.

Arminius himself was made professor of theology at Leiden and remained in that post until his death in 1609, despite the objections of the senior professor of theology, Gomarus, to his unorthodoxy. Because of the hospitality of Leiden to Arminians, the orthodox faction opened their own university at Groningen in 1614. At the Synod of Dort, 1618–19, the Arminian faction, the Remonstrants, were with finality judged to be heretics, after which the persecution of their leaders was greatly intensified. One, Oldenbarnevelt, was put to death. Another, Hugo Grotius, the great theorist of international law, made a dramatic escape from imprisonment. Arminius' follower and successor at Leiden, Vorstius, was harassed and humiliated there, excluded from teaching, charged with Socinianism, and finally, after the decision of the Synod, expelled from his professorship.[162] In England the struggle in the churches of the Netherlands was followed with great interest. Ironically, while the preachers of Arminian persuasion were being hunted down in Holland, English Puritans, regarding that country as a sanctuary, were fleeing there from the hostility of James I.

In one respect the Arminians taught doctrines that were quite congenial to English authority: as a religious minority with more influence among powerful lay politicians than they had among the clergy, they naturally turned to doctrines of church-state relationships that favored civil

[162] *Ibid.*, pp. 52–59; cf. Harrison, *The Beginnings of Arminianism,* Chap. VI.

authority over religious affairs and denied any independent ecclesiastical jurisdiction. In their view the state was entitled to inspect and maintain the purity of the church—a doctrine most repugnant to Calvinists—but was not to act in any controversial matter to enforce the will of the majority or to interfere with individual conscience.[163] James I, for all his hostility to the Puritans, had been a Calvinist, and had thrown the weight of English influence on the side of the orthodox faction at the Synod of Dort. Under Charles I and Laud, however, the Arminian combination of liberal theology, secular autocracy, and stern church discipline became extremely congenial to the reigning trend, and the high-church party became deeply affected by Arminian ideas. Laud favored the Arminians for places in the church to the degree that when a divine asked what it was that the Arminians held, the answer was: all the best benefices and livings in England. From the standpoint of our present interest, what is important is that Arminian thought worked as a powerful leaven among the leading English clergy for religious rationalism and toleration. This is not to say that the first English Arminians were primarily interested in the philosophy or practice of toleration. But such ideas, latent in the theology they had adopted, began to be asserted. Nor is it to say that the English theologians were incapable of thinking up their own objections to Calvinism and that every deviation from orthodoxy can be attributed directly to Arminian sources. Arminianism became, in fact, a rather loosely used word for latitudinarian thinking, and in the American colonies, as we shall see, was an indiscriminate epithet for any variety of latitudinarian heresy. But Arminianism was an important opening wedge for the later development of English rationalism and English toleration. The latitudinarian theologians of the seventeenth and early eighteenth centuries found in it an important starting point. One finds traces of its influence in the Cambridge Platonists, in liberal Puritans like Milton, in later rationalists like Locke, and in the Unitarians and Universalists. From this latitudinarian tradition, which was the tradition of greatest influence for liberalism in the American colonies, stems the development of much of the liberalism of Harvard and of the later American Episcopal colleges.

Slow as the principles of toleration were to win adherence in the field of civil policy, they were still slower to make headway in the universities, with their traditional religious commitments. For university studies the

---

[163] Arminian political theory is discussed by Douglas Nobbs, *Theocracy and Toleration* (Cambridge, 1938), esp. Chap. II.

first consequences of the Reformation were disastrous.[164] Under the territorial confessional states the last remnants of corporate autonomy disappeared, and the long process by which the secular state had been encroaching upon the university reached its climax. The same formula that had been used to bring peace at Augsburg was the effective formula governing intellectual life: *cuius regio, eius universitas*. The king or the prince determined what faith was to be professed by his subjects and by those who taught or studied in his university; such freedom as was to be had could be found only by migrating. The university was now a completely confessional institution; and while the same might indeed have been said of the medieval universities as well, it meant something far more rigid and inflexible now that confessional allegiances and dogmatic differences were everything. A certain pluralism in philosophical tradition, as we have seen, enlarged and liberated the intellectual life of the medieval universities, despite their theoretical doctrinal unity. But in the full flush of the Reformation confessional considerations were dominant and everything could be a confessional consideration. When the Duke of Prussia, for instance, was disposed to take with full seriousness the Lutheran hostility to Aristotle, the study of the Peripatetic, and with him practically all study of philosophy at Königsberg, was suppressed.[165]

Exceptions there were, of course, to the dominant practices of the hidebound universities with their confessional oaths, but these came only toward the close of the sixteenth century. Leiden, founded in 1575 by William the Silent to honor the city for its resistance to the Spanish, reflected the liberalism and cosmopolitanism of the Netherland towns, and became "the earliest university of Europe to follow an intentional and consistent policy of academic freedom." [166] Professors were not required to make any doctrinal commitments in their simple oath of loyalty to the university and the city; Jews were admitted as students and private teachers; a Catholic professor, driven to resign by Protestants in the town because he defended religious persecution, was invited by the burgomasters and curators to return; and the university began to have the reputation as a refuge of learned men that it continued to keep during the seventeenth

[164] D'Irsay, *Histoire*, Vol. I, Chap. XIII, emphasizes the unfortunate consequences of the Reformation; see also Paulsen, *The German Universities*, pp. 36–37.

[165] D'Irsay, *Histoire*, I, 324–26.

[166] Robert B. Sutton, "European and American Backgrounds of the American Concept of Academic Freedom, 1500–1914," unpublished doctoral dissertation (University of Missouri, 1950), pp. 41–42.

century. The liberalism of Leiden was severely impaired after the Synod of Dort, when the Arminians were driven out, and it went into eclipse after 1676, when a professor was expelled for espousing Cartesianism.[167] Helmstedt, founded at about the same time as Leiden in the domains of the dukes of Brunswick-Wolfenbüttel, primarily to propagate Lutheran orthodoxy, nonetheless enjoyed at the end of the century a modest reputation for freedom, and retained the services of the liberal theologian Calixtus. That it was, however, far advanced on the path to liberalism later taken by the German universities is dubious.[168]

In England the Reformation was an act of state that began with the humbling of the universities. Henry VIII extracted favorable judgments on his divorce by employing threats against the universities, and followed his initial victory with the sweeping Royal Injunctions of 1535. These injunctions, which involved political interference beyond anything the universities had experienced, called for an oath of loyalty, set some of the conditions of lecturing, threw out the *Sentences* of Peter Lombard and required that all divinity lectures be given directly on the Scriptures, proscribed the "frivolous questions and obscure glosses" of Duns Scotus and his followers, and banned the study of the canon law.[169] It has been said that when the king's commissioners at Oxford found the torn leaves of Scotus' works driven by the wind through the quadrant of New College they were witnessing the final downfall of scholasticism in England. Like most attempts to draw sharp lines in intellectual history, this is an exaggeration; but what is true is that the divorce question and the Royal Injunctions put an end to whatever was left of the insulation and repose of the university scholars. From the time of the Lutheran controversy, when the early Protestant sympathizers at Cambridge had held secret meetings,[170] to beyond the middle of the seventeenth century, controversial theology was the most vital interest of university men and the story of university life was so intimately interwoven with the development of the English Reformation that the history of academic controversy is al-

[167] On Leiden see *ibid.*, pp. 42 ff., and Harrison, *Arminianism,* and *The Beginnings of Arminianism.*

[168] Sutton, "European and American Backgrounds," pp. 50 ff.

[169] See the account of the Reformation in Mullinger, *The University of Cambridge . . . to the Royal Injunctions of 1535,* Chap. VI, and for the injunctions see pp. 629–32.

[170] The Cambridge scholars who were infected with Lutheranism, many through smuggled books, met outside the colleges in the White Horse Inn, where it was felt they would be safer. On this episode see Mullinger, *ibid.*

most identical with that of the Reformation itself. During the religious upheavals of the Tudor era the men of the universities who did not conform to the reigning orthodoxy enjoyed no more immunity or peace than other dissenters or other clerics. They found themselves in a world of harassments, visitations, enforced confessional oaths, and burnings. Under Edward VI a vigorous and oppressive visitation took place that led to the exodus of many Romanist divines, while under the Marian reaction the leading Protestants left in large numbers and the universities became theaters and even agencies of the latest persecutions. Still another wave of exiles, now Catholics, left with the coming of Elizabeth, and at the beginning of the Elizabethan era the universities reached one of their low points.

With the growing moderation of the Elizabethan age and the return to the universities of many of the Marian exiles who had been in Holland or Switzerland, Calvinism took firm root among the theologians of the church, and in its wake came the Puritan breed. While Oxford, although not without its Puritans, became the stronghold of episcopacy, Cambridge was significantly infiltrated by the theologians of the Puritan party. Thomas Cartwright, the intellectual leader of the growing Puritan party, held forth at Cambridge for a few years, but for his doctrine of church government was removed from his professorship in 1571 over the opposition of the majority of the younger masters of arts. This action was supplemented by the imposition upon the university of a number of statutes that effected a constitutional reorganization, weakening the university organization in favor of the colleges and replacing the liberal and broadly representative mode of government by an oligarchy.[171] Many Puritans, among them Walter Travers and William Ames (whose theology was to be so influential in New England), sought safety in exile. Ames went from Christ's College to the University of Franeker, where as professor of theology he had a broad influence upon European Protestantism.[172] Still Puritanism was not rooted out of Cambridge. In 1584 Sir Walter Mildmay, Chancellor of the Exchequer and Elizabeth's trusted adviser, established Emmanuel College as a training ground for the ministry. His sympathy for the Puritans was quite properly suspected;[173] the college

[171] On Cartwright and the Elizabethan statutes see James B. Mullinger, *The University of Cambridge from the Royal Injunctions of 1535 to the Accession of Charles I* (Cambridge, 1884), pp. 207–41.
[172] *Ibid.,* pp. 510–12.
[173] "I hear, Sir Walter, you have been erecting a Puritan foundation," said

became a center of Puritan thought, and incidentally the primary nursery of the learned minds of New England.[174] By 1596, when a controversy raged between Calvinists and Arminians, the Calvinists at Cambridge were strong enough to oust from his post as Lady Margaret Professor of Theology an Arminian opponent, Peter Baro, who had offended them in one of his sermons.[175] As yet no quarter was given by either side in academic controversies, and no broadly accepted sanctions existed to prevent opposing sides from using naked power as a means of settling disputes. The theological disputants of the late sixteenth and early seventeenth centuries felt that the points at issue were far too grave to leave much room for the pale decencies of intellectual freedom. But some freedom did survive,[176] not because men believed as yet that the universities ought to be committed to it, but because so many and so complex and rapid changes had taken place in the religious life of England that there was persistent doctrinal uncertainty. Moreover it was the good fortune of the English that their bitterest conflicts arose not so much over broad theological issues as over questions of church government and liturgy, and men who were ready to conform on the latter could often find some intellectual elbow room for the former.

The end of the Catholic threat, however, only freed the Puritan and episcopal factions in the English church for a fuller expression of their mutual animosity, and as the breach widened the position of the Puritans became increasingly difficult. Under James I an oath of loyalty to the episcopal form of church government and the liturgical practices of the Church of England was imposed on all candidates for university degrees, confirming a requirement of the Act of Supremacy (1559) and fixing upon the conscience of the universities a blight that was not satisfactorily removed until 1871.[177] Now earnest Puritans could no longer complete a course of university studies. In 1628 all disputations on the Thirty-nine

---

Elizabeth. "No, Madam," was the answer, "far be it from me to countenance any thing contrary to your established laws, but I have set an acorn, which when it becomes an oak, God alone knows what will be the fruit thereof." *Ibid.,* p. 312; cf. pp. 310–14.

[174] On Emmanuel College and Harvard see Samuel Eliot Morison, *The Founding of Harvard College* (Cambridge, 1935), Chap. VI.

[175] Mullinger, *The University of Cambridge . . . to the Accession of Charles I,* pp. 347–50.

[176] See Mallet, *History of Oxford,* II, 89, on the views of contemporaries.

[177] The governing ideal was succinctly stated in the royal letter to the Chancellors: "The universities are the nurseries of learning and should be free from all factions." Mullinger, *The University of Cambridge . . . to the Accession of Charles I,* p. 457.

Articles of the Church of England were forbidden at either university, thus curtailing discussion of many of the matters that were most central in university intellectual life. Archbishop Laud's intensified campaign against the Puritans brought him to look closely into the orthodoxy of his own Oxford and stamp out the remnants of Puritanism there. As chancellor of the university after 1629, Laud patronized it liberally with one hand while doing his best to suppress its remaining freedoms with the other. He enriched it with benefactions, adorned it with buildings, and at the same time assured that it would be "the headquarters of the Arminian faith in England, an institution of orthodoxy, decorous, disciplined, and correct." [178] From its vice-chancellor he required a detailed weekly report of its discipline and doctrine, for there was hardly a matter so small as to be beneath his notice. In the Laudian Statutes, confirmed in 1636, the life of the university was codified and its government and conduct minutely prescribed; a measure of oligarchy was introduced such as the Elizabethan statutes had brought to Cambridge.

Such, in barest outline, was the state of the English universities in relation to the problem of religious freedom at the time of the founding of Harvard and the beginnings of collegiate education in America. The impact on America of later English developments may be seen from the colonial point of view in Chapter II, but one further development in English education may be anticipated here—the emergence of the dissenting academies. With the Restoration and the Act of Uniformity (1662) about a fifth of the divines of England who would not conform were ejected from their pastoral or academic positions (among them, it may now be noted, twelve who had been educated at Harvard and had returned to England during the Commonwealth or Protectorate). The university men among them set about to build new lives for themselves tutoring the sons of the dissenting nobility and gentry and educating the nonconformist ministers of the future. Out of these activities emerged a series of remarkable educational institutions whose value to subsequent English education, especially during the palsied days of the universities, was profound, and whose influence on American collegiate education was far from negligible.[179]

[178] H. R. Trevor-Roper, *Archbishop Laud* (London, 1940), p. 116; for Laud's chancellorship see also Chap. VIII and Mallet, *History of Oxford,* Vol. II, Chap. XVII.
[179] Irene Parker, *Dissenting Academies in England* (Cambridge, 1914), and H. McLachlan, *English Education under the Test Acts* (Manchester, 1931), are in-

From the Restoration to the beginning of the nineteenth century the academies employed the best educational energies in England. At first staffed each by a single tutor, and only afterwards by larger faculties, they grew and prospered and multiplied, and passed from an early phase of suppression by the authorities into one of recognized public existence. Their student bodies, at first composed of the sons of clerics and others primarily interested in religious issues, expanded to include a large middle-class public and even many children of conforming Anglicans. Their moral regimen and academic standards were higher, their fees lower, than the universities, and they offered work of university grade. Soon they were competitors sufficiently formidable to provoke agitation by the universities for their complete suppression. As for their course of studies, their original founders were too well versed in the classical studies to abandon them, but as one might expect of dissenters, were somewhat more hospitable than the universities to scientific and practical learning, so that the curricula of the academies combined classicism with a not excessive dash of utilitarian flavor.[180] Studies suited to budding clerics were in time somewhat subordinated to those suited to the budding middle class of England. In these institutions were educated such men as Daniel Defoe, Bishop Joseph Butler, the dissenting educator Philip Doddridge, Joseph Priestley, the Reverend Thomas R. Malthus, William Hazlitt, and James Martineau, among a distinguished list of leaders in politics, learning, and business. Students in some of the academies during their heyday were treated to a measure of liberality in thought and pedagogical practice that would have been altogether unfamiliar in the universities.[181] Locke was widely read among them at a time when the *Essay*

formative on these institutions, and their American impact is discussed by T. J. Wertenbaker, *Princeton: 1746–1896* (Princeton, 1946), pp. 81–89. See also Eugene D. Owen, "Where Did Benjamin Franklin Get the Idea for His Academy?" *Pennsylvania Magazine of History and Biography,* LVIII (1934), 86–94.

[180] Students of the history of the curriculum will be interested in comparing the early eighteenth-century course of studies at Yale or Harvard with that taught, say, at Sheriffhales Academy. See Parker, *Dissenting Academies in England,* p. 70, McLachlan, *English Education under the Test Acts,* p. 46.

[181] Priestley, who went to Northampton Academy, recalled: "In my time the Academy was in a state peculiarly favourable to the serious pursuit of truth, as the students were about equally divided upon every question of much importance, such as liberty and necessity, the sleep of the soul, and all the articles of theological orthodoxy and heresy; in consequence of which, all these topics were the subject of continual discussion. Our tutors also were of different opinions; Dr. Ashworth taking the orthodox side of every question and Mr. Clark, the sub-tutor, that of heresy, although always with the greatest modesty. Our lectures had often the air

concerning Human Understanding was forbidden at Oxford, and much of their work was carried on in a spirit of modified rationalism and modified Puritanism.[182] From them and their graduates, as from that solid middle-class England that they so capably served, there came to America during the early eighteenth century an unmeasured stream of influence and example which could hardly have been other than liberalizing and which must in some degree have been responsible for the notable gains of American education during the earliest years of the American Enlightenment.

By the early eighteenth century, when collegiate education in America was just beginning to proliferate outside the limits of Cambridge, Massachusetts, the European universities were still largely bound by confessional requirements. At the peak, judged by standards of freedom, was such an interdenominational institution as Leiden, which in its hour of glory stood almost alone. On the Continent, where the Reformation had made its mark, the scholar could free himself from the limits of the confessional university only by migrating to the region where the religion of his choice was enforced (by 1648 the formula *cuius regio* had been extended to include Calvinists as well as Lutherans and Catholics). In England the nonconformists could leave or ignore the universities and teach in the dissenting academies. By and large, one could not exchange views and freely discuss fundamental confessional matters within the walls of a single institution, although there were a number of extrafundamental matters that one might safely exercise one's mind upon. On the margins of theology there was a greater and growing freedom for philosophical speculation, insofar as the principle of *libertas philosophandi* was winning recognition.

---

of friendly conversations on the subjects to which they related. We were permitted to ask whatever questions and to make whatever remarks we pleased, and we did it with the greatest, but without any offensive, freedom. The general plan of our studies which may be seen in Dr. Doddridge's published lectures was exceedingly favourable to free inquiry, as we were referred to authors on both sides of every question, and even required to give an account of them." Parker, *Dissenting Academies in England,* p. 103.

[182] At the close of the eighteenth century these academies turned toward the work of propagating the principles of particular nonconformist bodies and away from the task of offering the best possible liberal education with the result that they lost much of their special distinction. Parker, *Dissenting Academies in England,* pp. 123, 136.

II: HARVARD COLLEGE FROM DUNSTER TO LEVERETT

THE COLONY AND THE COLLEGE

THE EARLY New England Puritans were a determined people whose religion was a stern school for the discipline of character. They had been able to take up their abode in a wilderness because they had the strength to risk all the uncertainties of the New World in order to realize religious principles. In this they were sustained by the belief that it was not their own wills but the will of God that had sent them to the American strand. They were picked, as Cotton Mather later asserted, "by no human contrivance, but by a strange work of God upon the spirits of men" that inspired them "to secede into a wilderness, they knew not where, and suffer in that wilderness they knew not what." [1]

If they were a chosen people—if God had sifted a whole nation to send choice grain into the wilds of North America—it must be for some high and significant purpose, they thought, and the Puritans believed that they well understood what that purpose was. They were here to demonstrate to all England, indeed to all Europe, that their ideals of religion and church policy were sound. They were here to found, under the auspicious conditions provided by a virgin continent, a Holy Commonwealth in which Puritan ideals could be sustained and realized as it was obviously impossible to do in England during the time of Archbishop Laud. They were to establish a community that would make them the vanguard of international Protestantism.

The Puritans saw themselves in a special relation to God which involved special privileges and obligations. Since they were doing God's work, it was only to be expected that particularly powerful efforts would be made by satanic forces to undermine them. They were prepared to make the strenuous efforts necessary to guarantee that the Holy Com-

[1] Cotton Mather, *Magnalia Christi Americana* (1702; Hartford, Conn., 1820), II, 219.

monwealth would not be subverted either from without, whether it be by pagan Indians or mad Quakers, or from within by the defection of some of their own breed. Under the stress of their holy task and their singular problems, it was hardly to be expected that they would be a tolerant people. True, they had been persecuted themselves,[2] and they did not embrace the idea of persecution without qualifications. They had simply withdrawn, they felt, to form their own society in the wilderness, and they had not invited or compelled men of other faiths who did not share their vision of the Holy Commonwealth to come with them to Massachusetts Bay. Baptists, Quakers, Antinomians, and other heretics could find places for themselves elsewhere in the wilderness—there was room enough. The characteristic Puritan punishment for heresy was banishment, and when they resorted to the more drastic expedient of hangings, as they did in the case of some Quakers in 1659 and 1660, it was after the victims, warned and banished, had returned to provoke them with their agitations.

Not surprisingly the Puritans held to the classic views concerning toleration and heresy. As Nathaniel Ward put it in his *Simple Cobbler of Aggawam,* anyone who was willing to tolerate the active propagation of a religion other than his own was simply not sincere in it. A state that would give liberty of conscience in matters of religion might just as well give liberty of conscience in its moral laws. Experience would teach Christians that it was far better to live in a united, if somewhat corrupt, state than in a state "whereof some Part is Incorrupt, and all the rest divided." One might (as the Puritans did) close one's eyes for convenience to the deviations of some citizens who did not openly challenge the established way, but one could not in any case concede their right openly to divide the conscience of the community.[3] Most of the Puritans seem to have accepted the distinction between fundamental points of doctrine, meaning those without which man cannot be saved, and others which were merely circumstantial points, on which men might differ in judgment

[2] The frequency of this experience among the first generation is attested by the biographies and family stories of the early presidents of Harvard. Henry Dunster seems to have left England because of his nonconformist principles. Charles Chauncy had been twice imprisoned for his opposition to Laud's regulations. Leonard Hoar had been silenced by the Act of Uniformity and had given up his ministry in Hants. Increase Mather, the first American-born president, was the son of Richard Mather, who had been suspended from his ministry in Lancashire.

[3] Perry Miller and Thomas H. Johnson, *The Puritans* (New York, 1938), pp. 227–32.

without prejudice to the salvation of either side.[4] In his famous argument with Roger Williams, John Cotton shrank from the accusation of persecution for conscience. It was not lawful, he said, to persecute anyone "for Conscience sake Rightly informed." But "for an Erronious and blind Conscience," once the apostolically enjoined double admonition (Titus 3:10) had been given, it was legitimate to proceed against the heretic; for, after all, in fundamental points the word of God was so clear that the heretic could not help but be convinced of the error of his ways after one or two admonitions, and hence any further persistence on his part was not really out of conscience but actually *against* his own conscience. Thus it was never for true conscience but only for sinning against his conscience that a man was persecuted.[5]

Those among the Puritan tribe who persisted in heresy—in the willful choice, that is, of false doctrine—must be prepared after due warning and argument to accept banishment if they would not stop uttering their beliefs. Those from outside, who like the Quakers tried to impose themselves upon the community, faced something worse than banishment. As a relatively homogeneous group that had not yet to reckon with the problem of a diversity of active faiths, the American Puritans were much firmer in their resistance to the idea of toleration than were their English counterparts. The English Independents had among them so many sects of various kinds that mutual toleration was a practical necessity if they were to hold together as a political party. The American Puritans saw this tolerance as a lamentable softness in their English friends. They felt as though they had been cut off from their roots and that they stood alone in their singleminded pursuit of God's way, for they had hoped that English Independency, which looked up to the writings of such New England intellectuals as Cotton, Hooker, and Shepard, would be the instrument through which their own success in God's work would be broadcast first to England and then to Europe. Thus while a liberal Independent like Milton was writing the *Areopagitica* his brethren in the New

---

[4] See John Cotton, "The Answer of Mr. John Cotton . . ." *ibid.*, pp. 217–18. An election sermon delivered by Urian Oakes in 1673 indicates the extent to which the more liberal New England Puritans might go. Compassion should be shown for the infirmities of men's minds, he said, and it was the duty of the magistrate to tolerate some errors, notably those that were "extrafundamental," small, or inconsiderable, and maintained in a "modest and peaceable" manner. Much depended also upon "the Condition of the State. . . . Hence that may be tolerable in one State, that is not in another." John L. Sibley, *Biographical Sketches of Graduates of Harvard University* (8 vols.; Cambridge, Mass., 1873–1951), I, 175–77.

[5] Miller and Johnson, *The Puritans*, p. 218.

World were determining to continue in their ways. The English Independents, on their side, were in fact embarrassed by having the New Englanders thrown in their faces when they advocated toleration. As George Downing, the former Harvard tutor, wrote in 1645 from England to his cousin, John Winthrop, Jr., "the law of banishing for conscience . . . makes us stinke every wheare." [6]

It may seem at first blush a startling paradox that Harvard College, founded in a community so dedicated to the enforcement of religious unity, should have become the university that for three centuries held the leading position for liberality of thought in American higher education. The historical developments that produced this paradox give the early history of Harvard a special significance for our story; for the seeds of Harvard liberalism were actually planted with Puritanism itself, and they sprouted not long after the first generation of American Puritans had passed on to their rewards.

Unquestionably Harvard was meant to be the orthodox instrument of the community and its faith. At the time of Harvard's founding there was a common anxious concern for the preservation of sound teaching. Boston had just been rocked by the antinomian controversy precipitated by Anne Hutchinson and her followers, a controversy perhaps most significant, so far as the difficulties of maintaining orthodoxy were concerned, for the fact that in its turbulent course Master John Cotton, one of the most authoritative expositors of the New England Way, narrowly escaped being disastrously involved. While many modern students will find in the Hutchinson movement a healthy note of religious individualism, it must be understood that to the Puritans Anne Hutchinson's teachings not only implied religious and social anarchy but were identified with a kind of popular anti-intellectualism.[7] At least three Puritan historians recorded that one of the reasons for the choice of Cambridge (first known as Newtown) for the site of the college was the fact that its pastor, Thomas Shepard, a preacher of great authority, influence, and appeal to the young, had succeeded in keeping Newtown "spotless from the contagion of the opinions" that had disturbed the people of Boston.[8]

But if Harvard was to be a center of orthodoxy, it was also to be the

---

[6] Quoted by Samuel Eliot Morison, *Builders of the Bay Colony* (Boston, 1930), p. 249.

[7] Samuel Eliot Morison, *The Founding of Harvard College* (Cambridge, Mass., 1935), Chap. XIII, esp. pp. 175–76.

[8] *Ibid.,* pp. 182–83.

home of a learned and rational ministry. Probably in greater measure than any other Protestant group the Puritans inherited the scholastic impulse to rationalize faith and the belief that learning has a high and vital place in religion. Puritan services emphasized neither ranting exercises in emotionalism nor the repetition of an esthetically appealing ritual, but rational discourses blending thought, piety, and scholarship. From an early date a strong effort was made to provide a common-school training good enough to produce a literate population that could follow the discourses of the clergymen and read Scripture for itself. There was an extraordinary number of university-educated men among the first generation of Puritans. Before 1646 about a hundred Cambridge men and about one third that number from Oxford emigrated to New England, so that the community in which they settled had one university-trained scholar for every forty or fifty families. From these men, says Professor Morison, were recruited the founders and first governors of Harvard College; from their loins sprang most of the first generation of Harvard students. These university-trained emigrants were the people who founded the intellectual traditions and scholastic standards of New England. They created a public opinion which insisted on sound schooling at whatever cost; and through their own characters and lives they inculcated among a pioneer people a respect for learning.[9] They expected their clergy to realize high standards of scholarship. All but 5 percent of the colonial clergymen of the New England Congregational churches were degree holders.[10] The

[9] Morison, *The Founding of Harvard College,* pp. 40–41; cf. pp. 358–410 for brief personal sketches of this body of educated immigrants. Among them were 100 from Cambridge, 32 from Oxford, 3 from Dublin, 2 each from Leiden and Franeker, and 1 from Padua; 87 held B.A.'s, 63 M.A.'s, 3 B.D.'s, and 1 M.D. In New England these men contributed (counting more than once any who had more than one occupation) 98 ministers, 27 magistrates, deputies, and lawmakers, 15 schoolmasters, 5 businessmen, and 3 physicians. Among the Cambridge colleges, Emmanuel was by far the most conspicuous, contributing 35 men, including John Harvard, John Cotton, and Thomas Hooker. Harvard's first president, Henry Dunster, came from Magdalene, its second, Charles Chauncy, from Trinity. *Ibid.,* pp. 360–62.

[10] Frederick Lewis Weis in *The Colonial Clergy and the Colonial Churches of New England* (Lancaster, Mass., 1936), finds that there were in New England 2,064 colonial clergymen of all denominations, from 1620 to 1776, of which 1,586 were Congregationalists. Figures for all denominations are not provided; but while Baptists and Separatists had clergies of which respectively 89 percent and 81 percent did not hold degrees, 95 percent of the Congregational ministers held degrees. Among the degree-holding clergy of all denominations up to 1776, 57 percent came from Harvard; 26 percent from Yale; 6 percent from Cambridge; 3 percent from Princeton; 2.5 percent from Oxford, and a scattering from other institutions, including not only American colonial colleges but Edinburgh, Glasgow, Dublin, Aberdeen, and Geneva. See the tables, *ibid.,* pp. 15–16.

B.A. degree by itself was not considered a sufficient attainment for a truly learned Congregational minister; the usual candidate for the clergy went on to take his M.A., for which he had to wait three years (not all of which, however, was required to be spent in study). During the seventeenth century Puritan clergymen were commonly addressed as "Master" in England and New England because they had commonly taken the Master's degree.

As early as 1636, when the population of Massachusetts Bay could hardly have been more than 10,000, the Puritans, "dreading to leave an illiterate Ministry to the Churches, when our present Ministers shall lie in the Dust," legally established a college which began instruction two years later. The fact that this fear of an illiterate clergy was the immediate and urgent motive for the founding of the college has led to some disagreement among historians over whether it was intended to be a theological seminary or a divinity school. The question is almost without meaning, for the theological seminary belongs to an age of specialized education of the sort the Puritans did not know. The tradition of liberal learning, as it had come down from the Middle Ages and had been broadened by the Renaissance, was the sole collegiate education they knew— and this was the fare of all students, whether their ultimate vocation was to be clerical or secular. That students planning for secular lives, notably for public leadership, would go to the college was undoubtedly expected, but no one thought that their interests required a different curriculum from those of future clerics. In 1650, when the General Court provided a charter for the college, the training of ministers was not mentioned among the specified purposes: "the advancement of all good literature, artes and Sciences" and "the education of the English and Indian youth of this Country in knowledge: and godliness." [11] Urian Oakes, the fourth president of the college, spoke common sentiments in his election sermon of 1673 when he called for "able instruments to manage church and state affairs" and to maintain "our civil and ecclesiastical state . . . in good plight and condition." [12] It is not surprising, then, to learn that during the seventeenth century only a little over 40 percent of all Harvard's students and about 52 percent of her graduates became ministers.

---

[11] See Morison, *The Founding of Harvard College,* pp. 247–51, on the early statements of the objects of the college. For an interesting defense of liberal education for ministers, see President Charles Chauncy's commencement sermon of 1655, as extracted in Miller and Johnson, *The Puritans,* pp. 705–7.

[12] Quoted in T. J. Wertenbaker, *The Puritan Oligarchy* (New York, 1947), p. 140.

Harvard may actually be considered less ecclesiastical than Oxford or Cambridge, in the sense that a smaller proportion of her students became clergymen.[13] It may be a just summation to say that while Harvard's purposes were not conceived to be secular—since nothing was entirely secular in a Holy Commonwealth—they were not entirely ecclesiastical. It was also implicitly understood that the teaching in the college would be committed to the doctrinal orthodoxy of the New England Congregational Way; and if no formal tests or oaths of conformity were imposed, it was not because conformity was not expected but because the community was at the beginning so homogeneous in religious conviction that such requirements were felt to be superfluous.

One of the primary problems in founding and maintaining the college was to secure a satisfactory president. From the beginning the presidency of Harvard College was intended to be a post of no mean status in New England, equal at least to the outstanding ministerial offices of the province. The president must be a learned clergyman, with a capacity for leadership. What made it difficult to meet these requirements was that the outstanding pastors were unable to get releases from their congregations; and when one considers the uncertainty of the college's finances it seems doubtful that many were willing to try. It became necessary to look to newly arrived young Masters, who came without congregational assignments, as was the case with the college's first "Master," the scapegrace Nathaniel Eaton, and its first president, Henry Dunster; or to find an eminent pastor who happened to be ready to move, like Charles Chauncy, the second president. The salaries paid by the poorly financed college were never alluring. The complaints of the presidents about their personal poverty and that of the college are a *leitmotif* of its early history. On the whole it must be said that after their original mistake with Master Eaton the Overseers did well. Six presidents were appointed during the seventeenth century, and four of these—Henry Dunster, Charles Chauncy, Urian Oakes, and Increase Mather—were notable men. The three admin-

---

[13] Morison, *The Founding of Harvard College,* pp. 247, 247–48n. Not only did students pass from the college into a wide variety of occupations, but their social recruitment itself was fairly wide. The sons of ministers and magistrates loom very large at first, but shortly after the middle of the century there is a notable increase in the proportion of sons of artisans, tradesmen, and modest farmers. The college from an early date in its history was an agency of social mobility in a society that seems on the whole rather stratified. See Morison, *Harvard College in the Seventeenth Century* (Cambridge, Mass., 1936), I, 74–75 and II, 450–51 for figures on the student body.

istrations of Dunster, Chauncy, and Mather covered forty-eight years, the greater part of Harvard's history before 1700.

The early Harvard presidents, like other American college presidents for more than two centuries afterwards, were not only administrative but teaching officers. For more than a hundred years, however, the primary teaching personnel at Harvard consisted of two or three young men designated as tutors. It was not until 1722 that the college had a professor, not until after 1720 that it had as many as four tutors in service at one time. Unmarried men in their early twenties, residents of the college hall who supervised the lives as well as the studies of undergraduates, the tutors were usually future clergymen waiting and studying for the required three post-baccalaureate years for their M.A. degrees. Normally they resigned their tutorships as soon as a ministerial call came to them, since their teaching careers were in their own minds no more than a way of marking time. Until near the end of the seventeenth century a tutor's pay was not sufficient to constitute an inducement to remain in the post. Tenures were brief. Henry Dunster complained in 1653 that tutors came and went at such a rate that "ever and anon all the work committed to them falleth agen on my shoulders." [14] Under his successor the average length of service was only two and a half years, and until the long absentee presidency of Increase Mather when the outstanding tutors, John Leverett and William Brattle, stayed for twelve years, a three-year tutorship was most typical. Thereafter the span of a tutor's teaching life began to lengthen. The average tenure of eighteen tutors hired from 1697 to 1742 comes to almost nine and a half years. [15]

[14] Morison, *The Founding of Harvard College*, p. 449.

[15] These calculations omit the unusually long and devoted career of the famous "Father" Flynt, which would distort the average. Henry Flynt, whose tutorship stretched from 1699 to 1742, was the son of a Dorchester minister. After receiving his Harvard M.A. he was invited to preach at Norwich, Connecticut, in 1695, but having discovered that he did not like preaching, he returned to Harvard a few years later to begin the career that won him the affections of generations of students. In 1718 he declined the rectorship of Yale. It is from his teaching that Shipton dates the end of the rapid succession of transient tutors that had been customary. Clifford K. Shipton, *Sibley's Harvard Graduates* (Vols. IV–VIII of John L. Sibley, *Biographical Sketches of Graduates of Harvard University*, 8 vols.; Cambridge, Mass., 1873–1951), IV, 163. But it was not until the term of another famous tutor, Thomas Robie (1714–23), that tenures regularly became extended to eight or nine years or more. Robie, like Flynt, tried preaching after graduation, but was accused of unorthodoxy because of his liking for the works of Tillotson. He turned to science, became skilled in meteorology and astronomy, and was admitted to the Royal Society. *Ibid.*, V, 452. Toward the close of the seventeenth and the beginning of the eighteenth century one finds a larger proportion of ex-tutors going into secular occupations,

The fugitive teaching careers of these early tutors is a matter of much moment for the history of American education. Since there were greater inducements in the ministry for learned young men, it was impossible to staff the college with anything but transient teachers, whose interest in the college and in teaching was secondary. Such teachers could hardly play a role of importance in the government of the college, nor were they likely to raise issues of intellectual or religious freedom. (If they had any deviations they were attached to, they were well advised to postpone airing them until they had established themselves in the affections and confidence of some congregation.) The early history of Harvard is silent as to matters bearing on the freedom of these young instructors,[16] and it is not until the period of the Great Awakening that a clear case arises among them. The only figure of importance among the instructional officers was the president himself. Here the record has something to tell, for controversies over intellectual freedom in American collegiate education begin with the first president of the first college, Henry Dunster.

THE DUNSTER CASE

In June, 1654, eighteen years after the enactment that created Harvard, its president, Henry Dunster, was obliged to present his resignation to the Overseers. Although the event naturally bears only the remotest resemblance to a modern academic freedom case, it was the first instance in American history in which a college official's tenure in his post was broken by a conflict between his personal beliefs and the established opinion of the community.

---

chiefly into public service. One also finds a significant number of men who, like Flynt and Robie, studied for and momentarily entered the ministry but gave it up out of incapacity or lack of enthusiasm. By contemporaries this might well have been taken as a sign of the times.

[16] The only stir in the college before the days of Increase Mather in which tutors were involved seems to have had little to do with religious or intellectual differences. President Hoar was forced to resign in 1675 under circumstances the precise causes of which were a mystery to contemporaries and remain one to historians. They seem to have involved personal issues. Hoar, it appears, alienated both students and tutors (who may have been whipped up against him by his successor, Urian Oakes, pastor of the church in Cambridge and evidently an aspirant to the presidency). Hoar was supported by the Overseers, magistrates, and ministers but when the entire student body deserted the college after the commencement exercises of 1674, his resignation became necessary. The case suggests, at least, that a president could not hold the college together, much less carry on with constructive

It is by a technicality, or perhaps by default, that Dunster can be called Harvard's first president. His regime was preceded by that of Nathaniel Eaton, designated "Master" rather than "President," whose brief stewardship had been cut short by his own mismanagement and brutality and by the slovenliness of his wife, who boarded the students. Eaton was dismissed by the magistrates of the province at the end of his first year. Harvard had been closed for the academic year 1639–40, its existence little more than a legal fiction after this abortive beginning, when the newly arrived young minister Henry Dunster, a graduate of Magdalene College, Cambridge, took charge of its fortunes. During the fourteen years of his administration, Dunster did well for the young institution. Working with meager funds, he established the curriculum and the institutional forms of the college, obtained its charter in 1650, and brought it to such repute that its students, who numbered upwards of fifty, included boys sent from Bermuda, Virginia, New Amsterdam, and even from England, where Oxford and Cambridge accepted its degrees, *ad eundem gradem*. "No American college president," writes Samuel Eliot Morison, ". . . has succeeded in doing so much with so little money." [17]

In 1653, when income reached a low point, Dunster appealed to the General Court for more ample funds for the coming academic year. The Court replied with an irritating financial investigation which seemed to cast his probity or competence into question; whereupon he sent the committee of inquiry a long memorandum rehearsing the various grievances that he had developed during his presidency. The investigation caused the Court to grant the Overseers some new financial prerogatives, which Dunster found "questionable and offensive." It may be that his difficulties with the Overseers weakened Dunster's attachment to his post and subtly prepared his mind for the espousal of a heresy that would be as irritating to the authorities as their intrusions had been to him. This is conjecture; what is undeniable is that Dunster, who had hitherto shown no signs of heresy and whose first three children had been baptized in the Cambridge Church, refused to present for baptism his fourth child, born in

---

plans of the sort Hoar had, if he did not enjoy some respect and confidence among tutors and students. For an account of the incident see Morison, *Harvard College in the Seventeenth Century*, II, 401–8.

[17] Morison, *Harvard College in the Seventeenth Century*, I, 38; for the most satisfactory account of the financial investigation of 1653–54 and the Dunster case, see pp. 302–19; see also Jeremiah Chaplin, *Life of Henry Dunster* (Boston, 1872), Chaps. IX–XIII.

the fall of 1653 just at the time when the General Court's unfavorable reaction to his petition was beginning to rankle. The community was soon excited by the sensational news that the president of Harvard College had become entangled, as Cotton Mather later wrote, in "the snares of Anabaptism." [18]

In denying the scriptural validity of infant baptism, Dunster was touching upon a sore issue. For some years the colony had been agitated over serious questions concerning who should be eligible for baptism and who could be members of the church. These questions, which as we shall see were not resolved until the Half-Way Covenant of 1662, went straight to the heart of the New England Church polity. The prevailing view was that while Scriptural evidence for the baptism of infants left something to be desired, the practice seemed to be a logical deduction from Scripture and from the necessities of Puritan institutions. Moreover, opposition to infant baptism was associated in the Puritans' minds with the Anabaptists, with "enthusiasm," with currents of religious feeling that they heartily detested.[19] In arriving at the conviction that no infants could properly be baptized, Dunster came to a conclusion that was considered dangerous and altogether unacceptable, but he came to it not as an Anabaptist or enthusiast but as a misguided member of the Congregational community who stumbled into an error in the course of contemplating the community's own problems. This fact alone makes intelligible some of the gentler aspects of the controversy in which he became involved.

When one compares it with the rancorous and cruel banishment of Anne Hutchinson and the banishment of Roger Williams, and the imprisonment and whippings that had already been administered to Baptists and the brutal treatment and final execution of Quakers that was to come a few years later, the treatment accorded Dunster seems considerate. The magistrates arranged in Boston a private debate, or "conference," after the fashion of the formal disputation, between Dunster and several champions of orthodoxy; this only had the effect of hardening the president in his heretical ways. A few months later the General Court, observing that "it greatly concernes the welfare of this country that the youth thereof be educated, not only in good literature, but sound doctrine," rec-

[18] Cotton Mather, *Magnalia Christi Americana,* II, 10.
[19] See the account of the situation in Perry Miller, *From Colony to Province* (Cambridge, Mass., 1953), Chap. VI.

ommended to the Overseers and the selectmen of the towns of the province that they refuse to keep as teachers or officers of schools or colleges any persons "that have manifested themselves unsound in the fayth, or scandelous in theire lives, and not giving due satisfaction according to the rules of Christ."

Dunster had not been dismissed, and he could have kept his job if he had promised to be silent about his unacceptable convictions, for everything in the case indicates that the magistrates and ministers never lost personal confidence in him.[20] Dunster, however, submitted a curious letter of resignation which made no clear reference to religious issues but dwelled at some length on the recent investigation of the college and the expansion of the powers of the Overseers at the expense of the Corporation. The General Court gave Dunster the opportunity to take a month to reconsider. Evidently they still hoped that he could be persuaded to swallow his heresy, and it may be inferred that the internal affairs of the college were, in the minds of all concerned, more vital than doctrinal issues. But a month later Dunster closed his presidency with the utmost finality when he interrupted a baptismal service at Cambridge with a startling speech against infant baptism and the "corupcions stealing into the Church."

His subsequent notice to the Overseers that he had not reconsidered was a formality. Accepting his resignation, the Overseers tendered the presidency of the college to Charles Chauncy, a learned pastor at Plymouth. Chauncy was sound on the baptism of infants but he held to a nettlesome deviation in the conduct of the ceremony itself: he believed in baptism by total immersion rather than sprinkling. This was a pardonable practice in doctrine, but, as Governor Bradford said, it was "not so conveniente in this could countrie"; and it threatened to have more bearing on infant mortality than infant immortality. Chauncy accepted the presidency with the condition attached that he remain severely silent on the alleged necessity of immersion, and on another of his peculiarities, his belief that the Lord's Supper could properly be celebrated only at evening.

[20] The extent to which Dunster had been esteemed is suggested in an earlier letter to John Winthrop from the Rev. Thomas Shepard, the trusted pastor of the church at Cambridge, in which he observed: "Your apprehensions agaynst reading and learning heathen authors, I perswade myselfe were suddenly suggested, and will easily be answered by H. Dunstar, if you should impart them to him." Chaplin, *Life of Henry Dunster,* p. 48.

As for Dunster, he continued to enjoy consideration at the hands of the Overseers; he was permitted to remain in the president's house for several months after his resignation took effect. But the county court at Cambridge found him guilty of having interrupted the baptismal service, for which he was publicly admonished. A few years later a debt of £40 that he owed to the Colony was forgiven by the General Court "as a gratuity for his good service" to the college. Dunster removed to the town of Scituate in Plymouth Colony which was hospitable to dissenters and where he seems to have found opportunities to preach. He often visited Massachusetts Bay, remained a member of the Cambridge Church, and in 1659 died, as Cotton Mather put it, "in such harmony of affection with the good men, who had been the authors of his removal from Cambridge, that he, by his will, ordered his body to be carried unto Cambridge for its burial, and bequeathed legacies to those very persons." [21]

Plainly the case of Henry Dunster was a gentlemen's disagreement. The offender was treated not as a subversive outsider but as a member of the inner elite who happened to fall out of line on one item of doctrine but whose discretion could still be trusted, even after all attempts at persuasion had failed.[22] His own mild acquiescence to the code that compelled his resignation is also illuminating, especially since it contrasts so sharply with his strong assertion of his views and rights both in matters of college policy and theological doctrine. Plainly he felt himself to be doctrinally on solid ground; but even to him, the victim of expulsion, there seems to have existed no sanction in the form of a code of educational or intellectual decorum to which he could appeal to justify his remaining in the presidency while publicly proclaiming an unpopular tenet. He did not say that he had, as the college's president, a right to his opinion; he could only stoutly maintain that his opinion was right. As a trusted and familiar figure in the community he was given a chance to argue for this opinion with other learned clergymen, although it must have been a foregone conclusion that he would not convince them.[23] The concept

---

[21] See Mather's account of Dunster in *Magnalia Christi Americana,* I, 367; the will is in Chaplin, *Life of Henry Dunster,* pp. 303–8.

[22] The Puritans made a distinction between the Baptists themselves, who were totally objectionable, and members of their own group who happened to oppose only their baptismal practices. Cf. Kenneth Murdock, *Increase Mather* (Cambridge, Mass., 1926), pp. 138–39, 142.

[23] The text of Dunster's debate with the orthodox ministers, transcribed evidently with several minor errors, may be found in Chaplin, *Life of Henry Dunster,* pp. 289–301. Of course the purpose of the debate was not to give Dunster a chance to

upon which his tenure at Harvard was based was presumably the same as that upon which the New England clergy held their offices. These men considered themselves engaged in a solemn covenant with their congregations which could be broken on either side only for the gravest reasons. It might well have been felt that accepting the presidency of Harvard College involved an implicit covenant under which the president was to remain loyal to the essential doctrines of the New England Way. Having departed at a significant point from these doctrines, and having failed to persuade New England's doctrinal leaders that his views were correct, it is understandable that Dunster may have thought his resignation obligatory under the terms of his covenant. He never argued that a college is a place in which the search for truth is to be carried on through free inquiry and the exchange of views. He apparently agreed with his opponents that it is a place in which the received truth is to be passed on, and so thinking, he quietly and gracefully accepted his defeat.

THE DECLINE OF THE HOLY COMMONWEALTH

In order to realize the purposes of the Holy Commonwealth the early Puritan leaders had striven to maintain complete unity in Massachusetts Bay, and they had done so with a firmness that ruled out all possibility of articulate dissent. By the 1660s it was clear that against those who would invade their community with an alien vision, whether they were complete outsiders like the Quakers and Baptists or would-be members of their own group like the followers of Anne Hutchinson or Roger Williams, the Puritans had maintained themselves with great success. What they could not do was to remain what they were, to preserve among themselves that unity and conformity which they had expected to retain. The pristine Congregational ideals were so demanding and the Puritan spirit was so dynamic that it proved impossible to freeze the spiritual and doctrinal life of Massachusetts Bay in the eternal pose that the sculptors of the Holy Commonwealth demanded. Plagued by internal differences over church polity and secular politics, and confronted by the besetting problem of relations with an uncongenial government in England, the guardians of the Puritan ideal conducted after 1660 a long strategic retreat. As they

---

persuade the others, but chiefly to give them a chance to persuade him. One of his former students, Jonathan Mitchel, had been swayed for a time by Dunster's views, but finally cast them off as coming from the Devil. Shipton, *Sibley's Harvard Graduates*, I, 148–49.

gradually backed into a policy of growing freedom and toleration, their college passed into the hands of those elements in the community whose liberal tendencies laid the foundations of the Harvard tradition of freedom.

As a chosen people, living under a special covenant with God, the Puritans did not believe that any of their fortunes were attributable to environmental circumstances or accidents. Since they were under the special charge and care of God, everything that befell them, they thought, had a divine meaning, a cosmological significance. If they were subject to an invasion of witches, it was because the Devil had special reason for trying to storm God's own bastion on earth. A pestilence, a famine, an Indian attack, a storm—these were signs of God's disfavor to the group, just as an accident, an illness, a business loss were signs of His disfavor to the individual.[24] It was characteristic, then, for the Puritan conscience to entertain a particularly lively sense of sin under conditions of adversity; for adversity itself was the surest proof to a covenanting people that sin was still within it. The hunger and insecurity of life in a raw wilderness made many occasions for the middle- and lower-middle-class Englishmen who led the Puritan settlements to give thought to the state of their souls. It was the hardness of life that was felt to be consistent with the Puritan temper at its most rigorous.[25]

But it was precisely at this point that the Puritan spirit, as it worked out its destiny in seventeenth-century America, contained the materials of its own destruction. If misfortune went hand in hand with sin, it followed that prosperity was a token of virtue. As the colony grew, as trade flourished and an urban aristocracy arose, the means of sin and luxury were provided. At the same time the very presence of these means seemed to betoken a state of grace that would permit some spiritual relaxation. Even had it been of any use, the Puritan preachers were not free under

---

[24] In the Puritan conscience the sense of guilt was heightened by adversity, which was interpreted as divine punishment. For vivid personal illustrations, see Murdock, *Increase Mather*, p. 51; Barrett Wendell, *Cotton Mather* (New York, 1891), p. 50.

[25] A view accepted by the author of an early (1630) promotional pamphlet urging settlers to go to New England on the ground, among others, that life was hard there. "If men desire people to degenerate speedily, and to corrupt their minds and bodies too, and besides to tole in theeves and spoilers from abroad, let them seek a rich soil, which brings in much with little labor: but if they desire that Piety and godliness shall prosper accompanied with sobriety, justice, and love, let them choose a Country such as this is—which may yield sufficiency with hard labor and industry." Quoted in Sanford H. Cobb, *The Rise of Religious Liberty in America* (New York, 1902), p. 154.

their own doctrine to rail against the coming of prosperity. God had provided well-being, as He had provided everything else. "Their gain is their godliness," as a current aphorism had it. But it was the surest evidence of human depravity that godliness was not well sustained after gain had been assured. The clergy who clung to the old dispensation found themselves in a merciless dilemma: "[They] could not demand that people stay poor, for their economic opportunities were specifically opened by the providence of God; on the other hand, they could not quietly acquiesce in letting New England go the way of all flesh." [26] As a consequence, the sermons of the New England clergy sounded a constant note of lamentation, heard even as early as the 1640s, which "swelled to an incessant chant within forty years. By 1680 there seems to have been hardly any other theme for discourse, and the pulpits rang from week to week with lengthening jeremiads." [27]

A further difficulty—not unrelated to the first—was that the Puritans had founded the Holy Commonwealth as a sect, and they were now in the process of becoming a church. They had started out with the hopelessly demanding notion that no one could become a member of their churches (and with that a full-fledged citizen, for suffrage ran with church membership) who was not, so far as any human agency could determine, a regenerate soul, a pure saint. Access to the sacraments—which they regarded not as instruments by which a man might be saved but only as instruments by which his Covenant with God could be sealed—was in strictest theory to be reserved for those who were spiritually prepared for them. Adults were considered to be prepared to partake of the Holy Communion only after they had undergone a religious conversion and had given a public account of their experience of regeneration. As for infants, while the Puritan fathers had some difficulties about the validity of baptizing them—it was on this question that Dunster fell—they thought they had Scriptural reason for believing that children could be fairly assumed to inherit, in a sense, the grace of their fathers. Hence, children of church members were eligible for baptism.

A problem arose with the passing of the first generation. Young people were growing to adulthood who had not experienced the persecutions of

[26] Perry Miller, *The New England Mind: The Seventeenth Century* (New York, 1939), p. 475.

[27] *Ibid.*, p. 472; for a full treatment of this theme see Chap. XVI, and the same author's *From Colony to Province*, Chaps. I–III. Cf. Herbert Schneider, *The Puritan Mind* (New York, 1930), Chap. III.

the Old World, the passage to the New, the trials of deracination, the hardships of the wilderness—who did not, in brief, share to the full the vision of the Holy Commonwealth or the stern temper that was required to realize it. For such persons, significantly, the rigors of the personal accounting demanded for access to Communion became embarrassing. They might well be willing to accept exclusion from Communion as a consequence, but what of their children? Would they be eligible for baptism? To deny baptism, and hence church membership, to such persons would have meant to have by far the greater part of the community outside the congregations. It would have torn up the fabric of the Holy Commonwealth. To permit baptism would be to make an inconsistent compromise with the original dream of a church of pure saints by filling the churches with presumably unregenerate persons.

After years of debate a compromise was reached at the Synod of 1662 in the Half-Way Covenant: the unregenerate could be half-way members of the churches; their children could be baptized, but neither they nor their children would be eligible for Communion. This was a workable compromise in practice, but it seemed to sacrifice theological consistency to considerations of church polity, and it was roundly opposed by a minority of the parsons and a majority of the laymen.[28] The adoption of the Half-Way Covenant marked the first serious formal departure from the old ways. Not only did it constitute in itself a relaxation from the pristine ideals and practices, but it left issues over which the community continued to be divided. Before very many years had gone by the Reverend Solomon Stoddard, one of the most influential men in the province, established an ecclesiastical empire of his own in the Connecticut Valley in which the practice was adopted of allowing professing Christians to take Communion even when they could not claim that they were in a state of grace. In some respects, notably in his emphasis on the irrational sovereignty of God, Stoddard's theology was more "conservative" than that professed by the clerics of Boston, but he opened the Lord's Supper to the unregenerate on the ground that it could be an instrument of conversion. Over this he waged with Increase Mather a bitter theological

[28] In view of the criticisms usually made of the Puritan clergy, it is worth noting that at this point the clergy espoused the "liberal" side of the issue while the laity opposed this extension of baptism. Perry Miller characterizes the opposition to the Half-Way Covenant as "an uprising of the crowd against the majesty of scholastical learning." *From Colony to Province*, p. 105.

battle which was of particular importance because it involved institutional practices as well as abstract issues. The controversy left a rent in the Holy Commonwealth that could not easily be mended.

The controversy over "Stoddardeanism" disturbed a community that was already in difficulties over its relations with the Crown. The Restoration in England had posed serious new problems for the Puritans by making it necessary for them to pretend—as they had not had to pretend under the Commonwealth or the Protectorate—to be something other than what they were. Oddly enough, while English policy after the Restoration was probably if anything less tolerant than that of the Puritans, its pressure on New England worked for toleration there. The Puritans had to walk carefully lest they offend the Crown and put their charter in jeopardy. In 1662 they had a letter from the king confirming the Massachusetts charter but demanding that Anglicans be free to worship, that persons of honest lives not be denied the Lord's Supper, and that religious restrictions on the suffrage be abandoned. These demands they were able to avoid or craftily evade, but only because of easy-going English administration. Again, however, the rent in the Holy Commonwealth was widened by the appearance of a party, chiefly mercantile, that was out of sympathy with efforts to realize the old ideals at the cost of angering the king. "By 1670 the holy society had become like any other society outside the national covenant, sundered into two opinions, not over a basic theological or even ecclesiastical question, but over one of political expediency." [29] Under the threat of external interference and internal disunity the defenders of the old New England Way found themselves unable to maintain the purity and unity of their society. Baptists and Quakers persisted in settling among them, and could not, as in the old days, be driven out. In 1665 a group of Baptists formed a church in Boston and carried on with it in spite of prison sentences.[30] Three years later the General Court sentenced the sect to banishment, but the law was never enforced. Quakers, who had begun in the early 1660s to have meetings in private homes, began to worship more openly in 1674. As early as 1665 a law was passed permitting them to go about their secular business, although it was not until 1697 that they were able to demonstrate

[29] Miller, *From Colony to Province,* p. 128; our account of the various factors in the decline of the Holy Commonwealth draws heavily upon Books I and II of this work.

[30] Cobb, *Rise of Religious Liberty in America,* pp. 228–29.

their acceptance by the construction of a solid brick meetinghouse on Brattle Street.[31]

As the trade of the Northern colonies became more important, and as the Crown became preoccupied with tighter organization for the sharpening imperial struggle with France, maintenance of the long-standing freedom and independence of New England became impossible. In 1684 the charter of the Massachusetts Bay colony was revoked. In 1686 the Dominion of New England was created under the autocratic governorship of Sir Edmund Andros, and the traditional agencies of colony government in Massachusetts were abolished. In the same year the Puritans, to their horror, saw the Old South Church occupied forcibly for the holding of an Anglican service, after which the first Anglican Church, King's Chapel (1688), was built in Boston.[32]

The establishment of the Dominion, catastrophic as it was, was at first accepted by most of the Puritans as a punishment for sin. Before long, however, the combined threat of the Dominion to trade, land titles, the liberties of Englishmen, and the promise of the New England Congregational Way turned almost the entire province bitterly against the Dominion and its governor. Even the pro-English faction fell apart. When the

[31] See Rufus Jones, *The Quakers in the American Colonies* (London, 1911), Chaps. V, VI; R. P. Hallowell, *The Quaker Invasion of Massachusetts* (Boston, 1887); Cobb, *Rise of Religious Liberty in America,* pp. 217 ff.

A high point in the progress of the free conscience in America had been reached in 1657, when a band of English Quaker missionaries was hospitably received at Newport and the commissioners of the other colonies requested their banishment, threatening reprisals if it were not forthcoming. To which the Rhode Islanders replied that they had no law among them by which the Quakers could be punished for exercising freedom of conscience. "And we, moreover, finde, that in those places where these people aforesaid, in this colony, are most of all suffered to declare themselves freely, and are only opposed by arguments in discourse, there they least of all desire to come, and we are informed that they begin to loath this place for that they are not opposed by the civill authority, but with all patience and meekness are suffered to say over their pretended revelations and admonitions, nor are they like or able to gain many here to their way; surely we find that they delight to be persecuted by civill powers, and when they are soe, they are like to gain more adherents by the conseyte of their patient sufferings, than by consent to their pernicious sayings: And yet we conceive, that theire doctrines tend to very absolute cuttinge downe and overturninge relations and civill government among men, if generally received." *Rhode Island Records,* I, 376 ff. In 1702, when Cotton Mather published his *Magnalia Christi Americana,* he accepted the Rhode Island approach to the Quakers. He would not, he said, defend the past persecutions of them. "I am verily perswaded these miserable Quakers would in a little while (as we have *now* seen) have come to nothing, if the civil magistrate had not inflicted any civil penalty upon them." *Magnalia,* II, 453.

[32] For the early growth of Episcopacy in Boston see Henry W. Foote, *Annals of King's Chapel* (Boston, 1882), Vol. I, Chaps. II–V.

news of the Glorious Revolution reached Massachusetts in 1689 it precipitated a local uprising that effectually dissolved the Dominion government. The newly established rapport with England, however, brought fresh issues. The Act of Toleration of 1689 seemed to indicate that the Puritans could be left alone, like other dissenters, with their church system, but they were reluctant to assume the position of an ordinary dissenting sect. The original ideal of the founders had been to purify the Church of England itself, and they had always professed—although the profession had grown increasingly hollow—to be still inside that body. It would be difficult to carry on this pretense and continue with the exclusion of Anglicans, difficult to live as the beneficiaries of a tolerating regime without extending to dissenters among themselves a little at least of the toleration now enjoyed by all Englishmen except papists. Such toleration was indeed demanded by their own new charter of 1691. Dissenters could no longer be treated as Anne Hutchinson and Roger Williams and the Baptists and Quakers had been treated by the first generation of New Englanders. Thus the proponents of the main line of tradition, for example Increase and Cotton Mather, began during the 1690s to sing the praises of a measure of toleration that their venerated ancestors would have scorned. Unfortunately, admitted Increase Mather, the people of New England had been "in some matters relating to Conscience and difference of opinion . . . more rigid and severe than the primitive Christians or the Gospel doth allow of." But "tell them," said his son Cotton, "That New England has Renounced whatever laws are against a Just Liberty of Conscience." [33] This swing toward a mood of tolerance may have been, at least in the beginning, an act of expediency more than a heartfelt change. But, for whatever reason, toleration was being preached by men who had good right to consider themselves the lineal inheritors of the ideals of the founding fathers. That the Mathers could find a good word for toleration was a measure of the distance that the New Englanders had come. They had paid, perhaps, no more than a reasonable price for the restoration of self-government and the liberties of Englishmen. But it must be observed that these were *secular* considerations. The Puritans had found themselves in a world too complex for the simplicities of the Holy Commonwealth, and they had yielded. The changes were too sweeping to leave their college untouched.

[33] Miller, *From Colony to Province,* pp. 166, 167.

THE EMERGENCE OF HARVARD LIBERALISM

The years from 1684 to 1707 saw the rise within Congregationalism of a "liberal" faction led by William and Thomas Brattle, the Reverend Benjamin Colman, and John Leverett. The struggle between this group and the "conservatives" led by Increase and Cotton Mather culminated, so far as Harvard was concerned, in 1707 when John Leverett was made president of the college. Any historian who wishes to portray this conflict in its full significance for the college runs the risk of exaggerating its significance for the community as a whole or misrepresenting the issues involved. What was at stake was not a matter of theology, for the liberals still considered themselves reasonably good Calvinists and could probably have subscribed to a common confession of faith with the conservatives without any sense of misrepresenting themselves. Moreover, the conservatives were exactly what that word in its better sense implies—they were not totally unenlightened or inflexible reactionaries.[34] The victory of the liberals was neither a revolution nor a *coup d'état;* it can best be compared to what happens in modern American politics when one of our two major parties—both adhering loyally to the same political system and a common set of presuppositions and each containing within itself elements of liberalism and conservatism—ousts the other.

The feud between the liberals and the conservatives thus had rather the quality of a family quarrel than a battle to the death. One cannot overlook the fact that the Mathers, with whatever misgivings, consented to preach when the liberals opened the Brattle Street Church, that Benjamin Colman remained an intimate friend of Cotton Mather and was charged by the aging Increase with the defense of the churches, that he delivered eulogies at the funerals of both the Mathers, and called Increase "a Father to us all." Nor is it desirable to forget the latter-day conversion of the Mathers to toleration, or that "liberal" tendencies in natural philosophy could be found in Increase Mather, and that many students have seen overtones of deism in his son's work *The Christian Philosopher.*[35]

---

[34] A serious attempt to do justice to the Mathers and to the New England clergy as a whole during the period from 1680 to 1725 that should be read by all students who have been raised, say, on V. L. Parrington's version of the Puritans, is Clifford K. Shipton's "The New England Clergy of the 'Glacial Age,' " *Publications of the Colonial Society of Massachusetts,* XXXII (Boston, 1937), 24–54.

[35] Cf. Shipton: "Both the Mathers were among the theological progressives of their generations, but they lived long enough to be passed by their swiftly moving times, and to have their seventeenth-century religious theatricals become ridiculous

The lines of controversy were vague and shifting, the issues usually more personal and factional than doctrinal. And if intellectual change was as inexorable as it was gradual, it may well be because Puritanism contained within itself some of the materials of the Enlightenment, as is believed by many modern students. Such considerations, at any rate, go far to explain why the very considerable intellectual changes that took place at Harvard between 1680 and 1720 were not symbolized by a single spectacular issue or *cause célèbre,* but by a series of relatively minor incidents and sly maneuvers.

What gave the liberals their significance for the fate of the Holy Commonwealth was not quite so much that they were radically liberal or that they won control of the college, but that they existed at all; for the original dream of the Commonwealth had not contemplated the emergence of parties but the maintenance of unity. It was the signal achievement of the liberals that they brought directly into the heart of Boston and the citadel of ministerial learning the great blessings of diversity and conflict. For Harvard College itself and for New England intellectual life their victory was truly momentous, for it set the institution on a path which it has never deserted and paved the way for a series of cumulative minor victories that established Harvard's place in the vanguard of intellectual liberalism.[36] Harvard began its existence at a time when one theology and one religious group held sway in the colony. By the beginning of the eighteenth century that sect split into two factions and students from both wings attended the college. Even the orthodox faction was taking a broader view of things than it had in earlier days. The college was well advanced in the transition from the Puritan age to the age of the Enlightenment. At Harvard the eighteenth century began, in a sense, with the inauguration of Leverett in 1707. Yet in all this there was no sudden abandonment of the covenant theology, no sudden onslaught against Calvinism. The real departure that was visible at the time of Leverett's succession was not in dogma, but rather in temper and in church prac-

---

in the eyes of younger persons who read the *Spectator* . . ." "The New England Clergy of the 'Glacial Age,' " p. 30. The character and significance of the difference between the liberals and conservatives in this era is discussed by Miller, *From Colony to Province,* Chap. XXVII.

[36] This is not to deny that Harvard had always been more liberal than the mean average of the Puritan community itself. For some eloquent remarks on the place of Harvard in Puritan liberalism see Clifford K. Shipton, "Puritanism and Modern Democracy," *New England Historical and Genealogical Register,* CI (July, 1947), 87–88.

tice. The new group did not at once drop the old tenets of the Congregational Way, but they did neglect conspicuously to show the full rigor of the pristine Puritans. Emotionally they relaxed. The liberals flourished among the wealthy, leisured, and aristocratic elements in the province, while the appeal of the conservatives was somewhat stronger in the villages where the old conditions were still more in evidence and folkish piety held its own. The liberals associated on terms of ease with the Anglicans in the province and began to intermarry with them. Some of them perhaps dipped more frequently into Tillotson than they did into Calvin. If they did not see any reason for espousing wholeheartedly the tenets of the latitudinarian writers, they saw no reason for not reading them or putting them under proscription.

During the last crucial phase in the fortunes of the Holy Commonwealth, Increase Mather, the most eminent defender of the faith, both in politics and religion, was also president of Harvard College. It was one of the pivotal facts of his regime that Mather was a nonresident president. Ironically, the college, which was languishing when he took over in 1685 and flourishing when he resigned in 1701, became the beneficiary of his salutary neglect.[37] The "teacher" of the Second Church in Boston, the theological and ideological leader of the old order, and long a fellow of the Harvard Corporation, Mather was the outstanding figure in New England. He found himself too busy ever to assume in full the responsibilities of his Harvard office. During the sixteen years of his presidency he was settled in Cambridge for only a few months. He gave up his pastorate in Boston only for a short period toward the end, and that at the urgent demand of the General Court; for four whole years he was absent on the colony's business in England. He had spent some of the pleasantest days of his life in England as a young man, and his appetite for English society was whetted anew by his four-year sojourn. He seems to have longed for any occasion that might present itself for his permanent removal to England, whether as agent for the colony or pastor of a congregation. After England the society of provincial Boston, not to speak of the mudholes of Cambridge, failed to satisfy his ambitions. He was a supremely able man, a fact appreciated by no one so well as himself and his son Cotton; but so far as Harvard College was concerned his pride was precisely the kind that goeth before a fall. The status quo at Harvard

---

[37] Morison, *Harvard College in the Seventeenth Century,* Vol. II, Chaps. XXII and XXIII, is severe in his interpretation of Mather's role at Harvard; Murdock, *Increase Mather,* defends Mather at all possible points.

was never so much in need of a watchdog as during his regime, when he was busy elsewhere trying frantically to repair the innumerable weak spots in the defenses of the Holy Commonwealth.

It had been the intention of the founders that Harvard College reproduce the English collegiate way of living, which required the common residence of both students and tutors and demanded, at its best, the constant supervision of a resident presiding officer. Mather, if we are to judge by the advice he gave at the founding of Yale, as well as by his own presidential conduct, had little respect for this conception of the college.[38] He bitterly resisted the many suggestions of the General Court that he take up residence in Cambridge, invoking his unwillingness to desert his pastorate (which he would readily have sacrificed, however, if a call had come from an English congregation), and several times offering to resign instead.[39] And although he understood its importance in the life of the colony, he had a certain unconscious disdain for the college itself, which he once revealed to the representatives of the General Court, when he asked: "Should I leave off preaching to 1500 souls . . . only to Expound to 40 or 50 Children, few of them capable of Edification by such Exercises?" [40]

This attitude was one of the causes of Mather's undoing so far as his aspirations for the intellectual role of the college were concerned. During his commuting presidency the sole tutors of the college, and during his absence its sole resident governors, were John Leverett and William Brattle, who became tutors and fellows of the Corporation in 1685 and 1686 respectively and remained together until 1697. Both were able men and good teachers, many of whose students were devoted to them. To them is attributable the progress made by the college during the last fifteen years of the century. Both were members of mercantile and magisterial families that were in short order to be aligned against Mather. They were relatively liberal in their attitudes, and for twelve years the future intellectual elite of the Bay Colony passed under their tutelage and theirs alone.

---

[38] Morison, *Harvard College in the Seventeenth Century*, II, 499–500.

[39] That these resignations were regularly refused is explained by Morison with the conjecture that it would have been difficult to prevent the election of Cotton Mather as Increase's successor, something that even Increase's partisans feared. "For Cotton Mather was a typical infant prodigy grown up, pedantic and conceited, meddlesome and tactless, unsympathetic to the aspirations of youth and intolerant of their failings. Cotton as President would have emptied Harvard College. . . ." *Ibid.*, pp. 502–3.

[40] Samuel Sewall, *Diary* (Boston, 1878), I, 493.

When Increase Mather returned from his four-year mission in England bearing the reluctantly accepted Massachusetts Charter of 1691, he confronted an intolerably complex set of tasks. On one side he was trying to fend off the formidable threat of Stoddardeanism to the old Covenant ways. On the other he had the emergent liberals of Boston and Cambridge to cope with—and this was most important for the college. But he also had to reconcile the province to the imperfect charter and with its royal governor—the best charter he had been able to secure. In this he was confronted with the opposition of a "popular" faction consisting chiefly of people who were dissatisfied with the concessions he had made in London.[41] This group, more out of concern with crippling his political power and preventing his return to England than love for the college, continuously made a point of invoking the residency requirements for the college president and ultimately succeeded in confronting Increase with the choice of giving up his office or residing in Cambridge.

Still another task that plagued Mather was that of securing a new charter for the college itself, which was considered to be legally dead inasmuch as it had been chartered under a now obsolete regime. However, this last was a delicate task and one that proved in the end to be too much for him, for it would be difficult to get a royal charter without Anglican visitation, and what he needed to fulfill his aims was an extremely sectarian instrument strong enough to fend off both the Anglicans from without and the liberals from within. Already, he knew, the college under the tutorship of Leverett and Brattle had suffered from too latitudinarian a management to suit his taste. Thus for ten years Mather tried, with draft after draft, to replace the legislative charter of 1650 with a royal charter that would satisfy his sectarian requirements.

The story of Mather's charter maneuvers is unbearably tedious. It may be enough to say here that they reached their climax in 1699 when he inserted into a proposed charter a provision that no one could be president or vice-president of the college or a fellow of the Corporation who would not declare himself to be and continue in adherence to the New England Congregational Way. No such sectarian requirement had been set forth in the 1650 charter, nor even in the various charter bills and

---

[41] For factional and ecclesiastical politics in this period, see Everett Kimball, *The Public Life of Joseph Dudley* (New York, 1911) and Clayton Harding Chapman, "Life and Influence of Rev. Benjamin Colman," unpublished Doctor of Theology dissertation (Boston University, School of Divinity, 1947), Chap. IV.

disallowed charters of the past seven years.[42] Not surprisingly the royal governor, Lord Bellomont, offended at the open exclusion of Anglicans (although the exclusion was actually aimed at the liberals), vetoed the charter.[43] In his desperation Mather indicated that since he could not obtain such a religious test he preferred to have no charter at all—which would have reduced Harvard to the level of an unincorporated divinity school without the power to award degrees.[44] His efforts were futile, and in 1707, after a legal interregnum of many years, the college reverted to the 1650 charter, which has been ever since its fundamental instrument of government.

In the meantime Mather had become embroiled in a new controversy involving not only his political opponents in the Governor's Council but also the tutors at the college. During his earliest years at Harvard he had maintained harmonious relations with his tutors. He had himself at first commended "the liberal mode of philosophizing" in the study of logic at Harvard, in accordance with which students were "pledged to the words of no particular master," but could consult Aristotle, Petrus Ramus, Descartes, or Bacon; and it may be no more than a coincidence that tutor William Brattle had made his slight innovations in the logical theses in 1689 shortly after Mather left for England.[45] It was not logic, however, but religion that was crucial, and here tutors Leverett and Brattle seem to have strayed out of the strait and narrow. One of their students, many years later, recalled that

they recommended to their Pupils the reading of Episcopal authors as the best books to form our minds in religious matters and preserve us from those narrow Principles that kept us at a Distance from the Church of England as apostates from the Primitive Faith . . . the Number of friends to the Church of England in that Country is at least ten times I may say twenty times more since these Gentlemen govern'd the college than they were before.[46]

[42] Morison, *Harvard College in the Seventeenth Century*, II, 524; see Murdock, *Increase Mather*, pp. 353–55.

[43] Many years afterward, in 1725–27, the rectors of the two Episcopal churches of Boston petitioned the Overseers for seats on that board on the ground that they qualified by virtue of being "teaching elders" of Boston churches, who, under a law of 1642, were automatically Overseers. Without incurring any difficulties with the representatives of the Crown the Overseers dismissed this application for what it was worth. See Josiah Quincy, *The History of Harvard University* (Cambridge, Mass., 1840), Vol. I, Chap. XVII and pp. 560–74.

[44] *Ibid.*, II, 526–27.

[45] See Miller, *The New England Mind*, pp. 118, 121; what Brattle had done was chiefly to translate the standard Ramist terms into Cartesian ones.

[46] Morison, *Harvard College in the Seventeenth Century*, II, 505–6.

Presumably Mather sniffed out the odors of latitudinarianism; at any rate, upon his return in 1692 we find him tightening up the teaching of theology and narrowing the studies: "I caused the masters of Art to begin disputations in Theological Questions, with a design to put down Arminianisme." [47]

Mather now saw more clearly than before the vital role of the college in staving off "Degeneracy & Apostasy," and the importance of "care that the Tutors there be such as shall make Conscience to Establish the Young Scholars in these Holy Principles of Truth." [48] In 1697 he wrote an Epistle to the Church and the scholars at Cambridge in which he reminded Leverett and Brattle that the well-being of the Church depended upon the college, and added:

Nor are the Churches like to continue pure Golden Candlesticks, if the Colledge, which should supply them, prove Apostate . . . You that are Tutors there, have a Great Advantage put into your Hands (and I pray God give you Wisdom to know it!) to prevent it. The Lord hath made you Fathers to many Pupils. You will not deny but that He has made me a Father to you. It was my Recommendation that brought you into that Station. And therefore, as my Joy will be Greater to see you Acquit your selves Worthily, so my earnest Sollicitudes for it must needs be the more, on that Account. [49]

Which was a slightly elliptical way of saying to the tutors that since they held offices upon his nomination, it was their duty to teach as he pleased. A few weeks later an association of ministers met in the college hall and expressed their awareness of "the tendencies which there are amongst us towards Deviations from the good Order wherein our Churches have . . . been happily established and continued." [50]

It was too late. Leverett and Brattle were already about to leave their tutorships for other posts, Brattle for the ministry and Leverett for politics. Their work had been done, had indeed already made a notable contribution to liberality of thought in Massachusetts. Moreover, they were already well involved with a group of well-to-do young men who were about to make the greatest breach in the church policy of New England since the Half-Way Covenant. They joined with William Brattle's brother Thomas, who was treasurer of the college, and other influential men in the group which in 1698 formed the new Brattle Street Church and called the Reverend Benjamin Colman, a student of Leverett's, as its pastor. The new church promptly abandoned the half-way

[47] *Ibid.*, II, 503; cf. I, 280 and 280n. [48] Murdock, *Increase Mather*, p. 330.
[49] Morison, *Harvard College in the Seventeenth Century*, II, 542.
[50] *Ibid.*, p. 543.

membership of the sort that had been institutionalized in 1662. Its members issued a challenging manifesto in which, despite their pledged loyalty to the Westminster Confession, they asserted that baptism would be given to the children of any professing Christians who wished to educate their children in the Christian religion; and that while Communion would be available only to those whose sanctity was ascertainable by the minister, the congregation would not "impose upon any a public relation of their experiences." Thus some of the worst aspects of Stoddardeanism had been brought right to Boston. The conservatives were now confronted with an organized liberal wing, fortified by a wealthy membership and close rapport with the governor and his circle.

A few years later Mather himself, after an enforced trial at residence in Cambridge which he found quite intolerable, indicated to the General Court that they would do well to think of another president. He was succeeded by Samuel Willard, one of his chosen colleagues on the Harvard Corporation, who followed his example in not surrendering his pastorate of the Old South Church. It seemed ironically inconsistent to have unseated Mather only to get another nonresident, and indeed the statutes called for a man who lived in Cambridge; but the members of the Court evaded the issue by the ingenious if transparent device of calling Willard the vice-president, which was the title he held until his death.

Willard, a graduate of the Harvard class of 1659, was quite as orthodox as Increase Mather but far less militant and powerful.[51] His six-year tenure proved to be an interregnum, which was abruptly ended one day in 1707 when he "cut his finger while eating oysters," fell into a convulsion, and died. The fellows of the Corporation (then a temporary body which had been gradually infiltrated by the liberals) nominated John Leverett for the presidency. The Mathers were horrified. "To make a lawyer, and one who never affected the study of Divinity, a praesident for a College of Divines, will be a very preposterous thing, a thing without precedent," wrote Cotton Mather who had hoped for the presidency himself. But "the Churches might yett be saved" if the General Court would reject Leverett.[52] Unfortunately for the position of the Mathers, the notion that Leverett represented a threat to the churches was not too widely shared. The General Court had before it an address from thirty-nine ministers (of whom nineteen or twenty had been Leverett's pupils

[51] Miller suggests, however, that the young men educated under Willard provided the last-ditch resistance to the catholic spirit of Colman. *From Colony to Province*, pp. 450–51.
[52] Morison, *Harvard College in the Seventeenth Century*, II, 552–53.

in Harvard College) endorsing him in affectionate terms and commending his ratification as a service to the religion and learning of the province. That the tutorship of Leverett and Brattle had proved to be a significant source of political power is manifest in the prominence of Leverett's pupils among the signers, as it is in the ministers' observation that "under the Wise and faithful Government of him and the Reverend Mr. Brattle of Cambridge the greatest part of the now rising Ministry in New England were happiely Educated." [53]

A deadlock seemed nonetheless to be impending in the General Court when the acceptance of Leverett's nomination by the Governor's Council was not concurred in by the House, which represented more closely the rural piety of the province. Governor Dudley then suggested an ingenious compromise; in return for the House's acceptance of Leverett, the governor and council would discard the temporary settlement under which Harvard had been governed since 1700 and restore the charter of 1650, a gratifying admission of the hitherto uncertain right of the General Court to charter a college without sanction from the Crown. Only after this bargain was consummated did the House realize that the restoration of the 1650 charter would automatically reduce the Corporation from seventeen members to seven, and put into the hands of the governor the power to select from the large temporary Corporation a small group acceptable to him and Leverett. [54]

John Leverett, born in the year of the Half-Way Synod, was forty-five. The grandson of Governor John Leverett and the son of a lawyer who "maintained but an indifferent character," he inherited wealth and readily took a place among the prominent men of affairs in Massachusetts. Before leaving his tutorship he had been elected representative for Cambridge in the General Court; he had subsequently studied law and served as justice of the peace and judge of the Supreme Court, speaker of the House, and member of the provincial council. An old friend of Governor Dudley, he had also served the province on important missions. A political conservative securely anchored in the dominant faction of the colony, befriended by a large part of the ministry, and favored by an amenable Corporation, he entered the presidency in a strong position. [55]

For the first time in its history, the college Corporation found itself

---

[53] *Ibid.*, pp. 551–52.   [54] *Ibid.*, p. 555.
[55] On Leverett see the sketch in the *Dictionary of American Biography* and Shipton, *Sibley's Harvard Graduates,* III, 180–98; for Leverett's conservative views, see Morison, *Harvard College in the Seventeenth Century,* II, 554.

consistently at odds with a significant portion of the community; and the very qualities that made it possible for Leverett to found "the liberal tradition of Harvard University" [56] kept Leverett's regime under the glare of criticism. The Reverend Benjamin Colman, who had resided at Oxford and Cambridge, thought that "no Place of Education can well boast a more free Air than our little College may." [57]

Much of Leverett's sixteen-year reign at Harvard coincided with the era of peace and prosperity that followed the Treaty of Utrecht in 1713. Harvard expanded with the colony, and a large part of the increase in its undergraduate body came from the well-to-do gentry of the seaport towns who were fattening on land speculation and the triangular trade. This inundation from the very element that had done the most to dilute the pristine spirit of Puritanism took the college a long way further in the direction in which it had been moving. Harvard men, who had traditionally been designated in a Biblical way as "Sons of the Prophets" and were now referred to simply by Leverett as "Sons of Harvard," were increasingly being educated simply as young gentlemen, and began to conduct themselves—with cards, horse races, and "profane swearing"— as young gentlemen of means usually did. In self-defense the more devout students organized societies for worship and discussion. But even the theological side of the college was relaxing. At a meeting of the Overseers in 1718 Leverett was attacked by Judge Samuel Sewall on the ground that there had been some "intermission of the Exposition of the Scriptures." [58] Leverett was also subject to occasional sniping by the Mathers, and although his position was too strong to make subversion of his regime possible, his financial support was somewhat constricted during a period of rising prices and he died heavily in debt. [59]

Leverett's regime was also disturbed by the battle over self-government by the Corporation, which will be discussed in the next chapter, and by one investigation by the Overseers, the first of a long series of heresy-

[56] Samuel Eliot Morison, *Three Centuries of Harvard* (Cambridge, Mass., 1936), p. 75.

[57] Ebenezer Turell, *The Life and Character of the Reverend Benjamin Colman* (Boston, 1749), p. 123; among the novelties was the award to Colman's young friend, an Italian Jew, Judah Monis, of the Master's degree in 1720; even before his conversion to Christianity, Monis became Instructor of the Hebrew Language, 1722–60. This was at a time when in most of the universities of the Western world, including Oxford and Cambridge, Jews along with dissenting Christians were barred from degrees by religious tests and oaths. Cf. Chapman, "Life and Influence of Rev. Benjamin Colman," pp. 142–43.

[58] Shipton, *Sibley's Harvard Graduates*, III, 188.   [59] *Ibid.*, pp. 189, 191–92.

hunts in the history of American higher education. The investigation (1723) seems to have been precipitated by charges made by Cotton Mather to the effect that students were privately reading "plays, novels, empty and vicious pieces of poetry, and even Ovid's Epistles, which have a vile tendency to corrupt good manners," that tutors were assigning books on theology "that have rank poison in them," and that a Harvard College education had become an impediment rather than an asset to a good ministerial career. The Overseers' Committee of Visitation was headed by the honorable Samuel Sewall—the same who in days past had humbly stood before his congregation in solemn repentance for his part in the witchcraft trials—and its report was a temperate affair which mentioned lapses both in orthodox instruction and in student morals but made no strong recommendation for change in the conduct of the college.[60]

One of Harvard's signal academic gains during Leverett's presidency was also intimately linked with the advance of tolerance when an endowment for a professorship of divinity was accepted from a Baptist layman. In 1719 and 1720 a London merchant, Thomas Hollis, gave generous gifts to Harvard for poor scholars and divinity students, gifts which were followed by a request from John Leverett and Benjamin Colman for funds to create a divinity professorship. Hollis, who seems to have been attracted by the growing liberalism of the college in a colony where his coreligionists had been persecuted in the past,[61] readily

[60] On the investigation see Quincy, *History of Harvard*, I, 316–21. The essential finding of the committee, so far as intellectual freedom is concerned, was: "That there does not appear to have been any greater recommendation of books in Divinity to the students, but that they have read promiscuously, according to their inclinations, authors of different denominations in religion; and by some information given, the works of Tillotson, Sherlock, Scott and Lucas, are generally most used." The strongest stricture on student morals was this: "That, although there is a considerable number of virtuous and studious youth in the College, yet there has been a practice of several immoralities; particularly stealing, lying, swearing, idleness, picking of locks, and too frequent use of strong drink; which immoralities, it is feared, still continue in the College, notwithstanding the faithful endeavors of the rulers of the House to suppress them."

Miller has concluded that the conservatives were chiefly agitated by the fact that the liberals, while still holding to Calvinism in its broad outlines, were quietly forsaking the particular offshoot of it, the Covenant theology, that had so long been the marrow of New England divinity. See *From Colony to Province*, Chap. XXVII.

[61] Such is Professor Morison's conclusion (*Three Centuries of Harvard*, p. 66). Murdock, however, points triumphantly to the fact that Hollis' interest in Harvard

omplied. The sole qualification attached was that no candidate for the professorship "should be refused on account of his belief and practice of adult baptism"—a stipulation not intended to exclude anyone but to assure the donor that men of his own denomination would not be objects of discrimination. He also required that during his lifetime the names of those nominated for the professorship be submitted for his approbation. The Corporation greeted this endowment, the first chair in Harvard's history, with enthusiasm, but the Overseers balked at accepting it without redefining Hollis' language in such a way as to make possible the exclusion of candidates other than those who adhered to the strict New England Way. Hollis' specifications had called for a Master of Arts and a communicant of the Congregational, Presbyterian, or Baptist church, and a man of "sound and orthodox principles." It could be said that the donation was not received in the best of faith. The Overseers, while they swallowed for policy's sake the eligibility of a Baptist, chose to construe the words "sound and orthodox" in their own way and not in Hollis'. Leverett's son-in-law Edward Wigglesworth, the first choice of the Corporation, was accepted for the Hollis Chair, but only after an examination into his orthodoxy commanded by the Overseers, in which he was specifically questioned (*pace* Mr. Hollis!) on "the divine right of infant baptism," as well as other dogmas. Although Hollis was not fully apprised of the Overseers' miscarriage of faith, he did grow alarmed as to the use to which his funds might be put; especially was he alarmed at "the late uncharitable reflections of some upon the Baptists as not orthodox." [62] Having been asked for his portrait for the college hall, he wrote:

---

dated from Increase Mather's four-year sojourn in England, and adds: "If Harvard's liberality was what appealed, it must, then, have been its liberality prior to 1690, or, its liberality under Mather!" (*Increase Mather,* pp. 276–78 and 278n.) Possibly, but it should not be forgotten that the liberality of Harvard under Mather was ascribable in large part precisely to Mather's absence and neglect, and to the presence of Leverett and Brattle. Over thirty years passed between Hollis' first expression of interest in Harvard and the creation of the Hollis Professorship of Divinity, and at the time of the donation Hollis was in correspondence with the liberal Colman. For a full account of the donation see Quincy, *History of Harvard University,* Vol. I, Chap. XII. This is not to say that the Mather dynasty did not still have its hand in the business. Cotton Mather, although he had sent his son Samuel to Harvard, seems to have been busy trying to divert Hollis' interest to Yale College! *Ibid.,* I, 226–29, 524–28. Chapman, "Life and Influence of Rev. Benjamin Colman," pp. 132 ff.

[62] Quincy, *History of Harvard University,* I, 258.

I doubt not but that they are pleased with my moneys, but I have some reason to think, that some among you will not be well pleased to see the shade of a Baptist hung there, unless you get a previous order to admit it, and forbidding any indecency to it . . . I pray to God [he charitably added], to allay the un-Christian heats, that have been among you of one sort and another. Be at peace, and continue not to divide and bite one another.[63]

Leverett and his Corporation had been forced to connive at the actions of the Overseers, but by not forcing the issue they won both the professorship itself and the occupant they chose to designate. Edward Wigglesworth proved to be a liberal and inquiring scholar and an effective teacher, and he lived to see most of the pulpits of Massachusetts and northern New England filled by ministers who had learned their divinity from him.[64] He was succeeded by his son Edward, the two in succession occupying the Hollis Professorship from 1722 to 1792. "It was the Wigglesworths," says Professor Morison, "who trained the pioneers of liberal Christianity in New England—the ministers who led the way out of the lush but fearsome jungles of Calvinism into the thin, clear light of Unitarianism." [65]

To make theology the touchstone of intellectual freedom is perhaps one-sided, for this was of course the exposed nerve of Puritanism. If receptivity to new ideas can be taken as an index of freedom, the receptivity of Harvard men in the areas of science and philosophy speaks well for the early college. The development of science will be discussed elsewhere, but it may be pertinent to point out here that the old ideal of *libertas philosophandi* was familiar and acceptable to both liberals and conservatives in the age of Increase Mather and John Leverett. "In philosophical matters," wrote Leverett in 1711,

Harvardians philosophize in a sane and liberal manner, according to the manner of the century; in logic as in Physics they are neither sceptics nor dogmatics. . . . For what is Natural Philosophy, unless a system in which natural things are explained; and in which that hypothesis is certainly the best by which the greater part of natural phenomena are most fully and clearly explained; these things are to be sought and required. Without any manner of doubt whatever, all humane matters must be tested by Philosophy. But the same license is not permissible to Theologians.[66]

[63] *Ibid.,* pp. 258–59.   [64] Shipton, *Sibley's Harvard Graduates,* V, 552.
[65] Morison, *Three Centuries of Harvard,* p. 68; the Hollis scholarships were also liberally administered by the Corporation. One of the first was given to John Callender, who became the Baptist minister of Newport.
[66] Morison, *Harvard College in the Seventeenth Century,* I, 168; cf. the sentiments of Increase Mather, p. 167.

Clearly the ancient distinction between philosophy and theology in respect to freedom of inquiry was still operative at Harvard at the beginning of the eighteenth century. That this philosophical freedom was actually exercised is clear from the readiness with which both the logical systems of Petrus Ramus, the intellectual guide of the Puritans, and Aristotle, his foe, were accepted and studied, and also by the ease with which the categories of Cartesian logic were introduced toward the end of the seventeenth century.[67]

To this philosophical latitude must be added a growing practical toleration. By the beginning of the eighteenth century the dominant sect had split into two factions, and students from both wings were present in the college; they were occasionally exposed to the work of Anglican theologians; they were joined by Baptist students (who were present on scholarships); the professorship of divinity, no less, bore the name of a Baptist merchant; a cleavage was beginning to appear between theology and ethics; and even the orthodox wing of Congregationalism was taking a broader view of religion than in the earlier days.

With all this change, the evidence that is available shows no sign that anything quite like modern notions of intellectual freedom had yet been formulated. Still less is there a specific justification for academic freedom. Men often spoke of liberty of conscience but never applied it to the teaching function. College teaching was not a recognized career, and tutors lacked even the faintest trace of a professional consciousness, for the very good reason that college teaching was as yet far from being a profession. It was not customary to say either that intellectual freedom was an asset to the community or that the individual had a right to free conditions for the growth and development of his mind. The Dunster case showed that in his day the only appeal was to the correctness of the individual's deviant opinion, not to his right to have one.

There is hardly more evidence for a clearly delineated rationale for freedom of inquiry at the opening of the eighteenth century than there was at the beginning of Harvard. But by that time two general sanctions had emerged: gentlemanliness and tolerance. When Judge Sewall accosted Leverett before the Overseers over the neglect of religious exercises at the college, Leverett responded, in the words of Sewall's diary,

---

[67] Morison, *Harvard College in the Seventeenth Century*, I, 187 ff. The logical compendium prepared in 1687 by William Brattle on the basis of Descartes was used as a textbook until 1765. *Ibid.*, p. 193.

by seeming "to be surprised at my treating him in this manner. I did not use to do so. Neither did he use to treat me so. This complaint was made twice at least. Many spoke earnestly, that what was said [i.e. by Sewall] was out of season." [68] The short account we have of this interchange says much about the social situation in which college practices under Leverett were challenged. The spokesman of orthodoxy was fended off by an appeal to the standards of good manners: he was treating another gentleman in less than courtly fashion and was "out of season"—a stratagem sufficient in this case to put Sewall on the defensive, but one that would have been swept aside by one zealot in the company of other zealots. A certain regard for gentlemanliness had always been one of the Puritan virtues, but it had not always been so powerful an inhibition on sectarian bigotry or brutality. [69] With the rise of a wealthy class of gentry this regard increased in strength to the point where decorum was beginning to be of roughly comparable importance with principle.

The advance in tolerance was another index of the decline of the religious scruples of the pristine Puritan age; for tolerance is, unfortunately, too often the virtue only of those who do not care excessively. It becomes a necessity of peace, trade, security, and culture not to care overmuch when a religious monopoly is replaced by religious duopoly or by diversity. The split within Congregationalism, the presence of Anglicans and Baptists, the pressure from England—all of these introduced such endless possibilities for bitter struggle that peace and quiet would have been totally impossible if religious differences had been pushed to the limit. Nor should it be imagined that the more orthodox were unaware of this. In 1718, when a pastor was ordained in the Baptist Church of Boston, three Congregational pastors took part. Among them was Cotton Mather, who preached a sermon in which he spoke of bygone religious persecutions in these terms:

Good men, alas! have done such things as these. New England also has in former times done something of this aspect, which would not now be so well approved: in which, if the brethren, in whose house we are now convened, met with anything too unbrotherly, they now with satisfaction hear us ex-

[68] Sewall, *Diary*, III, 202–3.

[69] Per contra, see F. A. Christie, "The Beginnings of Arminianism in New England," *Papers of The American Society of Church History*, Second Series, III (New York, 1912), 157: "To be orthodox one did not need to be fanatic or disrespectful, and certainly politeness is no sure proof of theological laxity." But when politeness is invoked as of comparable importance with good dogma and sound practice, something has happened to the Puritan spirit.

pressing our dislike of everything which looked like persecution in the days that have passed over us.[70]

And even old Increase, who died in 1728, liked to boast in his last days that Harvard College "forever indifferently Instructs and Rewards all Scholars of whatever different Perswasions in Christianity among us." [71]

[70] Cobb, *Rise of Religious Liberty in America,* p. 223.
[71] Miller, *From Colony to Province,* p. 481.

III: THE COLONIAL COLLEGES

THE AMERICAN PATTERN:
DENOMINATIONAL SPONSORSHIP

B Y THE MIDDLE of the eighteenth century there had emerged an American system of collegiate education different not only from the English
models with which Americans were most familiar but from all others as
well. In three features the early American system was unique. First, while
American collegiate education, like that of Europe, was the ward of religion, its pattern of essentially private denominational sponsorship, with
a modest admixture of state supervision, was new. Second, unlike the
European universities, American colleges had no connection with professional and advanced faculties—that is to say, they were colleges but not,
strictly speaking, universities. American colleges did not, like those of
Oxford and Cambridge, multiply and cluster at great centers of learning;
they were small and scattered, and after the Revolutionary era they were
to become numerous as well, so that the educational effort of the American people was increasingly diffused. In the nineteenth century, as we
shall see, this tendency got completely out of hand. The third unique
characteristic was that the early American colleges developed a system
of lay government—that is, a system in which the major decisions were
made by boards of nonresident governors who were not teachers [1]—that
remains characteristic of American higher education to this day. In order
to understand later developments in the colleges insofar as they affected
the status, the freedom, and the initiative of teachers, we must first understand the origins of lay government and the emergence of America's
distinctive pattern of denominational sponsorship, a pattern which was
not modified or replaced on any considerable scale until after the Civil

---

[1] The term *lay government* threatens to be confusing when applied to this early
period when ministers were so prominent on governing boards. What we mean by
lay government of academic institutions is simply government by persons other than
the faculties—i.e., nonautonomous government. Applied to churches, the same
term, of course, means government by those who are not clergymen.

War. Later, in analyzing the nineteenth-century colleges, we will trace the consequences of the diffusion of effort in American education.

The first three colleges, Harvard (1636), William and Mary (1693), and Yale (1701), were founded by the established churches of their respective colonies.[2] Then, after the settled churches had become too austere, too doctrinal, and too remote from the religious needs of the people, the religious scene was revitalized by the Great Awakening, inspired by the preaching of such men as Theodore J. Frelinghuysen, William Tennent and his sons, Jonathan Edwards, and by the five rousing evangelistic trips of the great English revivalist, George Whitefield. This series of revivals led to splits in the Congregational, Presbyterian, and Baptist groups that had important consequences for education. Princeton (1746) was founded by New-Side Presbyterians who hoped to show that they too, for all their revivalist fervor, could continue the New England tradition of an educated ministry. Both Brown (1764) and Queen's College (1766, later Rutgers) were founded by revivalistic groups, the first among the Baptists of Rhode Island, the second among Frelinghuysen's followers in the Dutch Reformed Church. Dartmouth (1769), the last of the colonial establishments, grew out of an Indian missionary school organized with Whitefield's help by Eleazar Wheelock, a Congregational pastor who had caught the current "enthusiasm." The two most secular of the colonial schools, King's College (1754, later Columbia) and the College of Philadelphia (1755, later the University of Pennsylvania) were still not untouched by religious rivalries, since both were shared and fought over by Anglicans and Presbyterians.

While the early colleges developed under religious sponsorship and a large measure of religious control, it does not follow that their religious purposes wholly account for their character. The common statement that they were in effect theological seminaries is altogether untrue. We have seen that Harvard was never a mere religious seminary with the sole purpose of training ministers. The stated purposes of other early institutions, as expressed in their charters, also included references to liberal education and the service of the public.[3] What is true is that the

---

[2] Dates, in all cases, are those of the first charters. In naming colleges whose titles later underwent a change, we have followed convenience rather than consistency.

[3] William and Mary's charter, unlike Harvard's, did say that it was to be a "seminary of Ministers of the Gospel," but added the more general goal "that the youth may be piously educated in good letters and manners." Yale's spoke of fitting youth "for publick employment, both in church & civil state," Princeton's simply of in-

desire to educate a suitable, orthodox body of native clergymen could be plausibly asserted to be the most urgent and immediate reason for founding the majority of the colonial colleges, perhaps seven out of nine. But it is equally true and equally important that their curricula were not those of divinity schools but of liberal arts schools, and that among those denominations that tried to maintain high standards for their clergy, additional postgraduate study in divinity was expected. It must also be remembered that early in the eighteenth century the clergymen graduates became a minority among all graduates. The proportion declined sharply throughout the eighteenth century, at the close of which about four fifths of all graduates were going into other vocations.[4] Not one of the colonial colleges required students to subscribe to a particular religious creed as a condition of admission. The founders of Brown, the most liberal college among them, not only ruled out sectarian differences as an object of classroom instruction but barred religious tests for members of the faculty.[5]

The sectarian allegiance of a college was usually expressed by the religious adherence of its president. The charters of King's College, Brown, and Queen's College specified that their presidents must be, respectively, an Anglican, a Baptist, and a member of the Dutch Reformed Church. And although their charters did not demand it, Yale and Harvard could hardly think of anyone but a Congregationalist, Princeton anyone but a Presbyterian.

---

structing them "in the learned Languages, and in the Liberal Arts and Sciences." If there was any trend among the later colleges in their statements of purpose, it was toward a more secular tone. See Edgar W. Knight, *A Documentary History of Education in the South before 1860* (Chapel Hill, N.C., 1949), I, 401; Franklin B. Dexter, *Documentary History of Yale University* (New Haven, 1916), p. 21; Thomas J. Wertenbaker, *Princeton, 1746–1896* (Princeton, 1946), pp. 396–97; Herbert and Carol Schneider, eds., *Samuel Johnson . . . His Career and Writings* (New York, 1929), IV, 222–24; Elsie Clews, *Educational Legislation and Administration of the Colonial Governments* (New York, 1899), pp. 303–8.

[4] Bailey B. Burritt, *Professional Distribution of College and University Graduates* (Washington, 1912), pp. 14, 22, 75, gives figures that should be good approximations. For figures on Princeton graduates to 1794 see Varnum L. Collins, *President Witherspoon: A Biography* (Princeton, 1925), II, 222. The importance of education for the ministry has been a source of some controversy. See, for example, Winthrop S. Hudson's angry polemic, "The Morison Myth concerning the Founding of Harvard College," *Church History*, VIII (June, 1939), 148–59.

[5] Walter C. Bronson, *The History of Brown University, 1764–1914* (Providence, R.I., 1914), pp. 3–4, 506; this liberality was practiced as well as professed, so far as choice of faculty was concerned. *Ibid.*, p. 101. In 1774 the Corporation at Brown added specifically that the children of Jews were free to enter the institution and enjoy the freedom of their religion. Reuben A. Guild, *Early History of Brown University* (Providence, R.I., 1897), p. 150.

The most noteworthy departure from the practice of the first three colleges to be made by those institutions that were founded around the middle of the century and afterwards is the introduction of interdenominational representation on boards of control. While the last six colonial colleges were all identified in varying degrees with a single dominant church, five had interdenominational representation. With the exception of Dartmouth they did not enjoy, as had the earlier colleges, the privilege of being founded by an established church.[6] The founders of the later colleges, in order to establish their institutions, had been forced to allay the hostility of other denominations by allotting them some place on governing boards, while their subsequent need to broaden the base of their financial support and enlarge their student bodies also contributed to softening their sectarian features. King's College, despite its Anglican affiliation, had among its charter members the pastors of four churches of other denominations in New York City. The College of Philadelphia, which grew out of a nonsectarian academy chartered in 1749, was reorganized and broadened in 1779 as the University of Pennsylvania (although it had already been infiltrated by the Presbyterians), an arrangement under which six of the twenty-four trustees were to be the senior members of each of the principal religious denominations of the city, including the Roman Catholic. The pretensions of the two most prominent denominations were recognized by making the first provost an Anglican divine and the first vice-provost a Presbyterian. At Brown, where the Baptists had a clear preponderance in both units of the dual governing board, the Congregationalists, Anglicans, and Quakers together held fourteen out of thirty-six seats among the trustees, while among the fellows only eight of twelve could be Baptists.[7] The spirit of interdenominational concession was least in evidence at Queen's College, yet even Queen's included four state officials among its forty-one trustees, and still others of the twenty-eight laymen named to its original board were not members of the Dutch Reformed Church.[8] Only a little less sectarian was Dartmouth, where three mem-

[6] This must be qualified for King's College insofar as the English and Dutch Churches shared a form of joint establishment dating from the promise of the English upon the surrender of New Amsterdam not to subvert the religion of the Dutch settlers. The first charter of King's College required that the president be a member of the English Church "as by law established."

[7] Clews, *Educational Legislation and Administration* . . . , pp. 259, 300–308; Edward P. Cheyney, *History of the University of Pennsylvania* (Philadelphia, 1940), pp. 122–25; Edward C. Elliott and M. M. Chambers, *Charters and Basic Laws of Selected American Universities and Colleges* (New York, 1934), pp. 415–16.

[8] William H. S. Demarest, *A History of Rutgers College, 1766–1924* (New Bruns-

bers of the first board were Anglican laymen and New Hampshire officials.[9]

The tendency toward interdenominational representation, although a sign of growing tolerance, did not mean that the denominations had composed their differences and forgotten their hostilities. On the contrary, interdenominational representation came about precisely because sectarian bickering was so acute that hostile factions had to be quieted in some diplomatic way if the new institutions were to have a chance of success. The founding of King's College seemed for a time to be seriously jeopardized by animosities between Anglicans and Presbyterians, while differences between the same groups affected the early development of the College of Philadelphia. Brown was founded only after an angry tussle between Baptists and Congregationalists. Sectarian pride kept the governing board of Queen's College from accepting union with Princeton at a time when Queen's was staggering toward total collapse. As for Dartmouth, the mere suspicion that the Bishop of London might be made an ex-officio trustee caused Eleazar Wheelock to consider removing his projected college from New Hampshire to another province. As late as 1779 the suspicion inspired in the dissenting sects of Virginia by the Anglican background of William and Mary destroyed Jefferson's plans to revamp the institution, even though these plans involved a diminution of its denominational character.[10]

In sum, the desire to dominate and the fear of being dominated had by no means died out in sectarian breasts, but the capacity to do mischief to each other had been greatly diminished, and the necessity of reckoning with outsiders brought about a greater flexibility in educational planning.

The later eighteenth-century colleges were opened at a time of ex-

---

wick, N.J., 1924), pp. 62, 74–76; Clews, *Educational Legislation and Administration . . .*, pp. 338–39. The early spirit of Queen's College was expressed by Theodore Frelinghuysen when he said of the other denominations, "We have no business with their colleges; they may erect as many as they please, and must expect to maintain them too, themselves. Let everyone provide for his own house." Demarest, *History of Rutgers*, p. 39. Perhaps it was this attitude that made it so difficult to keep Queen's College alive.

[9] Frederick Chase, *A History of Dartmouth College and the Town of Hanover* (Cambridge, 1891), pp. 121n, 642.

[10] On these developments see *A History of Columbia University* (New York, 1904), Chap. I; Dorothy Rita Dillon, *The New York Triumvirate* (New York, 1949), Chap. II; Cheyney, *History of the University of Pennsylvania*, pp. 122–23; Bronson, *History of Brown University*, pp. 122–23; Chase, *History of Dartmouth*, pp. 114–20, 125–26; Sadie Bell, *The Church, the State, and Education in Virginia* (Philadelphia, 1930).

panding religious liberty. To be sure, this expansion was for the most part neither planned nor welcomed. The articulate Protestant leaders of colonial settlement had been—with few notable exceptions like Roger Williams and William Penn—firmly opposed to toleration. But while they rejected it as a principle they yielded increasingly to it out of necessity or expediency. A large number of sects poured into or emerged within the colonies during the eighteenth century, and none was strong enough to attain dominance. In the absence of a majority strong enough to exercise coercion, some mutual forbearance became a simple necessity. Indeed the situation of the various sects provided an example for free political organization that was not lost upon American observers. "In a free government," wrote Madison in Number 51 of *The Federalist,*

the security for civil rights must be the same as that for religious rights. It consists in the one case in the multiplicity of interests, and in the other of the multiplicity of sects. The degree of security in both cases will depend on the number of interests and sects.[11]

Also working for tolerance were the example of English opinion and English law under Cromwell and after the Act of Toleration of 1689, as well as the influence of English governors who reflected the preference of the mother country (and of some of the Catholic and Quaker proprietors) for economic prosperity rather than sectarian bickering. The developments of the eighteenth century accentuated the trend toward tolerance, as the sects moved somewhat closer together in the face of common problems—the threat of an Anglican episcopate and the rise of rationalism and Deism. Even the development of revivalistic factions among the Presbyterians, Baptists, and later the Methodists contributed surprisingly to the atmosphere of religious latitude. The New-Side apostles, despite their intolerant impulses, realized that their type of emotional religion would only benefit by the destruction of the formal institutions and establishments that had been created by their predecessors and opponents; such destruction would clear the way for movements that exalted the force of spirit over external discipline and traditional arrangements. Finally, the growth of rationalism itself created a liberal-minded elite, the flower of which were such men as Franklin, Adams, Jefferson, and Madison, and which was fundamentally indifferent to doctrinal issues and impartially tolerant of all the sects.[12]

[11] *The Federalist,* ed. by Edward Mead Earle (Washington, 1937), pp. 339–40.
[12] The forces working for religious liberty are discussed by W. W. Sweet, "The American Colonial Environment and Religious Liberty," *Church History,* V (March,

THE AMERICAN PATTERN: LAY GOVERNMENT

Of great significance for later struggles over intellectual freedom was the American system of academic government which had taken on its essential features by the middle of the eighteenth century. Nowhere outside the United States and Canada are modern universities governed by boards of laymen. The system of lay government has created special problems for free teaching and scholarship in America. The essence of lay government is that the trustees, not the faculties, *are,* in law, the college or university, and that legally they can hire and fire faculty members and make almost all the decisions governing the institution. This has hampered the development of organization, initiative, and self-confidence among American college professors, and it has contributed, along with many other forces in American life, to lowering their status in the community. Other professional groups have far greater power to determine the standards and conduct of their own professions.[13]

To contrast without qualification the European system of academic self-government with the American system of lay government would, however, be misleading. While European universities, particularly those of the Continent, are formally self-governing, they are still not entirely free from the influence of church and state. American universities and colleges, particularly the best private institutions, have developed a system under which the balance of governmental power is actually distributed among trustees, administration, and faculty. Formally empowered with almost all the prerogatives of government, trustees in such institutions have in fact delegated most of them to the administrations or the faculties, retaining chiefly the prerogative of budgetary decisions and the right of intervention in broad policy. Faculties have a very large voice, often in effect the controlling voice, in matters of appointment, promotion, and curriculum. Legally still powerless, they are nonetheless potent agencies of academic government in the most reputable colleges and universities.

1935), 43–56, and Perry Miller, "The Contribution of the Protestant Churches to Religious Liberty in Colonial America," *ibid.,* pp. 57–66. Cf. Evarts B. Greene, *Religion and the State* (New York, 1941), Chap. III.

[13] American academic government is discussed in relation to the problems of academic freedom by Robert M. MacIver in *Academic Freedom in Our Time* (New York, 1955), Part II. See also the discussion of the freedom and status of American professors by Richard Shryock, "The Academic Profession in the United States," *Bulletin of the American Association of University Professors,* XXXVIII (Spring, 1952), 32–70.

How this measure of informal self-government has grown up within the framework of the plenary legal powers of the trustees is an important part of our story.[14]

When all necessary qualifications have been made, however, the fact remains that lay government has been one of the most decisive factors in the problem of academic freedom in America, and its origin and development are central to our concern. The American system of lay government was not planned by the founders of the colonial colleges, who were themselves familiar chiefly with the altogether different system of the English universities. Rather it grew out of the conditions of religious and social life in the New World.[15]

In at least three important respects the American situation was unique. The first was that while the European universities had been nurtured for centuries on the medieval gild traditions of faculty self-government, the American colleges were not only Protestant institutions but had been founded in a totally Protestant milieu, sharply cut off from many medieval traditions. The medieval universities were ecclesiastical agencies founded at a time when the Church was still effectually guarding its institutions from the incursions of lay power. Both the church principle of ecclesiastical independence and the gild principle of corporate self-government provided the universities and society at large with dominant models of autonomy. This autonomy the Protestant Reformation had

[14] See below, Chap. V, pp. 232–38; Chap. VI, pp. 308–9.
Lest the American system be excessively depreciated, one may add that it is naive to suppose, whatever the formal and traditional sanctions underlying freedom of teaching and scholarship, that any universities anywhere can be altogether free from the pressures that the community brings to bear. One need only look at the interplay between the "autonomous" medieval universities and the Church, at the impact of the Reformation upon universities, or even to probe a little at the genial facade of German *Lehrfreiheit,* to see that European practices of academic government have hardly eliminated inhibitions from academic life. In justice to the role of laymen in education, it should also be said that their intervention has on occasion been salutary. After academic self-government had led to stagnation and decay at Oxford and Cambridge, Parliamentary intervention in the middle of the nineteenth century led to admirable reforms. See A. I. Tillyard, *A History of University Reform* (Cambridge, 1913). In the United States many colleges were being rescued at the same time by the intervention of their alumni. See below, Chap. VI.
[15] It is suggestive, in this respect, that the Protestant universities of Canada have undergone a parallel constitutional evolution, embracing an original scheme of lay government later qualified by the growth of a considerable degree of informal faculty government. In the early Canadian institutions the roles of ex-officio trustees drawn from political positions seems even more important than in the American colleges, and political events—elections, the changes of governors—had decisive influence on the fortunes of Canadian colleges.

sharply circumscribed. As we have seen, the proud self-sufficiency, and with it much of the intellectual freedom, that had been characteristic of the medieval universities at their zenith went into decline. Moreover, the principle of the freedom of the church hierarchy from intervention by laymen was sharply challenged—not least by the Puritans, of whom it has been remarked that they gave the layman a larger part in the control of the local church than he had enjoyed since the Roman emperors became Christian.[16] Now it was not a very drastic step from admitting men who were not clerics into the government of churches to admitting those who were not teachers into the government of colleges. Just as gild self-government and church autonomy were models for the organization of the medieval universities, so nonconformist Protestant church government provided new and different models for the American colleges. In England itself, while the method of founding colleges at Oxford and Cambridge was not changed by the Reformation, educational foundations of lower than university grade had begun to be placed under the control of incorporated bodies of lay trustees in the sixteenth century.[17]

American Protestants did not consider that they were destroying intellectual freedom by extending the policy of lay government from churches to colleges. Indeed they considered it one of their contributions to civilization that they had broken up the priestly autonomy of advanced education and had brought it under the control of the community.[18] Of course the early founders of American colleges did not depart very far from

[16] Samuel Eliot Morison, *Three Centuries of Harvard* (Cambridge, Mass., 1936), p. 71.

[17] See Edward H. Reisner, "The Origin of Lay University Boards of Control in the United States," *Columbia University Quarterly*, XXIII (March, 1931), 68–69.

[18] "Since the Reformation from Popery, the Notion of the Sanctity of Colleges and other Popish Religious Houses has been exploded. . . . The Intention herein was not to destroy the Colleges or the Universities, and rob the Muses, but to rescue them from Popish Abuses, and reduce them to a Constitution more agreeable to the Original Design of Universities [i.e., in antiquity], and more dependent upon the Civil Power. From this time they have been considered as Lay-Communities. . . . And in forming new Universities, and Colleges, the British Nation has perhaps made them a little more pompous, in Compliance with Customs introduced into the ancient Universities in *Popish* Times; which Customs being of long Standing they chose to suffer to continue in them. But the Protestant Princes, and Republicks, and States, in whose Territories there was no University before, had no Regard to any Popish Usages or Customs in erecting Colleges, and Universities, and only endowed them with such Privileges and Powers, and Officers, as were properly School Privileges, Powers and Officers." [Benjamin Gale] *A Reply to a Pamphlet Entitled the Answer of the Friend in the West* (n.p., 1755), pp. 47–48. Significantly, the author of these remarks was a partisan of the somewhat more liberal faction that sought to wrest the control of Yale from Thomas Clap.

the traditional assumption that institutions of higher learning should be run largely by clerics, but if clerics were expected to share the government of churches they might also be expected to share the government of colleges. Such early efforts as were made to increase the corporate autonomy of teaching bodies were not identified with any movements toward greater liberality in thought, but rather with narrow clerical interests, conservatism, and orthodoxy. As we shall see, Mather at Harvard in the seventeenth century and tutors Sever and Welsteed in the early eighteenth century sought to augment corporate autonomy for reasons that had little to do with freedom, while the clerics at William and Mary seem to have been interested only in their own salaries and privileges. Likewise, Thomas Clap at Yale, defending the independence of that institution against the intervention of the Connecticut legislature, was fighting for conservative theology and sectarian purity. Paradoxical as it may seem to those who read the situation with twentieth-century values in mind, the growing religious and intellectual liberalism of eighteenth-century America was identified in the colleges not with corporate autonomy but with lay government. Not until the nineteenth century, when lay government had been long established, was this situation reversed.

The second reason for lay government was that while the European universities evolved out of long-established communities of scholarship and teaching, the first American colleges were created, in a sense, as artifacts by communities that had to strain very limited resources to support them. This meant that infant institutions in the American colonies had to be carefully nursed for many years before they developed into stable colleges capable of standing on their own feet. During this period of infancy the lay boards of control exercised sweeping powers that they were later reluctant to give up, being, like other parents, unwilling to accept the fact of their own obsolescence. Moreover, the prominent role of private benefactions guaranteed that this obsolescence would never be complete; institutions dependent upon renewed surges of good will in the lay community were more sensitive to lay opinion than were those that relied upon stable clerical livings or regular parliamentary appropriations.

Finally, while in Europe a body of men belonging to what could be called a teaching profession existed before the emergence of the universities, the colleges in America were created first, and only afterwards did a considerable body of professional teachers emerge. The idea of the self-governing university had been based upon the assumption that teachers were mature professionals; the first American teachers were preponderantly youthful amateurs. In a raw community like early colonial America the opportunities for a man of learning outside the realm of teaching were too great to leave many first-rate men available for the ill-compensated, low-status positions that were the lot of those whose whole lives would be given to the instruction of boys. As we have seen in Chapter II, the first teaching staffs at Harvard were composed of future ministers for whom teaching was only a temporary occupation, a preamble to a clerical career. In the later colleges this was also the case, with the exception, as we shall see, of William and Mary. So long as the bulk of college teaching was in the hands of groups of youngsters for whom teaching was only a by-path to more desired careers, faculty self-government was bound to seem less acceptable, indeed less meaningful, than it did in European universities numbering among their masters many great and influential men of learning. For over a century and a half American collegiate education relied chiefly on young tutors, having in all its faculties only a handful of professors of some maturity and length of tenure.[19] Harvard had been established for more than eighty-five years, Yale for more than fifty, and Princeton for more than twenty before each had its first professor, and it was to be many years more before regular professors outnumbered transient tutors. The only secure and sustained professional office in American collegiate education was that of the college president himself. He alone among the working teachers of the early colleges had, in the community and before the governing boards, the full stature of an independent man of learning. To this situation can be traced the singular role and importance of the American college or university president.

Lay government created more problems than it solved, and to these problems the college president provided an answer—at least the best answer that could be found. Lay boards of trustees were absentee proprietors, and in the bustling America of colonial days they usually had very little leisure to devote to their colleges. Small as they were, these colleges had promotional problems, staff problems, disciplinary problems,

[19] From the standpoint of ecclesiastical organization one might say that while in Europe the clerics who were responsible for education were the teachers themselves, in America the clerics responsible for education were trustees and the teachers were only *future* clerics.

servant problems, curricular problems—and to none of these could the busy trustees consistently give enough attention. Thus between the trustees, who had the legal capacity but not the time or energy to govern, and the teachers, who were considered too young and too transient to govern, there was created a power vacuum. This vacuum the presidents quickly began to fill.

The early college president played a multiple role. As a cleric and learned man he taught. As a member of the governing board he participated in major decisions. As a leading citizen of his community he promoted his institution. As a faculty member he led the teaching staff. As a preacher he prayed and sermonized for the students. Since he was subject in most cases to dismissal by governing boards, he was the subordinate of the trustees, and yet as the man most familiar with college affairs he was also the leader of the governing board. In relation to his tiny teaching staff he was a leader or a boss, depending upon his situation and temperament. Unlike the European rector, he was not elected by the teachers nor in any formal way accountable to them. Teachers came and went as a matter of course. The president remained until he died or resigned or, in rare cases, was ousted by his board. The tutors, being temporary servants, had little reason to resist or hamper his authority.[20] The trustees, although they appointed and could replace him, could not displace him. In legal theory they were the college, but in the eyes of the community, and often in his own eyes, the president was the college. Upon his reputation and his promotional energies its place in the community chiefly depended. He became at once its dynamic center of authority, its symbol, and its spokesman. He occupied and in a sense created an office which has no equivalent in academic systems outside the United States. The prestige and pride that elsewhere were vested in the faculties came to center in him—and there, with some modification, they have remained to this day.

For a long time, in most colleges, the president was the only teacher who possessed enough status, power, and confidence to wage a battle with the trustees or repressive forces in the community on behalf of religious or intellectual freedom. Thus, from the time of Henry Dunster down to the Civil War period, the outstanding college controversies of this sort involved presidents more often than professors, and tutors

---

[20] The president might make a practice of consulting tutors, however, and his absence or illness might leave them with large powers of discretion.

hardly at all. In some of these cases it is hard to determine to what extent the controversy was a purely administrative affair and to what extent it involved intellectual issues. But the fact remains that in the transition of both freedom and power from lay trustees to faculty members, insofar as that transition has taken place, the president played an important and constructive part. In the early days of the colleges it was quite difficult for trustees to find a man endowed with all the qualities needed for vigorous college leadership. Those institutions that could not find a strong president or would not give him sufficient powers frequently languished. The man who had the necessary qualifications thus found himself in a good bargaining position, and if he was astute, he often saw to it that he came into his office with a strong hand.[21] Strong presidents, to be sure, could make great difficulties, as the opponents of Mather and Clap could testify; but strong presidents, like Ezra Stiles and John Witherspoon, made strong colleges, and ultimately—though this was much later indeed—they made strong faculties. In the transit of powers of decision to the faculties, as in the struggle for freedom of thought, many of the outstanding college presidents contributed their full share.

THE BEGINNINGS OF LAY GOVERNMENT

The development of the first two colonial colleges, Harvard and William and Mary, suggests that their founders intended to emulate the governmental conditions of the English colleges with which they were familiar, but that circumstances impelled them in the direction of lay government. Oxford and Cambridge were governed by their own faculties. The scholars made their own rules and appointed their own officers, and neither the Crown nor the donors of college properties normally made claims to participate in academic government. The colleges, which had grown out of student residence halls, were managed by the elected col-

[21] A good illustration in the Revolutionary period is that of Ezra Stiles, who made an extremely canny reconnaissance of the terrain before he accepted the presidency of Yale. Almost a hundred years later James Burrill Angell made the trustees of the University of Michigan all but stand on their heads before he went from Vermont to Michigan. One of his predecessors at Michigan, Henry L. Tappan, had been treated harshly by the trustees and in a manner very unfavorable to the freedom of the institution. This was one factor in Angell's caution. See the fascinating letters in Wilfred B. Shaw, ed., *From Vermont to Michigan: Correspondence of James B. Angell* (Ann Arbor, 1936).

lege heads and the "fellows"—and in English usage no one who was not a college fellow taught in a college. College and university authorities ran their own affairs and administered their own finances. There seems to be no evidence that the founders of Harvard College at first intended to depart from these familiar and respected practices of academic government. But when Harvard was created by legislative enactment in 1636, it seemed impossible to commit to a group of men as yet unknown and unchosen the full powers of management of the resources that were to be put at the disposal of the college by the General Court. (The wisdom of the founding fathers, from their own point of view, in keeping control in their own hands was shown by the early history of the institution, for its first head, Master Nathaniel Eaton, was a scapegrace and its first president, Henry Dunster, turned heretical.) Hence the college was placed under the control of a board of Overseers consisting of six magistrates and six ministers. Until a charter was granted in 1650, the Overseers were the sole governing body of the college. In 1642 the legislature reorganized them, appointing as members of the board all the magistrates of the province, its governor and deputy governor, the president of the college and the "teaching elders" of the churches of the six adjoining towns.[22] The first board under this statute numbered, in addition to the president, eleven public officers and nine ministers.

The disadvantages of trying to manage a college through such an external agency, with scattered members of whom only one, the college president, was in close and continuous contact with college business, soon became clear; and it seems to have been at President Dunster's insistence that a corporate charter was secured. The disparity between the position of the college teachers, who were no more than transient employees of the Overseers, with much responsibility but no power, and the autonomous position of the English universities was painfully obvious. The charter of 1650 seems to have been meant in part to eliminate this anomaly by creating the Corporation of the college as a separate governing body, to be composed of the president, the treasurer, and

[22] Magistrates meant the Assistants of the province who were annually elected by the freemen. Teaching elders meant both the "pastors" and the "teachers" of the churches involved. A fully staffed church was expected to have two ordained ministers. On the reorganization of 1642 see Samuel Eliot Morison, *The Founding of Harvard College* (Cambridge, Mass., 1935), pp. 325–28. Subsequent measures changing the composition of the Overseers are printed in Edward C. Elliott and M. M. Chambers, *Charters and Basic Laws of Selected American Universities and Colleges* (New York, 1934), pp. 216–24.

five fellows. The power to elect their own successors, to manage the college's property and act for it in law, to hire college servants, and to make rules and by-laws was vested in the Corporation—but that body was to secure the consent of the Overseers on all important decisions and to submit to its arbitration in cases of disagreement. The charter thus seems to have embodied a compromise between the familiar English conditions of faculty self-government and the practice that had prevailed at Harvard since 1636. The Corporation was to take the initiative in all matters, but the Overseers were endowed with a veto.

Thus the disparity between the inherited English ideal of self-government and the conditions of provincial life led to a system of dual control; and, as we shall see in the case of William and Mary, dual control was to result there also from the action of the same forces. In one respect this dual system formally emulated English practice, for it was customary for English colleges to have an external agent of government called the Visitor. But usually the function of the Visitor was only to act as an umpire when disputes arose, and many English colleges actually had no Visitor in 1600. Plainly the role of Harvard's Overseers would have been far greater than the traditional visitorial function, even if the provisions of the charter of 1650 had been observed.

In fact, those provisions were not observed, and Harvard was not governed in accordance with the charter. In spite of its mandates, the Overseers, not the Corporation, elected the two presidents who followed Dunster, hired and paid the fellows, and issued orders governing the college servants. The Overseers, after fourteen years of ascendancy, were evidently not prepared in 1650 to yield their prerogatives to a very small group of very young men.[23] Nor, evidently, were the young men, who were destined in any case to be teachers for only a few years, especially interested in challenging this usurpation by the Overseers of the Corporation's charter prerogatives. Faculty self-government was thus forestalled at the beginning by the simple fact that there was as yet no teaching profession. Nothing could be more misleading than to describe early Harvard College, as one student of academic government

---

[23] Professor Morison points out that in 1650 President Dunster himself had just turned forty, the treasurer was twenty-six, and the average age of the five fellows was about twenty-four. *Harvard College in the Seventeenth Century* (Cambridge, Mass., 1936), I, 11. On early Harvard government see *The Founding of Harvard College,* Chaps. XV, XXII, and *Harvard College in the Seventeenth Century,* Chaps. I, XXIII, XXIV.

has done, as a "tutor's college." [24] Not only did the early Corporation neglect to exercise most of the fundamental powers of academic government, but even within the Corporation the place and power of the tutors was severely limited at the outset. As Morison puts it, "the Harvard Corporation never functioned like an English collegiate body, and began to evolve into something else before the ink was scarce dry on the Charter." [25] It had evidently been Dunster's intention to follow the English pattern: every teacher of undergraduates was to be a fellow, and no nonresidents were to be fellows. (Some residents might be fellows, without teaching, if they were present at the college in some scholarly role.) As it turned out, some of the teaching fellows began to resign shortly after the granting of the charter, and the revenues of the college proved far too meager to provide stipends for the five fellowships mentioned in the charter. During the rest of the seventeenth century there were apparently never more than three tutors at the college (often only two), and hence never more than three resident fellows.[26] The rapid turnover of the tutors made the Corporation an unstable body, despite the longer ex-officio tenures of the presidents and the treasurers. Even in Dunster's time neighboring ministers who had been tutors began to get seats on the Corporation; beginning in the 1670s it became customary to give seats to ministers who had never been tutors. Morison concludes that until the Corporation was reorganized under President Leverett in 1707 "the President governed the College with the aid of such Overseers as were interested, and treated the tutors as senior students assisting him in discipline and instruction, rather than his fellows." [27]

After 1707 it became a regular practice to appoint tutors without granting them the status of fellows of the Corporation. Finally, in 1780, the Corporation became a totally nonresident body, except, of course, for the president himself. Businessmen and lawyers began to be elected to the Corporation, and with this development the functions of the Over-

[24] John E. Kirkpatrick, *The American College and Its Rulers* (New York, 1926), Chap. I.

[25] Morison, *Harvard College in the Seventeenth Century*, I, 14.

[26] For the tutors, fellows, and other officers, with their terms of office as nearly as they can be determined, see Albert Mathews in *Publications of the Colonial Society of Massachusetts*, XV (1925), lxvi, lxvii, and clii, ff. On the meaning of the word "fellow" see pp. cxxxii–cxxxv. Before 1690 there were only three fellows appointed who were not tutors, but there were additional fellows whose tenures as fellows was far longer than their resident careers as tutors. From 1690 to 1728 there were seventeen fellows who never served at any time as tutors.

[27] *Harvard College in the Seventeenth Century*, I, 15.

seers became more and more vestigial.[28] With only minor qualifications it can thus be said of the Harvard Corporation that while it was in any serious measure a resident body of teachers it did not govern, and that when it finally took on the functions of government it was a group of nonresident men who were not teachers.[29]

William and Mary, the second colonial college to be chartered, resorted, like Harvard, to a dual system of government that included one unit that was expected to take charge in the absence of a body of teachers and another unit that was expected at length to embody the will of the faculty. But while at Harvard the supposed "faculty" unit, the Corporation, contained non-teaching members from very early times and became the real agency of government only after it had become almost entirely a body of laymen, at William and Mary the faculty unit, the President and Masters (or Professors), was always a body of resident masters in the English tradition. Its right to control the college, how-

[28] The primary reason for the initial steps taken to replace ministers by businessmen in 1779 and 1784 seems to have been the financial difficulties faced by Harvard in the Revolutionary period and immediately after. Josiah Quincy, *The History of Harvard University* (Boston, 1860), Vol. II, Chap. XXXI; Morison, *Three Centuries of Harvard*, pp. 153–60.

[29] In 1721 a constitutional issue arose out of the antagonism between Leverett and the conservatives. Two tutors, Nicholas Sever and William Welsteed, claimed that by virtue of being resident teachers and stipendiaries of the college they were entitled to seats on the Corporation. In presenting their case to the Overseers, they relied upon the alleged meaning of the charter of 1650 and the intention of its framers to follow the English practice of including all "fellows" in the management of colleges. While their conception of the intent of the founders was probably correct, it ran counter, of course, to long-standing Harvard usage. At the time the conservative faction had great strength in the Overseers and the General Court, and the entire move represented an effort through Sever and Welsteed to remove from the Corporation two recently appointed ministers of the liberal faction, Benjamin Colman and Nathan Appleton, who would have to leave if the others were seated. Fortunately for Leverett, the Royal Governor, Samuel Shute, was feuding with the legislature. He took the side of the liberals and made it clear that he would invoke Royal authority if necessary to prevent any further attempt to alter the traditional practice to the disadvantage of Leverett's Corporation. The fullest account of the controversy is in Quincy, *History of Harvard*, Vol. I, Chaps. XIII and XIV, with documents, pp. 546–56. A briefer and more detached account is that of Morison in *Three Centuries of Harvard*, pp. 69–73. See also the comments by Shipton in *Sibley's Harvard Graduates*, V, 92–93, and VI, 154–55, and the text of Sever's argument before the legislature in *Proceedings of the Massachusetts Historical Society*, XVI, 54–67.

For a later effort to minimize the power of the Overseers and strengthen the Corporation, see Shipton's sketch of Nathan Prince in *Sibley's Harvard Graduates*, VI, 272–73, and Nathan Prince, *An Account of the Constitution and Government of Harvard College* (n.p., n.d. [1742]).

ever, was always under dispute by the lay unit, the Visitors—and in the end the Visitors won a complete victory.

From the early seventeenth century there had been talk of a college for Virginia, but it was not until 1693 that the Reverend James Blair, commissary for the Bishop of London and head of the Anglican church in Virginia, returned to England and secured the royal charter that authorized the creation of the college.[30] Financed by aid from the Crown and the provincial government, as well as by subsequent private gifts, William and Mary was an agency both of the church and the state. The charter created four schools: a common school for Indian children; a grammar school at which Greek and Latin were to be taught to post-elementary students; a "philosophy school," or college; and a divinity school. In addition to the president, who was not expected to teach, there were to be six "professors," two each in the divinity school and college and one to head each of the lower schools. A board of Visitors was established, consisting of fourteen laymen and four clergymen, with the power to appoint the president and the masters and to make the rules and statutes of the college. They were to co-opt their successors. The Reverend Blair was made both a Visitor and the president of the college for life, while Governor Francis Nicholson was among the Visitors. In the English tradition a chancellor—i.e., a protector, adviser, and agent at the court —was included, an office filled by the Bishop of London. It was further provided that when the college was founded and established its properties and revenues should be transferred from the Visitors to the President and Masters, and that the latter body was to be a body politic with perpetual succession, empowered to conduct the college's business affairs.[31]

[30] Basing his argument partly on Commissary Blair's familiarity with the universities of Aberdeen and Edinburgh, A. Bailey Cutts has made a case for the importance of a Scottish influence on the American pattern of lay government. "The Educational Influence of Aberdeen in Seventeenth Century Virginia," *William and Mary Quarterly,* Second Series, Vol. XV (July, 1935), pp. 229–49. However, his parallel between the academic senate at Aberdeen and the William and Mary system is not very convincing. The real clash at William and Mary seems to have been between Oxford ideals and American realities. See Courtlandt Canby, "A Note on the Influence of Oxford upon William and Mary College in the Eighteenth Century," *William and Mary Quarterly,* Second Series, Vol. XXI (July, 1941), pp. 243–47.

[31] So large a part of the records of William and Mary have been lost, especially for its earliest years, that its history cannot be written with the thoroughness that is possible in the case of the other colonial colleges. However, from the beginning of the *William and Mary College Quarterly,* First Series, Vol. I, and in the pages

Teachers and members of the governing board were required to take an oath subscribing to the Thirty-nine Articles of the English church.

The text of the charter suggests that the college government was intended to follow the English pattern so far as possible—it even provided for a representative of the college in the House of Burgesses to be named by the President and Masters (not, it should be noted, by the Visitors)—which leads one to suspect that its founders assumed that the ultimate transfer of the college properties into the hands of the President and Masters would carry with it the fundamental power of control, leaving the Visitors in some such incidental position as that occupied by Visitors in England. However, if this was the intention, the charter failed to anticipate the effects of American conditions upon the power structure of the college. So long as the right to make the statutes and choose personnel was in the hands of the Visitors, they were in a position to govern if they chose to do so.

Revenues were inadequate, and the institution was long in getting under way. Indeed, while its charter was the second to be granted in the colonies, William and Mary became the third college in actual operation, for Yale was graduating students long before William and Mary was able to offer a college curriculum. There is no evidence that anything resembling the regular college curriculum of the time was offered before 1729, when the full complement of teachers as provided by the charter was at last engaged, a body of statutes drawn up, and the transfer of college properties and revenues from the Visitors to the President and Masters was finally made.[32]

By this time, however, the Visitors had been engaged in the active and

---

of its successor, the *William and Mary Quarterly,* documents shedding much light upon its history have appeared. It is inexpedient to cite all these items in detail. The text of the charter, together with many of the most important surviving documents, is printed in Edgar W. Knight, *A Documentary History of Education in the South before 1860,* I, 368–552. See also *Virginia Magazine of History and Biography,* IV (October, 1896), 161–75. A good brief historical sketch may be found in Lyon G. Tyler's *Williamsburg* (Richmond, 1907), pp. 110–204. See also the anonymous sketch, *The History of the College of William and Mary from its Foundation, 1660, to 1874* (Richmond, 1874), and Herbert Baxter Adams, *The College of William and Mary* (Washington, 1887).

[32] The grammar school was open by 1694, the Indian school by 1711. The sole faculty member who had served any length of time at "college" teaching, the Rev. Hugh Jones, asserted in 1724 that William and Mary "at present . . . scarcely merits the name of a college." See Knight, *Documentary History of Education in the South,* pp. 493, 498, and *The Official Letters of Alexander Spotswood* (Richmond, 1865), pp. 166–67. Cf. Samuel Eliot Morison, "American Colonial Colleges," in *Rice Institute Pamphlet,* XXIII (October, 1936), 261n.

detailed supervision of the embryonic college and its associated schools for almost thirty-five years, and a precedent for their continuous interference had been firmly established. Even after the transfer was made, the right to make the laws and statutes of the college was still theirs, and later they seem to have construed from this a right to intervene in academic affairs when they chose.[33] As a consequence the legal structure of the college was utterly anomalous: the faculty found itself formally empowered to exercise control of its business transactions, while the Visitors were legally left (through their control of the statutes) with broad and intrusive rights of intervention in academic matters. That such a condition had been the intent of the charter seems very doubtful. However, there seem to have been few difficulties of much academic importance for some years after the transfer. From 1729 to about 1755 the President and Masters probably enjoyed more self-government than did the faculty of any other early American college.[34] Having surmounted its early period of poverty and neglect, the college flourished between the middle of the century and the time of the Revolution, a period in which Thomas Jefferson and many other distinguished students graduated.

During the 1750s William and Mary became the center of a series of contentions between the faculty and the Visitors that was a part of a larger struggle over clerical salaries between the clergy and laymen of the province. The right of individual members of the faculty to marry and reside outside the college and to combine professorships with church functions became the subject of occasional disputes, while the right of the faculty body as a whole to appoint college officers and servants, bestow scholarships, manage revenues, and control college discipline without interference precipitated a running argument over the constitution of the college. The peculiar ambiguities of the charter and the sweeping powers exercised in the past by the Visitors gave ample cause for confusion.[35] The faculty, consisting almost entirely of Oxford men

[33] This in spite of the injunction made by the two survivors of the original board of Visitors when they drew up the Statutes of 1728 to the effect that the Visitors should "not suffer themselves to be troubled, except in Matters of great Moment, where there is some Difficulty to be got over, or some Corruption or ill Practice to be reformed, or a new Statute to be made, or some other weighty business to be transacted." Knight, *Documentary History of Education in the South,* p. 507.

[34] See Lyon G. Tyler, "Early Courses and Professors at William and Mary College," *William and Mary College Quarterly,* First Series, Vol. XIV (October, 1905), pp. 71–83.

[35] The clearest account of the controversies is that of Tyler, *Williamsburg,* pp. 144 ff. See also H. J. Eckenrode, *Separation of Church and State in Virginia* (Rich-

accustomed to far greater academic autonomy, put up a spirited resistance to lay control, insisting that beyond the making of the statutes the Visitors had enjoyed no rightful powers over the college since 1729 except in cases in which violation of the statutes was alleged. Since the faculty could appeal to the Bishop of London against the decisions of the Visitors they were not without recourse, and they won a number of concessions. But in the end it was inevitable that the powerful gentry of Virginia would win out over a handful of stubborn clerics. Whatever vestiges of faculty autonomy remained after the 1760s were swept away by the Revolution, during which Jefferson, as governor of Virginia and a member of the Visitors, attempted to transform his alma mater into a state university. In this he failed because of the hostility of the dissenting sects of Virginia to an institution with Anglican traditions.[36] But he did manage to reorganize and in a considerable measure to secularize it. In 1790 a legal action taken by a dismissed master resulted in a decision of sweeping importance by the Virginia Court of Appeals which in effect reaffirmed the extensive powers that had long been exercised by the Visitors and confirmed their right to remove professors.[37] Thus ended at William and Mary the only sustained attempt by college teachers to reproduce in the colonies the English pattern of academic autonomy. The independence and militancy of its faculty had been remarkable, but they had rested on forces outside the American milieu—the Privy Council, the Church of England, the Bishop of London—and no comparable situation was possible after the Revolution.

THE ARCHETYPES OF LAY GOVERNMENT

Harvard and William and Mary had one significant experience in common: the early emergence of a dual system of control, followed by the

mond, 1910), Chap. II; John E. Kirkpatrick, "The Constitutional Development of the College of William and Mary," *William and Mary Quarterly,* Second Series, Vol. IV (April, 1926), pp. 95–108; William S. Perry, *Historical Collections Relating to the American Colonial Church* (Hartford, 1870), I, 456–57, 468–69, 473, 517–18, 523–24 and *passim;* "Journal of the President and Masters of William and Mary College," *William and Mary College Quarterly,* First Series, Vol. V (October, 1896), pp. 85–89; Vol. V (April, 1897), pp. 224–29. Some light is shed on the relation of the faculty of William and Mary to the Visitors by H. L. Ganter, ed., "Documents Relating to the Early History of the College of William and Mary," *William and Mary Quarterly,* Second Series, Vol. XX (1940), *passim.*

[36] For an account of the impact of the Revolution on William and Mary see Bell, *The Church, the State, and Education in Virginia,* pp. 171–88.

[37] Bracken *v.* the Visitors of William and Mary, 1 *Call* 495–514 (1790).

ultimate concentration of power in the hands of the lay board and the subordination of the faculties. At William and Mary, unlike Harvard, the faculty body had after 1729 the character if not the strength of a group of resident masters in the English tradition, a unique situation explained in part by the ample resources that made possible six teachers of professorial stature and in part by their strong outside support. At Harvard the primary teaching officers, the tutors, played a much smaller role; and there the president became the only effective spokesman for the faculty. William and Mary illustrates more clearly the transition from the medieval university ruled by a clerisy to the modern American college ruled by laymen; while Harvard, more distinctively Protestant and distinctly American from the outset, had neither the hierarchical-gild model of control nor the resources and faculty to emulate the English colleges. Despite their support in England, however, the scholars at William and Mary, like the Virginia clerics generally, failed to command enough respect and assent in the local community to maintain their control of the college. Therefore, neither Harvard nor William and Mary, with their transitional forms and their dual boards of control, provided the characteristic models for American college government. For the most part, early American colleges, like modern American universities, were governed by unitary lay boards of control formally endowed with absolute and unqualified powers of decision. In the establishment of this pattern the most powerful models and centers of influence were the third and fourth colleges to be chartered, Yale and Princeton, and it is the government of these schools in the eighteenth century that we must now examine to see how the American mold was formed.

Yale was a creation of Harvard men. Its ten original trustees were clergymen, nine of whom had the benefits of a college education at Harvard. Its first five presiding officers were Harvard graduates. But while Harvard was enmeshed in administrative entanglements and ambiguities for more than seventy years after its founding, the legal distribution of authority in early Yale was simple: its first charter, granted by the legislature in October, 1701, gave to its trustees the authority to "erect, form, direct, order, establish, improve, and at all times in all suitable ways for the future to encourage" [38] the "collegiate school" which later was named for Elihu Yale. Their powers embraced

[38] For the text of the first charter of 1701, as enacted by the General Court of Connecticut, see Dexter, *Documentary History*, pp. 20–23.

the choice of their successors (who were to be Connecticut ministers over the age of forty), the choice of the rectors and teachers of the school, the payment of these and other employees, and the management of all properties and finances. In law, and for a long time to come in fact, their powers of government were absolute.

The chief problem confronting the Connecticut clerics who founded Yale was to safeguard the legal future of their college. It was on this account that they were troubled by the events at Harvard during the previous fifteen years. When the charter of the Massachusetts colony itself was vacated in 1684, the charter that had been granted to Harvard College by the Massachusetts legislature automatically became a legal nullity. Thus despite the several attempts that had been made in the meantime to secure a charter for Harvard, the older institution was still, at the time of Yale's founding, in law (although not, of course, in fact) a dead institution. While Connecticut, unlike Massachusetts, had not had its charter annulled when it was brought into the Dominion of New England, it had before it the ominous example of the Bay Colony. At that very moment there was a bill before Parliament to annul the charters of the New England colonies. Thus the Connecticut clerics faced a dilemma: to get a charter from the legislature was to risk the total dissolution of the college, as the charter might readily be voided by the Crown if the college received unfavorable attention; but to seek a royal charter was to run the risk, as the Massachusetts men had learned, of inviting royal and episcopal interference. Yale's founders decided to solve this problem as best they could by getting a charter from the colonial legislature and by masquerading their college under the most trivial guise, hoping that English indifference to or ignorance of colonial affairs would leave it unmolested.[39] Hence they called it not a "college" but by the more modest title "collegiate school"; hence they called its head not the president, as at Harvard, but the "rector"; hence they ambiguously authorized its trustees to issue "degrees or licenses," whatever that might mean. They had every intention of founding a college of the same grade and merit as Harvard, but for the time at least had no desire to proclaim it as such.

It has often been said that Yale was started because its founders

[39] The clearest statement of this problem is that of William L. Kingsley in William L. Kingsley, ed., *Yale College: A Sketch of its History* (New York, 1879), I, 21–24.

were primarily concerned with having a center of orthodoxy that would serve Congregationalism more faithfully than did the backsliding college in Cambridge.[40] While there can hardly be any doubt that Yale's founders meant to establish a sound orthodox institution, it is unlikely that the emergent latitudinarianism of Harvard frightened them excessively or that it provided the primary impulse for a Connecticut college. The desire for a college less expensive, nearer to home, and more satisfying to local pride had been expressed in Connecticut more than fifty years earlier and seems never to have disappeared.[41] Perhaps the most significant departure from Harvard's practice that was made at the beginning was the dropping of the dual form of government urged upon the Connecticut men by their Massachusetts correspondents and advisers. One can only hazard the guess that the planners of Yale found no merit in the periodic tug-of-war that they knew had gone on at Harvard between the Overseers and the Corporation, and that they intended to keep as tight-reined a control as possible over their own school. Whatever their reason, their decision marks a momentous break in the origins of American academic government, the dividing line between the dual system of the first two charters and the single board that was to be the almost universal pattern ever afterwards. That they did not admit non-clerics to the Yale Corporation (in this they spurned another recommendation from Massachusetts) may have been the consequence of their interest in upholding the legal proposition that they had already founded an institution when they applied to the General Court of Con-

[40] An interpretation expressed by Quincy, *History of Harvard University*, I, 197–200, and elaborately refuted by Prof. James L. Kingsley of Yale in *American Biblical Repository*, Series 2, Vol. VI (July, 1841), pp. 177–95; Vol. VI (October, 1841), pp. 384–404; and Vol. VII (January, 1842), pp. 175–207.

[41] The traditional conservatism of Yale may have originally made the older view plausible, and it is true that Moses Noyes, a brother of one of the first trustees and himself a trustee for many years, observed in 1723 that the initiators of Yale had given as their reason that Harvard was "under the Tutorage of Latitudinarians." Dexter, *Documentary History*, p. 242; cf. Simeon E. Baldwin, "The Ecclesiastical Constitution of Yale College," *Papers of the New Haven Historical Society*, III (New Haven, 1882), 406–8. But Connecticut was at the time far less troubled than Massachusetts by latitudinarian tendencies. Also it seems significant that the recommendation of some of the Massachusetts conservatives that the diligent study of the Westminster Confession and Ames' *Medulla* should be prescribed for all scholars was quietly ignored at Yale. Dexter, *Documentary History*, pp. 8–9, 15–19. See also Dexter, "The Founding of Yale College," *Papers of the New Haven Colony Historical Society*, III (New Haven, 1882), 1–3, and "Yale College in Saybrook," *ibid.*, VII (New Haven, 1908), 129–30.

necticut for a charter. To admit new members to the board of trustees might be to reopen the question.[42] It has also been suggested that laymen were excluded "because there were really so few active educated men then in Connecticut outside of the clergy, so few laymen who would endure labor and sacrifice for the ideal of higher education." [43]

So far as the powers of the president were concerned, Yale's experience was quite similar to Harvard's, and this is the more striking when we realize that the original group of trustees, who well knew what difficulties had been created for Harvard by the dominating person of Increase Mather, intended to keep the rector a subordinate figure. Their first set of rules allowed tenure on good behavior to the rector and other officers. During the early days of the fledgling collegiate school, when a permanent site had not yet been agreed upon, its first two rectors were trustees who combined ministerial duties with supervising the tutors and teaching. In 1718 the school was at last settled at New Haven and given the name of Yale College. It was not very long after the secure establishment of the school that its rector loomed very large in its affairs. The first rector not chosen from the original group of trustees was the Reverend Timothy Cutler, who as we shall see had to leave because of his conversion to episcopacy. The second, the Reverend Elisha Williams, whose rectorship began in 1726, was admitted to the board of trustees, and after some years began to preside at meetings of the Corporation.

The larger, the more complex, the more prosperous the college grew, the more did the prestige and power of its presiding officer grow. The emergence of the rector as the dynamic force in the college merely had to wait upon the appearance of a tactful or forceful man who enjoyed the confidence of the trustees.[44] Williams was succeeded in 1739 by the Reverend Thomas Clap, an able and domineering man, who quickly enlarged the position of the rector by assuming as a right the leadership of the Corporation that had been delegated as a privilege to Williams. Clap's influence led to the new charter of 1745, which transformed the Corporation, now styled the President and Fellows, into a body in which the president became in law what Clap had made him in fact, the dy-

[42] Dexter, "The Founding of Yale College," p. 23; see also the considerations urged by J. L. Kingsley in *American Biblical Repository,* VI, 186.

[43] Dexter, "The Founding of Yale College," p. 16.

[44] An extremely illuminating study of the growth of the rector's and then the president's powers is Dexter's "An Historical Study of the Powers and Duties of the Presidency in Yale College," *Proceedings of the American Antiquarian Society,* New Series, Vol. XII (October, 1896), pp. 27–42.

namic center and the head of the governing body.[45] Clap's arbitrary conduct later became unpopular and led to a movement among some of the gentry of Connecticut to subject the college to a committee of visitation from the legislature. Clap was able to forestall this by an ingenious defense of the autonomy of the college,[46] but finally in 1792, long after his day, an arrangement was concluded under President Ezra Stiles that settled the antagonism and for a time ended the separation of the college and the state. The governor, the lieutenant-governor, and six senior assistants in the council were admitted into the Corporation in return for material benefits to the college, including funds for a new dormitory and future professorships. For eighty years Yale was governed by a Corporation of such a mixed composition of private and public fellows; state officers were at last replaced by six Yale alumni, elected by their peers.[47]

Princeton, Yale's offspring, reproduced Yale's basic pattern by vesting all powers of government in its trustees, but its organization was in several respects a new departure in American academic history. It was the first college chartered after the impact of the Great Awakening and the enlarged toleration of eighteenth-century life had been felt. It was the first non-Anglican college to get a royal charter, the first case in which the Crown unambiguously recognized the existence of a distinctive American system of lay government for colleges; it was the first to be chartered in a province that had no established church, and the first to have a strong intercolonial influence that raised it from the beginning above the level of a local agency.

In one respect Princeton was an outgrowth of the expansion of New

[45] For the text of the charter of 1745, under which, with its amendments, Yale is still governed, see Elliott and Chambers, *Charters and Basic Laws,* pp. 588–93. The laws drawn up by Clap for the college in 1745 anticipated the later emergence of faculty participation in Yale's government insofar as they required the president to consult with the tutors "in all cases of difficulty and importance." However, "the participation of the Tutors in Faculty deliberations was far more a matter of form than of reality" in Clap's time. Dexter, "An Historical Study," pp. 36–37. For later faculty participation see George W. Pierson, *Yale College: An Educational History, 1871–1921* (New Haven, 1952), Chaps. VII and VIII, esp. pp. 133–35.

[46] Thomas Clap, *The Annals or History of Yale-College* (New Haven, 1766) esp. pp. 69–76. See Dexter, "The Founding of Yale College," pp. 10 ff. and 22–23, and "Thomas Clap and His Writings," *Papers of the New Haven Colony Historical Society,* V (New Haven, 1894), 247–74. For a contemporary critique of Clap's position from a legal standpoint see [Samuel Whittlesey Dana] *Yale-College Subject to the General Assembly* (New Haven, 1784).

[47] The negotiations of 1792 are accounted for in F. B. Dexter, ed., *The Literary Diary of Ezra Stiles,* III (New York, 1901), 452–58, 460–69; for later changes see Elliott and Chambers, *Charters and Basic Laws,* p. 589n.

England. For years before its founding the Puritans had begun to leave Massachusetts and Connecticut, spreading out across Long Island, down into New York, and on into New Jersey. In the middle colonies the Yankees rubbed elbows with the older stocks and the new immigrants, with the Dutch, Scots, Germans, and Scotch-Irish of these provinces; and Congregationalists found themselves confronted for the first time with a complex religious environment in which they encountered Presbyterians, Quakers, Baptists, Lutherans, Mennonites, and members of the Dutch Reformed Church.[48] In this new environment Congregationalism itself tended to change, chiefly toward acceptance of the Presbyterian form of church organization; for the loose form of organization that prevailed in New England had been fostered by the religious homogeneity of the early days, by the system of town organization, and by the advantageous position of the established church. While even Connecticut Congregationalists had shown some tendencies toward closer organization, those who went farther south found it all but an imperative necessity. The township system and the privileged position in the state legislatures that gave Congregationalists the cohesion they had had in New England were lacking in New York, New Jersey, and Pennsylvania, while the presence there of several other religious bodies seemed to make cohesion more necessary than ever. Thus New England Calvinism, with the expansion of New England, tended to become Presbyterian in government, and it was more in the Presbyterian than the Congregational form that it propagated itself throughout the country. In adopting Presbyterianism, the New Englanders found themselves in the same synods and presbyteries with the Scots and Scotch-Irish, to whom this form of organization was long familiar. Princeton was in a measure the joint product of the traditional New England educational enthusiasm and the political and organizational strength of Presbyterianism.

It was the product, too, of a religious schism brought by the Great Awakening. The Presbyterians were divided into two factions by a difference in attitude toward the new religious "enthusiasm," the integrity of the minister's domain, and the education of the ministry. The Old-Side faction disapproved of the religious excitements of the Awakening. Their staid traditional clergy were troubled by the revivalist practices of itinerant ministers who frequently confronted them with competing agents of

---

[48] Thomas J. Wertenbaker, *The Founding of American Civilization: The Middle Colonies* (New York, 1938), Chaps. IV and V.

salvation who not only invaded their territories but often attacked the settled clerics themselves as cold and unregenerate. There was, moreover, the issue of education: the Old Side, insisting upon regular training at colleges and universities, were opposed to licensing ministers who fell short of the traditional standards.[49] Those New-Side men who had Congregational backgrounds were particularly sensitive to the charge that their faction was rearing a substandard ministry. It was a group of such men in New York and New Jersey, determined to set adequate educational standards and discouraged by the hostility of Yale under President Clap to the Awakening, who made the first movement to found Princeton. (Six of the seven trustees named in the original Princeton charter were Yale men, while one was from Harvard.)

In 1746, despite the opposition of the Anglican clergymen of the middle colonies, Governor John Hamilton granted a charter to a small group of New York and New Jersey ministers and laymen to found the College of New Jersey (the name was not legally changed until 1896). In this first charter three prominent New York laymen of unimpeachable New-Side Presbyterian affiliations and four New Jersey clergymen were named trustees with power to co-opt other trustees to the number of twelve. The trustees were given the full powers of management, including the hiring and firing of the president and all faculty members. Two years later, after the institution had already been feebly launched, the new royal governor, Jonathan Belcher, persuaded the trustees to accept a second charter. Belcher was a good Calvinist, but he feared that the college might be attacked by the other religious denominations if it did not have a closer affiliation with the province. With some difficulty, he was able to persuade the trustees to accept an enlargement of the board from twelve to twenty-three; this step added the governor and four members of his council, together with three prominent Pennsylvania laymen, and preserved the clerical majority by adding eight ministers. It was also required that the trustees (not the faculty or the students) take an oath of loyalty to the Hanoverian succession, which could be adopted by anyone but recusant Catholics.

In other vital respects the text of the charter was the same as that of two years before. Retained but slightly reworded was the provision of the 1746 charter that the trustees could not exclude

---

[49] John Maclean, *History of the College of New Jersey* (Philadelphia, 1877), I, 24–60.

any Person of any religious Denomination whatsoever from free and Equa^l Liberty and Advantage of Education, or from any of the Liberties, Priviledge: or immunities of the Said College on account of his or their speculative Sentiments in Religion and of his or their being of a Religious professior Different from the said Trustees of the College.[50]

This clause, the first such statement of tolerant principles in an American college charter, reflected at once the necessity of placating the Anglicans and Quakers and the difficulties of a dissenting church that was securing a charter from an Anglican monarch. But the fact of primary significance is that with Princeton we have the first instance of a college founded under the characteristic conditions of the America of the eighteenth, rather than the seventeenth, century: religious and ethnic heterogeneity, schismatic differences brought by the Awakening, and growing mutual accommodation and tolerance. Harvard, William and Mary, and Yale, being colleges chartered for established churches, had had an intimate relation in each case with the state, receiving substantial amounts of financial assistance and becoming subject, especially in the case of the two New England schools, to a great deal of intervention by the state legislatures.[51] Of necessity Princeton carried on without state aid and was substantially free of state control.[52]

The appearance in Princeton's charter of a clause opening the college to students who were not of the trustees' religious persuasion should not, however, be taken as mitigating the sectarian commitment of the institution. Even after the breach within the Presbyterian church had been outwardly healed, the New-Side faction kept its hands upon the reins. The Old-Side leaders proposed in 1766 that in return for the election of a president chosen by them and the appointment of a genuine faculty of professors they would guarantee substantial donations.[53] This proposal

[50] The text of both charters can be found in Wertenbaker, *Princeton,* pp. 396–404. The text of the first charter, which was lost for over a century and a half and hence unknown to Princeton historians before Wertenbaker, is not conveniently available elsewhere. For later constitutional changes see Elliott and Chambers, *Charters and Basic Laws,* pp. 431–33. The non-denominational clause was thought to be required to conform to the 1664 charter of the province. See Charles W. Shields, "The Origin of Princeton University," *Memorial Book of the Sesquicentennial Celebration of the Founding of the College of New Jersey* (New York, 1898) pp. 455–60, on the role of Governor Belcher in working for the liberality of the college.

[51] William Wallace Smith, "The Relations of College and State in Colonial America," unpublished doctoral dissertation (Teachers College, Columbia University, 1949), Chaps. II–IV.

[52] Maclean, *History of the College of New Jersey,* I, 67–68.

[53] Varnum L. Collins, *Princeton* (New York, 1914), pp. 67–68.

the trustees rejected, fearing synodical control; instead they chose as their new president the distinguished Scottish theologian, Dr. John Witherspoon. This proved a strategic choice, for the new president was a man of such caliber as to enable the college to put its stamp upon the church instead of being merely controlled by it.[54] Witherspoon, who promptly Americanized himself, became a figure of much ecclesiastical and political influence (he was a delegate to the Continental Congress from New Jersey for most of the period from 1776 to 1782), and proved to be acceptable to both Presbyterian factions.[55]

With the development of Princeton we have the characteristic pattern for American private college government: control through a unitary board of nonresident, nonacademic persons; [56] the presence on the board of clergymen either in equal numbers to laymen or in predominant strength; a denominational affiliation of some kind, but hospitality to matriculants of other sects; the centrality, in the institution's governance and development, of the strong president; the essential independence, despite the occasional presence of state officials on boards of control, from either control or support by the state. The later colonial colleges might vary this formula to a greater or lesser degree. But after the Revolution, and during the first decades of the nineteenth century, as the American college system emerged from the eastern states and spread through the South and West in the wake of settlement, it was the pattern begun by Yale and set by Princeton which was most emulated. In the early national period the work of founding and managing colleges remained primarily in the hands of the churches, and two main

[54] See *ibid.*, pp. 62–93 for the best discussion of factors bearing on college control in this period.

[55] Varnum L. Collins, *President Witherspoon: A Biography* (Princeton, 1925), is an important study. Such was the confidence of the trustees in Witherspoon that in 1770 they resolved to turn over to him "the sole direction as to the Methods of Education to be pursued in this Seminary" (*ibid.*, I, 134–35).

[56] Among the colonial charters one, that of Brown, reverted to the dual board of control. It seems uncertain whether the model in this case was the bicameral legislature of the state or the Harvard system, which Brown's closely resembled. Brown's board consisted of a group of trustees, who resembled Harvard's Overseers, and a body of fellows, resembling the Harvard Corporation. The president was an ex-officio member of the Fellows. Basic policy decisions were made by the joint concurrence of the two boards, as in a bicameral legislature, although the awarding of degrees and the "Instruction and immediate Government of the College" were vested in the president and fellows; so also was the drafting of college statutes, subject to the approval of the trustees. Aside from the president, no faculty members were fellows. Walter C. Bronson, *A History of Brown University, 1764–1914* (Providence, R.I., 1914), pp. 500–507. Bowdoin, among the later New England colleges, also adopted a dual board, in this case a clear imitation of Harvard's.

streams of influence can be discerned, one emanating from Yale and
spreading into the Northwest and the other emanating from Princeton
and spreading into the South and the Southwest.[57] The diffusion of the
influence of Yale and Princeton might be illustrated in several ways
Perhaps none is more dramatic than the prominence of their graduates
among college presidents. Among 110 presidents of 75 colleges in operation before 1840, 36 were graduates of Yale and 22 of Princeton—the
two institutions together providing more than half the total.[58]

SUPPORT AND CONTROL

The earliest colleges had been founded at a time when private resources
were much too feeble to maintain them, and support by the state was a
necessity. The close of the colonial period saw the ideal of the private
college well established. The intimate relations between the first colonial
colleges and the states have caused one student of the subject to declare
that the first three colleges were in effect under state control, and to imply a vague analogy with the state universities of a later age.[59] But since
all three institutions were founded under the aegis of established churches,
this statement can easily be misleading. It is hardly more valid than the
assertion that the colleges were controlled by the churches. It is perhaps
less startling but more correct to say that the colleges were governed
by the church-state complex. In Massachusetts the magistrates usually
consulted and often deferred to the ministers. Anne Hutchinson, for instance, was condemned and excommunicated by a church synod, but she
was tried and banished by civil authorities. Similarly, the clergy took the
initiative in the prosecution of the Quakers, but the legislation controlling

[57] George P. Schmidt, *The Old Time College President* (New York, 1930),
pp. 25–28; Wertenbaker, *Princeton*, pp. 113–17. Donald R. Come has written an
illuminating account of the diffusion of Princeton's example, "The Influence of
Princeton on Higher Education in the South before 1825," *William and Mary
Quarterly*, Third Series, Vol. II (October, 1945), pp. 359–96.

[58] Schmidt, *The Old Time College President*, p. 96. The others were recruited
as follows: Union 13, Brown 12, Dickinson 10, Dartmouth 9, Harvard 8, and a
scattering accounting for the remainder. Dickinson itself, however, was profoundly
influenced by Princeton, as Dartmouth was by Yale.

[59] Smith, "Relations of College and State in Colonial America," pp. 1–4, and
passim. The author confounds his own thesis with respect to Massachusetts when
he points out that the suffrage act of 1631 guaranteed "that the affairs of the civil
government would remain largely under the control of the Church" (*ibid.*, p. 9).
It is confusing when a college is "controlled" by a state that in turn is "controlled"
by the church.

them was enacted by the General Court and enforced by the magistrates.[60] In similar fashion the General Court often interfered in the affairs of Harvard—and not merely through the Overseers, on which board it was represented, but also directly through legislative action. It was the General Court, not the Overseers, that took action against President Dunster and received his resignation, and that called upon Increase Mather either to reside in Cambridge or vacate the presidency. In Connecticut the Assembly, although not represented on the governing board of Yale, showed its interest by ordering the trustees to finish a building at New Haven, intervening in the choice of a rector and the permanent location of the school, examining finances on many occasions, and looking into the religious condition of the college. Dependent as they were upon state aid, the two New England colleges were in no position to resist such interference even if they so chose. William and Mary, in a stronger position because of its larger fixed income, was subjected to less detailed intervention; but the personnel of the board of Visitors there was closely interlocked with the membership of the Governor's Council and the House of Burgesses. The college's situation at Williamsburg, the capital of the province, was a token of its intimate relation with the state, as well as a great academic advantage.[61]

In the last thirty years before the outbreak of the Revolution both state aid and state interference diminished as the burden of support shifted from government to private individuals. The first three colleges had relied chiefly upon governmental support in the form of annual grants or assigned revenues from a particular source. But the later schools, largely because of sectarian hostilities and inhibitions, could not safely call upon the state governments, and thus benefited from state aid only in a marginal and incidental way. King's College got some public help, the College of Philadelphia less, and Dartmouth only two very small grants, while Princeton, Brown, and Queen's College received nothing.[62]

The founding and continuation of the later colleges were made possible by the development of a widespread interest in higher education among

---

[60] Greene, *Religion and the State,* pp. 42–46.

[61] For state action bearing on the colleges see Smith, "Relations of College and State in Colonial America," Chaps. I–III.

[62] Smith summarizes state aid to the colonial colleges, *ibid.,* pp. 33–38, 58–64, 77–80, 89–114, 142–43; cf. the table compiled by Clews, *Educational Legislation and Administration . . . ,* p. 501, which represents schematically and approximately the grants and appropriations of the colonial governments to colleges and schools.

the well-to-do, an interest intense enough to bring contributions from thousands of individuals in the colonies, the British Isles, and other parts of the Empire. Important bequests were still quite rare; most of the funds were raised through subscriptions, some through the riskier and less popular means of private lotteries.[63] The pressing need for private funds gave prestige to trustees like Gilbert Tennent of New Jersey and Morgan Edwards of Brown and administrators like William Smith of the College of Philadelphia and John Witherspoon of New Jersey, all of whom were outstandingly successful as fund raisers. It also underlined, however, the importance of the churches, through which a great deal of the solicitation was carried on, especially in the British Isles. British contributors were often impatient of American sectarian disputes, and the necessity of raising funds from them added some leverage to the movement toward tolerance in the colleges.[64] Colonial assemblies seem not to have been disposed to intervene officiously in the management of educational institutions that they were not supporting, and the later colonial colleges manifest a decided shift toward private control along with private support. Harvard and Yale, with their traditional involvements with the states, became disentangled more slowly, receiving their last grants in 1823 and 1831 respectively.[65] They were legally relieved of their liability to substantial state intervention after 1819 by the implications of the Dartmouth College case.

Direct legislation was not, of course, the only measure of state interest in the colleges. With the exception of Yale, Brown, and the College of Philadelphia, the colonial colleges had ex-officio representatives of the state officialdom, including the governors, on their boards of control, a relationship which arose out of the necessity either of securing a state charter or a royal or proprietary charter with some governor's benevolent intervention. Where political matters, factional feuds, church differences, or the interests of the state or Crown were involved, trustees representing

[63] For the sources of college support in the period 1745–75 see Beverly McAnear's valuable account, "The Raising of Funds by the Colonial Colleges," *Mississippi Valley Historical Review,* XXXVIII (March, 1952), 591–612. McAnear estimates that over £20,000 was raised in the colonies by private subscriptions and about £12,000 through lotteries. Bequests accounted for £7,402, public grants for £2,776. More than £21,000 was netted from British sources, whose aid was widely considered indispensable to the success of a colonial college. Suggestive but frequently inaccurate on the support of the colleges is Jesse B. Sears, *Philanthropy in the History of American Higher Education* (Washington, 1922).

[64] See, for example, Maclean, *History of the College of New Jersey,* I, 234.

[65] Smith, "Relations of College and State in Colonial America," pp. 137–38.

he political order were thus on hand to express themselves. On the Harard Overseers and the governing board of Dartmouth the state officials omprised about half the membership.[66] At Philadelphia after 1779 and Yale after 1792 state officials were added, leaving only Brown, an ineritor of Rhode Island's church-state separatism, without such a relationhip.[67]

The respective places of laymen and clerics on boards of control also deserve notice. By the terms of the charters (and these arrangements ended to perpetuate themselves for long periods), four of the colonial olleges—Harvard, Princeton, Brown, and Dartmouth—had governing boards on which clerical and lay trustees were quite evenly balanced. Three—William and Mary, King's College, and Queen's College—were mixed but clearly dominated by the laymen, while one, the College of Philadelphia, consisted entirely of laymen.[68] Yale's board, until its reconstitution in 1792, was the only one composed entirely of clergymen.[69]

A mere enumeration of the number of clerical and nonclerical trustees, however, perhaps underestimates the religious character of the colleges.

[66] At William and Mary only the Governor was an ex-officio representative of the state on the Visitors, but the overlapping of the province's governing groups provided others informally. At Princeton the governor was the sole state member. Twelve political officials were ex-officio members of the King's College board, including the first Lord Commissioner for Trade and Plantations, ten state officers, and the Mayor of New York City. Four out of forty-one trustees at Queen's College were in this category. Six of Dartmouth's twelve trustees were state officials (five from New Hampshire, one from Connecticut), but were not designated as ex-officio members.

[67] The revision of the College of Philadelphia's constitution in 1779 made six state officers ex-officio members of a board of nineteen, but the other members named were almost all state officers also. Another revision in 1791 maintained similar state representation. Yale, of course, added eight state officials to its board of eleven members in 1792.

[68] The statement concerning the College of Philadelphia needs some qualification. One of the original trustees, Richard Peters, had taken orders in the Church of England and had come to America as a clergyman. Differences between himself and his rector caused the suspension of his license by the Bishop of London. Although he remained a figure of some influence in the church in Pennsylvania, he had been living the life of a layman for twelve years before becoming a trustee of the academy out of which the college grew. Thomas H. Montgomery, *A History of the University of Pennsylvania from Its Foundation to* A.D. *1770* (Philadelphia, 1900), pp. 92–95.

[69] William and Mary had four clerics out of eighteen trustees; Queen's, thirteen out of twenty-eight (and a charter provision specified that ministers must not be over one third of the Board); King's College, seven clerics (including the Archbishop of Canterbury and the president of the college) out of forty-four. Brown may be said to have had a balanced board by virtue of the fact that ministers had a clear preponderance among the fellows, laymen among the trustees.

Ministers tended to be more assiduous in their attendance at meetings. The presidents who, as we have seen, provided so much of the dynamic leadership, were clergymen. And laymen themselves were very commonly chosen with their denominational affiliations clearly in mind, and often with reference to their position as pillars of their church communities. Perhaps most important of all, the college itself seems to have been thought of very largely in the light of its religious relationships, and the role of a college trustee had more of the pastoral character than it came to have in later times. Trustees, while governing the business affairs of the colleges, thought of themselves also as the moral and spiritual guardians of the students, and indeed often of the faculties; and pious laymen, leaving their businesses to attend board meetings, seem to have shorn themselves, to a degree, of their usual roles to assume the moral and intellectual garb of pastors-for-the-moment, inquiring closely into the regularity and character of religious services at the college and examining the spiritual nature and moral discipline of the undergraduates.

Thus even though the colleges were committed to the governance of laymen, these laymen found in the role and demeanor of the clerics a subtly influential archetype for their own behavior; the religious inheritance of the colleges created a kind of priesthood of the trustees. This was a process that could also work in the opposite direction, for the responsibilities of fund raising and administration tended to make men of affairs and business managers out of the clerics who became college presidents.[70] The management of colleges was indeed one of the many areas of life in which the unspecialized society of the eighteenth-century colonies created its versatile men.

One may find difficulties in disentangling the roles of church and state in college sponsorship, but one thing seems clear: aristocratic control and aristocratic values were universal. Colonial America may have been a more democratic society and may have offered more opportunities for class mobility than the contemporary societies of Europe. But as compared with the open and fluid society of the first half of the nineteenth century, or with the image of "frontier democracy" that is all too often freely pictured in general books on American history, the society of the American colonies was one dominated by an aristocracy of land and commerce, an aristocracy difficult of access to rising members of the middle class and all but closed to those who started very poor. To be

[70] This was notably true at Princeton and Brown.

sure, opportunities to earn an independent livelihood, to be free from poverty and gross insecurity, were exceptionally good for those who started in life with little but a willingness to work; but this was a far cry from opportunity to enter the ranks of the rich and powerful. A privileged class, strengthened by ties of intermarriage, existed in each province and at length spread across colonial boundaries; it seems to have grown stronger and become more sharply defined in the eighteenth century than in the seventeenth. "There was, in fact," writes a distinguished student of the colonial period, "in almost every colony a definite ruling class [which] dominated the local political machinery, filled all or nearly all the important local offices, . . . spoke on public matters in behalf of all . . . [and] used its power very largely for the benefit of its own members. . . ." [71] Attached to this ruling class were the outstanding professional men of the colonies, and on its periphery were the most acceptable leaders of a class of solid citizens of the sort represented by Benjamin Franklin.[72] It was to serve the traditional and aristocratic needs of this upper crust that the colonial colleges, with their conservative adherence to the classical curriculum, were designed, while the middle classes beneath them, whose base was small shopkeeping and special crafts, were generally satisfied to send their children to good private academies with curricula based less upon the classics and more upon a program of practical studies.[73]

It was the aristocracy that was primarily concerned with the colonial colleges, the well-to-do class that gave the bulk of private support, and the ruling group that provided the trustees.[74] When a governing board sat down to consider the affairs of the colonial college, there was usually assembled at the same table a group of men who were accustomed to seeing each other frequently at the counting houses, in each others' homes, and in the vestries of the churches, and whose family relationships could

[71] Leonard W. Labaree, *Conservatism in Early American History* (New York, 1948), p. 2. Chap. I of this volume has a brilliant account of the ruling families of what Labaree calls the conciliar aristocracies of the colonies. See also James Truslow Adams, *Provincial Society, 1690–1763* (New York, 1927), Chap. III, and Henry Graff's forthcoming study of the backgrounds of the signers of the Declaration of Independence.

[72] Carl and Jessica Bridenbaugh, *Rebels and Gentlemen* (New York, 1942), Chap. I.

[73] *Ibid.*, Chap. II; cf. Clifford K. Shipton, "Secondary Education in the Puritan Colonies," *New England Quarterly*, VII (December, 1934), 658–61.

[74] Cf. the comments of Cheyney, *History of the University of Pennsylvania*, pp. 30, 104, 111, 123, 131, 148; Demarest, *History of Rutgers College*, pp. 61–64; Guild, *Early History of Brown*, pp. 54–58.

be represented only by a complicated network of crisscrossing lines.[75] Even in Connecticut, which a man like Samuel Johnson considered hardly better than a mobocracy,[76] and which was in fact less clearly aristocratic than many other colonies, the bonds of kinship were conspicuous, and the clerical founders of Yale were quite elaborately interrelated.[77]

[75] A study of the members of the first Board of Trustees of the College of Philadelphia provides us with a microcosm of the economic and social world of the colonial elite. There were twenty-four trustees, of whom three quarters were Anglicans. At least fourteen were wealthy from investments in trade or land or a combination of the two, and many had inherited such wealth. Four were lawyers, four physicians, one an ex-clergyman turned to public service and the Indian trade, and one, Benjamin Franklin, was a scientist, inventor, author, and diplomat, as well as a man of business. No fewer than twenty-one held public offices at one time or another; most of them held multiple offices during their lives, including many of the highest positions in the provincial government and the municipal government of Philadelphia. Fourteen of the trustees were closely related to other trustees, either directly or through their siblings or children. Their interwoven connections become doubly complicated when family relationships are carried down a few generations and when they are compounded with business partnerships. One trustee, for instance, Thomas Lawrence, was associated in the shipping business first with another trustee, James Logan, and then with the elder brother of a second fellow-trustee. One of Lawrence's sons married the daughter of a trustee, while his daughter married a trustee's son. Samuel McCall, Jr., was a brother-in-law of two trustees, while two of his daughters married trustees (one of whom was the son of a trustee). The zenith of this kind of interrelationship is represented in the life of Charles Willing, the son of a Bristol merchant who came to Philadelphia in 1728 after his elder brother had already established a mercantile business there. In 1731 Willing married the sister of Dr. William Shippen, Sr., another of the original trustees. Of their four daughters, two married trustees, one married the son of a trustee, and the fourth married Col. William Byrd of Westover. They also had a son, Thomas, who became Chief Justice of the Supreme Court and joined the Board of Trustees in 1760. Thomas married the daughter of a trustee, and had a son who became a trustee in 1800 and a daughter who married a trustee. It is interesting that while many of the original trustees had good educations, only one held a college degree and that exposure to any portion of the undergraduate curriculum of the time was rare among them. No doubt this heightened their sense of the community's need for a college. In later years the kinship network left its mark upon the college staff. The daughter of trustee William Allen married into the famous DeLancey family of New York, and her grandson was William Heathcote DeLancey, Provost of the University of Pennsylvania, 1828–33. Dr. William Shippen's son, William Shippen, Jr., took his M.D. at Edinburgh and became the first professor of anatomy and surgery at the new medical school of the college. Trustee Philip Syng's grandson was Professor of Surgery, then Anatomy, at the University, 1805–31. Trustee Thomas Hopkinson's daughter married Dr. John Morgan, who was the first medical professor at the college. Data on the trustees was compiled by Mr. F. W. Smith, chiefly from sketches given in Montgomery, *History of the University of Pennsylvania,* pp. 53–108.

[76] Labaree, *Conservatism in Early American History,* p. 66.

[77] "The youngest trustee was Joseph Webb," remarks Dexter. "The fact he and Mr. Chauncy married sisters reminds us that the bonds of family connection between these early trustees were remarkably numerous. The same relationship existed

In sum, each of the early colleges was under the governance of men representing a fairly homogeneous social class and sharing a common conception of education. Although colonial politics was often the field of sharp partisan dispute, the social homogeneity of the immediate sponsors of the colleges, together with the absence from the curricula of topical economic or political subjects, kept the colleges relatively free from urgent controversy of this sort. The chief problems to appear within them— and they were by no means negligible—were those arising out of religious and intellectual differences within the governing group. On the whole the colonial elite need not have been ashamed of its educational achievement, for the colonial colleges, with all their weaknesses, made remarkable gains during the eighteenth century, not only in the direction of higher standards but of greater liberality. The sponsorship of an enlightened aristocracy has often been identified with such gains in American higher education.

---

between Mather and Andrew; Pierpont was the nephew of Pierson by one marriage, and the stepson of Buckingham by another; Noyes and Woodbridge were cousins; the children of Pierson and Woodbridge intermarried. . . ." "The Founding of Yale College," p. 31.

IV: RELIGION, REASON, AND REVOLUTION

SECTARIANISM AND RESTRAINT

IN THE DEVELOPMENT of the American colleges, freedom of thought as a consciously formulated goal appeared first as religious freedom for students. Long before anyone spoke of freedom for teachers, the existence of religious freedom or toleration for undergraduates was commonly boasted as an outstanding asset of the eighteenth-century colleges. Princeton, summing up its own virtues for the public in 1764, was only repeating claims that had grown common among the other colleges when it asserted that its students were encouraged to exercise the right of private judgment and that the faculty did not dictate to them with "an air of infallibility." [1] Such a claim was a general point of pride among the colleges throughout the latter part of the century; and a college that openly violated this governing principle, as Yale did under President Clap, was bound to suffer for the breach. [2]

The tendency of the colleges to take pride in the toleration they accorded undergraduates, although observable at Harvard even in the late seventeenth century, was quickened after 1746 by competition among the colleges for students. In the financing of the colleges student fees were of crucial importance, and around the middle of the century an active competition for students emerged among the colleges from Phila-

---

[1] *An Account of the College of New Jersey* (Woodbridge, N.J., 1764), p. 28. Again in 1802, in the course of an appeal for funds, Princeton's sponsors looked back with pride to the fact that in the more than fifty years of its existence "we never, indeed, have been so attached to the dogmas of any religious sect as to impose them on our pupils. . . . No pupil with us has ever been questioned on the subject of his political creed, nor withheld from a full and free avowal of his sentiments, nor received any censure or disapprobation for making known his opinions either in speech or writing." John Maclean, *History of the College of New Jersey* (Philadelphia, 1877), II, 37–38.

[2] Even Thomas Clap paid lip service to it. See his claims in *The Annals or History of Yale-College* (New Haven, 1766), pp. 83–84.

delphia to Cambridge. While sectarian considerations did play some role in the choice of colleges by students and parents, low fees and sheer proximity seem to have been more decisive factors. Most college administrations, feeling that a single sect was unlikely to furnish enough students for the prosperity of their institution, chose in their public statements to advertise their nonsectarian character and to supplement this quietly by a more sectarian form of recruitment carried on by denominational pastors among the bright boys of their congregations.[3] The plea of sectarian loyalty, which might offend potential donors as well as potential students, was a risky one to use as a public argument. Once committed by their public announcements to nonsectarian conduct, however, the schools were mortgaged to it as an ideal.[4]

Educational theorists were much concerned that young men should have an education conducive to piety and good morals, to personal development, and to the wellbeing of society as a whole. But the needs and rights of faculty members were not commonly discussed in similar terms; teachers were assumed to be instruments rather than ends in themselves. It was expected of them that they be persons suitable for the development of the undergraduates in their tutelage and care—that is, they had to have some minimum of competence as teachers and they had to display piety and good morals because they were the exemplars of the young.[5] Beyond this, little was said of them. Even a man so sensitive to the necessary conditions of work for craftsmen in all spheres and so liberal in his ideas as Benjamin Franklin could write a little tract on the type of academy education best suited to the youth of Pennsylvania which included no more than a single perfunctory sentence on the men

[3] An excellent analysis of the problem is Beverly McAnear's "The Selection of an Alma Mater by Pre-Revolutionary Students," *Pennsylvania Magazine of History and Biography*, LXXIII (October, 1949), 429–40, esp. p. 435.

[4] Avoiding discrimination against students of sects other than the one that chiefly sponsored a college was not, however, quite identical with failure to proselytize among them. For instance, the Anglican atmosphere of the College of Philadelphia and the alluring inducements of Anglican orders seem to have swayed some of the Presbyterian youth, even though the faculty itself was largely Presbyterian. See Leonard J. Trinterud, *The Forming of an American Tradition* (Philadelphia, 1949), pp. 215–16.

[5] William Smith, in his *A General Idea of the College of Mirania* (New York, 1753), remarked (pp. 28–39) that all the masters must be of irreproachable character because the youth will emulate them. "The Masters . . . are truly affable, indefatigable and patient. . . . *Learning* in them, tho' universal, is but a secondary Qualification. Their amiable temper, mild Behavior, Forebearance and Placability, have long since struck Envy and Calumny dumb" (pp. 65–66). Good men and true, but rather subdued!

who were to teach them: "That the Rector be a man of good Understanding, good Morals, diligent and patient; learn'd in the Languages
and Sciences, and a correct pure Speaker and Writer of the *English*
Tongue: to have such Tutors under him as shall be necessary." [6]

One of the earliest signs of recognition of the liberties of faculty members dates from 1772, when President John Witherspoon of Princeton,
appealing to Englishmen in the West Indies for support, made a point
of what he claimed was the atmosphere of liberty at that college. He
made the conventional observations about the absence of religious discrimination, remarking that many students had completed the entire
course without his ever becoming aware of their denominational preference.[7] But something of a landmark in educational discussion was his
additional reference to the independence of the teachers:

There is no fear of being obliged to choose Teachers upon Ministerial [i.e.,
governmental] recommendation, or in compliance with the over-bearing weight
of family interest. On the contrary the Trustees are naturally led, and in a
manner forced to found their choice upon the characters of the persons and
the hope of public approbation.

Thus, he assured his potential benefactors, those concerned in the government and instruction of the college were free from temptation "to a
fawning cringing spirit and mean servility in the hope of Court favor or
promotion." [8] Although a seminary of learning should not enter deeply
into political contention, it should have an internal spirit of liberty,
which is "infinitely preferable to the dead and vapid state of one whose
very existence depends upon the nod of those in power."

The fact that Princeton did not derive its support all from one source,
but was compelled to appeal to many interests, Witherspoon considered
a distinct asset, since it conduced to freedom and tolerance: "Having
no particular prop to lean to on one side, we are obliged to stand upright
and firm by leaning equally on all." [9] The teachers in the college, too,
being of varying religious principles, had had to adjust to each other.[10]
Possibly this statement did not mean as much as it might have seemed on
the surface—"court favor" had not been much of a problem in American
education, and Witherspoon did not care to specify how widely the teach-

---

[6] Benjamin Franklin, *Proposals Relating to the Education of Youth in Pensilvania*
(Philadelphia, 1749), p. 9.

[7] John Witherspoon, *Address to the Inhabitants of Jamaica and Other West-Indian
Islands* (Philadelphia, 1772), pp. 25–26.

[8] *Ibid.*, p. 20.   [9] *Ibid.*, pp. 20–21.   [10] *Ibid.*, p. 25.

ers in the college actually differed in religion—but so far as it went, it represented a distinct advance over past expressions of college policy; at least a measure of freedom for college teachers was posited as an educational advantage of some importance.

During the greater part of the century, however, close religious conformity by teachers was commonly demanded as the norm. Such conformity was secured by what has always been the primary instrument of control, *restraint by recruitment:* that is to say, in the making of appointments an effort was commonly made to be sure at the beginning that the incoming president, professor, or tutor was one who accepted the requisite theological doctrines. That this method was quite self-consciously adopted at a very early stage can be seen in the case of President Chauncy, who was required to agree to keep quiet about his little doctrinal deviations before he was installed at Harvard in 1654. Again, when Edward Wigglesworth was appointed to the first professorship of divinity at Harvard, the Overseers forced the Corporation to test his orthodoxy.[11] Similarly, in 1756 the installation of Yale's first divinity professor, Naphtali Daggett, was attended by such an examination.[12] Yale not only indulged in such a practice but had also formalized its requirements in the laws drawn up by President Thomas Clap in 1745 by exacting of all incoming officers a public statement of assent to the Westminster Confession and the ecclesiastical discipline of the Connecticut Congregational churches as laid down in the Saybrook Platform of 1708.[13] Professors and tutors were subjected to some detailed examina-

[11] Shipton, *Sibley's Harvard Graduates,* V, 549; Josiah Quincy, *The History of Harvard University* (Cambridge, Mass., 1840), I, 253–56.

[12] The Corporation seems to have spent the better part of a day at this task. F. B. Dexter, *Biographical Sketches of the Graduates of Yale College,* 6 vols. (New York, 1885–1912), II, 154, 400. Daggett was examined "as to his principles of religion, his knowledge and skill in divinity, cases of conscience . . . and various other qualifications. . . . On the next day he preached in the College Hall, and then gave his assent to the Westminster Catechism and Confession of Faith, and to the Saybrook Platform; declared his belief that the Apostle's Creed, the Nicene Creed, and the Athanasian Creed agree with the Word of God; assented to the ninth of the Thirty-nine Articles of the Church of England, being that which relates to original sin; and ended by presenting an extended confession of his faith from his own pen, in which he renounced all the errors and heresies which commonly go under the name of Arianism, Socinianism, Arminianism, Pelagianism, Antinomianism, and Enthusiasm." William L. Kingsley, ed., *Yale College: A Sketch of Its History* (New York, 1879), I, 83–84.

[13] *Ibid.,* II, 16. While Clap put this test into the college laws, he did not introduce the practice, which was instituted by the Corporation after the startling apostasy of Rector Cutler in 1722. His own installation as rector in 1739 included giving proof of his orthodoxy, although he was himself probably much closer to orthodox

tion of the state of their faith even as late as the presidency of Ezra Stiles, which began during the Revolution.[14] The practice of careful recruitment and prior examination did not stop at Harvard with the elder Wigglesworth, as is shown by the discussions concerning the orthodoxy of President Holyoke before his installation in 1737 and the fact that the younger Wigglesworth, seated in the Hollis Chair of Divinity in 1765, went through an examination somewhat similar to that suffered by his father forty-three years earlier.[15] John Winthrop, the second occupant of the Hollis Professorship of Mathematics and Natural Philosophy, was treated more indulgently: the Board of Overseers twice voted down a proposal to examine him on his religious principles before ratifying his nomination. They examined him only on his competence in mathematics.[16] Princeton, like Harvard and Yale, made appointments with religious persuasion in mind. Its New-Side trustees firmly refused in 1766–67 to appoint the distinguished Francis Alison as president, even at the cost of much-needed financial support from the Philadelphia Old Side.[17] It is hard to say, however, whether or not this rejection was more attributable to dogmatic considerations than to factional stubbornness; for instead of Alison the trustees took John Witherspoon, who did not share their preference for the "New Divinity" of the Edwards-Bellamy-Hopkins school.[18]

The candid examinations of prospective appointees suggest that the consideration of doctrinal acceptability was all but universal; and where a president, professor, or tutor was installed without prior examination, the omission is more plausibly explained by the presumption that his principles were already well known than by the assumption that the boards of governors were liberal or indifferent to such matters. In interdenominational colleges more latitude existed for variety of belief, but no one seems to have contested the principle that a college officer's beliefs could properly be scanned before his appointment.

It might be inferred from the prevalence of restraint by recruitment that where clashes did take place between governing boards and college

---

Calvinism than the members of the Corporation that elected him. Shipton, *Sibley's Harvard Graduates,* VII, 31.

[14] Ezra Stiles, *Literary Diary* (New York, 1901), III, 18.

[15] Quincy, *History of Harvard,* II, 5–11, 131–32.   [16] *Ibid.,* II, 26–27.

[17] Thomas J. Wertenbaker, *Princeton, 1746–1896* (Princeton, 1946), pp. 48–51; Trinterud, *Forming of an American Tradition,* Chap. XII.

[18] Trinterud, *Forming of an American Tradition,* pp. 223–25.

officers over matters of belief, it would be because the officers underwent a change of mind during their tenures and announced for new principles that could not have been predicted at the time of their appointment. Such was in fact the case. It will be remembered that Henry Dunster's espousal of Antipedobaptism came suddenly and as a surprise to the Overseers after he had served Harvard for many years. A second such case occurred at Harvard in 1735, when Louis Langloiserie, who had been granted permission by the president and tutors to teach French to such students as desired it, was excluded from instruction at the college. A French Canadian immigrant who had embraced Protestantism, Langloiserie had been offering French instruction for almost two years when word got about that he held unsound doctrines. The Overseers authorized an investigation which showed that the instructor had recently been affected by some of the same tendencies toward "enthusiasm" that were associated with the Awakening, and that he had been proselytizing among some of the resident graduates. The Overseers resolved that the faculty had no authority to permit students to take French lessons from Langloiserie and that they must break off the relation immediately. They further resolved that they, the Overseers, had a right

to Examine into the principles of all those that are Employed in the instruction of the Students of the College upon any Just Suspicion of their holding dangerous tenents altho no Express Charge be Layed in against them. . . . and that no person chosen into such an office shal be accepted or Continued who refuseth when desired to give Satisfaction to this board as to their principles in religion.[19]

This resolution the faculty did not contest.

But undoubtedly the most celebrated case of an unexpected conversion was that of Rector Timothy Cutler at Yale in 1722, which shook the entire colony of Connecticut. Three years earlier Cutler, at thirty-five, had been called from his ministry at Stratford to become rector of the college, which at last had seemed to leave behind its infant struggles and had begun to experience a period of growth and prosperity. However, Yale had recently acquired the famous collection of books secured for it by Jeremiah Dummer, including those of the leading Anglican writers. Whatever

---

[19] The best account of the case is that of Albert B. Mathews, "Teaching of French at Harvard College before 1750," *Publications of the Colonial Society of Massachusetts,* XVII (1914), 216–32. Cf. the brief account in Edward Wigglesworth, *A Letter to the Reverend Mr. George Whitefield* (Boston, 1745), pp. 6–8, and Quincy, *History of Harvard,* I, 394–95, 574–76.

the real cause of the interest in episcopacy at Yale, these books seem to have quickened it, and it was not long before rumors were circulating that, as Cotton Mather put it, "Arminian books are cried up in Yale College for eloquence and learning, and Calvinists despised for the contrary." At the Yale commencement of 1722, when these suspicions had already been spread abroad, Cutler confirmed them in the most dramatic way by ending his prayer with the Episcopal form: "And let all the people say, Amen." The next day, Cutler, two of the tutors, and four ministers, including Samuel Johnson of West Haven, who was to become the first president of King's College, appeared in the college library to discuss with the Corporation their doubts of the validity of Presbyterian ordination. Once again, as in the Dunster case, what was at issue was not the right of the rector and tutors to hold simultaneously their offices and their unacceptable tenets, but simply who was right about the substantive theological issues.[20] Eventually Cutler, Johnson, and two others decided to leave Congregationalism and took Episcopal orders. The Corporation accepted the resignation of tutor Browne and "excused" Cutler from further service. They also provided that henceforth formal confessions of faith and examinations were to be demanded of future rectors and tutors. A tradition of candid watchfulness was begun at Yale.[21]

At Harvard the supervision of the religious and theological life of the college by the Overseers continued to be fairly severe through President Holyoke's regime, and for a time in 1747 there was even some talk in Massachusetts of an oath bill to impose Calvinism on Harvard.[22] Holyoke had not been president two years when the Overseers, who still represented far more accurately than the Corporation the conservative religious sentiments of the colony, intervened at a commencement by altering

[20] Also comparable with the Dunster case was the absence of abiding rancor. Cutler was by nature a difficult man; but Johnson, far from holding a grievance against his alma mater, maintained a friendly interest in it; and Episcopal ministers continued to attend there. W. L. Kingsley, *Yale College*, p. 54.

[21] F. B. Dexter, *Documentary History of Yale University*, pp. 231–34; *Yale Biographies and Annals*, I, 260, 270–73. For Samuel Johnson's account of the affair, Herbert and Carol Schneider, *Samuel Johnson . . . His Career and Writings*, (New York, 1929), I, 6–16. Shipton in his sketch of Cutler points to indisputable evidence that the rector had been guilty of duplicity in his dealings with the Yale Corporation, inasmuch as he had been planning to announce his conversion to episcopacy under circumstances which would cause the greatest consternation in Congregational ranks. "I now declare publicly," Cutler wrote to Thomas Hollis, "what I before believed privately." Shipton, *Sibley's Harvard Graduates*, V, 51–52.

[22] Samuel Eliot Morison, *Three Centuries of Harvard* (Cambridge, Mass., 1936), p. 87.

the form of the *quaestiones,* the Masters' disputations, forcing the Masters to put into an affirmative form of statement three theses raising questions concerning the trinity and other Christian doctrines.[23] Almost twenty years later a New-Light minister, who had been excluded from a place among the Overseers, stalked out of a commencement because he was outraged to hear the Masters arguing: Whether knowledge of even contingent singulars is appropriate to God. Unable to restrain his indignation, he wrote two anonymous letters to President Holyoke protesting against allowing the Masters to sport with the idea of God's omnipotence. Being at length forced to reveal his identity, he was answered gently by Holyoke, who pointed out that very challenging *quaestiones* (for instance, Intermediate knowledge is not premised of God) had been debated even in the days of Chauncy, Oakes, and Mather.[24]

While the greater part of the history of the colleges in the eighteenth century is one of progressive liberalization, at least in academic theory and curricular content if not in formal academic practices, there was one period in which this advance was checked in New England by the first developments connected with the Great Awakening: the decade falling approximately between 1740 and 1750. Ultimately the cause of toleration, and with it opportunities for liberalism in the colleges, was advanced by the schismatic tendencies of the Awakening in New England, but only after a period in which the first impact of the New-Light enthusiasms had brought a wave of sectarian and factional antagonisms and some efforts at repression. In all this the colleges were intimately involved. Not only were Harvard and Yale under the control of the Old-Light factions in their respective colonies, and thus knit into the fabric of the established order, but they were the centers for the supply of orthodox ministers; and one of the crucial issues of the Awakening—perhaps the most important practi-

---

[23] Quincy, *History of Harvard,* II, 23–25. The objectionable theses were: Whether the trinity of persons in the deity is revealed in the Old Testament, Whether creation from eternity involves a contradiction, and Whether to explain mysteries serves the cause of religion.

[24] Although the cleric insisted that he had no intention of harming the college or striking a blow at learning (the critics of freedom in the colleges never *meant* to harm them), this did not stop him from publishing his criticisms in a pamphlet, along with Holyoke's tactful, but to him unsatisfactory, answer. It is noteworthy that Holyoke took personal responsibility for the particular *quaestiones* introduced, and pointed out that they were in line with those debated in foreign Protestant universities. See A[ndrew] Croswell, *Testimony against the Prophaneness of Some of the Publick Disputes on the Last Commencement-Day* (Boston, 1760), esp. pp. 4–9. On Croswell's extremely contumacious career, see Shipton, *Sibley's Harvard Graduates,* VIII, 386–407.

cal issue—was the question of criteria for the ministry. In a colony like New Jersey, where there was neither an established church nor an established college, it was relatively simple for those attracted by the revivals to found their own schools and rear satisfactory ministers; but in Massachusetts and Connecticut, where the governance of the church order by the legislatures made possible the official repression or harassment of the New Lights, factional disputes took on an especial bitterness. So long as the Old Lights dominated it was difficult to found new churches of New-Light persuasion and impossible to found competing colleges. As pillars of the established order, the colleges naturally fell under criticism.

Since the New Lights represented a stern breed of Calvinism and the Old Lights were affected, if not by liberalism, at least by the decadence of the ancient principles, the modern student may be tempted to see in the battle between them some signs of a struggle between liberalism and reaction. It seems unlikely, however, that tolerance was in the beginning very thoroughly understood by either side; and if attempts to criticize or bully the colleges came chiefly from the ranks of the New Lights, one suspects that this was, while perhaps in part a product of their anti-intellectualism, still more attributable to the fact that, so far as control of the colleges was concerned, the New Lights were the Outs while the Old Lights were the Ins. Had the shoe been on the other foot, similar criticism of the colleges would probably have come from the opposite direction. But the more enlightened college authorities could hardly help but learn one lesson: there were grave disadvantages for serious educational work in too intimate a sectarian connection.

The first effect on the colleges of the factional antagonisms in the churches was to bring them under a wave of criticism for religious laxity and unorthodoxy. And this criticism came not merely from the more ignorant and ranting itinerant preachers of the revivals. No less a man than Jonathan Edwards in his *Some Thoughts concerning the Present Revival of Religion in New England* (1742) attacked the colleges in narrow terms as divinity schools gone sour. "The original and main design" of the colleges, he felt, was

to train up persons and fit them for the work of the ministry. And I would say in general, that it appears to me care should be taken, some way or other, that these societies should be so regulated, that they should, in fact, be nurseries of piety. Otherwise they are fundamentally ruined and undone as to their main design and most essential end. They ought to be so constituted that vice and idleness have no living there. . . . It seems to me a reproach to the land, that ever it should be so with our colleges, that, instead of being places of the greatest advantages for true piety, one cannot send a child thither without great danger of his being infected as to his morals. It is perfectly intolerable; and any thing should be done, rather than it should be so. . . . They should be . . . fountains of piety and holiness. There is a great deal of pains taken to teach the scholars human learning; there ought to be as much and more care thoroughly to educate them in religion, and lead them to true and eminent holiness. . . . And I cannot see why it is not on all accounts fit and convenient for the governors and instructors of the colleges particularly, singly, and frequently, to converse with the students about the state of their souls. . . .[25]

Such were the respects paid to the colleges by one of the most distinguished minds of the age. Presumably these strictures would have been less severe if the New Lights themselves had not been struggling to advance their persuasions under considerable pressure. We may wonder what Edwards' later tenure of the presidency of Princeton would have been like had it not been cut short after two months by his death.

More offensive than Edwards' criticisms were those made by George Whitefield a few years later. In 1744–45 Whitefield spent more than a year in New England during which he was drawn into furious controversy with the local orthodox ministers and the faculties of the colleges. His belief that the light of the New England colleges had now become "darkness that may be felt" and his charge that their spirit was ungodly received such wide currency that the faculties of both Harvard and Yale felt obliged to answer. The Harvard faculty issued a "testimony" in which they met Whitefield's charges with countercharges: he was an enthusiast, and hence an unreliable spiritual guide; he was "uncharitable, censorious, and slanderous"; he had accused the college of irreligion without giving evidence; he had cited the opinions of certain "godly ministers," but the ministers he was best acquainted with were those of Boston—who were themselves, as Overseers, a part of the government of the college. The faculty implied that Whitefield had drummed up his charges, and that in this as in many other respects he was a deluder of the people.[26] Whitefield replied with a hypocritical pamphlet full of half-disavowals and half-

[25] Jonathan Edwards, *Works* (New York, 1830), IV, 264–65.
[26] *The Testimony of the President, Professors and Hebrew Instructor of Harvard College . . . against the Reverend Mr. George Whitefield* (Boston, 1744), pp. 4, 8, 9–11.

regrets, ending with the statement that he still believed his assertions to be essentially true. Bad books were being read at Harvard College, and the failure of the tutors to pray with and examine the hearts of their students was, if nothing more, a sign of the general religious laxity of the times.[27]

This brought from Edward Wigglesworth a lengthy and formidable reply in which the entire state of the college was reviewed and Whitefield's charges laboriously and effectually refuted. Wigglesworth cited the Langloiserie case as evidence of the harmfulness of revivalist enthusiasm within a college. Pointing to Langloiserie's dismissal and the firing for his drunken habits of Isaac Greenwood, first Hollis Professor of Mathematics and Natural Philosophy, as illustrations of doctrinal and moral purity, Wigglesworth suggested that a college which was so unsparing with its own officers would hardly be indifferent to the morals of the children under its care. As to the latitudinarian theologians whose works were allegedly read there, the library records showed that Tillotson had not been borrowed once during the nine years from 1732 to 1741, nor Clarke for the past two years. The graduate divinity students read the orthodox Puritan divines far more than they did either Tillotson or Clarke. Finally, if it had been Whitefield's intention, as he said, merely to contribute to the religious reformation of Harvard, why had he not communicated his thoughts privately to its president or officers? Did he give a public airing to his views because he wished to discourage students from coming or potential donors from giving? [28]

The Yale faculty, then consisting of President Clap and three tutors, followed with a little counterblast of its own which in essence duplicated the Harvard countercharges and denials. This document was colored, in addition, by one of Clap's obsessional notions, namely that Whitefield had come to New England intending in the end to turn all its ministers out of their pulpits and "to introduce a Sett of Ministers into our Churches, by other Ways and Means of Education." Naturally one of the most effective ways of destroying the existing ministry of New England was "to vilify and subvert" its colleges, which would be a prelude to bringing in clergymen educated elsewhere. Certainly anyone who believed that the

[27] George Whitefield, *A Letter to the Reverend the President, and Professors . . . in Answer to a Testimony Published by Them* (Boston, 1745).

[28] Wigglesworth, *A Letter to the Reverend Mr. George Whitefield,* esp. pp. 6–8, 26–34. Whitefield seems indeed to have harbored no permanent grudge against Harvard. Almost thirty years afterward, when the Harvard Library was burned, he helped obtain books for a new library.

colleges were as bad as Whitefield charged would hardly believe them capable of supplying adequate ministers.[29]

These exchanges offer the novel spectacle of college faculties acting in a body to defend the reputation of their schools. It can hardly be said, however, that they were defending the existence of heterodoxy in the colleges; they were simply denying the truth of the charges and countering with charges of their own. Wigglesworth's satisfaction at Langloiserie's dismissal as evidence of Harvard's caution shows how far from the Harvard faculty's thoughts was the suggestion that a deviating teacher ought to be defended. The only matter of academic conduct on which there was a difference of opinion was whether tutors should indeed privately pray with and examine into the hearts of their students. Wigglesworth asserted that the tutors prayed with the students in church and that that was enough; it was the duty of every man to examine his own heart. Finally, it must be understood that the faculties were in this case simply acting in concert with a large part of the orthodox ministry in New England that had been outraged by some of Whitefield's preachings and accusations.[30] There was no flavor of independence in their acts of self-defense, merely a zeal to join the war of the factions that had been excited by the Great Awakening in New England.

SECTARIANISM AT YALE

The severest repressions growing out of the Great Awakening occurred in Connecticut. Yale under the regime of Thomas Clap as rector and president (1740–66) provides us with a case study in illiberalism, for there all the animus of sectarian passion was unleashed and there the restrictive measures that were being taken informally, partially, and sometimes rather apologetically at other colleges were made a formal part of the college laws and were openly defended. There an attempt was made to reduce one of the major colonial colleges to the status of a severely sectarian agency, foreshadowing many of the small church-dominated colleges that were to spring up in such profusion throughout the country in the early nineteenth century. The ultimate defeat of Clap's

[29] *The Declaration of the Rector and Tutors of Yale-College in New-Haven against the Reverend Mr. George Whitefield* (Boston, 1745), esp. pp. 8–12.

[30] For an account of the larger pamphlet war of which these college pamphlets were but a part, see Luke Tyerman, *The Life of the Rev. George Whitefield* (London, 1877), II, 123–42.

effort sheds light on the conditions that tended to broaden the horizons of higher education in the eighteenth century; for while Clap was certainly not the last tyrannical college president nor the last bigot, he was the last man in an eighteenth-century college to be powerful enough to go to such lengths.

Why did it happen at Yale, and why at that time? If the explanation which immediately comes to mind is correct—that Yale more or less accidentally came under the leadership of an exceptionally powerful and exceptionally bigoted sectary—then the incidents of Clap's regime have no more explanatory value than any other historical accident. It is undeniable that some of the acerbities of the situation are traceable to Clap's personal peculiarities, for he was more than ordinarily despotic and stubborn, and he had a streak of meanness.[31] It may also be allowed that the choice of this particular minister for Yale's rectorship in 1739 was an historical accident, in the sense that Clap's religious views were not a direct reflection of those of the Corporation that chose him: the Corporation consisted of vaguely liberal Old-Light men, while he was a vigilant and orthodox Calvinist.[32] It must be allowed, too, that the choice of such a man was perhaps a slight anachronism, because Yale had prospered for thirteen years under Elisha Williams, his predecessor, a man of more liberal and compromising spirit than Clap would have thought desirable. A member of a prominent Connecticut Valley family and a graduate of Leverett's Harvard, Williams was akin to Leverett in his versatility; he had studied law before turning to the ministry, and was actively interested in business and public affairs. His resignation from the college rectorship was widely attributed to his aspirations for the governorship. In 1744, while his successor was zealously harassing the young "enthusiasts" in Yale College and attempting to withhold a degree from a senior who had taken up a subscription to reprint one of Locke's letters on toleration,[33] Williams, as a sympathizer of the New Lights, wrote an extremely able pamphlet on religious liberty in which he argued from a Lockean

---

[31] See the sketch by Shipton in *Sibley's Harvard Graduates,* VII, esp. 48–49.

[32] That the Yale Corporation was dominated by moderates as early as 1723 is suggested by the fact that in that year they offered the rectorship to Edward Wigglesworth, who declined, evidently because of growing deafness. Dexter, *Yale Biographies and Annals,* I, 290, 312; Shipton, *Sibley's Harvard Graduates,* V, 550.

[33] The senior, however, forced Clap and the Corporation to award the degree by threatening to carry the matter to the king in council. Nothing was more frightening to college authorities. Benjamin Trumbull, *A Complete History of Connecticut* (New Haven, 1818), II, 183n.

standpoint the case for separation of church and state and denied the right of the civil magistrate to "make any penal Laws in Matters of Religion." [34]

But if Clap's point of view—or perhaps more accurately, his consecutive points of view—had not been rooted in the soil of Connecticut religion, it is doubtful that he would have held on as long as he did. Moreover, it seems a fact of striking significance that Yale under Clap was going through a process very similar to what Harvard had experienced under Mather, and the two situations have more in common than the presence of two forceful and rather doctrinaire old men. Harvard and Yale were both founded as colleges of sectaries and both had the problems incident to evolving into colleges of gentlemen. Both were Congregational, and both were founded under established churches. Both were founded under conditions of sectarian monopoly and each went through a period of strife when its religious environment became more pluralistic. One might be tempted to say that the troubles of Yale were due to consecutive attempts to make a college a partisan agency of a single religious faction. But Princeton was as much dominated by a single faction of Presbyterians as Yale was by a single faction of Congregationalists; and yet Princeton, founded as it was in the midst of greater religious diversity and without the benefits or disadvantages of an established church, was never plagued by the problems that beset Yale under Clap. (Indeed, competition from Princeton, where, as we have seen, quite a promotional asset was made of liberality toward the religion of students, was probably one reason for the later relaxation at Yale, since that liberality appealed to some of the same religious constituency in the same region.)

The essential reason for the acuteness of the situation at Yale was the existence of a religious establishment challenged by the sudden development of religious diversity in the Awakening. The presence of an establishment created the legal conditions of suppression, and the college became one of the agencies through which the two larger factions sought to make life difficult for each other and for the smaller dissenting groups. Yale was, in short, experiencing some of the same growing pains that Harvard had undergone earlier, but Connecticut, being more rural and less

---

[34] [Elisha Williams] *The Essential Rights and Liberties of Protestants: A Seasonable Plea for the Liberty of Conscience* (Boston, 1744), p. 1. On the authorship of this work see Shipton, *Sibley's Harvard Graduates*, V, 593; on Williams, see Shipton's sketch, *ibid.*, pp. 588–98, and Francis Parsons, "Elisha Williams," *New Haven Historical Society Papers*, VII (1908), 188–217.

commercial than Massachusetts, was slower to develop a critical aristocracy. Hence the change took place there at a later date and was attended
by sharper conflict.

In 1708 a representative group of Connecticut ministers had met at
Saybrook and adopted a confession of faith and a system of ecclesiastical
discipline under which the colony had enjoyed religious peace until the
period of the Awakening. There were in the province only small handfuls
of dissenters from the regime established in the Saybrook Platform, and
these dissenters—a few Baptists, Quakers, Episcopalians, and Rogerenes
—were granted liberty to worship in their own way while contributing to
the support of the established church; but the peace of the province
may be laid more to its fundamental homogeneity than to the breadth of
its tolerance.[35] The most formidable of these dissenting groups at the time
of the Awakening was the Episcopal, which, although practically non-
existent at the time of Rector Cutler's horrendous apostasy, had been
gaining in numbers and organizing new congregations for the past fifteen
years.

The Awakening alarmed the supporters of the standing order far more
deeply than had the rise of any of the pre-existing dissenting denominations, because it cut into the Congregational churches themselves. Although less infected with liberalism than the churches of Massachusetts,
many Connecticut congregations had shown signs of the same relaxation
that had been complained of so loudly in the sister colony since 1680.
Accordingly, when the Awakening came, even many of the essentially
conservative churchmen of Old-Light persuasion, despite their distaste
for extreme manifestations of "enthusiasm," could not resist seeing some
good in the great outpourings of the spirit of God that seemed to be
accompanying the revivals. Nor were the "liberal Calvinists" particularly alarmed at the tendencies toward stricter Calvinism that marked the
theological emphasis of the revivals. Two things, however, at length set
the greater part of the Old-Light men firmly against the revivals: one was
the tendency toward an extravagant amount of uninvited itinerant preaching by the revivalists (who were often far more exciting to local parish-
ioners than the sometimes dull clerics whose domains they were invad-
ing); the other was the tendency of the revivalists openly to discredit the
standing ministry, to insist that many of its members, being unregenerate,

[35] See M. Louise Greene, *The Development of Religious Liberty in Connecticut,*
Chaps. VI and VII. The Rogerenes were a tiny sect that had split off from the
Sabbatarians or Seventh-Day Baptists of Rhode Island.

were unworthy of their offices, and to charge them with various heresies, chiefly Arminianism. Thus while Whitefield had at first been greeted with cordiality by a large portion of the established ministry, his own censoriousness and the even less restrained preaching of men like Gilbert Tennent and James Davenport, soon created a multitude of enemies. It was one thing to welcome a visitor who might bring a new infusion of religious zeal to a complacent congregation; it was another to countenance itinerants who declared, in the words of Gilbert Tennent, that the regular ministers were "hirelings, caterpillars, letter-learned Pharisees, Hypocrites, Varlets, Seed of the Serpent, foolish Builders whom the Devil drives into the ministry, dead dogs that cannot bark, blind men, dead men, men possessed of the devil, rebels, and enemies of God." [36]

The ministers, who felt that they must fight back, were supported by many eminent Old-Light laymen who might have taken tolerant views of broad differences in theology had it not been for their belief that civil order could not be maintained without a large measure of religious conformity. Such men were alarmed not only because the established church was split into two factions, but because a body of Separatist Congregationalists had emerged. The church seemed to be threatened by disintegration; and this probably explains why the Consociated Congregationalists were for a time spurred to greater intolerance for deviant members of their own religious tradition than they were for Quakers or Episcopalians. In May, 1742, the Connecticut Assembly passed a series of restrictive laws: even regularly ordained ministers were not to preach in parishes other than their own except on invitation of the settled minister, at the risk of forfeiting the support of all the colony laws made for the benefit of the ministry; no church association was to license any minister to preach outside its precincts; bonds of a hundred pounds were levied to guarantee against a second offense of unauthorized itineracy; and strangers from outside the colony found guilty of this offense were liable to expulsion as vagrants.[37] The toleration enjoyed by some dissenters since 1708 was repealed by the Assembly in 1743.

A time of troubles came to the religious life of the colony: there were excommunications and arrests; church members were imprisoned for

[36] *Ibid.*, pp. 237–38.
[37] Benjamin Trumbull, *Complete History of Connecticut,* II, 162–65. Under this law Samuel Finley, later to become president of Princeton, was arrested on his way to preach to a Separatist congregation in New Haven without legal standing, and expelled as a vagrant.

attending Separatist meetings or refusing to be taxed for the support of the establishment; officials who held New-Light beliefs were removed from public offices; ministers were rebuked and expelled from their churches; others had their salaries withheld. Baptist and Anglican churches gained recruits from the ranks of those who were disgusted by the factionalism and bitterness of the Congregationalists. Connecticut won a reputation for persecutions.[38]

At best this was a sorry milieu for a college, and it was Yale's misfortune to be under the leadership of an able but contentious man hardly capable of picking his way through the tangled briars of sectarianism. In formal theology Clap was actually closer to the troublesome New Lights than to the dominant Old Lights who controlled the Assembly and the college; but in his position on ecclesiastical politics and discipline he was for some years after his induction a pillar of the standing order. Unfortunately for Yale he conceived of the college primarily as a theological agency; and once this assumption was granted, the full involvement of the institution in factional struggles became inevitable, for the college was thus committed to enforcing the point of view of one or another of the participants instead of standing open as a school available to all. Clap's first move was an attempt to clamp down on New-Light tendencies in the college.

In this enterprise Clap had the support of the trustees, who, alarmed by the signs of interest in the revival within the college, resolved at the commencement of 1741 that any student who called a college officer or trustee "carnal" or "unconverted" should be required to make a public confession, and for a second such offense should be expelled. Later that year, young David Brainerd, who was destined to become one of the saints of New England Protestantism and to be immortalized in a modest way by Jonathan Edwards, made the mistake of saying of one of the tutors who had just been praying with the students, "He has no more grace than the chair I am leaning upon." It was characteristic of the atmosphere that had already been created by these controversies that a freshman who overheard Brainerd took the story to one of the women of the town, who reported it in turn to Rector Clap. And it was charac-

[38] Mary Hewitt Mitchell, *The Great Awakening and Other Revivals in the Religious Life of Connecticut* (New Haven, 1934), pp. 12–19. The fullest account is that of Benjamin Trumbull, *Complete History of Connecticut*, Vol. II, Chap. VIII. Cf. Maurice W. Armstrong, "Religious Enthusiasm and Separatism in Colonial New England," *Harvard Theological Review*, XXXVIII (April, 1945), 111–40.

teristic of Clap to call those who were reported to have been with Brainerd at the time and compel them to inform on their friend. When Brainerd refused to make a humiliating public confession in the college hall for a remark made in private conversation, he was expelled; and not even the intercession of such godly ministers as Aaron Burr, Jonathan Dickinson, and Jonathan Edwards, coupled with an apology from Brainerd, would cause Clap to relent and readmit him.[39]

In 1744 a new measure was taken against the New Lights: the trustees ruled that no one over twenty-one could be admitted as a freshman without special permission, an ordinance that was intended to bar some of the New Lights, many of whose most assertive adherents were over twenty-one at their entrance.[40] In the same year two students, John and Ebenezer Cleaveland, were reproached for attending Separatist church services with their parents while at home on vacation. Upon refusing to make the required confession in the college hall, they too were expelled.[41] The case aroused so much criticism that Clap and the tutors issued a pamphlet stating their side of the case. They pointed out that the Cleavelands had absorbed corrupt principles and dangerous errors, including that of antinomianism, from the "lay exhorters" whose services they had attended, and asserted "it would be a Contradiction in the Civil Government to Support a College to Educate Students to trample upon their own laws." [42] The logic of this was hardly answerable, given the repressive laws and the assumption that the college was to be as vigilant as possible an agent of the Old-Light faction. During the same year a member of the Corporation, being asked to account for his New-Light leanings, resigned rather than undergo an examination by his fellow trustees.[43]

It was at this point that Clap, taking advantage of the good favor he had with the Old Lights, secured the permanent charter of 1745; and the newly styled President now drew up a set of severe college laws which "smelled more of the Test Act and the English Cambridge than the laxity and theological vagueness of the new Cambridge in which he had stud-

[39] Jonathan Edwards, "Memoirs of the Rev. David Brainerd," in *Works* (New York, 1829), X, 50–51.

[40] Dexter, *Yale Biographies and Annals,* I, 754.

[41] *Ibid.,* p. 771; cf. Dexter, *Documentary History of Yale University,* pp. 368–72.

[42] *The Judgment of the Rector and Tutors of Yale-College concerning Two of the Students who were Expelled* (New London, 1745), esp. pp. 1–3, 10. Many years later, when the power of the New Lights had grown considerably, both Cleavelands were awarded their degrees. Dexter, *Yale Biographies and Annals,* II, 29 ff., 149 ff.

[43] Leonard Bacon, "The Corporation," in W. L. Kingsley, ed., *Yale College,* I, 177–78.

ied." [44] For some years there was quiet in the college. But by the middle 1750s, the continued growth of the New Lights put them in a position of approximate parity with the Old Lights in the Assembly; Clap, in the meantime, having fallen out with Joseph Noyes, the stubborn Old-Light pastor of the New Haven First Church, shifted his position until he was classified in the parlance of the time as a "political New Light." Thus the second half of his administration was spent in a feud with the Old Lights. Clap's first moves were to withdraw the students of the college from Noyes' church and to ask for the establishment of a professorship of divinity so that the college would have its own preacher. First, however, the Corporation resolved that every future officer of the college, including members of the Corporation itself, must declare for the Westminster Confession, and went on to prescribe quite elaborately just what it was proper to believe at Yale in matters theological. It was clearly stated that these principles were to govern Yale in perpetuity, and it was explicitly provided that a member of the Corporation could be examined if any other fellow suspected him of deviation from the prescribed articles. Of the professor of divinity a particularly elaborate confession of faith was demanded, in which he was to "renounce all such errors as shall in any considerable measure prevail at the time of his introduction." [45]

Clap's divinity professor, Naphtali Daggett, was examined and installed in March, 1756, and the college church was organized the following year. The next step in the campaign, an attempt on Clap's part to use against Joseph Noyes the new resolve of the Corporation concerning examination of its own fellows, miscarried badly. The Corporation tamely resolved in favor of the examination, but Noyes refused either to be examined or to resign from his position, and the proposal was too unpopular to be pushed any further in the face of such a determined stand.[46] By holding his ground, and thus setting bounds to heresy-hunting within the Corporation, Noyes undoubtedly did the college a great service,

[44] Shipton in *Sibley's Harvard Graduates,* VII, 33; the laws are reprinted in Dexter, *Yale Biographies and Annals,* II, 2 ff.

[45] The text of these resolutions, adopted in 1753, is given by Trumbull, *Complete History of Connecticut,* II, 316–19. Significant of the dogmatic confidence of the fellows was their promise to use Yale to maintain these tenets forever: "That we will always take all proper and reasonable measures, such as christian prudence shall direct, to continue and propagate the doctrines contained in these summaries of religion, in this college, *and transmit them to all future successions and generations;* and to use the like measures to prevent the contrary doctrines from prevailing in this society." *Ibid.,* p. 317; italics added.

[46] Dexter, *Yale Biographies and Annals,* II, 442–43.

although one of the historians of the Corporation has pointed out that he might have served it still more effectively and more consistently if he had objected twelve years earlier, when one of his New-Light opponents, Samuel Cook, had been forced to resign from the Corporation under the threat of just such an inquisition.[47]

The events of the 1750s aroused a storm of opposition in Connecticut. The movement to establish a professorship of divinity and a separate college church started a pamphlet war which had hardly died out when the attempted examination of Noyes began another. Many of the details of these controversies are beyond our concern; but some of the arguments shed light upon the conceptions of the college entertained by both sides, for the controversy raised many broad questions about the place of higher education in society and the relations of education to religion.

The clearest statements of the conservative position were in the writings of Clap himself. It is plain from an examination of his pamphlets that if he had had his way he would have forever frozen the development of the colleges in their original sectarian phase, for to him colleges were simply sectarian agencies, whose fundamental aim was not to teach the arts and sciences but to train orthodox and pious ministers.[48] They were religious societies, but of a special character because they reared the religious elite, the clergy. Thus the most vital thing in a college education was the internal religious life and the doctrinal soundness of the institution.

Should students, then, be permitted to worship variously and separately in accordance with their own choice, or that of their parents? To Clap this was inconceivable; no monitor could supervise the worship of students outside the college; their parents could not do so, so long as they committed them to the care of the college; but, above all, the uniformity, the conformity, which Clap's vision of a college unqualifiedly demanded,

[47] Bacon, "The Corporation," pp. 176–78. Dexter suggests that the move against Noyes was a bid on the part of the Corporation for support from the New Lights in the Legislature, where they were now a majority. Because of its Old-Light past, the college was not popular among the New Lights; but a show of concern for orthodoxy, and a personal blow at one of the leading members of the opposition, might win them over. *Yale Biographies and Annals,* II, 443.

[48] "Colleges are *Religious Societies* of a Superior Nature to all others. For whereas Parishes are Societies, for training up the *common People;* Colleges are *Societies of Ministers,* for training up Persons for the Work of the Ministry. . . . The great Design of Founding this School, was to Educate Ministers in our own Way." Thomas Clap, *The Religious Constitution of Colleges* (New London, Conn., 1754), pp. 4, 15.

could not be reconciled with diversity of religious practice. This led him to challenge commonly accepted parental prerogatives, as he had indeed done earlier in the Cleaveland case. For, as he said, if the parents were to say how their children should worship and thus take this decision out of the authority of the college, then there would be as many kinds of worship at college as there were different opinions of parents.[49] Such a state of affairs, which might seem quite acceptable to many who were steeped in the idea of tolerance, was to Clap simply shocking. He was aware that he might be reproached for violating liberty of conscience, but this he denied. "Under the Limitations of the Law," after all, any man could found such a college as his conscience might think fit. (This may have been formally true, but Clap must have known that at that time the liberty was more formal than real; one is reminded of Anatole France's famous remark about the majestic equality of the law.) In such a college, it would be fit and proper, once again, that uniformity should prevail in accordance with the will of the founder, which should always be followed. Any outsider who contributed funds to such a college should be aware—and this applied, said Clap, to the Anglicans who had given to Yale—that their money would be used to realize the purposes of the original founders, whose views differed from their own.[50]

In the realm of doctrine, Clap went on in another work to justify the system of tests that had been adopted at Yale for faculty members and Corporation fellows alike. He pointed out that a new scheme of divinity had been winning acceptance; this amounted in effect to a system of natural theology in which the doctrines of Calvinism were totally subverted.[51] After reflecting upon this system he insisted that minor deviations from orthodoxy could not safely be trifled with, because it could not be left up to heretics to define the significance of their own deviations. This was why the orthodoxy of teachers could not be satisfactorily established by anything short of a full and specific confession of faith.

[49] *Ibid.,* p. 14.

[50] *Ibid.,* pp. 14–20. These remarks were no doubt occasioned by some discontent with Clap's refusal in 1753 to allow the Episcopalian students in the college to attend regularly the Sunday services in the new Episcopal church. F. B. Dexter, "Thomas Clap and His Writings," *Papers of the New Haven Colony Historical Society,* V (New Haven, 1894), 256–57. Cf. the protest of Samuel Johnson against this policy. Schneider and Schneider, *Samuel Johnson,* I, 176–77. Episcopalian students, of course, never ceased to be welcome at Yale. Even Clap's primary concern was with the internal discipline of Connecticut Congregationalism.

[51] *A Brief History and Vindication of the Doctrines Received and Established in the Churches of New-England* (New Haven, 1755), pp. 19–23.

For a man may suppose or pretend, that the Ten Commandments are the most substantial Part of the Catechism, and that the Doctrines of the Divinity and Satisfaction of Christ, Original Sin, &c are but meer speculative *circumstantial* Points, upon which no great Weight ought to be laid. Such persons ought at least to declare what particular Articles they do *except,* that so others may judge, whether they are meer Circumstantials or not.[52]

It was dangerous, after all, to give up any one of a series of articles of faith, since they were a logical tissue and stood or fell together. Clap believed that the received doctrines of the Congregational churches were "of the utmost Consequence to the Salvation of the Souls of Men." He felt himself therefore duty bound "to do all that lies in my power, to continue and propagate those Doctrines; especially in the COLLEGE committed to my Care, since that is the Fountain from whence our Churches must be supplied." [53]

Uncompromising as they were, Clap's apologetics were of the sort to convince those already convinced and to alienate still more those who were opposed to him. Even before Clap's assault upon Noyes' position in the Corporation, the legislature had begun to falter in its annual financial support to Yale, and the college had fallen under attack because of its demand for a divinity professor.[54] After the movement against Noyes there was a fresh outburst of criticism in the course of which the entire concept of a narrow sectarian school was very closely examined. A broadminded Old-Light spokesman argued that the Corporation ordinance was unjust because a member could be called up on the suspicion of a single accuser; because the very election of Corporation members should have been taken as presumptive evidence of their worthiness to serve until some act gave evidence to the contrary; and because the mere fact of an examination would damage a man's character, even if he were acquitted. If "a Set of Narrow-Spirited Bigots" got on the Corporation, the writer warned, they would be in a position to harass other members and college officers who were "moderate, catholick, charitable Calvinists." [55] This was a clear warning to fellow Old Lights that to yield on this issue might be to sacrifice the entire control of the college to the most inquisitorial members of the opposing faction.

The author went on to attack Clap's concept of a college as a religious

[52] *Ibid.,* p. 37. Presumably Clap was referring to the Arminian distinctions between fundamental and non-fundamental doctrines of religion.

[53] *Ibid.,* p. 40.

[54] Dexter, *Yale Biographies and Annals,* II, 320–22, 366–68, 399.

[55] [Shubael Conant], *A Letter to a Friend* (New Haven, 1757), p. 10.

society. The president of Yale, he conceded, was a minister, but he presided as legal head and governor of the school, not as a clergyman. The fellows of the Corporation were, to be sure, ministers; but many trustees elsewhere were laymen and there was nothing intrinsically clerical in that office; moreover, they acted not in their capacity as ministers but under a civil appointment coming from a governmental charter. The tutors were not ministers, nor were the undergraduates; and of the latter it could safely be said on the basis of recent graduating classes that less than one quarter of them ever would become ministers. The sole member of the college who acted at the institution in his capacity as minister was the divinity professor. How then was Yale a society of ministers? In the curriculum? About three fourths of that was given to languages and arts, the rest to the study of divinity. No, a college was not simply a religious society, because it had other purposes than worship—some purely civil, others mixed. And while a church could conceivably be set up *within* a college, the right to do so did not lie, according to Congregational practice, in the president and fellows acting in their *political* capacity as governors of the college.[56]

What is displayed in such documents is an increasing critical awareness of the problems involved in the church-college relationship, and an emergent recognition of the fact that this relationship must be somewhat loosened if two or three religious factions were to use the college without continuous internecine strife. It is amusing to find some of the Old-Light worthies, now that they were themselves under pressure, dragging out arguments for tolerance and restraint that they had neglected to think of a few years before when they had driven a New-Light fellow off the Corporation and had been applauding Clap's reprisals against New-Light students. (It is similarly amusing to find Anglicans protesting bitterly against restrictions that were much less severe than those applied against dissenters at Oxford and Cambridge.) And yet the mere groping for these broader and more catholic principles had an independent value of its own; for after resorting to them instrumentally for a while, men began really to feel and believe them, and the road was opened for mutual peace.

The rest of the story of Clap's regime may be told briefly. He was besieged by rising restlessness in the colony at large, and by renewed petitions from formidable citizens for regular legislative visitation of Yale. Within the college itself his illiberalism continued, but it was met by stu-

[56] *Ibid.,* pp. 23–32.

dent rebellions (possibly stimulated in good part by parents or other persons outside the college interested in getting rid of the president), and in the end by desertions among the unhappy tutors.[57] Among Clap's final gestures of authority was the refusal of a gift of books because they included the works of an English divine of doubtful orthodoxy,[58] and the dismissal of two tutors for having espoused the grave heresy of Sandemanianism.[59]

After 1760 Clap's regime was under almost continuous pressure from two sides: on one there was the legal movement in the legislature to change the Yale charter by introducing legislative visitation into its government; on the other there was the more informal harassment of the college government by resident students, by parents, and in the end by the withdrawal of tutors. As we noted in Chapter III, the able old president successfully resisted the movement toward legislative changes in 1763 when he presented his effective but now discredited legal-historical account of the founding of Yale. But the growing unpopularity of the college in the community, a reaction not only to Clap's highhandedness, expulsions and discipline, and student fines,[60] but also to increased tuition

[57] See Dexter, *Yale Biographies and Annals,* II, 636–37, 723–24, 777; III, 167–68.

[58] *Ibid.,* II, 565–66; the potential donor was a Newport Baptist, the objectionable author the Reverend James Foster. Ezra Stiles felt that this act justified the charges of bigotry against Clap, and wrote him a powerful letter appealing for freedom of inquiry. "It is true," he conceded, "with this Liberty Error may be introduced; but turn the Tables the propogation [sic] of Truth may be extinguished. Deism has got such Head in this Age of Licentious Liberty, that it would be in vain to try to stop it by hiding the Deistical Writings: and the only Way left to conquer and demolish it, is to come forth in the open Field & Dispute this matter on even Footing. . . . Truth and this alone being *our* Aim in fact, open, frank and Generous we shall avoid the very appearance of Evil." Woodbridge Riley, *American Philosophy: The Early Schools* (New York, 1907), p. 217.

[59] Dexter, *Yale Biographies and Annals,* III, 93; the resignation was demanded of the two tutors in accordance with the test laws of 1753. The third tutor resigned with them in 1765, and the new tutors hired to replace them found themselves so uncomfortable that they, too, resigned. Kingsley, *Yale College,* p. 92. The Sandemanians were a tiny sect whose doctrine of salvation deviated drastically from that of Calvinism and allied theologies.

[60] John Trumbull, who was an undergraduate during Clap's last years, concluded that the fines were an anticipated part of the college's income (in "The Progress of Dulness," *Poetical Works* [Hartford, Conn., 1820] II, 38):

> Where kind instructors fix their price,
> In just degrees, on every vice,
> And fierce in zeal 'gainst wicked courses,
> Demand repentance of their purses;
> Till sin, thus tax'd, produces clear
> A copious income every year
> And the fair schools, thus free from scruples
> Thrive by the knavery of their pupils.

and poor fare in the college commons, was more than he could forever fend off. On the eve of commencement in 1765 a mob of students and townspeople assailed the home of the president, broke most of his windows, and slightly injured Clap himself.[61] During the following year students became so disorderly that life became impossible for the tutors; both tutors and students withdrew, and college functions were temporarily suspended.[62] Having brought the college to the brink of ruin, Clap resigned in 1766.

Clap's defeat ended the last attempt to impose upon one of the major colonial colleges the most restricting implications of a narrow sectarian commitment. It is noteworthy that the effective instrument of this defeat was the student body, which acted, one suspects, with parental backing. Clap had forestalled the movement in the assembly toward legal intervention; but there was no substitute for students, and when it appeared that the college was in danger of being all but emptied, it was clear that surrender must follow. By aligning the college vigorously first with one religious faction and then another, instead of holding it open to all in a catholic spirit, Clap had succeeded only in making for it too numerous and too determined a body of enemies. Had he merely tyrannized over tutors, he might have come to no difficulties; but to infringe conspicuously upon the religious liberties of students was to violate a sanction widely accepted in the community and necessary to the health of the college. The whole experience was an object lesson in the limitations of despotism and bigotry in a college whose role was as important as that of Yale in the mid-eighteenth century.

Clap was succeeded by Daggett, who was made president *pro tempore* for an interregnum that stretched out to eleven years. Although some signs of the same kind of student discontent that had plagued Clap were in evidence during Daggett's time, the man himself seems to have governed the college very loosely, being busy much of the time with the duties incident to his divinity professorship. Finally the Corporation, feeling the necessity of repairing some of the damage that had been done to the repu-

[61] Alexander Cowie, *Educational Problems at Yale College in the Eighteenth Century* (New Haven, 1936), pp. 21–25.

[62] Dexter, *Yale Biographies and Annals,* III, 167–68. Clap was on his way toward emptying the college of students. The class that entered in 1766 and graduated in 1770 numbered only 19 at the time of its commencement, as did the class that followed it. These were the smallest graduating classes in 16 years. Over the quarter of a century prior to 1770 graduating classes had had an average of 29 students.

tation of the college under Clap, elected to the presidency a man who was in many ways his antithesis, the Reverend Ezra Stiles of Newport. A graduate of the class of 1746 and a moderate Calvinist, Stiles was a man of broad tolerance and wide interests. He accepted the presidency after a visit with the Corporation during which he obtained from them the promise that they would repeal the religious restrictions enacted in 1753 and attempt as soon as possible to provide permanent professors for the college.[63] Stiles was unalterably opposed to any continuation of the internecine squabbles of Clap's era. "There is so much pure Christianity among all sects of Protestants," he wrote,

> that I cheerfully embrace all in my charity. There is so much defect in all that we all need forbearance and mutual condescension. I don't intend to spend my days in the fires of party; at the most I shall resist all claims and endeavors for supremacy or precedency of any sect; for the rest I shall promote peace, harmony, and benevolence. I honor all Protestant churches so far as they are reformed, and even the Church of England as a sister, by no means a mother, church. But I conscientiously give the preference, in my own choice, to the Congregational churches as nearest the primitive standard, and most purified from the corruptions of the Latin church.[64]

Two weeks after his installation the seniors were disputing forensically, "Whether a Toleration of all Religions is beneficial to the State?"[65]

UNITARIANISM AT HARVARD

The period of more than twenty-five years during which Yale was under Clap's domination represents no more than a temporary reversal of the underlying trend toward liberalism in the eighteenth century. In most places theology was affected by an increasing breadth and liberality, whether in the form of Arminianism, emergent Unitarianism, or even Deism. Theology itself ceased to have such an inclusive claim on men's interests, as the growth of commerce, the enlargement of the well-to-do classes, the importation of the ideas and concerns of the European Enlightenment, and the development in America of the absorbing

---

[63] W. L. Kingsley, *Yale College*, p. 104. Stiles was in a position to make a good bargain. His election was the occasion of an elaborate reconsideration of the relationship of Yale to the Assembly, which reached its fruition in 1792. See Stiles, *Literary Diary*, II, 224–69, *passim*, for the relevant entries.

[64] Quoted by W. L. Kingsley, *Yale College*, p. 104. Stiles, however, accepted the Saybrook platform and promised to teach accordingly.

[65] Stiles, *Literary Diary*, II, 287.

eighteenth-century middle-class passion for pure and applied science, for practical improvements, comforts, and conveniences, broadened enormously the range of intellectual preoccupations. All these things were reflected, on the whole rather promptly, in the colleges themselves. With the exception perhaps of the forward role of Harvard in the growth of a liberal theology, it would be too much to claim that the colleges took the initiative in many of these developments. It is probably nearer the truth to say that the colleges followed closely but at a safe distance; that their leaders were prompt to take an interest in the new concerns of the Enlightenment, but for the most part showed no special daring in pushing them to the forefront.

Necessarily the climate of the Enlightenment brought with it a somewhat greater concern for a free intellectual atmosphere in education. This did not result, to be sure, in the development of any highly self-conscious or formal sanctions for academic freedom for teachers, or in any open pulling and tugging at the inherited system of restraint which was so notable wherever fundamental religious interests were touched upon. But a new degree of latitude seems very slowly to have developed even in the absence of any such formal rationale. *Am Anfang war die Tat:* men exercised a measure of freedom before the formulation of any body of ideas with which they were prepared to challenge the traditional limitations. One can sense this new freedom in reading the history of the colleges in the eighteenth century; one sees some of its evidences in changes in the curriculum, which in most places were instituted by, or at the suggestion of, the presidents and professors themselves. It seems a safe conclusion that where intellectual changes of the magnitude suggested by these curricular innovations took place without being imposed externally by trustees or overseers, a certain amount of vital intellectual initiative had passed to the faculties. What is most impressive, however, is the quietness and gradualness with which the change took place. It was a long, slow advance, characterized by opportunism rather than daring, preceded by a careful reconnaissance of the terrain, and marked by few explosions.

A part of the story of the unfolding of the Enlightenment in America was the growing intrusion into the curriculum of a new interest in the utilitarian and the scientific; another was the change in theology itself, which was slowly and all but imperceptibly being liberalized. Among Anglicans this process took place with perhaps the least excitement, as the writings of latitudinarian theologians who had long been dominant in the more advanced thought of England were imported; but among

Congregationalists and Presbyterians the process was attended by more alarums and excursions, and the development in New England of that theological liberalism which came to be so important for Harvard deserves some attention.

The Puritans, it must be recognized, had begun to delimit and soften Calvinist predestinarianism even before Massachusetts Bay Colony was securely established. Calvin, although he was of course studied by the founding fathers of New England, was not in fact the sole fount of the characteristic Puritan theology. From the beginning the standard work, the one prescribed for study in the Puritan colleges, was William Ames' *Medulla Theologiae,* which had appeared in 1623, sometimes supplemented by his book of casuistry, *De Conscientia* (1632). These works were used until well into the eighteenth century, when they were often supplemented by Johannes Wollebius' *Compendium Theologiae Christianae* (1626). Predominant theological opinion, then, among the New England Congregationalists followed what was known as the Federal, or Covenant, Theology, which was predestinarian with modifications.[66] The Puritans had made an attempt to reduce somewhat the role of the arbitrariness of God by positing that God had voluntarily entered into a covenant with man in which He engaged to abide by certain principles governing salvation. While this view did not abandon the core of the predestinarian position, it had the effect of encouraging men to believe that the terms governing the gift of grace to man were, after all, infused with some principles of order amenable to human reason; and it encouraged them to cultivate whatever seeds of grace they might imagine they found in themselves. It was the first crack, however tiny, in the formidable dikes of Calvinist doctrine. Until the fourth decade of the eighteenth century the Covenant Theology was the only thing that could be spoken of as the orthodox position of New England Congregationalism. Only after the established churches had shown what the New Lights felt to be signs of advanced decay did a return toward orthodoxy take place.

There were doubtless several reasons why this turn to high Calvinism took place, but the one with which we must be most concerned was a reaction against the rise within the Congregational churches of a tendency toward liberal speculation which was generally stigmatized by the name "Arminianism." Now "Arminianism," like the terms "agrarianism" and

---

[66] The character of New England theology is carefully delineated by Perry Miller in "The Marrow of Puritan Divinity," *Publications of the Colonial Society of Massachusetts,* XXXII (1937), 246–300.

"anarchism" in the nineteenth century and "communism" in the twentieth, was a seventeenth- and eighteenth-century swear word; it is not always correct to conclude that a preacher accused of it by contemporaries actually espoused Arminian doctrines. The number of doctrinal points upon which one might choose to quarrel either with high Calvinism or the Federal Theology was quite large, and it would take the patience of a Harnack to trace in full the tortuous development of theological liberalism in eighteenth-century New England and to assess with any precision the extent to which this or that clergyman was really an Arminian. Understandably the gross evidence is confusing.[67] We have already seen how Increase Mather felt it necessary to take steps to "put down Arminianisme" among the Masters at Harvard in the 1690s; and yet his son Cotton is on record as congratulating the New England Congregational churches in 1726 because not one of their pastors was guilty of this abominable heresy.[68] Only eight years later, nonetheless, Jonathan Edwards was troubled by "the great noise that was in this part of the country, about Arminianism"; and yet a modern student of the subject stoutly insists, concerning the fountainhead of liberal New England theology, that "either deism or Arminianism in Harvard College before the Revolution is a myth." [69]

The confusion derives partly from the fact that much of what was called Arminianism was a shade of belief only a trifle more liberal than the pristine New England orthodoxy—an exploitation, as it were, of the germs of liberalism that could be found in the Covenant Theology itself.[70] The Covenant Theology, with the passage of time, slowly shaded off into Arminianism, just as Arminianism later shaded off into Unitarianism. What really aroused men like Edwards was not so much a clear and classifiable trend toward doctrinal deviation but something far more serious: an unmistakable continuation of that decline in religious morale that had been troubling the pastors of New England for two generations. This was a matter that went beyond doctrine, and was far more palpable.[71] Even

[67] The prevalence of Arminianism is minimized by F. A. Christie, "The Beginnings of Arminianism in New England," *Papers of the American Society of Church History,* Second Series, Vol. III (New York, 1917), pp. 153–72.

[68] *Ibid.,* pp. 154–55.   [69] *Ibid.,* p. 159.

[70] Some of the complexities of the problem are illustrated by Conrad Wright in his discussion of "Edwards and the Arminians on the Freedom of the Will," *Harvard Theological Review,* XXXV (October, 1942), 241–61, in which he finds large areas of agreement between Edwards and his opponents.

[71] The significance of this trend and its rather broad relation to Arminianism is assessed by Perry Miller, *Jonathan Edwards* (New York, 1949), pp. 101–26.

among those pastors who did not trouble themselves to challenge the old
doctrines, those doctrines themselves had lost their original meanings;
and the pulpits of New England—at least in the large seaboard towns
and the centers of trade—were being filled with substantial but dull liberal intellectuals like Charles Chauncy, the great-grandson of the
seventeenth-century President Chauncy. Such men hobnobbed with the
great merchants, defended avowed Arminians if they did not actually
join them, enjoyed the works of Tillotson, and put off afternoon services
for an hour in order to allow time for the luxurious dinners served by
members of their congregations.[72] It was against the social atmosphere
that produced such men that the New Lights revolted and the Edwardians
protested.

Whatever the efficacy of the protest in the inland counties, it did not
check the course of events around Boston. In 1791, when Ashbel
Green, who was later to become president of Princeton, visited the Boston Association, the local organization of clerics, he reported that the
prayer with which the meeting opened was the only religious event in the
course of the meeting.

But, as I understand, they are so diverse in their sentiments that they cannot
agree on any point in theology. Some are Calvinists, some Universalists, some
Arminians, some Arians, and one at least is a Socinian. How absurd it is
for men of such jarring opinions to attempt to unite. How much more con-

---

[72] See the excellent sketch of Chauncy by Shipton, *Sibley's Harvard Graduates,*
VI, 439–67, esp. p. 443. One cannot help but conclude that religion in New England
mercantile centers must have reached a stage similar to that treated so disdainfully
by Milton, when he discussed in the *Areopagitica* the relations between rich men
and eminent divines: "A wealthy man, addicted to his pleasure and to his profit,
finds Religion to be a traffic so entangled, and of so many piddling accounts, that
of all mysteries he cannot skill to keep a stock going upon that trade. What should
he do? fain he would have the name to be religious, fain he would bear up with
his neighbors in that. What does he therefore, but resolve to give over toiling, and
to find himself out some factor, to whose care and credit he may commit the whole
managing of his religious affairs? some Divine of note and estimation that must
be. To him he adheres, resigns the whole warehouse of his religion, with all the
locks and keys, into his custody; and indeed makes the very person of that man his
religion; esteems his associating with him a sufficient evidence and commendatory
of his own piety. So that a man may say his religion is now no more within himself,
but is become a dividual movable, and goes and comes near him, according as that
good man frequents the house. He entertains him, gives him gifts, feasts him, lodges
him; his religion comes home at night, prays, is liberally supped and sumptuously
laid to sleep, rises, is saluted, and after the malmsey, or some well-spiced brewage,
and better breakfasted than he whose morning appetite would have gladly fed on
green figs between Bethany and Jerusalem, his Religion walks abroad at eight, and
leaves his kind entertainer in the shop trading all day without his Religion."
Areopagitica (1644; ed. Chicago, 1949), pp. 44–45.

ducive to improvement and to pleasure, that the parties should divide, and that those who are agreed should walk by themselves. Yet this plan I know would be esteemed by them as the effect of bigotry and narrowness of mind; and so they will meet, and shake hands, and talk of politics and science, and laugh, and eat raisons and almonds, and apples and cake, and drink wine and tea, and then go about their business when they please.[73]

As a social occasion, Green remarked, he saw nothing objectionable in the meeting, but for the purposes of church government it was "ludicrous."

Possibly so. This is the comment of a Presbyterian with consistent notions of church government upon a group of latitudinarian Congregationalists who, he thought, had no church to govern. It may also be the reaction of a man who had not yet learned poise in the presence of a difference of opinion and could not entertain two conflicting ideas without acute discomfort. To a modern observer the combination of unity and diversity achieved by the Boston clergy might seem highly desirable; and their ability to prevent doctrinal differences from becoming the causes of internecine squabbling might be regarded as a signal accomplishment of civilized men. As the background for the government of a college, the temper of the Boston clergymen, who were characteristic clerical members of the Overseers, seems wholly admirable; and it may be worth pointing out that the Harvard which reflected their attitudes and those of their sons was soon to go on to some of its highest achievements, while the Princeton of Ashbel Green's regime reached a point that has been described by its historian as "Princeton's Nadir." [74]

Most of the liberal ministers who flourished during the period of change were former students of the first Edward Wigglesworth, who held his divinity professorship for over forty years and lived to see the great majority of the pulpits of Massachusetts and northern New England filled by ministers whom he had trained.[75] In his theology Wigglesworth was hardly more than a moderate liberal whose views corresponded very closely to those prevailing among the more sophisticated clergy; he was considerably less radical, for instance, than Ebenezer Gay, whose ministry at Hingham began five years before Wigglesworth's induction, and

[73] Quoted by James King Morse, *Jedidiah Morse: Champion of New England Orthodoxy* (New York, 1939), p. 36.
[74] The title of Wertenbaker's chapter on Princeton under Green in his *Princeton,* pp. 153–83; cf. the author's comments, pp. 121–22, 160–62, 164, 169–70, 172.
[75] Shipton, *Sibley's Harvard Graduates,* V, 552.

who is usually classified as a pioneer of Unitarianism.[76] But although Wigglesworth opposed Arminianism he refused to join Edwards in a crusade against it; he taught his students that such weighty arguments could be made on both sides of the controversy that mutual charity was clearly in order, and recommended, with admonitions, that they critically read the works of Tillotson.[77] He seems, in short, to have been something of an intellectual diplomat. And if his opinions were not notably advanced for Boston, they were at first well ahead of those of the older ministers who held forth in the rural churches; his intellectual leadership was thus important for the countryside, as had been that of Leverett and Brattle before him.

While there were complaints against Wigglesworth's habit of presenting to students both sides of the controversy rather than hammering home the orthodox position, his long tenure was on the whole untroubled. His position was strengthened by the offer of the Rectorship at Yale; his original five-year appointment under the terms of Hollis' endowment was made more secure, and in later days his financial needs were amply met.[78] Thus the first person in the history of American collegiate education to hold a major professorship can be said to have enjoyed a notable measure of intellectual freedom in his academic post, despite the inauspicious examination that preceded his election. His son, the second Edward Wigglesworth, maintained his father's tradition until 1794, and marked a further step away from the original scheme of Puritan divinity when he dropped Wollebius in favor of the lectures of the liberal English dissenting educator, Philip Doddridge. During this period the leadership of the clerics among the Overseers was in the hands of Jonathan Mayhew, the first openly avowed Unitarian among the clergy, and his friend, Charles Chauncy, who belatedly espoused Unitarianism in 1784.[79] In 1789 the executors of the estate of one John Alford, a Charlestown

---

[76] Shipton demurs from this classification, *ibid.*, VI, 62; cf. the sketch by Samuel A. Eliot, *Heralds of a Liberal Faith* (Boston, 1910), I, 1–8. W. B. Sprague, in his *Annals of the American Pulpit*, Vol. VIII (New York, 1865), lists Gay as the first Unitarian in an American pulpit. Sprague finds that there were seven preachers who took up their ministries before 1750 who can be called Unitarians, including Gay and Chauncy; there were ten more between 1750 and 1775, and thirty during the last quarter of the century.

[77] Shipton, *Sibley's Harvard Graduates*, V, 549–50, 553.

[78] *Ibid.*, pp. 550–51.

[79] See the somewhat indignant account by Charles Lyttle, "A Sketch of the Theological Development of Harvard University, 1636–1805," *Church History*, V (December, 1936), 301–29.

merchant who had left large sums for charitable purposes upon his death twenty-eight years before, established the Alford Professorship of Natural Religion, Moral Philosophy, and Civil Polity. The duties of the incumbent were prescribed by Alford's executors in considerable detail, but in such broad terms that a Deist could easily have fulfilled them.[80] These terms would of course be balked at by a modern professor of philosophy, but in the context of the time they represented a distinct and explicit enlargement of the scope of theology.

The culmination of Unitarian advance came in the years 1804–06, when Harvard University (so styled after 1780) was taken over by the Unitarians. David Tappan, the successor of the younger Wigglesworth and a moderate Calvinist, died in 1803, and for two years the election of the next Hollis Professor was in doubt. A battle took place between the liberals and the conservatives in the Corporation in which high feelings were aroused on both sides. Tappan's ten-year occupancy of the Hollis Professorship had not been distinguished by any brilliancy of the sort to reconcile the liberals to the idea of another Calvinist divine, and after much maneuvering and many heated words the Corporation nominated the Reverend Henry Ware, against whom it had been objected that he was not a Trinitarian. The presentation of this choice to the Overseers was the occasion of a thorough but angry review of the whole question of the doctrinal commitments of the college. The essence of the conservative position was that the first Thomas Hollis, who had endowed the professorship, had been a Calvinist and that the provisions of his endowment called for a man of sound and orthodox principles—a phrase which, even granting Mr. Hollis' famed liberality, surely excluded Arminians, Arians, and Socinians.[81] The liberals argued that the terms

---

[80] ". . . . whose principal duty it shall be . . . to demonstrate the existence of a Deity or First Cause, to prove and illustrate his essential attributes, both natural and moral, to evince and explain his providence and government, together with the doctrine of a future state of rewards and punishments; also to deduce and enforce the obligations which man is under to his Maker, and the duties which he owes him, resulting from the perfections of the Deity, and from his own rational nature . . . interspersing the whole with remarks, showing the coincidence between the doctrines of Revelation and the dictates of reason. . . ." Quincy, *History of Harvard,* II, 502. This professorship was not filled until 1817, when sufficient funds had accumulated. It was first occupied by Levi Frisbie.

The earlier benefactions of the second Thomas Hollis, who had done his best to stock the Harvard library with Unitarian books, also deserve mention. See Caroline Robbins, "The Strenuous Whig: Thomas Hollis of Lincoln's Inn," *William and Mary Quarterly,* Third Series, VII (July, 1950), 444 ff.

[81] The best account of the controversy is that of James K. Morse, *Jedidiah Morse,* Chap. VII; cf. Quincy, *History of Harvard,* II, 284–88, and Samuel Eliot Morison,

"sound" and "orthodox" ought to be construed according to the changing sentiments of the times; by this criterion Ware could be held to qualify. While the liberals were accused of undermining sound faith and planning to convert Harvard into an Arminian university, the conservatives were charged with narrowness and bigotry. The liberals had the majority, and Ware was confirmed. In 1806 Samuel Webber, whose views verged on Unitarianism, was elected president and the Unitarian victory was complete.

Had the victory of the Unitarians simply meant the domination of the university by a new sect as intractable as the old, it would have had little to do with the advance of a free intellectual climate at Harvard. But tolerant principles were far more central to the religious views of the Unitarians than they had been to those of even the moderate Calvinists, and the victory of the Unitarians was a genuine gain for the principle that different shades of belief could coexist under the roof of the same institution. It was much more likely, for instance, that an institution dominated by liberals would choose a Calvinist as its professor of divinity (as Harvard did in the case of Tappan) than that an institution dominated by Calvinists would choose a liberal. Similarly, it was the liberals who stood for a broad and catholic presentation of religious beliefs in the teaching of divinity, while most Calvinists held out for firm indoctrination.

THE SECULARIZATION OF LEARNING

The most significant trend in collegiate education during the eighteenth century was the secularization of the colleges.[82] By opening up new

---

Three Centuries of Harvard (Cambridge, Mass., 1936), pp. 187–91. The conservative argument is expounded at length by Jedidiah Morse, *The True Reasons on Which the Election of a Hollis Professor . . . Was Opposed at the Board of Overseers* (Charlestown, Mass., 1805), esp. pp. 9–12. Morse was combating, as he said, "an opinion now avowed, and becoming too fashionable among us, that the Professor of Divinity should not disclose his own particular religious sentiments to the students, but only place fairly before them all the tenets of the different sects of Christians, with their respective arguments, and leave each student to form his own creed." *Ibid.,* pp. 17–18. That the conservatives were thrown on the defensive during this period may be shown by Morse's subsequent denial that he wished to interfere with "the right of private judgment and freedom of inquiry." *An Appeal to the Public on the Controversy Respecting the Revolution in Harvard College* (Charlestown, Mass., 1814), p. 185.

[82] For the background see Michael Kraus, *Intercolonial Aspects of American Culture on the Eve of the Revolution* (New York, 1928), Chap. IX.

fields for college study, both scientific and practical, by rarefying the devotional atmosphere of the colleges, and by introducing a note of skepticism and inquiry, the trend toward secular learning inevitably did much to liberate college work. Secularization was evident in several ways: in the more commercial and less religious tone of newly founded colleges; in the rapidly rising number of college graduates who went into occupations other than the ministry; and in vital changes in the curriculum, notably the rise of scientific studies and the modification of theology to include freer philosophical speculation.

The relative advancement of secularism in the two gentlemen's colleges founded in the 1750s, Philadelphia and King's, is perhaps less important than the changes in the older institutions. Neither of these colleges achieved during the eighteenth century the importance they were later to have among the institutions of the East Coast. At a time when Harvard's graduating classes had more than forty young men, Yale's more than thirty, Princeton's about twenty, and William and Mary's only a few less, Philadelphia averaged about seven seniors and King's College about five.[83] The reasons for the early failure of these colleges to grow more rapidly are complex; at Philadelphia, at least, stagnation, as E. P. Cheyney has suggested, was the price paid for secularism.[84] Both Philadelphia and King's were ruled by predominantly Anglican boards of trustees, although they had been founded on interdenominational bases; both were afflicted by sharp antagonisms between Anglicans and Presbyterians; and the Presbyterians of the region might well prefer to go to Yale or Princeton. Moreover, the possibility of importing Anglican divines from England made the role of clerical education in these schools less important than it was in the institutions dominated by dissenting bodies, and schools located in cities offered fewer living attractions than those situated in small towns.

However, although in size Philadelphia and King's were hardly comparable to the earlier institutions, educational literature produced in connection with their establishment revealed a temper so different from that shown in the founding of the dissenting colleges as to demand some notice here. Despite the part taken by the Anglican gentry in their organization, and the appointment at both institutions of Anglican divines as

[83] Thomas H. Montgomery, *A History of the University of Pennsylvania from Its Foundation to* A.D. *1770* (Philadelphia, 1900), p. 268.

[84] Edward P. Cheyney, *History of the University of Pennsylvania* (Philadelphia, 1940), p. 177.

heads, the dominant note in the discussions preceding the establishment of these institutions was practical and secular. Franklin's *Proposals Relating to the Education of Youth in Pensilvania* had been notable for its emphasis on civic needs, private careers, and practical goals. In 1753, when the prospects of a college for New York were under discussion, the Reverend William Smith drew up a scheme for an ideal college in which educational aims were set forth unaccompanied by those pious remarks commonly found in statements of purpose by the earlier schools.[85] Citing Tillotson to the effect that knowledge of anything that would not make better men would be knowledge of trifles, he called for the abandonment of study in the tomes of rabbis and schoolmen, metaphysicians and theologians, in favor of studies that would simply produce virtuous and tolerant citizens.[86] He also devoted much attention to the necessity of education in the mechanical arts, to be organized in a separate but related school under the governance of the same trustees.[87]

Probably the most remarkable statement in pre-Revolutionary educational discussions also appeared in 1753 when William Livingston, a New York lawyer and Presbyterian leader, published a series of essays on the proposed King's College in a weekly newspaper, the *Independent Reflector*. These essays, although products of a sharp sectarian conflict, are somewhat different from the writings provoked by the Great Awakening in the sense that they are more concerned with political and less with ecclesiastical matters. Livingston, fearing ultimate educational and religious domination by the Anglicans, cast his argument in the form of a plea for a liberal, nonsectarian college. His intentions were not quite as disinterested as his arguments, for he seems to have been more concerned with making certain that there should be *no* college controlled entirely by Anglicans than with insuring that there would be a liberal college controlled without regard to sect.[88] But what is most significant for our

[85] William Smith, *A General Idea of the College of Mirania*, pp. 9–10.

[86] *Ibid.*, pp. 11–12. "Men blest with such an Education will, in all probability, be good Men of any Protestant Church; nor will they think the different modes of professing the same FAITH, and paying the same HOMAGE to the DEITY, of Consequence enough to occasion the least Dispute, or Breach of Charity, between Fellow-Citizens" (p. 68).

[87] *Ibid.*, pp. 14–15.

[88] Livingston refused to act in the office of trustee of King's College, evidently tendered in order to mollify him and his associates, and despite the fact that its educational practices conformed in some considerable measure to his own prescription he never became reconciled to the institution. He was pleased that he had been instrumental in diverting some support from it and relished the fact that "it makes

purpose is not his intent, but the arguments he chose to employ. That his factional passions should have become transmuted into pleas for disinterestedness is another illustration of those ironic processes by which sectarian zeal finally became translated into an understanding of tolerance. Even though Livingston was making his case from a prejudiced point of view, it remains important that he should have felt it expedient to argue in the terms he chose and that he made his case so clearly.

The true use of education, he began, taking from the outset a secular tack, was "to qualify men for the different employments of life, to which it may please God to call them. . . . [and] to render our youth better members of society." [89] Youthful minds were tender and susceptible to almost any impression, and it was impossible to be too careful in shaping them. The colleges were more important in this than the lower schools, because in colleges the students took a more active role in confirming the ideas presented to them and incorporating them into their personal outlook. Unfortunately the colleges were "generally scenes of endless disputation," but seldom places of "candid inquiry."

> The students not only receive the dogmata of their teachers with an implicit faith, but are also constantly studying how to support them against every objection. The system of the college is generally taken for true, and the sole business is to defend it.[90]

It was important to alter this practice of teaching so many things that later had to be unlearned. Unless the constitution and government of the proposed college "be such as will admit persons of all protestant denominations upon a perfect parity as to privilege, it will itself be greatly prejudiced, and prove a nursery of animosity, dissention and disorder." There were so many sects in New York that it seemed certain that the domination of the college by any one of them would draw the animosity of all the others and thus operate to impair its development. In such a state of things, Livingston argued (although he must have known that Episcopalians, however uncomfortably, sent their children to Harvard

---

indeed a most contemptible Figure." Dorothy R. Dillon, *The New York Triumvirate* (New York, 1949), pp. 39–40.

Much new information about the controversial background of King's College may be found in Milton M. Klein, "The American Whig: William Livingston of New York," unpublished doctoral dissertation (Columbia University, 1954), Chaps. IX, X.

[89] Schneider and Schneider, *Samuel Johnson*, IV, 120.
[90] *Ibid.*, p. 122.

and Yale), no children would be sent to the college except those of the sect that controlled it. This would not only damage the institution itself, but would cause many youths who would want higher education to be deprived of it.

Moreover, Livingston said, such a party-college, by spreading only its own ideas, would lead to domination of the entire province by members of a single sect. In any case, it would be commanding support from the legislature at the expense of the whole people while serving only a part.

A public academy is, or ought to be a mere civil institution, and cannot with any tolerable propriety be monopolized by any religious sect. The design of such seminaries [is] entirely political, and calculated for the benefit of society, as a society, without any intention to teach religion, which is the province of the pulpit.

Furthermore, if the college were only founded "on the plan of a general toleration" it would prosper by drawing students from the neighboring provinces where the colleges were church-dominated.[91]

Livingston went on to sketch the outlines of a plan for the kind of college he thought desirable. He opposed a royal charter, warning that the freedom of the college might easily fall victim to some future practitioner of "the tyrannical arts of James," and urged instead that it have an assembly charter. A royal charter would put the trustees of the college out of reach of the people and their representatives, and establish them in a position from which they could propagate their own civil and religious principles by choosing "such persons to instruct our youth, as would be the fittest instruments to extend their power by positive and dogmatical precepts." [92] A college incorporated by an act of the assembly would be in the hands of the people or their guardians, and this would preserve the essential "spirit of freedom."

For as we are split into so great a variety of opinions and professions; had each individual his share in the government of the academy, the jealousy of all parties combating each other, would inevitably produce a perfect freedom for each particular party.[93]

That Livingston did not rely upon the initiative of the faculty itself to produce such freedom in diversity was clear when he expounded his conception of the role of faculty officers:

[91] *Ibid.*, pp. 124–28.   [92] *Ibid.*, pp. 129–35.
[93] *Ibid.*, p. 138; readers will notice the similarity to the rationale of the *Federalist,* Number 10, and the whole theory of balanced government.

Every officer in the college being under the narrow aspect and scrutiny of the civil authority would be continually subject to the wholesome alternative, either of performing his duty with the utmost exactness, or giving up his post to a person of superior integrity.[94]

Like most other writers on education of the period, he meant, when he spoke of a free college, a free college *for students;* his concept of the teacher was simply that of an obedient instrument of the welfare of the students and the community. He assumed without question that teachers would reflect the "positive and dogmatic precepts" of the trustees who chose them. He did not ask whether this was desirable: it was certain to happen, and the way to provide the students with the benefits of diversity and freedom was not to underwrite a free faculty, but to put both the trustees and the faculty under the pressure of so many conflicting elements in the community that they would be forced to accept the community's diversity. Livingston was arguing for a kind of free consensus through a plurality of pressures. This is a defensible model of freedom indeed, but because it assigns to the faculty a purely passive role, it bears little resemblance to the concept of academic freedom with which we are familiar today. It neglects to count the interest of the teachers themselves as within the plurality of legitimate interests.

In offering his positive notions as to how the prospective college should be set up, Livingston specified that no person of any Protestant denomination should be disqualified by virtue of his religion from holding any office in the college; that the choice and removal of the president by the trustees be subject to confirmation by the legislature, so that the head of the college would have greater independence of the trustees in his educational duties than if he were answerable to them alone; that college by-laws be ratified by the legislature, and that the legislative constitution provide for as many details of the government of the college as foresight could make possible; that "no religious profession in particular be established in the college, but that both officers and scholars be at perfect liberty to attend any Protestant Church at their pleasure respectively"; that the prescribed public prayers offered twice daily at the college follow forms all Protestants could subscribe to; that divinity should not be taught at the college, that the corporation be constitutionally barred from electing a professor of divinity and degrees be offered only in arts, medicine and civil law; that

[94] *Ibid.,* p. 139.

the officers and collegians have an unrestrained access to all books in the library, and that free conversation upon polemical and controverted points in divinity, be not discountenanced, whilst all public disputations upon the various tenets of different professions of Protestants be absolutely forbidden;

and finally, that disputes among the inferior officers of the college be settled by the trustees, while those of the trustees be settled by the legislature.[95]

Livingston's proposals may be profitably contrasted with Clap's intentions at Yale which, even as he wrote, was on the eve of its severest trials. And yet one cannot help but observe that Livingston, in his zeal to secure a nonsectarian institution, was far from solving his problem in the freest way. His confidence in the superiority of the wisdom of a public legislature to that of private trustees, for instance, has not been borne out by the histories of state and private universities in the United States. His attempt to reduce the religious commitment of the college to vague public prayers held twice a day (and made compulsory for the students) was in itself a liberating suggestion, as were some other religious provisions. But to free the college of sectarianism by barring the teaching of divinity and banning the clash of theologies would be to deprive undergraduates of the chance to consider some of the most important intellectual currents of the eighteenth century, and it seems far inferior to the solution that was gradually emerging at Harvard—i.e., of discussing, not too dogmatically, at least some of the different systems of divinity and presenting the students with differences and choices. The context in which these proposals were presented, however, shows that Livingston, for all his factional zeal, had a good understanding of and an honest belief in the principles of toleration and religious liberty as many men of enlightenment saw them in his time. He simply lacked confidence (and perhaps with reason) that a plurality of religious systems could be taught under one college roof without producing deleterious sectarian bickering; and, being determined that no single profession should dominate the institution, he preferred to go almost all the way toward establishing a secular college. In this fashion sectarian antagonisms tended to modulate themselves in the eighteenth-century climate.[96]

[95] *Ibid.,* pp. 142–46.

[96] Note that even Bishop Madison, the head of the reorganized William and Mary, wrote Ezra Stiles almost thirty years later that the professorship of divinity there had been given up because it was deemed incompatible with a republic. Stiles, *Literary Diary,* II, 447.

At the time that men like Franklin, Smith, and Livingston were writing, piety in the older colleges was declining. A tendency extremely significant for the role of higher education was the precipitate fall in the proportion of undergraduates destined for the ministry. The percentage of future ministers among graduates, which had always been over 50 percent and often over 60 percent in the closing decades of the seventeenth century at Harvard and in the opening decades of the eighteenth at Harvard and Yale together, declined steadily until the early 1740s, when it was around 40 percent. The percentage of future ministers in all but two of the colonial colleges fell from a little over 40 percent in 1751 to about 20 percent in 1791, which represented the nadir for the eighteenth century.[97] The course of Yale's development is illuminating. Among the graduates whose occupations were known to Dexter, ministers vastly outnumbered physicians and lawyers together up to 1777. But in the classes from 1778 to 1805, Dexter found 350 lawyers, 238 ministers, and 94 physicians. In the period after 1792 businessmen, teachers, farmers, and planters appeared in sufficient numbers to warrant separate enumerations.[98] As future ministers increasingly shared the college halls with men destined for other occupations, both the tone and the curriculum of the college changed. The impulse of presidents and professors to catch up with the new currents of thought of the Enlightenment was strengthened by the growing complexity and receptivity of the undergraduate bodies.[99]

Changes in the curriculum bear directly on the origins of academic freedom, for in this sphere the initiative was passing into the hands of the faculties, especially where strong presidents reigned. If we look first at the schools in the Congregational-Presbyterian tradition, we find that

[97] See the table in Bailey B. Burritt, *Professional Distribution of College and University Graduates* (Washington, 1912), p. 75, and the explanation of his sample, p. 74.

[98] Dexter, *Yale Biographies and Annals,* gives a brief statistical résumé of the occupations at the end of each volume. For comparable figures on the shift at Brown between its founding and 1802, see Walter C. Bronson, *The History of Brown University, 1764–1914* (Providence, R. I., 1914), pp. 129, 154; for Princeton from 1761 to 1794, see John Maclean, *History of the College of New Jersey* (Philadelphia, 1877), I, 274–357. There, under President Finley, 45 percent of the graduates became ministers, whereas under Witherspoon 24 percent did.

[99] One good index of the development of the colleges is the change in student intellectual interests. Valuable sidelights on this subject may be found in Edward J. Young, "Subjects for Master's Degree in Harvard College from 1655 to 1791," *Proceedings of the Massachusetts Historical Society,* XVIII (1881), 119–51, and David Potter, *Debating in the Colonial Chartered Colleges* (New York, 1944), Chaps. I, II, III.

Harvard was the first to undergo an important curricular reformation; this occurred during the regime of President Holyoke, 1737–69. While Wollebius was still studied in divinity up to about the middle of the century, he had been dropped by 1759. In 1742–43, the college faculty resolved to use Locke on the human understanding and to use 'sGravesande's natural philosophy, a popular statement of Newtonianism, Isaac Watts' astronomy, and other such works.[100] Yale clung to Wollebius and Ames right up to the time of the Revolution, but these writers were supplemented during the second half of the century by Wollaston's *Religion of Nature Delineated,* so that during that period at least the Yale students could contemplate and compare both the old Federal Theology and the new natural theology. Edwards' *Enquiry into the Freedom of the Will* was also used for a time, but was dropped, evidently because it gave offense. During the last quarter of the century the college studies became thoroughly infused with the influence of Newton and Locke and their popularizers.[101] Princeton took cognizance of the new philosophy almost from the beginning.[102] Princeton was also profoundly influenced, as was Yale and to a lesser degree Harvard, by the textbooks of the English dissenting divine and hymnist, Isaac Watts, who in the reckoning of American Protestants was accounted an important thinker and whose works on astronomy, logic, theology, and philosophy mingled the traditional dissenting theology with the new concerns of the age. Even Watts, however, was alleged to be tainted with the heresy of Arianism, and at Yale the relevant volume of his work did not become available to students for a century after it was received by the library in 1730.[103]

The New York and Philadelphia colleges, whose advantage it was to have been founded in the midst of the Enlightenment, were burdened

[100] Louis F. Snow, *The College Curriculum in the United States* (n.p., 1907), pp. 47–48; Morison, *Three Centuries of Harvard,* p. 89. The only full-length study of the subject, Colyer Meriwether, *Our Colonial Curriculum 1607–1776* (Washington, 1907), is lamentably inadequate.

[101] John C. Schwab, "The Yale College Curriculum, 1701–1901," *Educational Review,* XXII (June, 1901), esp. 4–8; cf. Snow, *The College Curriculum,* pp. 41–45, 79–81; Benjamin Rand, "Philosophical Instruction in Harvard University from 1636 to 1900," *Harvard Graduates' Magazine,* XXXVII (September, 1928), 29–45. See also G. Stanley Hall, "On the History of American College Textbooks and Teaching in Logic, Ethics, Psychology, and Allied Subjects," *Proceedings of the American Antiquarian Society,* IX (April, 1894), 137–74.

[102] For an excellent study of Princeton, see Francis L. Broderick, "Pulpit, Physics, and Politics: The Curriculum of the College of New Jersey, 1746–1794," *William and Mary Quarterly,* Third Series, Vol. VI (January, 1949), pp. 42–68.

[103] Anne Stokely Pratt, *Isaac Watts and His Gifts of Books to Yale College* (New Haven, 1938), pp. 13–14.

with somewhat less of the traditional theological and metaphysical baggage that Harvard and Yale sloughed off. Both, at their beginnings, made rather strong gestures toward supplementing the usual classical studies with many practical subjects, but neither in practice went quite so far. At King's College, presided over by Samuel Johnson, one of the first colonials to perceive the importance of Locke's philosophy and to grow weary of Ames and Wollebius,[104] students were introduced to Whitby and Hutcheson, Grotius and Pufendorf.[105] At Philadelphia Provost Smith drew up a program of studies requiring considerably more science, theoretical and applied, than had been common. His was, Cheyney points out, the first systematic arrangement in America "of a group of college studies not following medieval tradition and not having a specifically religious object." [106] The tenor of his educational program was also shown in the materials recommended for additional reading by the students in their "private hours"—the *Spectator,* the works of Watts, Newton and the Newtonian popularizers, and Locke, Pufendorf, Hutcheson, and others.[107]

The rise of science was the most impressive aspect of curricular changes in the eighteenth century. While less than one tenth of the Harvard curriculum of the seventeenth century had consisted of scientific subjects, the typical curriculum of 1760 gave to them one fifth or more of the students' classroom time.[108] In the sixty years from 1640 to 1700 there had been little advance in the teaching of science at Harvard, but in the quarter of a century after 1725 the two holders of the Hollis Professorship of Mathematics and Natural Philosophy, Isaac Greenwood and John Winthrop, had revolutionized the teaching of science and mathematics and had made of Harvard a center of Newtonianism.[109] The

[104] Schneider and Schneider, *Samuel Johnson,* I, 6.

[105] Snow, *The College Curriculum,* pp. 56–60.

[106] Cheyney, *History of the University of Pennsylvania,* p. 82.

[107] Horace Wemyss Smith, *Life and Correspondence of the Rev. William Smith* (Philadelphia, 1879), pp. 58–59, 124–25; for an estimate of the practical significance of this curriculum see Cheyney, pp. 81–87, and for its origins, Theodore Hornberger, "A Note on the Probable Source of Provost Smith's Famous Curriculum," *Pennsylvania Magazine of History and Biography,* LVIII (1934), 370–77.

[108] Theodore Hornberger, *Scientific Thought in the American Colleges, 1638–1800* (Austin, Texas, 1945), pp. 23, 29. The development of science in the colonial curricula is traced in Chap. IV.

[109] On the advance of Newtonian science see Frederick E. Brasch, "The Newtonian Epoch in the American Colonies," *Proceedings of the American Antiquarian Society,* New Series, Vol. XLIX (October, 1939), pp. 314–32. The progress of early Harvard science is the theme of I. Bernard Cohen's *Some Early Tools of American Science* (Cambridge, Mass., 1950).

other colleges made comparable progress. Jefferson's mentor, Dr. William Small, although not a creative scientist of Winthrop's stature, taught science and mathematics inspiringly at William and Mary, while Presidents Clap and Stiles devoted themselves to the advancement of science at Yale.[110] And while neither President Johnson of King's College nor Provost Smith of the College of Philadelphia was able to realize his ambitious plans for scientific and practical studies, their institutions were founded in the midst of a lively interest in the new science. From its very beginning the College of Philadelphia had a science professor, inherited from the Academy that preceded it, while King's College acquired one eight years after the date of its charter. By the beginning of the Revolution six of the eight colonial colleges that were actually open (Rutgers being temporarily defunct) had professorships of mathematics and natural philosophy; and by 1788 all eight were so staffed. While astronomy and physics were the central subjects of study, other sciences were beginning to receive a share of attention, and the subsequent founding of medical schools in association with Harvard, King's, and Philadelphia gave an impetus to the study of botany and chemistry.[111] Considering their size and limited funds, the colleges appropriated generous sums for demonstration equipment and orreries.[112] Trustees were well aware that a good lecturer in science and a spectacular piece of equipment—like the famous orrery made by David Rittenhouse for Princeton—were assets in the reputation of a college. The possession of such items soon began to be mentioned prominently in college promotional literature.

The greatest creative activity in colonial science, of course, took place outside the colleges, being carried on chiefly by gifted amateurs and sponsored most notably by scientific societies.[113] Mathematical education in American colleges had started from too negligible a base to provide good groundwork for advanced study in physics or astronomy, and biology

[110] On Small see Hornberger, *Scientific Thought*, pp. 61–62; on Clap and Stiles, Louis W. McKeehan, *Yale Science: The First Hundred Years, 1701–1801* (New York, 1947), Chap. II.

[111] Medical schools were founded in 1765, 1767, and 1782 at Philadelphia, King's, and Harvard. Cheyney, *History of the University of Pennsylvania*, pp. 96–104; Morison, *Three Centuries of Harvard*, pp. 167–69. For the early development of medical education, see W. F. Norwood, *Medical Education in the United States* (Philadelphia, 1944); for the biological sciences, W. M. and M. S. C. Smallwood, *Natural History and the American Mind* (New York, 1941), Chaps. II, X, and XI. I. B. Cohen, *Some Early Tools of American Science*, Chaps. IV and V, traces early chemistry and biology at Harvard.

[112] Hornberger, *Scientific Thought*, p. 37.

[113] See Ralph S. Bates, *Scientific Societies in the United States* (New York, 1945), Chap. I.

and chemistry were late additions to the curriculum. The names of the outstanding colonial scientists—men like Bartram, Franklin, Logan, Garden, Rittenhouse, and others—are for the most part names of men who were not on college faculties; Winthrop alone among the academic scientists was of comparable stature.[114] But the same thing can be said for the most part about the universities of Europe, which with only a few exceptions had not been important centers for advanced scientific work since the decay of the medieval universities. Considering the university standards of the time, and their limited resources, the record of the colonial colleges is in this respect far from discreditable; and it must also be said of them that unlike the European universities of the seventeenth century they never showed antagonism to the work of the scientific societies.[115]

However one may assess its scientific value, the growth of science teaching had an important effect on the colleges. In all the colleges the first professor of mathematics and natural philosophy was the first professor of a secular subject. Often he was also the first professor whose personal background was secular. While an able professor of science was like an able professor of divinity in the sense that he had something distinctive to bring to the college, something besides mere conformity, he was different in that he introduced the *discovery* of knowledge into the classroom. In education, the study of science, one may admit, is by no means intrinsically or universally a liberating discipline: it can be made as hidebound or formularized as the pedagogue wills. But eighteenth-century science breathed an air of freshness and discovery that seems not to have been lost upon either pupils or professors.[116] Teaching itself was freshened. While in the study of the classical languages recitation from the textbook was almost the sole method of instruction, the science teachers relied in great measure upon lectures, often accompanied by

[114] Rittenhouse, it should be observed, served very briefly on the faculty of the College of Philadelphia, but his most sustained relationship with it was that of trustee. Among those listed by Raymond Phineas Stearns in his "Colonial Fellows of the Royal Society of London, 1661–1788," *William and Mary Quarterly,* Third Series, Vol. III (April, 1946), pp. 208–68, are the names of five American academic men: William Brattle, John Leverett, and Thomas Robie of Harvard, all three of whom were elected after their teaching years were over; Dr. John Morgan, Professor of Medicine at the College of Philadelphia; and John Winthrop. Twenty-two non-academic scientists were elected from the American colonies.

[115] Martha Ornstein, *The Role of Scientific Societies in the Seventeenth Century* (Chicago, 1938), Chap. VIII.

[116] Cohen, *Some Early Tools of American Science,* pp. 12–17.

demonstrations. It may have done the students some good to memorize whole paragraphs of Locke's *Essay concerning Human Understanding;* it seems to have done them more good to be able to ask questions of the professors of natural philosophy.[117] Before the creation of the science professorships the divinity professors were usually the only men of stature on the college faculties who normally did more than check on the students' knowledge of some particular text. Now the undergraduates were exposed also to men of science who had posts of comparable stature and something of their own to impart. While the divinity professors continued to preach to the undergraduates and educate the masters for the ministry, the science professors now spoke from their secular pulpits with authority equal to that of the divines, and often reared the undergraduates in that passion for nature which was so much a part of eighteenth-century religion. Where the college had been in the past directed, even in its science teaching, toward the conservation and inculcation of existing knowledge, the science professors began to acquaint undergraduates with the idea of inquiry, to encourage the feeling that it was the business of the mind to discover things hitherto unknown.

The student of the history of intellectual freedom will observe that the intellectual changes resulting from the development of the Enlightenment in American colleges came about almost completely without incident. A whole world of new ideas was opened to the minds of undergraduates without struggle on the part of the old order, and frequently with the active interest and enthusiasm of governing boards. The only case in which a science teacher seems to have become involved in a controversy over his scientific teachings occurred in 1755. The scientist was John Winthrop, and the resolution of the issue is worthy of note because in this case it was the scientist who took the offensive and because his victory was so complete.

In November, 1755, Boston was shaken by a severe earthquake, which provoked a great deal of speculative literature. Notable among the reactions were a pamphlet by the Reverend Thomas Prince and a lecture given by John Winthrop in the Harvard College chapel. It was Prince's thesis that earthquakes were above all tokens of God's "just Displeasure," a familiar clerical theme. But in addition to giving currency once again to this now obsolescent reaction, Prince ventured to suggest that earthquakes were made more severe around Boston because the town con-

[117] *Ibid.,* p. 15.

tained so many lightning rods. It was his notion (and one not unknown among distinguished scientists at that time) that the severity of earthquakes was increased because the lightning rods drew "the Electrical Substance" out of the air. To erect lightning rods, Prince thought, was blasphemous: "O! there is no getting out of the mighty Hand of God! If we think to avoid it in the *Air,* we cannot in the *Earth.* . . ." Winthrop, provoked by some fallacies in Prince's reasoning, added an appendix to his own published lectures on the earthquake in which he effectively castigated the minister's arguments. When this drew from Prince an amiable but befuddled partial retraction, Winthrop replied with a withering communication which attacked still further the poor preacher's confusions. In the end the minister retreated in total disorder, amid a flurry of phrases in praise of Winthrop's family.[118] This public spanking administered to a cleric by a scientist (and to an Overseer by a professor) is a minor landmark in the intellectual history of New England, a token of the rising prestige of science and the vulnerability of some of the old providential interpretations of nature that had once held undisputed sway. It was not, however, an episode in any "war" between science and religion. Like so many of the Puritan clergy, Prince was himself a well-informed amateur scientist, not an opponent of science as such; he was simply trying to combine scientific with theological explanations in a way that the more rigorous Winthrop would not let pass. He had, moreover, the wit to know that he had been outargued, and the grace to admit it.

What is truly remarkable, indeed, is the absence of a "war" between religion and science during this great period of scientific advance, as well as the atmosphere of freedom in which the new science was introduced into the colleges.[119] In this respect the American colonial colleges compared very favorably with European universities of the period and with some later American institutions in the Darwinian age. All this is not to say that there was no tension between religion and science; all systems of faith are likely to contain tendencies hostile or inhibiting to scientific

[118] See the account of the affair by Eleanor M. Tilton, "Lightning-Rods and the Earthquake of 1755," *New England Quarterly,* XIII (March, 1940), 85–97; cf. Theodore Hornberger, "The Science of Thomas Prince," *ibid.,* IX (March, 1936), 26–42, and the comments by Cohen, *Some Early Tools of American Science,* pp. 127–28.

[119] Cf. Cohen, *Some Early Tools,* p. 127: "During the 18th century at Harvard, as throughout New England, and indeed the rest of America, there was a general freedom from clerical opposition to science."

inquiry, among them an exclusive preoccupation on the part of some persons with the supernatural. But the absence of overt clash, the development of so much positive support for science, may be ascribed in good measure to the fundamental hospitality of Puritanism to scientific inquiry. Many students of Puritanism have commented on its relationship to a high state of working morale in business and industry; this same devotion to work in the Puritan ethos carried over into leisure time and encouraged the spirited pursuit of knowledge in such areas as history and natural science. Diligence in the pursuit of knowledge, like diligence in one's calling, was congenial to the Puritan spirit, for the acquisition of knowledge about God's world was another means of glorifying Him.[120] It is now a familiar fact that in the remarkable creative activity that characterized English science in the seventeenth century, the number of Puritan backgrounds and convictions was far out of proportion to the number of Puritans in the population.[121]

The American Puritans were secure in their conviction that the knowledge of nature, far from undermining religion or contravening the glory of God, could only add to man's sense of the grandeur of His work. "Science was not merely tolerated because faith was believed to be secure, whatever physics or astronomy might teach, but it was actually advanced as part of faith itself, a positive declaration of the will of God, a necessary and indispensable complement to Biblical revelation." [122] In valuing science partly for its revelation of divine power, Increase Mather took quite the same position as Isaac Newton.[123] It is true that the Puritans had, especially in the early days, a strong need to see natural events as divine

[120] While there seems to have been no interference in the substantive teaching of science at Harvard, the Corporation itself did resolve in 1788 that the Hollis Professor of Mathematics and Natural Philosophy "be directed, while he is delivering his Philosophical and Astronomical lectures, to make such incidental reflections upon the Being, Perfections and Providence of God, as may arise from the subjects, and may tend seriously to impress the minds of youth." *Ibid.*, p. 12.

[121] The relation between science and Puritanism is discussed at length by Robert K. Merton, "Science, Technology, and Society in Seventeenth Century England," *Osiris,* IV (1938), 360–632, esp. Chaps. IV, V, VI; see also Richard Foster Jones, *Ancients and Moderns* (St. Louis, 1936), Chaps. V, VI, VII. James Bryant Conant in an essay on "The Advancement of Learning during the Puritan Commonwealth," *Proceedings of the Massachusetts Historical Society,* LXVI (1942), 27–31, points out that there were Puritans and Puritans, and that the ultra-doctrinaire Calvinists seem to have been far less interested in science than the Puritan moderates.

[122] Perry Miller, *The New England Mind* (New York, 1939), p. 211.

[123] See E. A. Burtt, *The Metaphysical Foundations of Modern Physical Science* (London, 1949), pp. 280–99.

symbols, or "providences." But they adapted an ancient and convenient dualistic conception of the universe under which events could be taken as having symbolic and providential significance and yet could be admitted to conform to natural laws.[124] Thus the transition from Puritanism to the dominant teleological defense of Christianity in the eighteenth century was an easy one.

From the very beginnings at Harvard, scientific innovations were viewed by many with enthusiasm and by the rest with tolerance. Although the first generation of undergraduates was taught the astronomy of the ancients, later the Copernican system, which was introduced at least as early as 1659, only ten years in the wake of Oxford, was accepted without fuss even by the orthodox. So conservative a preacher as the Reverend John Davenport of New Haven, presented with a copy of an almanac prepared by a Harvard tutor that gave an exposition of the new astronomy, observed that the work contradicted Scripture, but said of its author, "let him injoy his opinion; and I shall rest in what I have learned, til more cogent arguments be produced then I have hitherto met with." [125] Others took a more positive view: the almanac was approved, for instance, by President Chauncy, and Professor Morison remarks of the Puritan clergy that "instead of opposing the acceptance of the Copernican theory," they "were the chief patrons and promoters of the new astronomy, and of other scientific discoveries, in New England." [126] Even those clerical leaders who have been identified with conservatism or reaction in theology had a consistent record of enthusiasm for science. Increase and Cotton Mather were notable promoters of science—the latter a very courageous one—as were Thomas Clap and Timothy Dwight at Yale. And Jonathan Edwards, far from rejecting the new science, was one of

[124] See, for instance, Kenneth Murdock, *Increase Mather* (Cambridge, Mass., 1926), p. 146. Perry Miller, *The New England Mind,* Chap. VIII, discusses the Puritan attempts to synthesize providences and natural uniformity.

[125] Samuel Eliot Morison, "The Harvard School of Astronomy in the Seventeenth Century," *New England Quarterly,* VII (March, 1934), 13. For an estimate of the strength and weakness of early Harvard science, see Morison, *The Puritan Pronaos* (New York, 1936), Chap. X. The relation between American Puritanism and science is discussed briefly in Perry Miller and Thomas H. Johnson, *The Puritans* (New York, 1938), pp. 729–38 and at length by Theodore Hornberger, "American Puritanism and the Rise of the Scientific Mind," unpublished Ph.D. dissertation (University of Michigan, 1934).

[126] "The Harvard School of Astronomy," p. 13; cf. Shipton's observation about the clergy of a later day in "The New England Clergy of the 'Glacial Age,'" *Publications of the Colonial Society of Massachusetts,* XXXII (1937), 37–39, 45–46.

the first in New England to see its significance, and seized upon it to re-
inforce a revival of Calvinism in a remarkable synthesis of science and
theology.[127]

While the leading clerics, then, were highly receptive to science, it
does not follow that science was not, in some degree, subversive of the
inherited religious outlook. Although most Puritans failed to anticipate
it, the rise of science did in the end contribute to the decline of orthodoxy.[128] Ingenious as were the logical reconciliations between natural
law and "providences," the greater familiarity with the one weakened
concern with the other. While the Calvinist system had put its stress upon
God's foreknowledge of everything that man would do and all that would
befall him, the progress of science, interpreted as the advancing knowledge of God's laws, gave men greater confidence in their own foreknowledge, so to speak, of what God would do. The difference, although not
perceived at first, was ultimately vital. As time went on the tenets of
Puritanism passed gradually but easily into the tenets of the Enlightenment, divine providences yielded to natural law, and theology rested more
and more upon teleology. Of course, defenders of orthodoxy ultimately
realized that the incursions of science had made things more difficult for
older forms of religion,[129] but the full force of this realization was not
felt until the reaction from the Enlightenment that came in the early nineteenth century.

POLITICS AND REVOLUTION

The political life of the American colonies quickened after 1750 as questions of large historical importance elbowed their way onto the stage. In

[127] Miller speaks of Edwards as "the last great American, perhaps the last
European, for whom there could be no warfare between religion and science, or
between ethics and nature." *Jonathan Edwards,* p. 72.
[128] Cf. Robert K. Merton, "Science, Technology and Society in Seventeenth
Century England," *Osiris,* IV (1938), 438: "The possibility that science, as means
toward a religious end, would later break away from such religious supports and
in a measure tend to delimit the realm of theological control, was seemingly un-
realized. The apparent conflicts between theology and science which arose when
scientific findings seemed to disprove various contentions of orthodox theologians
occurred later with each extension of scientific inquiry into realms which were
hitherto regarded as sacred. . . . the Reformers did not anticipate the full actual
consequences of their teachings, consequences which did not coincide with their
expectations."
[129] For the beginnings of this realization, see Hornberger, *Scientific Thought in
the American Colleges,* pp. 80–85.

the earliest days of the American colleges, politics as a subject of study had its place only as an incidental part of courses in ethics or moral philosophy; but with the development of the eighteenth-century curriculum a large part of such courses was avowedly given over to the broad principles of politics, law, and civil ethics. Students were introduced to the writings of Grotius, Pufendorf, Wollaston, Locke, Hutcheson, and others. In the curriculum itself the studies were directed toward moral and political philosophy rather than to topical problems, and while it is reasonable to assume that the college presidents, who usually offered the relevant courses, used current issues to illustrate general principles, little is known about the details of classroom teaching.[130]

An incident involving Provost Smith at Philadelphia suggests that comments made by a teacher of politics about current issues were most likely to involve him in difficulties if he was at the same time an active figure in political controversies. Smith, who was an ardent champion of the interests of the proprietors in the struggle between them and the Quaker faction, was the object of much criticism in the newspapers, most of it in the form of anonymous letters; his teaching was alleged to be both irreligious and un-Pennsylvanian. The trustees, fearing that these charges would damage the reputation of the college, ordered an investigation in July, 1756. They were soon presented with strong testimony on Smith's behalf signed by the only four members of the senior class who were then present in town. The undergraduates averred that Smith's teaching had been nonpartisan as to the current provincial struggles and that

in the whole Course of his Lectures on Ethics, Government and Commerce, he never advanced any other Principles than what were warranted by our standard Authors, Grotius, Puffendorf, Locke, and Hutcheson; writers whose sentiments are equally opposite to all those wild notions of Liberty that are inconsistent with all government, and to those pernicious Schemes of Government which are destructive of true Liberty.

Moreover, said these young laymen of their clerical preceptor, his teachings embraced both morality and religion.[131]

The committee of trustees charged with the inquiry issued a report which expressed their conception of the problem of biased instruction:

. . . on examination, it must appear to everyone, as it really does to us, that no single Master can, by the Constitution of the College and Academy, carry

[130] See Anna Haddow, *Political Science in American Colleges and Universities, 1636–1900* (New York, 1939), Chaps. I–VII.
[131] Horace Wemyss Smith, *Life . . . of the Rev. William Smith*, I, 126–27.

on any separate or party-Scheme, or teach any principles injurious to piety, Virtue and good Government, without an evident failure of Duty in the whole Body of Trustees and Masters; the general Scheme of Education being fixed, a part of it assigned to every Master, The Visitations of the Schools by the Trustees monthly, and in the Interim between their Meetings, the Government, the Morals, and the Education of the whole Youth committed to the Faculty, which consists of the Provost, Vice-Provost, and Professors, who have it in charge to examine into and report to the Trustees at their Stated Meetings whatever shall appear wrong in any of the Professors, Masters or Scholars.[132]

The entire government of the college thus being a system of mutual espionage and counterespionage, it seemed that any misdemeanors on the part of the Provost would have become known to the trustees; and having closely examined Provost Smith's record, the committee found him whole. Indeed, having gone to the trouble, they said, of looking into the lecture notes of the four students who were in town as well as receiving their friendly representations about their teacher, they concluded that he had "discharged his Trust as a capable Professor and an honest man," and had given ample evidence "of the goodness of his Principles." [133] Although Smith was thus vindicated, the incident gives illuminating evidence of some of the limitations under which he carried on his work in this closely governed college. His situation, however, was untypical, not only because of the exceptionally intimate government of the college by its trustees but because of the acrimony of Pennsylvania's factional politics and his active role in it. Teachers of politics and ethics elsewhere, who paid the price of remaining aloof from current controversies, seem not to have been similarly troubled by criticism of their teaching.

While faculties do not seem on the whole to have been notable for their daring or importance in political speculations, much effort was made to encourage among the students a keen taste for controversy about political principles. It is no accident that the generation of acute political controversialists that led the pre-Revolutionary colonial agitations were men who had been for the greater part educated in the free and inquiring atmosphere of the colleges.[134] A primary source of vigorous and contro-

---

[132] *Ibid.,* p. 127.   [133] *Ibid.,* p. 127.

[134] See James J. Walsh, *The Education of the Founding Fathers of the Republic* (New York, 1935) which emphasizes the continuity with the scholastic tradition (especially Chap. X). Morison suggests that the schooling of the colonials in dissenting politics may have owed more to their traditional classical studies than to current eighteenth-century writings on politics. *Three Centuries of Harvard,* pp. 135–36.

versial thinking was the student disputations, which offer additional grounds for the conclusion that the undergraduates in these early colleges were freer men than the faculty members. As the eighteenth century wore on there was greater and greater evidence of ardent political argumentation, and many of the recorded theses show that urgently controversial topical questions were argued along with questions of political theory; among them were the value of paper-money issues, the lawfulness of resisting the supreme magistrate, the compact theory of government, the legality (debated after the Stamp Act) of collecting taxes by military force, and the moral propriety of slavery.[135]

An indulgent view was taken of these student exercises in all colleges about which we have sufficient evidence for conclusions. "The young gentlemen," wrote the Reverend Andrew Eliot, a member of the Harvard Corporation, to an English benefactor of the college in the early 1770s,

are already taken up with politics. They have caught the spirit of liberty. This has always been encouraged, but they have sometimes been wrought up to such a pitch of enthusiasm that it has been difficult for their Tutors to keep them within due bounds; but their Tutors are fearful of giving too great a check to a disposition, which may, hereafter, fill the country with patriots; and choose to leave it to age and experience to check their ardor.[136]

This was Harvard; but much the same might have been said at Princeton or William and Mary. The seniors at Yale under Stiles could debate such questions as "Whether polygamy is lawful?" and in 1780, despite the local bitterness excited by a recent British invasion of New Haven, they were freely arguing "Whether America would be more happy as a part of the British Empire, than as an Independ't Republick? or Whether America would be more happy in a subordinate connexion with Great Britain . . . ?"[137] They also debated such moot questions as whether

[135] On disputations see Haddow, *Political Science in American Colleges,* Chaps. III, VII; Potter, *Debating in the Colonial Chartered Colleges,* pp. 43–53.

[136] Morison, *Three Centuries of Harvard,* p. 138.

[137] Stiles, *Literary Diary,* II, 434. The diary affords frequent illustrations of the latitude allowed for disputation subjects. Cf. Reuben A. Guild, "The First Commencement of Rhode Island College and American Independence," *Collections of the Rhode Island Historical Society,* III (Providence, 1895), 267–98. Some readers have questioned whether allowing students to debate liberal-sounding issues in theology or politics was actually as liberal as it seemed, since in some instances —say, the lawfulness of polygamy—a ritualistic resolution of the argument on the "correct" side was expected. Even when this objection is taken into account, the intrinsic liberality of the brave effort constantly to rationalize one's conclusions and beliefs must be admitted. So long as *pro forma* debate is allowed, there is always the possibility that the "incorrect" conclusion may become functional to

there should be amnesty for Tories (1783) and whether the Federal Constitution should be ratified (1787). Men of Stiles' stamp evidently realized that even in a time of crisis it is educational wisdom to give free rein to the dissents and questions of eighteen-year-old minds.

The coming of the Revolution led, of course, to many severities and injustices to Loyalists, including some violations of civil liberties. This is in itself a large and important story—no doubt a more important one than the history of the colleges themselves during the revolutionary period—but it involves issues distinct from that of academic freedom. Civil liberties and academic freedom often suffer together from the same causes, but they are not identical. Another of Provost Smith's unhappy experiences provides an excellent case in point. In 1757 his friend (and subsequently his father-in-law), Judge William Moore, became embroiled with the dominant Quaker faction in the Pennsylvania Assembly. Out of this conflict there came a sharply worded counterattack written by him and published by Provost Smith in a German newspaper which Smith had established. Moore and Smith were both charged with libeling the Assembly, and in the course of events were jailed.[138] The incident is pretty clearly a case of political persecution,[139] and as such doubtless marks one of the low points in the history of civil liberties in the province. But oddly enough it turned out to be a landmark in the history of academic freedom; for the trustees of the college, upon hearing that the provost had expressed a desire to continue his classes, and his students a like desire to go on under his tutelage, gave permission to have his classes carried on "at the usual Hours in the Place of his present confinement." For several weeks Smith met his twelve students in his cell in the jail at Sixth and Walnut streets. Later the trustees gave him leave to go to England to carry an appeal from the Assembly to the Crown, which proved to be successful although it brought Smith no redress. Inasmuch as three of the trustees were members of the Assembly and one was a

---

some personal or social interest, and that Arminius' experience of being converted to the view he was engaged to refute may be repeated.

[138] The most ample account from Smith's standpoint is that of Horace Wemyss Smith, *Life . . . of the Rev. William Smith*, Vol. I, Chap. XII. The provost had an opportunity to escape sentence through a retraction, but he told the Assembly: "I cannot make acknowledgements or profess contrition. No punishment which this Assembly can inflict on me would be half so terrible to me as suffering my tongue to give to my heart the lie."

[139] See the detailed critical analysis by William R. Riddell, "Libel on the Assembly," *Pennsylvania Magazine of History and Biography*, LII (1928), 176–92, 249–79, 342–60.

judge who had denied habeas corpus to the provost, the action of that body involved, for some of its members at least, an element of self-denial.[140] As an episode in American academic history it may provide an interesting precedent for the determination of trustees to draw a line of demarcation between educational decisions and political controversy. The Philadelphia trustees did not raise questions about Smith's legal status, but they acted upon the ineluctable fact that it had no bearing upon his competence as an educator.

In nationalist and colonial revolutions college and university students have always played an aggressive part, and to this the American college students were no exception. At the dissenting colleges trustees, faculties, and students were so strongly committed to the patriotic cause from the time the controversies with the mother country became acute that there was little likelihood that any interference with the academic freedom of a patriotic student or professor would occur. As for the few Loyalists on academic faculties, they suffered, when they suffered at all, violations of civil rather than academic liberties, which, serious though they were, fall outside the necessary limits of our story. Most notable of the incidents in this category was the case of Myles Cooper, the second president of King's College and a resolute Loyalist, who would have been tarred and feathered in 1775 if young Alexander Hamilton, then an undergraduate and an activist in the patriotic cause, had not delayed an angry mob long enough to facilitate his escape. Hamilton's conduct, which suggests that he may have learned something about the principles of civil freedom at King's College, saved the president from a humiliating experience but it did not save his post; he was forced to flee to England, where he remained for the rest of his life.[141] A man like William Smith, however, who had been active in the early patriotic movement but could not follow the patriot cause to the point of demanding outright independence, found it possible when his college closed to retire to his country home at the Falls of Schuylkill without molestation.[142] Later he returned to educational administration both in Maryland and Pennsylvania.[143] The Anglican insti-

---

[140] Cheyney, *History of the University of Pennsylvania,* pp. 107–9.

[141] *A History of Columbia University* (New York, 1904), pp. 46–49; Nathan Schachner, *Alexander Hamilton* (New York, 1946), pp. 41–42. For a similar instance of persecution see E. Alfred Jones, "Two Professors of William and Mary College," *William and Mary College Quarterly,* Second Series, Vol. XXVI (April, 1918), pp. 221–31.

[142] Horace Wemyss Smith, *Life . . . of the Rev. William Smith,* Vol. I, Chap. XXXV.

[143] The only non-Anglican president who got into difficulties was Eleazar Wheelock

utions themselves not only lost their affiliation with the English church but narrowly escaped losing their private character as well. The reorganiration of William and Mary completed the victory of the Virginia laymen over the Anglican faculty. Both King's College and the College of Philadelphia underwent rather complex reorganizations which almost resulted in their having the legal status of state universities governed by combined boards of politicians and denominational representatives. Both drifted back, however, into their old private status.

Aside from the immediate effects of war, invasion, and inflation, and the temporary suspension of most of the colleges, the long-range effects of the Revolution upon higher education were far from favorable. The financial support which the colleges had had from private philanthropy in England was, of course, largely cut off both during and after the fighting. This was something that could be remedied at home; indeed the fact that sixteen institutions of higher education were chartered in America between the end of hostilities and the year 1795 suggests that the American states had resources enough to maintain and extend their system of higher education. Unfortunately they had already begun to scatter their resources. More serious than the financial loss was the fact that the close cultural ties with England, which had so long been a restraining hand on provincialism and sectarian bigotry, were now considerably loosened.[144] Possibly the benefits of this connection would have been lessened in any case after the reaction from the French Revolution began in England. At any rate, the political life of the American states themselves was troubled and often acrimonious from the end of the Revolution until the period of expansion that followed the War of 1812. Had there been a professoriat actively devoted to Republican principles, it is hardly likely that it would have survived the period of the Alien and Sedition laws, during which the major colleges north of Virginia were all committed to Federalism, without yielding many casualties to political persecution.[145]

---

of Dartmouth, but in his case a false and malicious accusation of disloyalty to the revolutionary cause was investigated by local Committees of Safety that not only cleared him but recommended that his accuser give satisfaction for slander. Leon Burr Richardson, *History of Dartmouth College* (Hanover, N.H., 1932), I, 159–62.

[144] Anglo-American cultural relations are treated in detail by Michael Kraus, *The Atlantic Civilization: Eighteenth Century Origins* (Ithaca, N.Y., 1949).

[145] The case of Josiah Meigs is suggestive. Having joined the Yale faculty as Professor of Mathematics and Natural Philosophy under his friend, Ezra Stiles, he became an ardent Republican and found himself completely at odds with Stiles' successor, Timothy Dwight, under whom Yale was imbued with Connecticut Federalism. In order to escape being dropped from the college, he found it necessary at

Despite all the gains that had been made by the emergent academic profession at the close of the eighteenth century, the American colleges had not reached the point at which a professor or tutor could be politically active in ways that did not meet with the approval of his president or board of trustees.

---

one point to make a formal statement of his political beliefs, which was interpreted as a recantation. In his letter to the Yale Corporation he declared that if he were in truth such an "enemy to the constitution and liberties of my country" as he had been alleged to be, it would be the Corporation's duty indeed to throw him out. He was kept in his post in return for making a public statement of his real views, but some two years later, having found the life of an ardent Republican in a Federalist community unbearable, he resigned, and went to the new University of Georgia—"an exile," as his wife put it, "to the backwoods . . . only twelve miles from the Cherokee Indians." Meigs was not attached to his position as president at Georgia ("I long to see the civilized part of the United States once more," he wrote in 1806), and soon fell out with the trustees, whom he denounced as "a damned pack or band of tories and speculators." After his dismissal there, Jefferson gave him jobs as Surveyor General and then Commissioner of the General Land Office. See William M. Meigs, *Life of Josiah Meigs* (Philadelphia, 1887), esp. pp. 38–42, 51–54; Richard Purcell, *Connecticut in Transition* (Washington, 1918), pp. 301–2; Charles E. Cuningham, *Timothy Dwight* (New York, 1942), pp. 198–99; E. M. Coulter, *College Life in the Old South* (New York, 1928), pp. 23–26.

V: THE OLD-TIME COLLEGE
1800–1860

THE GREAT RETROGRESSION

During the last three or four decades of the eighteenth century the American colleges had achieved a notable degree of freedom, vitality, and public usefulness and seemed to have set their feet firmly on the path to further progress. The opening decades of the nineteenth century, however, brought a great retrogression in the state of American collegiate education, a decline in freedom and the capacity for growth that universally afflicted the newer institutions and in all but a few cases severely damaged the older ones. While advances had been made in curricula and teaching methods from 1730 to about 1800, the succeeding forty years, despite much educational unrest and considerable experimentation, could show only modest improvements in the best institutions, to be weighed against the inadequate and unprogressive system of collegiate education that was being fixed upon the country at large.[1]

Perhaps the root cause of the retrogression was the pervasive national reaction from the Enlightenment. But one of the primary factors in the backsliding of the collegiate system was that the sponsors of collegiate education, instead of developing further the substantial and altogether adequate number of institutions that existed in 1800, chose to establish new institutions far beyond the number demanded by the geography of the country. Although it was partly a consequence of the physical growth of the young republic and of its feverish local rivalries, this multiplying and scattering of colleges was primarily the result of denominational

[1] Francis Wayland, comparing the pulpit and the bar of the 1840s with those of the revolutionary generation, concluded that intellectual training had considerably deteriorated. *Thoughts on the Present Collegiate System in the United States* (Boston, 1842) pp. 79–80. He attributed this in large part to the severance of educational relations with England after the Revolution, which deprived the cultivated American world of Oxford and Cambridge teachers as well as laymen familiar with English standards. *Ibid.,* p. 78.

sponsorship and sectarian competition. The gains of the colonial colleges had depended in part upon their tendency to break free from the sectarian limitations that men like Thomas Clap would have imposed upon them and their impulse to move into the mainstream of intellectual life.[2] The most advanced educational thinkers of the late eighteenth and early nineteenth centuries hoped that the interdenominational pattern of the later colleges would presage the development of larger, well-financed institutions, basically secular in their mode of operation, where some advanced studies and allied professional education would be available. Instead, the intellectual and religious reaction fostered a host of little institutions in which doctrinal and sectarian considerations were rated above educational accomplishment. Where serious attempts were made to achieve the university ideal, notably in the "state universities" chartered in the South, these attempts were defeated by sectarian rivalries. Throughout the country educators who had carried into the nineteenth century the liberal habits of mind of the eighteenth—men like Samuel Stanhope Smith at Princeton, Asa Messer at Brown, and still later, Thomas Cooper at South Carolina—found themselves out of harmony with their new environment.

From the outset the severely denominational institutions neither aspired to nor pretended to foster academic freedom; and very commonly—although not universally—their teachers lived and worked placidly within this framework. In a certain sense the problem of academic freedom as it is understood in the modern university did not yet exist in these colleges, or existed only in a rudimentary form. This fact itself elicits a few further observations. Perhaps the most significant is that the general absence of what we consider academic freedom was associated in the old colleges with a lack of advanced work, with certain severe limitations upon the colleges' educational achievement and their public value. In this chapter we will attempt to show how really advanced university studies failed for a long period to develop in American education, and, further, that this failure occurred not simply because the old denominational colleges ex-

[2] For a short time, to be sure, toward the close of the century, deistic and rationalistic rebellion among undergraduates reached such a pitch that almost everyone familiar with the situation became alarmed. This, of course, was an ephemeral result of turbulent times and heady new ideas. But the reaction that followed it was far from ephemeral. On this aspect of college history see G. Adolph Koch, *Republican Religion* (New York, 1933), Chap. VIII; Vernon Stauffer, *New England and the Bavarian Illuminati* (New York, 1918), Chap. I; Herbert Morais, *Deism in Eighteenth Century America,* pp 159–63.

isted as an alternative to real universities, but because the same cultural conditions that fostered such colleges operated to stultify the efforts that were made to achieve all the conditions of true university work, including the necessary condition of freedom. The worst thing that can be said of the sponsors and promoters of the old colleges is not that they failed to foster sufficiently free teaching and research in their own colleges, but that when others attempted to found freer and more advanced institutions the denominational forces tried to cripple or destroy their work. In the contemporary American educational system the great universities and leading colleges call the tune, and even the smaller church-related institutions (the heirs of the old denominational colleges) very often share to some degree their ideals of academic freedom. In the denominational era, the small denominational colleges set the pattern, and even the would-be sponsors of universities were hamstrung by that circumstance.

When we speak of American colleges down to 1780 we are speaking only of nine institutions, which varied in size and fiscal strength but which had roughly comparable goals. When we look at the college system in 1799, we find that sixteen more institutions had been added. In this period of nineteen years the area of the country had also grown, however, and such regions as the South Atlantic states, the growing areas of Tennessee and upstate New York, hitherto lacking in such educational centers, had begun to be served. Thus there had been no more than a moderate extension of the earlier system. But when we total the number of colleges in 1830, we find, counting only those that were strong enough to survive, that another twenty-four had been added; and by 1861, it is clear, the situation had gotten completely out of hand, for there were by then an additional 133—a total of 182 *permanent* colleges had been founded throughout the country down to the eve of the Civil War.

This figure itself is enough to give one pause, but it is trifling as compared with the number of colleges founded in the same period that failed to survive. Donald G. Tewksbury has found records of 516 colleges that were established before the Civil War in sixteen states of the Republic, and of those 104, or only 19 percent, survived! [3] The further one looks into the West or South the worse this record becomes. Of 36 colleges founded in New York State, 15 survived. In Ohio it was 17 out of 43; in North Carolina, 7 out of 26; in Missouri, 8 out of 85; in Texas, only 2 out of 40.

[3] Tewksbury, *The Founding of American Colleges and Universities before the Civil War* (New York, 1932), p. 28.

Physically, the great continental settlement of the United States in the pre-Civil War era was carried out over the graves of pioneers; intellectually, over the bones of dead colleges.

The experiences and findings of Philip Lindsley, one of the best educators of the first half of the century, illustrate the process of diffusion and fragmentation that went on in American collegiate education. A graduate of Princeton (1804), Lindsley had preached for a time and served as tutor, professor, librarian, vice-president, and acting president of his alma mater. After declining several presidencies, he finally yielded to the call from Cumberland College, soon to be rechartered as the University of Nashville. It appears that he accepted chiefly because he was attracted by the educational needs and opportunities to be found in the lower Mississippi Valley. He was impressed, when he first went to Nashville in 1824, by the fact that in the immense valley of the lower Mississippi, which had at least a million inhabitants, there was not a single college.[4] But within less than twenty-five years thereafter he found that thirty small, competing institutions had been founded in a radius of 200 miles of Nashville and nine within a radius of 50 miles.[5] Colleges, he protested,

rise up like mushrooms on our luxuriant soil. They are duly lauded and puffed for a day; and then they sink to be heard of no more. . . . Our people, at first, oppose all distinctions whatever as odious and aristocratical; and then, presently, seek with avidity such as remain accessible. At first they denounce colleges; and then choose to have a college in every district or county, or for every sect and party—and to boast of a college education, and to sport with high sounding literary titles—as if these imparted sense or wisdom or knowledge.[6]

Only a few of these denominational schools were equal to good second-rate grammar schools, Lindsley charged, and he scorned their "capacious preparatory departments for A, B, C-*darians* and Hic, Haec, Hoc-*ers*—promising to work cheap; and to *finish off* and graduate, in double quick time." [7] Although Lindsley was able to accomplish a good deal in his years at Nashville, he was perpetually plagued by the competition of these fly-by-night colleges, as was every educator in the newer regions who attempted to maintain serious educational standards.

[4] John E. Pomfret, "Philip Lindsley," in Willard Thorp, ed., *The Lives of Eighteen from Princeton* (Princeton, 1946), pp. 163–64.

[5] Philip Lindsley, *Speech about Colleges Delivered in Nashville on Commencement Day, October 4, 1848* (Nashville, 1848), p. 13.

[6] Philip Lindsley, *Paragraphs . . . from a Baccalaureate Address . . .* (n.p., n.d. [1829]), pp. 17–18.

[7] Lindsley, *Speech about Colleges,* p. 14.

This fragmentation of higher education was devastating in its consequences both for the quality of academic work and the position of the professor, but it was an all but inevitable response to the conditions of American life. The area of the Union was, of course, extensive, and travel was uncomfortable and costly. No doubt a country such as the United States needed a certain geographic dispersion of its colleges and universities. But geography alone hardly accounts for the extreme diffusion and wastefulness of educational effort in the denominational era. Travel in Europe was difficult in the Middle Ages and early modern times, and yet when men were sufficiently moved by a hunger for knowledge they traveled hundreds of miles to sit at the feet of a great master—often, incidentally, bypassing a nearer and lesser university—and wandered from university to university when they thought it would help them. In the American milieu the expense and inconvenience of travel loomed larger in the minds of most parents and students than the quality of the education to be received. Some educators complained bitterly that Americans expected to come by their collegiate education far too cheaply.[8] The cost of traveling a considerable distance to college and back was often higher than the tuition fee. One student who came to Amherst in the 1820s from a distance of 300 miles spent $60 a year in transportation at a time when tuition ran about $25 a year in such colleges and a student could get a year's board for considerably less than $60.[9]

Other popular attitudes militated against concentrating the educational effort in a few colleges: there was the notion that it was better for a young man's morals that he be educated in a country college than reside in the city, and the feeling that the social atmosphere of some of the older colleges and the more recently chartered state "universities" was excessively aristocratic.

The two factors that were far more important than geography in determining that American education should be fragmented were denominational sponsorship of colleges and local pride. The multiplicity of colleges was a product of the multiplicity of Protestant sects compounded by the desire of local bodies, religious or civic, to promote all kinds of enterprises

---

[8] See Francis Wayland's complaint that despite all the charitable investment in public education, "we cannot induce men to pursue a collegiate course unless we offer it vastly below its cost, if we do not give it away altogether." *Thoughts on the Present Collegiate System,* p. 16. Cf. Albea Godbold, *The Church College of the Old South* (Durham, N.C., 1944), pp. 54–60.

[9] On travel and other expenses, see Clarence F. Birdseye, *Individual Training in Our Colleges* (New York, 1907), Chap. IX.

that gratified local pride or boosted local real-estate values. Counting only those institutions that he classed as permanent, Tewksbury listed 49 institutions founded under Presbyterian auspices, 34 founded by the Methodists, 25 by the Baptists, 21 by the Congregationalists, 14 by the Roman Catholics, 11 by the Episcopalians, 6 by the Lutherans, and 20 by miscellaneous sects; there were as well 21 state institutions, 3 semi-state institutions, and 3 municipal ones.[10]

The denominations not only desired to educate their ministers locally and inexpensively, but wished to keep their co-sectarians in colleges of their own lest they be lured out of the fold. They entered, accordingly, into an intense rivalry to supply every locality with a cheap and indigenous institution that would make it possible for local boys who desired degrees to get them easily.[11] This denominational fervor was supplemented by civic loyalties, the measure of which can be taken by the pall of gloom that sometimes spread over a community at the news that its neighbor was about to become the seat of another country college.[12]

A fact that confronts every student of American educational history is that the American system of collegiate education was qualitatively almost as heterogeneous in the first half of the nineteenth century as it is today, and that the name "college" was given to a multitude of institutions ranging from those that respectably upheld the name of college to some that would not quite honor the title of high school. What was mischievous in all this was the competition that enabled the low-grade institutions, backed by the political strength of denominational sponsors, to offer "college" degrees.[13]

The great retrogression in education which we are considering did not occur only where this vast proliferation of third-rate and fourth-rate col-

[10] Tewksbury, *Founding of American Colleges and Universities,* p. 90; these figures do not allow for the occasional duplication or triplication of sponsorship, which the author has indicated.

[11] The factors in this rivalry are discussed by Tewksbury, *ibid.,* pp. 66–91.

[12] An attitude by no means confined to the West or South. When Amherst was chartered, a panic "seized the public mind and extended to the college" at Williamstown, in the words of its president. "The heavens were covered with blackness; and during the awful syncope that succeeded in vacation, we often looked up and inquired *'Is this death?'* " Leverett Wilson Spring, *A History of Williams College* (Boston, 1917), p. 128. The people of Williamstown had only recently extended themselves to raise over $18,000, a very substantial sum for such a town at the time, to keep Williams College from being moved to Northampton. *Ibid.,* p. 113.

[13] A number of institutions that took the more modest title of academy probably offered a sounder education than the weakest "colleges."

leges was most extreme. It occurred in varying degrees almost universally, although at different times. It tainted the older colleges as well as the new, the East as well as the West and South. It was in good part the outcome of the epidemic of revivals, the rise of fundamentalism, and the all but unchecked ragings of the denominational spirit. Along with revival meetings and a growing counterattack against skepticism came a concerted effort on the part of the Protestant churches to expand their influence and tighten their control over spiritual and intellectual life. New colleges were kept under tight supervision; old ones were infused with new piety. Theological seminaries were founded to train an abler and more combative ministry, and their work was kept free from the corrupting influences of ordinary undergraduate life.[14] Sunday schools, Bible societies, and missions were founded, and the influence of piety was brought into the newly settled regions of the West. The barbarism of the age was softened by humanitarian reforms espoused by the pious. Morals, too, were tightened: dancing, horse racing, card playing, and liquor were frowned upon, and the zealous energy of "temperance" was set in motion. Puritan earthiness and realism

[14] The early history of Andover Theological Seminary, established by Massachusetts Calvinists in 1808 to defend orthodoxy through scholarship, suggests, however, one of the dilemmas confronted by defenders of the Puritan tradition. Wherever orthodoxy wanted to further serious scholarship, it was compelled to make some concessions to the working needs of the scholars, for even under the best of circumstances serious scholarship and absolute rigidity of dogma were incompatible. The leading scholar at early Andover was the great Hebraist, Moses Stuart, who promptly fell under suspicion for his devoted interest in German biblical scholarship, which the trustees found in 1825, "has evidently tended to chill the ardor of piety, to impair belief in the fundamentals of revealed religion, and even to induce, for the time, an approach to universal skepticism." Daniel Day Williams, *The Andover Liberals* (New York, 1941), p. 17. What was poor Stuart to do? Could he maintain his hard-won eminence in this field without drinking deeply at the fountains of the most advanced scholarship of the time? Although formally orthodox enough, he seems to have concluded that he could not. The Seminary was and ought to be, he said, liberal in its mode of work. "We profess to shrink not from the most strenuous investigation. I am bold to say there is not a school of theology on earth, where a more free and unlimited investigation is indulged, nay, inculcated and practiced. The shelves of our library are loaded with books of Latitudinarians and Skeptics, which are read and studied. We have no apprehension that the truths which we believe are to suffer by such an investigation." Henry K. Rowe, *History of Andover Theological Seminary* (Newton, Mass., 1933), p. 19. Are we not getting close again to the "Averroistic" compromise? One attempts to secure a wide range of freedom for investigation by promising that if one is allowed to range through latitudinarian and skeptical scholarship, probing its arguments and ideas, one will always end with a formal commitment to the proper dogma. That is to say, one wins a certain freedom to philosophize in return for the guarantee that one will ultimately profess the right belief.

gave way to Victorian prudery, as throughout the country the little candles of the Enlightenment guttered or failed.[15] Between 1790 and 1830 the intellectual and moral temper of the country was drastically transformed.

An excellent illustration of the impact of the great retrogression upon enlightened scholarship in an older college is the later career of Samuel Stanhope Smith at Princeton. A graduate of Witherspoon's Princeton, the son-in-law and protégé of the Scottish educator, Smith tempered his piety with a certain amount of speculative boldness and independence of mind.[16] He had been a tutor and professor in the college, and in 1795, after Witherspoon's death, the trustees unanimously elected him to the presidency, an office whose duties he had in fact largely fulfilled for seven years. An outstanding personality, Smith had formulated educational policies that, as Professor Wertenbaker remarks, were far ahead of his time. Had he been given the same magisterial powers that the trustees had allowed his father-in-law, the progress Princeton had long been making might well have gone on. But the tide of trustee sentiment had turned and Smith was treated in a way that would have been unthinkable had he been Witherspoon. Not only did the trustees turn a deaf ear to most of Smith's proposals for improvement, but they began to assert their own powers of government obtrusively and in small matters as well as large. They had grown increasingly concerned with sectarian considerations, particularly with the fight against Episcopalianism. Some of the more eager watchdogs of orthodoxy among them became far more interested in establishing a Presbyterian theological seminary than in maintaining the college, which they anticipated could not be linked in harmony with the seminary and might actually be a rival.[17] A few of the trustees, notably Ashbel Green, became

[15] The religious reaction of the early nineteenth century is traced by Merle Curti, *The Growth of American Thought* (New York, 1943), Chap. VIII, and John A. Krout and Dixon Ryan Fox, *The Completion of Independence, 1790–1830* (New York, 1944), pp. 162–75. See also the penetrating comments by E. B. Greene, "A Puritan Counter-Reformation," *Proceedings of the American Antiquarian Society,* New Series, Vol. XLIII (1932), pp. 17–46, and Dixon Ryan Fox, "The Protestant Counter-Reformation in America," *New York History,* XVI (January, 1935), 19–35. For some illuminating comments on the state and influence of American religion in the 1830s see Alexis de Tocqueville, *Democracy in America* (New York, ed. 1912), I, 328–39; II, 488, 510–13.

[16] He had also a capacity for diplomacy that makes him appear sometimes to be two-faced. Compare his very enlightened letters to Jefferson on the relation of sectarianism to education (*The Papers of Thomas Jefferson,* Julian P. Boyd, ed., II [Princeton, 1950], 246–49, 252–55) with his later correspondence with Jedidiah Morse in the Princeton Library manuscript collections.

[17] As one of the leading trustees, Samuel Miller, put it, they wanted "to have the divinity-school uncontaminated by the college, to have its government unfettered,

impatient to get rid of the ill and aging president. Green, who was head pastor at the Second Presbyterian Church in Philadelphia, a figure of much influence in church politics and a leader in the movement for establishing the seminary, took the initiative in undermining Smith's authority. He set a tutor and some of the divinity students to informing on him, and the word was spread about that the President of Princeton had endorsed polygamy, recommended Arminian essays, expressed doubts about the efficacy of baptism, and inspired among the divinity students an open denial of the doctrine of total depravity.[18]

In spite of such molestations, Smith did manage to improve scientific instruction and restore the college after the disastrous fire that destroyed the college hall in 1802. But the usual differences with trustees over student discipline and the decline in enrollment finally led to drastic faculty retrenchment; and at the dawn of the second decade of the century Princeton stood about where it had been thirty years before. The resources of the Presbyterian church were thrown behind the newly founded theological seminary at Princeton, whose clerical trustees soon began to dominate the college. In 1812 the trustees, by suggesting that a vice-president was needed to run the college, succeeded in provoking Smith's resignation; they replaced him with Ashbel Green, who was far less equipped than he to solve Princeton's problems in the new milieu. The college continued to decline under Green and his successor, and might have had to close its doors altogether had it not been rescued by some of its alumni during the 1830s.[19] Thus the institution that had flourished under Witherspoon's direction during the full tide of the Enlightenment was nearly destroyed in the ebb of the great retrogression.

The early history of Dickinson College, another Presbyterian institution, founded in 1783 at Carlisle, indicates that any attempt to repeat Princeton's fortunate experience with Witherspoon was likely to be doomed. Benjamin Rush and the other early trustees made such an attempt

---

and its orthodoxy and purity perpetual"—for all of which a separate establishment seemed to them to be necessary. Samuel Miller, *The Life of Samuel Miller* (Philadelphia, 1869), I, 242; cf. pp. 192, 240–44.

[18] Thomas J. Wertenbaker, *Princeton, 1746–1896* (Princeton, 1946), Chap. IV, is most illuminating on Smith's presidency; cf. Samuel Holt Monk, "Samuel Stanhope Smith," in Thorp, *The Lives of Eighteen from Princeton,* pp. 86–110. For further light on the trustees of the period, see George Adams Boyd, *Elias Boudinot* (Princeton, 1952), and Gilbert Chinard, "A Landmark in American Intellectual History," *Princeton University Library Chronicle,* XIV (Winter, 1953), 55–71.

[19] Wertenbaker, *Princeton,* Chap. VII.

when they brought to Carlisle the Reverend Charles Nisbet, another learned Scot from whom they had no doubt similar expectations. Both Nisbet and the trustees were bitterly disappointed. Some of the reasons were purely personal, but the breach caused by the president's dislocation and his shock at first seeing an American college was made hopelessly wide by the continued interference of the trustees in Dickinson's affairs. Rush, who had plenty of excellent ideas that he was in no wise ready to try to put into practice—among them the belief in a great measure of faculty government [20]—was no less ready than some of the less celebrated trustees to condemn Nisbet; and it was long before the institution achieved any significance. One of the most remarkable episodes in the history of higher education occurred at Dickinson in the years 1799–1801 when, after the students' demand that the entire college course be completed in one year had been denied by the president, the trustees reversed his decision and permitted the travesty.[21] Maladministration by the trustees continued at Dickinson for many years. As late as 1815 the entire faculty resigned in protest, and the college was temporarily closed.

While it was being demonstrated in the opening decades of the nineteenth century that the Princeton tradition could neither be sustained in New Jersey nor reproduced in Pennsylvania, the rest of the colonial colleges were for the most part marking time or actually losing ground. The exceptions were Yale, which was laying the foundations of its scientific eminence under presidents Dwight and Day, and Harvard, which was beginning to achieve the literary stature which was so long to be the source of its reputation. William and Mary, which had never recovered from the removal of the capital from Williamsburg, was hit again by the creation of the University of Virginia, and sank to the level of the small country colleges. The University of Pennsylvania, never altogether prosperous, went through her lowest ebb during the years from 1791 to 1828, when the obtrusions of the trustees upon all facets of college life reached a point that "would have been incredible except for

[20] See his letter to the trustees, October 21, 1786, in *Letters of Benjamin Rush,* Lyman H. Butterfield, ed. (Princeton, 1951), I, 397. "When our professors cease to be qualified to share in the power of the College, it will be proper to dismiss them, for government and instruction are inseparably connected."

[21] Harry G. Good, *Benjamin Rush and His Services to American Education* (Berne, Ind., 1918), Chap. IV. On trustee interference and its consequences, see also James Henry Morgan, *Dickinson College* (Carlisle, Pa., 1933), pp. 131–44.

the testimony of the written records." [22] Until the 1820s Pennsylvania's graduating classes remained pitifully small. Columbia College was described by its trustees, in a petition to the New York legislature in 1814, as "an Object of Curiosity and Remark to Strangers . . . a Spectacle mortifying to its friends, humiliating to the City, and calculated to inspire opinions which it is impossible your enlightened body wish to countenance." [23] It was only in the 1840s that it ceased to present this pathetic aspect, and only in the post-Civil War period that the effects of the trustee changes of the late 1850s were sufficiently felt to lay the groundwork of its modern distinction in American education. Rutgers carried on in the state of half-existence that had characterized it almost from the beginning. In 1816 it was for the second time closed for lack of funds, and it did not reopen for nine years.[24] Brown under the presidency of Asa Messer, who served from 1802 to 1826, fared better than most of its sisters, but even there the president eventually ran into trouble with the trustees for his Unitarian opinions; after several years of harassment by his religious opponents in the community and the Corporation, he resigned.[25]

At Dartmouth, the last of the colonial colleges, there began a quarrel that was destined to have an important effect on the history of higher education in the United States. The school had been founded and maintained during its earliest days by the immense exertions of Eleazar Wheelock, and its presidency had been bequeathed by him to his son John. This singular dynastic procedure had aroused little comment or objection, and for some years the Wheelock autocracy continued unmolested by the trustees or the community precisely because the college itself was an institution of such little significance that no one who lacked the personal stake of the Wheelocks cared to contend for it. But by 1814 Dartmouth had become a thriving country college with a faculty of three professors and two tutors, a well-regarded little medical department, and students drawn from all the states of New England.[26] Toward

[22] Edward P. Cheyney, *History of the University of Pennsylvania* (Philadelphia, 1940), p. 178; see his Chap. V for a general account of this period.

[23] *A History of Columbia University, 1754–1904* (New York, 1904), p. 100.

[24] William H. S. Demarest, *A History of Rutgers College, 1766–1924* (New Brunswick, N.J., 1924), pp. 242–44, 277–78; as late as the 1840s the graduating classes usually had fewer than twenty students. *Ibid.*, p. 343.

[25] Walter C. Bronson, *The History of Brown University, 1764–1914* (Providence, R.I., 1914), pp. 186–92.

[26] Leon B. Richardson, *A History of Dartmouth College* (Hanover, N.H., 1932), Vol. I, Chap. V.

the closing years of John Wheelock's administration began a quarrel whose central issue was whether the college was to remain under the control of the Wheelock dynasty or to be governed by its trustees. Although there seem to have been no serious theological or political differences between Wheelock and the trustees, the conflict took on a political character because the president's cause was opportunely espoused by the local Democratic politicians while the Federalists generally stood by the trustees.[27] In 1816, the Democrats, who had captured the legislature, passed a law modifying the Dartmouth charter and changing the institution from a college to a "university." The college trustees refused to accept the change, and for more than a year both the old college and the new university functioned side by side in Hanover until the propriety of the legislation was finally passed upon by the Supreme Court in the famous Dartmouth College Case. The Court, of course, decided in favor of the college, and the university was disbanded. This decision, which occupies a celebrated place in the history of American constitutional law for its sweeping protection to corporations and encouragement to corporate business, was of comparable importance in the history of American higher education; it offered to the founders of private colleges the assurance that once they had obtained a charter from a state legislature they were secure in the future control of the institution.

Although the proliferation of small colleges was already well under way in 1819, the Dartmouth College decision provided a secure legal base for the host of private and denominational colleges that were about to emerge.[28]

As the American educational system expanded throughout the West and South, the most pervasive influence upon its character was the denominational affiliations of the small colleges and the struggle of these institutions and the churches that supported them against the larger nonsectarian or intersectarian "universities" or colleges that occasionally appeared. This struggle took on a somewhat different aspect in the

[27] *Ibid.*, Chap. VII; for the relation of the controversy to local politics, see William G. North, "The Political Background of the Dartmouth College Case," *New England Quarterly*, XVIII (June, 1945), 181–203.

[28] Tewksbury, *Founding of American Colleges and Universities*, pp. 64–66. The most valuable documentary source on the case is Timothy Farrar, *Report of the Case of the Trustees of Dartmouth College against William H. Woodward* (Portsmouth, N.H., 1819), which contains the opinions and arguments in both the Superior Court of New Hampshire and the Supreme Court. Of particular interest here is Daniel Webster's argument that college presidents and professors have freeholds in their offices. See pp. 269–72.

Southern states, especially those of the seaboard, than it did in the West. In the South several state universities were chartered at a time when the liberal thought of the Enlightenment was still widely current, especially among planter and merchant aristocrats, and when denominational colleges had not yet taken a foothold. There the story, as we shall later show, is one of persistent struggles between sectarian forces and the emerging church colleges on one side and the educationally more ambitious state institutions on the other. In the West the denominational colleges, except, notably, in Michigan, generally took root quickly and were often established by the time the state universities were chartered; and here the principal type of institution before the Civil War was represented by such private colleges as Illinois, Kenyon, Antioch, Knox, Beloit, Denison, Shurtleff, De Pauw, Wabash, and Lawrence. The dominant educational influences were those of the Presbyterians and Congregationalists, who, despite gestures toward union, did not always get along too well. Western educators carried with them preconceptions derived from such eastern schools as Yale, Princeton, Dartmouth, Union, Amherst, and Williams. Many of them also brought the Puritan temper which in the pre-Civil War period so often found its expression in reform agitations. Thus, while sectarian controversies and repressions were by no means absent from the Western colleges,[29] some of the most interesting academic controversies arose out of abolitionism. The implications of these will be treated later. But

---

[29] Among educators whose work was hampered by sectarian pressures was Horace Mann, president of Antioch College from 1852 to 1859. E. I. F. Williams, *Horace Mann: Educational Statesman* (New York, 1937), Chap. XV, and George A. Hubbell, *Horace Mann in Ohio* (New York, 1900), esp. pp. 48–50. Good accounts of sectarian influences upon Middle Western colleges are given in Frederick C. Waite, *Western Reserve University: The Hudson Era* (Cleveland, 1943), and Charles H. Rammelkamp, *Illinois College* (New Haven, 1928). Sectarian influences on the state university are discussed by Wilfred Shaw, *The University of Michigan* (New York, 1920), Chaps. III and IV; Andrew Ten Brook, *American State Universities* (Cincinnati, 1875), pp. 209–10, and Merle Curti and Vernon Carstensen, *The University of Wisconsin* (Madison, Wis., 1949), I, 87 ff. One of the more notable academic controversies in the region, however, was chiefly administrative —that aroused by the dismissal of President David Bates Douglass from Kenyon. See George Franklin Smythe, *Kenyon College: Its First Century* (New Haven, 1924), Chap. XIV; D. B. Douglass, *Statement of Facts and Circumstances . . .* (n.p., 1844), and *Further Statement of Facts and Circumstances . . .* (Albany, 1845); *Reply of Trustees of Kenyon College . . .* (Philadelphia, 1844). For controversies at a New England college involving the removal of an Episcopalian and a Universalist, see Richardson, *History of Dartmouth*, II, 446–52, and Benjamin Hale, *Valedictory Letter to the Trustees of Dartmouth College* (n.p., 1835); "Alumnus," *Professor Hale and Dartmouth College* (n.p., n.d.); *Remarks on a Pamphlet Entitled "Professor Hale and Dartmouth College"* (n.p., n.d.).

first it is necessary to look at the old college as a whole and attempt to understand some of the internal institutional factors bearing upon intellectual freedom.

THE OLD COLLEGE SYSTEM

"It is, sir, as I have said, a small college,—and yet there are those who love it," declaimed Webster in the bathetic peroration to his famous argument in the Dartmouth College Case. As the institutions of the world went, Dartmouth was no doubt a small college; but on the American educational scene it was a giant whose graduating classes had in recent years run close in size to those of Harvard and well above those of Yale. On the scale by which Dartmouth could be reckoned a small college there were none but small colleges in the United States, and there were to be none but small colleges for more than a generation to come. As late as 1839, if we may judge from the loosely gathered and poorly reported statistics of the period, the average college would be most closely represented by a school like Randolph-Macon, with its 98 students, the modal college by Kenyon and Waterville (later Colby), with their 55 students apiece; while Dartmouth, which had very promptly recovered from the ill effects of its litigation, was still second in size among undergraduate bodies, with 321 students.[30]

Size, of course, is not to be taken as the primary key to the quality of an educational institution. But there is such a thing as a college so excessively small as to be unable to afford adequate standards. Certainly, in the absence of a generous endowment, the faculty maintained by a college of 50 or 75 students could hardly be a distinguished one, nor could it be very lavishly maintained. Such a factor as size, which bears on the quality of the college education, also has much to do with problems of academic freedom and government; for these problems have an important relation to the growth of the faculty body. Larger faculties

[30] For figures on undergraduates, medical students, professors and other instructors, total graduates, and library volumes in 93 institutions in 1839 see *American Quarterly Register*, XIII (August, 1840), 110–16. At that time the leading ten colleges, each of which had over 150 undergraduates, were in this order: Yale, Dartmouth, Princeton, University of Virginia, Harvard, Union, Brown, Amherst, College of South Carolina, Bowdoin. Bacon College in Harrodsburg, Kentucky, claimed 203 students, which would put it in this group, but its claim to be a genuine college, even by the American standards of the time, is dubious.

tended to have more self-government and to be more self-assertive. Prospering colleges could defend freedom more readily than poverty-stricken ones shuddering at every gust of criticism that might cost them a few students or a handsome benefaction. Other things being equal, then, it was the larger and more prosperous institutions that had the greater power to protect dissent. Hence the small size and impoverished character of the American college is a major part of our story.

By 1839 some faculties had, to be sure, grown to a respectable size for the time. Harvard was most imposing, with twenty-one professors and two tutors, followed by Yale with sixteen professors and seven tutors, Dartmouth with an aggregate faculty of fifteen, and Transylvania, New York University, Hampden Sydney, Union, and Columbia, each of which had from ten to thirteen.[31] The representative faculties, again, were those of the smaller institutions: Randolph-Macon, say, with its six professors, or Waterville with five professors and one tutor, or Kenyon with six professors and one tutor. By and large the humble tutor was disappearing in favor of more permanent and august teachers labeled "professors" or occasionally "instructors."[32] In the country at large tutors were outnumbered by men in the other teaching categories by more than six to one, and the colonial conditions that had made faculty government impossible because of the youth and impermanence of teachers were gone.

To found a great many small colleges rather than to build up a modest number of larger ones meant to fill the country with precarious little institutions, denomination-ridden, poverty-stricken, keeping dubious educational standards, and offering little to teachers in freedom or financial rewards. The evidence is overwhelming that during the de-

[31] These figures include teachers in medical departments or other divisions who offered little or no instruction to regular undergraduates. Omitted are eight Catholic colleges which had a somewhat different way of reckoning faculty members, often counting "the novices and younger members of the Order . . . [as] professors and officers of the college." Francis Patrick Cassidy, *Catholic College Foundations and Development in the United States, 1677–1850* (Washington, 1924), p. 25. Teaching by priests with pastoral duties was supplemented by the work of lay faculty members. *Ibid.*, pp. 85–86. Thus a college like St. Mary's, with only 70 students in 1839, had 25 persons attached in some way to its instructional staff.

[32] Harvard began to recognize the justice of advancing tutors early in the regime of President Kirkland, when the principle was adopted that a tutor must be advanced to a college professorship, with increased compensation, after six years of satisfactory service. Josiah Quincy, *The History of Harvard University* (Cambridge, Mass., 1840), II, 354.

nominational era a great proportion of the schools in the United States that called themselves "colleges" were in fact not colleges at all, but glorified high schools or academies that presumed to offer degrees. As the president of the University of Georgia told his trustees in 1855, the American people were generally satisfied with the *name* of a college, and sought for their sons not so much an education as a degree.[33] Americans and Europeans alike who were familiar with the educational systems of the Continent and England tended to agree that "American colleges characteristically (not at their worst) were rather more like the German *Gymnasium,* the French *lycée,* or the English public school than like either the university or college of these countries.[34] It should be borne in mind, too, that the colleges were trying to handle student bodies with a considerably wider age range than the student bodies of our own time. Students were on occasion admitted into some institutions at the age of thirteen or fourteen, although the better institutions were successfully raising the compulsory age level for entering freshmen to sixteen.[35] Since it was not at all uncommon for men in their twenties to begin

[33] Alma Pauline Foerster, "The State University in the Old South," unpublished Ph.D. dissertation (Duke University, 1939), pp. 242–43.

[34] The evidence on this point is too voluminous to cite. See, however, *Journal of the Proceedings of a Convention of Literary and Scientific Gentlemen. . . . October, 1830* (New York, 1831), *passim.* In 1858 F. A. P. Barnard spoke of "the grade of the German gymnasium—which is precisely our grade of today," and an immigrant German professor declared, perhaps more accurately, "Our colleges, compared to the learned institutions of Germany, occupy a place between the gymnasia and universities, being generally similar to the three highest classes of the gymnasia and comprehending, also, some of the studies of the university." Richard J. Storr, "Academic Overture: The American Graduate School . . . ," unpublished Ph.D. dissertation (Harvard University, 1949), pp. 272, 304. Page references are to this version; a shorter version has been published as *The Beginnings of Graduate Education in America* (Chicago, 1953). Henry P. Tappan, *A Discourse . . . on the Occasion of His Inauguration . . . December 21st, 1852* (Detroit, 1853), p. 37. Schmidt, *The Old Time College President,* pp. 102–5, is illuminating on educational standards.

[35] Birdseye, *Individual Training in Our Colleges,* Chap. III; trends in the last half of the nineteenth century are discussed by W. Scott Thomas, "Changes in the Age of College Graduation," *Popular Science Monthly,* LXIII (June, 1903), 159–171. The factor of age explains much of the disciplinary problem. "They admit into college, children of 13 and 14 years," wrote Thomas Ruffin, Jr., to his father from Chapel Hill in 1843, "and the consequence is that they are compelled to reduce the standards of scholarship in order to get them through. The [student] Societies are a humbug for their members have not the sense, it cannot be expected that they should have at their age, to keep them straight, and there are some here really so young that they do not know how to take care of themselves." Quoted by Foerster, "The State University in the Old South," p. 262. Cf. John Fulton, *Memoirs of F. A. P. Barnard* (New York, 1890), pp. 163–64.

college in order to gain advancement in the professions, the colleges were dealing with a very large spread in the ages of undergraduates that added to the acuteness of their disciplinary problems.[36]

While the system of American higher education in effect in the pre-Civil War period offered studies of considerable variation in quality, the American college, in structure and government, was for the most part the same everywhere. Even those institutions that were called "universities," whether private or state, consisted, at the core, of a college, and often had no more than the core. It sufficed for the time that the founders were enamored of the name university, and therefore adopted it; or that they intended ultimately to establish a genuine one; or that there was appended to a college—this was the most frequent circumstance—a medical department. Occasionally there was also instruction in law, or there was an associated theological seminary; but most education for the law, ministry, and medicine was unfortunately dissociated from a genuine university structure and carried on either in separate schools (which for law and medicine were generally very poor and venal), or informally by individual practitioners.[37] Even the state universities were notably different from the huge organizations of the present day. American universities bore no resemblance to the great German universities that were beginning to inspire the admiration of almost all the great educational reformers. In some respects the American colleges resembled the English colleges from which they stemmed; but while the English colleges clustered at the great university centers, the American colleges were scattered.[38] Like the English university colleges, the American colleges aimed to be residential, an aim which they achieved wherever they

---

[36] See Wayland, *Thoughts on the Present Collegiate System* (Boston, 1842), p. 31; F. A. P. Barnard, *Letters on College Government* (New York, 1855), pp. 58–60. On the role of student discipline in academic government see below, Chap. VI.

[37] Wayland noted the existence, in addition to 101 colleges, of 39 theological seminaries, 10 law schools, and 31 medical schools. *Thoughts on the Present Collegiate System*, p. 8. For early medical education see Abraham Flexner, *Medical Education in the United States and Canada* (New York, 1910), Chap. I; for the law, Alfred Z. Reed, *Training for the Public Profession of Law* (New York, 1921), and Willard Hurst, *The Growth of American Law* (Boston, 1950), Chap. XII; for theology, Robert L. Kelly, *Theological Education in America* (New York, 1924), Chap. I.

[38] For some comparative comments by a student familiar with both Yale and Cambridge, see Charles A. Bristed, *Five Years in an English University* (New York, 1874), pp. 19–23, 445–515; see also the critical comments by Francis Bowen in *North American Review*, LXXV (July, 1852), 47–83, 75–80.

had the means for buildings. But they differed profoundly from the English colleges in their academic achievement, for they could expect much less from students in the way of secondary preparation and cultural background, and they were equipped to carry their students a much shorter part of the way toward profound knowledge or serious scholarship.[39] One of the most serious obstacles to university development in the United States was the fact that higher education had no organic relation to careers in civil service and diplomacy, as it had in England and some continental countries. Thus the spoils system and "democratic" rotation in office deprived American higher education of much of the potential importance of university work, while lax standards of professional training in medicine and law hurt it from another side.

The standard college curriculum was the program of classical-mathematical studies inherited from Renaissance education. To enter upon it at most institutions the student needed some minimal competence in Latin, Greek, and mathematics, requirements to which geography, history, English grammar and composition, algebra, and geometry were widely added during the decades from 1800 to 1870.[40] At college these attainments were supplemented by much further reading in standard Latin and Greek writers; mathematics up to plane and spherical trigonometry and analytical geometry; a smattering of mechanics, optics, and astronomy; some chemistry, botany, and biology (and geology if the college was fairly advanced and not overawed by the book of Genesis); and varying amounts of rhetoric, ethics, logic, metaphysics, political economy, history, and constitutional or legal lore.[41] Although the standard course took four years, it was not uncommon for the well-prepared academy student or a student who had been privately tutored to enter at a level above the freshman class.[42]

[39] Perhaps the crux of the difference rested here: "The Englishman's tardiness of development is in a great measure intentional. He is kept back to take a good start. He leaves [preparatory] school at the period of life when the American leaves College." Bristed, *Five Years in an English University*, p. 465.

[40] See Edwin C. Broome, *A Historical and Critical Discussion of College Entrance Requirements* (New York, 1902).

[41] On the curriculum see R. Freeman Butts, *The College Charts Its Course* (New York, 1939), and William T. Foster, *Administration of the College Curriculum* (Boston, 1911). For a brief contemporary characterization, see Wayland, *Thoughts on the Present Collegiate System*, pp. 32–42.

[42] Unfortunately the college too often repeated a large part of the work of a good academy, adding at first very little. Wayland, *Thoughts on the Present Collegiate System*, p. 108. Cf. Bristed, *Five Years in an English University*, p. 19: "During the first year I did little but read novels and attend debating societies. . . .

While there was much dissatisfaction with the old college curriculum among educators and many attempts at reform were made, it was not until the university era that the prescribed classical curriculum really broke down. Educational reformers argued that the common course of studies was too rigid, that a large measure of election should be introduced, that alternative scientific programs should be set up, and that the community demanded greater concessions to practical and vocational needs and less liberal education. While much of this argument was undoubtedly well advised, it seems also true that those social classes that commonly sent their sons to college were not as wholeheartedly attracted to experimentation as educational reformers implied, and that those who called upon the colleges to reform gave them inadequate support when they tried to do so. One of the most ardent and capable of the reformers, Francis Wayland of Brown, admitted as much in 1842 when he remarked that the colleges that had yielded to public demands by enlarging or altering their requirements had not been supported well enough to sustain the reforms: "And thus have we been taught that the public does not always know what it wants, and that it is not always wise to take it at its word." [43]

So much damage was done in later years to the cause of liberal education when the educational reformers finally got their way, threw out the prescribed curriculum, introduced the elective "system," and ultimately cluttered up undergraduate education with a mass of trivial "practical" courses, that the modern historian of education may in reaction be tempted to sentimentalize the old college and overestimate its value.[44] Since we have many strictures to make on the old college as a center of free thought or professional gratifications for its teachers, it is only just to say in passing that at or near its best it was very far indeed from a negligible agency of education. Men of considerable intellectual distinction came in reasonable numbers from its halls. It tried seriously to

---

This is the case with most boys who enter well prepared at a New England College; they go backwards rather than forwards the first year."

[43] Wayland, *Thoughts on the Present Collegiate System*, p. 13.

[44] For an account of some of the difficulties caused by the dissolution of the old curriculum see George W. Pierson, "The Elective System and the Difficulties of College Planning, 1870–1940," *Journal of General Education*, IV (April, 1950), 165–74. The faculty of Yale College, in their famous defense of the standard curriculum, understood one thing that was for long forgotten in American education: "There are many things important to be known, which are not taught in colleges, because they may be learned anywhere." *The American Journal of Science and Arts*, XV (1829), 308.

cultivate both the minds and the characters of its students. Its classical curriculum exposed them to great writers, great ideas, and fine expression. It encouraged articulate writing and thinking, and indicated that these abilities were to be put to work in civic as well as private affairs. It introduced its students to the problems of philosophy and theology. By inculcating serious application to mental, if not always intellectual, work, it does seem to have bred in its students a capacity for persistence and effort that modern education frequently fails to produce. It was not entirely lacking in inspiring teachers, who left a lifelong impress on their students. Perhaps most important of all, its student literary clubs and debating societies acquainted young men, who had perhaps had very little other contact with the life of the mind, with the fact that ideas and civic problems and literary values were proper objects around which men might associate. It rubbed the raw edges off many a country boy, taught him to write and talk and wonder, and sent him into life with advantages he could have found nowhere else.[45]

And yet when all these things have been said it must be added that the old college had grave failings as an instrument for the development of both students and teachers. Many contemporaries, in and out of the colleges, saw this. Many prescriptions for remedying the deficiencies of the old college were offered. Altogether too many of these stemmed from a persistent dissatisfaction with the prescribed classical curriculum. What was wrong with the curriculum, however, was not, as so commonly argued then and now, that it was a classical or a prescribed curriculum, for just such a curriculum had long contributed enormously to the rearing of the best minds in Western society. What was really wrong with the old college was that this curriculum was more often than not drably and unimaginatively taught. What was wrong was not that it still emphasized the classics so heavily—had not that great generation of superbly educated American leaders of the late eighteenth century been reared on the same classical writers?—but that it trained no good classi-

<hr>

[45] For some evaluations see Carl Becker, *Cornell University: Founders and the Founding* (Ithaca, N.Y., 1943), pp. 16–22; Walter P. Rogers, *Andrew D. White and the Modern University* (Ithaca, N.Y., 1942); Richard Hofstadter and C. DeWitt Hardy, *The Development and Scope of Higher Education in the United States* (New York, 1952), Chap. I and pp. 53–56; Schmidt, *The Old-Time College President*, pp. 146–49. The old college is defended by George F. Whicher in his preface to William Gardiner Hammond, *Remembrance of Amherst* (New York, 1946), pp. 1–18. There is an excellent account of contemporary dissatisfactions with the system in Storr, "Academic Overture," *passim.*

cists, that it reduced the study of classics to grammar and linguistics, that it usually failed to convey the spirit of the cultures of antiquity, that it often failed, indeed, even to teach very much Latin.[46]

Thus while the curriculum bore the brunt of the criticism, the great failure of the old college probably lay less in its course of studies than in its pedagogy and its pedagogues. The root of the matter was that most teaching was carried on by the recitation method—what one Harvard professor described as "the humble and simple, old-school, tedious business of recitation." [47] The job of the student was to address himself to a text, memorize it or master a translation, and reproduce it in class to the best of his ability, while the job of the instructor was to see that he got it right. While some advanced subjects were taught by lectures, and science courses at their best required some demonstrations, recitation was the true base of the old college's pedagogy, and this the students found tiresome and the faculty stultifying. The average teacher was closely bound to the text and had to spend the greater part of his time ascertaining whether the student had done his work. This left him no time to plan his own course, no incentive to add to his knowledge, for, as Wayland observed, "He already knows more than he has the opportunity to communicate." [48] This system dulled the minds of students and blunted the edge of faculty scholarship; and such well-educated students as the colleges turned out were usually triumphs of the human spirit over bad methods.

From the point of view of instructors, the lean monotony of the recita-

---

[46] Cf. Edward Everett in 1817: "It fills me with indignation that a person may pass through all our schools, academies and colleges, without being taught to speak a Latin sentence. . . . But our poor schoolmasters and preceptors and tutors are not to blame, they cannot teach what they never learned." Orie Long, *Literary Pioneers: Early American Explorers of European Culture* (Cambridge, 1935), p. 71. Cf. *Life, Letters, and Journals of George Ticknor* (Boston, 1877), I, 363.

[47] Storr, "Academic Overture," p. 6.

[48] Wayland, *Report to the Corporation of Brown University on Changes in the System of Collegiate Education* (Providence, 1850), p. 19. Cf. Wayland's *Thoughts on the Present Collegiate System*, pp. 84–86. Samuel Eliot Morison points to the case of the gifted Hellenist, Cornelius Conway Felton: "He was only a cog in the Quincy machine. He conducted recitations for at least twelve hours a week of the three upper classes, in alphabetical sections, and could not escape the requirement to hear and grade them on lessons from prescribed texts. It was not until the Class of 1852 entered College [Felton had then served for 23 years] that the Greek department had sufficient staff to permit Professor Felton to lecture once a week for half the year." *Three Centuries of Harvard* (Cambridge, Mass., 1936), p. 263. Cf. the experiences of Longfellow related in James Taft Hatfield, *New Light on Longfellow* (Boston, 1933), pp. 66, 82–83.

tion system was but one failing of a profession that was hardly professionalized. To become a college teacher required only a B.A. degree plus a modest amount of more advanced training, perhaps in theology. College teachers, although they might at the beginning of their careers earn slightly more than a fledgling in some other profession, soon lost ground by comparison. New England professors earned from $600 to $1,200 a year in the 1840s, but the former figure was more common in the country as a whole; on the eve of the Civil War salaries of $1,000 were more customary.[49] A good private instructor, not to speak of men in other professions, could earn a great deal more. Moreover, there was no system of rewards for competence; salaries were commonly inflexible, there was no system of raises, no hierarchy of promotion; once installed, the professor was treated much the same whether he was an eminent success or a substantial failure as a teacher.[50] Although a professor usually held office indefinitely on good behavior, his tenure depended upon usage and had no legal status: he could be fired at will by the governing board; in many institutions a hearing was not required.[51] Since there was no system of graduate education, no advanced work to look forward to, and no pecuniary reward for distinction in scholarship, the professor tended to settle into the groove of the recitation system and the policing of the students in which he was frequently required to join at much expenditure of time and energy and sometimes at the cost of humiliation.[52]

Those teachers whose energies led them to additional effort were tempted into literary work unconnected with their colleges or with schol-

[49] Although low in relation to some of the opportunities in business and the professions, this is not as low as it may seem. A highly skilled worker like a watchmaker or printer could earn a little over $600 a year in 1860 if he had a full year's employment. Thus the professor earning $1,000 a year in 1860 had a higher relative standing compared with a skilled worker than would the average professor today, when annual earnings in the two groups are about on a par. This, of course, does not apply to top professorial salaries today. Nor would it in 1860, when the highest salaries were about $2,000.

[50] It should also be noted that the dependence of the small college on tuition fees gave faculties a pecuniary ground for consenting to lower academic standards in order to entice more students.

[51] For the situation of the professor see Wayland, *Thoughts on the Present Collegiate System*, pp. 25, 26–27, 59, 62–76, 84–86, 136–37.

[52] Francis Lieber, one of the best-paid professors in the United States during his stay at South Carolina College, was once overheard to exclaim, after plunging over a pile of bricks on a nocturnal excursion after some aberrant students, "Mein Gott! All dis for two tousand dollars!" Frank Freidel, *Francis Lieber* (Baton Rouge, La., 1947), p. 140.

arship. But even had they been determined to carry out advanced work, the library of the typical college forbade it. When George Ticknor was at Göttingen in 1816 he noted with envy that while at Harvard there were twenty professors and fewer than 20,000 volumes, there were at the German university forty professors and more than 200,000 volumes. A taste of scholarly life under German conditions, Ticknor thought, would be enough to arouse the Cambridge professors to permanent discontent with their lot.[53] Such was the situation at Harvard, whose library was far better stocked than any other. By 1839, when Harvard had 50,000 volumes, there was only one other institution (Yale, with 27,000) that had more than half as many, and only sixteen that had more than 10,000 apiece. College libraries with as few as 1,000 volumes were by no means rare [54] at the time when Ticknor was building a personal library of 13,000 books.[55]

The absence of professional standards and rewards had its compensations from the standpoint of the individual teacher. Precisely because his profession required so little preparation beyond the B.A. degree and because it was so ill compensated both in money and in intellectual satisfactions, he was not as much attached or committed to it as is the modern teacher. If he was excessively troubled by his duties or by some administrative controversy, he could resign and go into some other walk of life more readily and easily than the modern professor. The transition to the law or the ministry was commonly not difficult, and business opportunities were many. An ex-professor might easily better his financial condition by opening a private academy.

In college teaching itself, moreover, new opportunities were multiplying in the expanding college system; and the antebellum college teacher, unlike his successor of today, did not face anything resembling a national code of political orthodoxy. One is impressed in reading over the histories of the early colleges by the readiness which which teachers and presidents at the smaller and less stable institutions turned in their resignations, accepting without apparent reluctance or anxiety the severance of a connection to which the modern professor will cling

[53] Orie Long, *Literary Pioneers*, p. 13. Cf. Wayland, *Thoughts on the Present Collegiate System*, p. 128: "The means do not exist among us for writing a book, which in Europe would be called learned, on almost any subject whatever." Cf. Godbold, *Church College of the Old South*, pp. 79–81, on libraries in small colleges.

[54] *American Quarterly Register*, XIII, 110–16.

[55] C. C. Jewett, "Statistics of American Libraries," in *Fourth Annual Report . . . of the Smithsonian Institution . . . during the Year 1849* (Washington, 1850).

desperately at the cost of many sacrifices.[56] However, these mitigating circumstances, which provided outlets for many spirited individuals, were unfortunate for the profession as a whole. The least enterprising and self-assertive, often the least able, members of an inferior faculty were those most likely to remain docile in their jobs under intolerable pressures. Any profession is in a bad way when its members can seek freedom most effectually by leaving it. The absence of mature professionalism contributed, as did denominationalism, fragmentation, and poverty, to the inadequacies of the old-time college. Professors suffered, but their students and the community often bore the greater share of the loss.

Changes, however, were beginning to take place in the management of the better colleges and in the status of scholarship. From the days of Ticknor's *Wanderjahre* and Jefferson's devotion to the projected University of Virginia, hardly a year went by in which some reform or experiment was not either proposed or quietly pushed forward. Many of these changes merely pointed to the debasement of liberal education by utilitarian studies that was to come in a later age. Others had genuine value for the students or the teachers.

Not the least of these changes was the slow transfer of college management from the hands of trustees through the presidents and into the faculty bodies. This process, which began in the larger and better institutions, seems indeed to have been closely related to the size of the faculties and the complexity of the colleges themselves. Trustees had long been in the habit of meeting either once a year (at commencement) or once a term.[57] Since this frequency was plainly insufficient for the

[56] Colleges were often chronically so near disaster that presidents or professors felt a moral obligation to resign when they became unpopular lest they bring upon their school its death blow. What is most interesting, in comparison with the attitude of the modern professoriat, is the absence of the feeling that their professional competence gave them any right to cling to their jobs. The general feeling seems to have been that strong criticism *obliged* them to resign. A man like Benjamin Hedrick was thought to be exceptionally willful and stubborn because he refused to resign his post at the University of North Carolina under pressure, and forced the trustees to fire him.

[57] On the role and function of trustees, see Wayland, *Thoughts on the Present Collegiate System,* pp. 43–62, 151–56. The history of academic government and of the transit of some governmental powers from trustees to faculties has never been written. It is for the most part ignored by Charles F. Thwing in his standard *History of Higher Education in America* (New York, 1906). The old college era is slighted in such studies as Samuel Katzin, "A Comparative Study of the Problem of Control

purposes of college management, the handling of details of policy was often delegated to committees of trustees, while individual members of boards on occasion exercised their right of visitation. Unfortunately this system seems often to have resulted in the settling of all but plenary powers upon committees composed of those trustees residing closest to the college—a principle of selection that might favor the most limited and provincial members and exclude the more sophisticated men of affairs. Thus the typical college was under the governance of a self-perpetuating board of absentee gentlemen, predominantly laymen but generally selected with an eye to their sectarian affiliations, who held their offices for life but were generally too busy to undertake the detailed management of the institution under their charge. Of necessity immense discretion had to be placed in the hands of the president, who was usually an ex-officio member of the board and by far its most important officer.

The situation of the president *vis-à-vis* his board and his faculty had somewhat changed since the days when faculties consisted predominantly of young tutors. In the colonial period it had not been too difficult for the strong president to overwhelm such a faculty—and even in the first half of the nineteenth century this doubtless remained the situation in the smallest colleges. But it was not in the larger ones. It was one thing for a president to sit down with one or two professors and a few tutors, and quite another to meet with a body of from six to ten or more professors, many of whom were men of some distinction and all of whom were likely to be approximately his peers in age and scholarship. As presidents came on occasion to be drawn from the ranks of the faculties rather than the ministry, they entered their offices with greater knowledge of the professors' problems. From being the spokesman of the board to the faculty, the president tended to become more the intermediary between the board and the faculty, obliged to find a substan-

---

in the Administration of Higher Education in the United States and Europe," unpublished Ph.D. dissertation (New York University, 1931), and Omer Stewart Williams, "Democracy in Educational Administration," unpublished doctoral dissertation (Northwestern University, 1940). See, however, W. H. Cowley, "The Government and Administration of American Higher Education: Whence and Whither?" *Journal of the American Association of Collegiate Registrars,* XXII (July, 1947), 477–91; George Bogert, "Historical Survey of Faculty Participation in University Government in the United States," in John D. Russell, *Emergent Responsibilities in Higher Education* (Chicago, 1946), pp. 107–18.

tial measure of harmony in both bodies in order best to carry out his work.[58] More and more, in the better institutions, the will of the faculty was something that had to be taken into account.

The history of the first beginnings of faculty participation in governing decisions has not yet been written. Since the early eighteenth century Harvard has had, in addition to the Corporation and the Overseers, a third body commonly called the "Immediate Government." This is, actually, the faculty sitting as a body to exercise those discretionary powers that were left to it by the Corporation.[59] How large and important the role of that body was before 1810 is doubtful; but under the presidency of John Thornton Kirkland (1810–28) the government of the College was left substantially in the president's hands and he showed an increasing reliance on his growing faculty. In the years 1823–25 an attempt was made by some spirited members of the faculty to revive the claim that the teachers alone were entitled to seats on the Corporation. Like Nicholas Sever's move more than a century before, this was doomed to failure, but it stimulated a thorough review of the process of college government. Although this movement was probably the most self-assertive act undertaken by any college faculty in the period, it was not based upon a desire to challenge the general powers of an absentee governing board. Indeed, the resident instructors, who had become irritated by some of the intrusions of the Corporation, were simply objecting to the presence of such a third body standing between themselves and the Overseers, and they strategically suggested that the Corporation, in addition to usurping functions that were properly their own,

[58] See John G. Palfrey's estimate of the president-faculty relationship in 1840: "The relation of the head of a college to the immediate associates of his cares is not without its delicacy. They are his equals, yet his inferiors; his inferiors, as sustaining individually a less share in the common responsibility, and subject in some respects to his supervision; his equals, as called by the public voice to be connected with him in the administration of a great public interest, as belonging to the same rank in society, and as his fellow-citizens of the commonwealth of letters. If they have a right to be where they are, they have a right to be treated with consideration and respect; and such undoubtedly needs to be the spirit of the intercourse maintained with them, if it concerns the public that their places should not cease to be attractive to such men as the public service requires." *A Discourse on the Life and Character of the Reverend John Thornton Kirkland* (Cambridge, Mass., 1840), p. 29. Cf. Andrews Norton, *Remarks on a Report of a Committee of the Overseers of Harvard College . . . Read May 4, 1824* (Cambridge, Mass., 1824), pp. 6–7.

[59] As early as 1708 there is evidence that the faculty of Harvard College acted on occasion as a body separate from the Corporation. In 1725 it began to keep records of its proceedings. Quincy, *History of Harvard*, I, 278–79, 391.

had also usurped the proper prerogatives of the Overseers.[60] Since the Corporation, however, was the dynamic agent in University government, its control by the faculty would have made a signal difference in the control of Harvard. In the light of the all but inevitable failure of the faculty claim, its true significance lies in the degree of self-consciousness on the part of the faculty that it showed, and the confidence with which it asserted the value of a large measure of self-government.[61] To collect as large and as able a faculty as that of Harvard in the 1820s was to invite faculty challenges to the inherited dominance of the colleges by nonresidents.

More influential than events at Harvard in American college government as a whole was the transition toward faculty participation at Yale under the regime of Jeremiah Day (1817–46). Coming to the presidency with many years of professorial experience behind him, Day adopted the practice of discussing and deciding all questions connected with college policy in a meeting of the assembled faculty. By the end of his regime a strong precedent had been established that even the Corporation should not take action without the recommendation or assent of the instructors. The principle that a new professor or other officer connected with instruction should not be appointed without the consent of his future colleagues seems to have been observed with particular scrupulousness.[62]

[60] Cf. Professor Andrews Norton in his *Speech Delivered before the Overseers of Harvard College . . . February 3, 1825* (Boston, 1825), p. xxi, and *Memorial to the . . . Overseers of Harvard* (Cambridge, Mass., 1824), presented by the members of the faculty, p. 20. For an account of the controversy, see Quincy, *History of Harvard*, II, 338–53. See also Edward Everett, *A Letter to John Lowell* (Boston, 1824); *Report of a Committee of the Overseers of Harvard College on the Memorial of the Resident Instructors* (n.p., 1825); [Andrews Norton], *Remarks on a Report of a Committee of the Overseers of Harvard College . . . Read May 4, 1824* (Cambridge, Mass., 1824); George Ticknor, *Remarks on Changes Lately Proposed or Adopted in Harvard University* (n.p., 1825); *Remarks on a Pamphlet Printed by the Professors and Tutors of Harvard University . . . by an Alumnus of That College* (Boston, 1824); *Further Remarks on the Memorial of the Officers of Harvard College by an Alumnus of That College* (Boston, 1824).

[61] Cf. Professor Norton: "Every one would be struck with the absurdity of entrusting the concerns of a mercantile body to those who were not merchants, or of an agricultural society to those who were not agriculturists; and the absurdity would be greatly enhanced, if the gentlemen who received the trust were, at the same time, so separated from the establishment which it was their business to govern, as to render it impossible for them to acquire any practical knowledge of its concerns." *Speech . . . February 3, 1825*, p. 22.

[62] William L. Kingsley, ed., *Yale College: A Sketch of Its History* (New York, 1879), I, 126–27; cf. George W. Pierson, *Yale College*, Chap. VII. On the early recognition of tutors as a part of faculty government at Yale, see Fulton, *F. A. P. Barnard*, pp. 65–66.

By 1830, at least the better Eastern colleges were following the practice of having new faculty members chosen upon the recommendation of the faculties.[63] In a great many places, however, this prerogative was still exercised by the president alone.

In 1837 the Reverend Jasper Adams, an Episcopalian who was at the time chaplain and professor of geography, history, and ethics at the military academy at West Point, and who had been for more than ten years an extremely successful president at Charleston College, delivered a lecture at Worcester which stated very effectively the more advanced thinking among academic administrators of the period. Although Adams pointed out that the legal status of faculty-trustee relations was an altogether cloudy one, he had a clear theory of his own as to what these legal and moral relations should be. Faculties were like quasi-corporations, grafted on the essential corporate bodies composed of trustees; they were, in any coherent conception of the nature of a college, the administrative body of such an entity, just as the trustees were its legislative body.[64] The purpose of a college, he said, was not simply to be incorporated, but rather to be incorporated in order that it might gather together a learned faculty and offer instruction. Since the assembling of the faculty was the end in view, to make the faculty subordinate to the trustees was "to reverse the usual order of things, to subvert first principles, to exalt the means above the end, instead of making them subordinate to the accomplishment of the end." [65] In the public mind the

[63] *Journal of the Proceedings of a Convention of Literary and Scientific Gentlemen,* pp. 79–86. Cf. Wayland in 1842: "But it may be asked, . . . how are appointments made. . . . Generally, I believe, upon the recommendation of the faculty. . . . Inasmuch as the Board to which this duty specially appertains, is unable to devote to it the attention which its importance usually demands, they [i.e., the faculty] are commonly obliged to perform an office which does not properly [i.e., legally] belong to them. . . . Thus they really nominate and the corporation appoint. But since where there is a good understanding between the parties, their nomination is almost always confirmed, they may be considered as in fact filling their own vacancies, and making their own appointments." *Thoughts on the Present Collegiate System,* p. 66. Wayland, it should be remarked, was most familiar with the better institutions, and even in these he had observed some sad violations of this practice. *Ibid.,* p. 67. On problems involved in faculty appointments, see pp. 67–75.

[64] Jasper Adams, "On the Relation Subsisting between the Board of Trustees and Faculty of a University," *American Institute of Instruction, Lectures . . . at Worcester, Mass., August, 1837* (Boston, 1838), pp. 144–46. Cf. Henry Davis, *A Narrative of the Embarrassment and Decline of Hamilton College* (n.p., 1832). For a later protest against the power of trustees see J. F. Jackson "American Scholarship," *The Knickerbocker,* XXVIII (July, 1846), 9–10.

[65] Adams, "On the Relation . . . between the Board of Trustees and Faculty," p. 147.

faculties inevitably got the credit or blame for the success or failure of instruction and discipline; hence they must be permitted to select their own means, agents, and associates, if they were not to be charged with responsibility without power.[66] Trustees should therefore not attempt to direct the instruction and discipline of the college.[67] The relation of the faculty member to the trustees, said Adams, is not that of a workman to his employer; it is rather like that of the lawyer to his client or the minister to his congregation—a relation in which the person retained has certain special skills, experiences, and qualities that put him in a position to advise and in a sense to direct the man who retains him.[68]

Generalizing from the experience of American colleges, Adams pointed out that "no college in this country has permanently flourished, in which the trustees have not been willing to concede to the faculty, the rank, dignity, honor, and influence, which belong essentially to their station." Contrariwise, "those colleges have been most flourishing, in which the instruction and discipline have been most exclusively committed to their faculties." The historical instances of obtrusive trustee interference in college management were all instances of failure.[69] Adams concluded by suggesting a functional allocation of powers: to the trustees should go the right of original organization under the college charter, the original choice of the faculty, the right of removal "for just and adequate cause," the right of managing institutional funds, and the duty of acting as the patrons and protectors of the faculty; to the faculty should go the determination of the course of study, including the choice of textbooks, and the right to decide all internal matters of instruction, discipline, and administration.[70] Perhaps the most impressive of Adams' remarks were his historical generalizations. His legal and moral observations were persuasively put, and in pointing out that those who expected to found colleges of repute that would survive and flourish must expect

---

[66] Cf. also Andrews Norton, *Speech . . . February 3, 1825,* p. iii.

[67] Adams, "On the Relation . . . between the Board of Trustees and Faculty," pp. 147–48.

[68] *Ibid.,* pp. 148–49.

[69] *Ibid.,* pp. 150–51. Cf. Norton, *Speech . . . February 3, 1825,* p. 13: "Every literary institution among us, other things being equal, has flourished in proportion as the government of it . . . has been virtually intrusted to the resident instructors." Trustees on occasion contributed in important ways to the management and reformation of colleges. The important point here is that they invariably failed when they tried to make themselves responsible for details of discipline and education.

[70] *Ibid.,* pp. 155–58. For a successful appeal by a president for enlarged faculty powers, see Fulton, *F. A. P. Barnard,* p. 204–5.

to delegate large powers to their faculties or fail, he was simply generalizing the whole experience of American academic life. For the main historical reason for the emergence of delegated faculty government within the framework of the plenary legal powers of the trustees was that complete trustee government had universally failed, while a division of powers among trustees, president, and faculty had in many cases conspicuously succeeded.[71]

PRESBYTERIANS AND PARTISANS

By the end of the eighteenth century and the beginning of the nineteenth the idea of freedom for the college or university scholar had received a rough formulation deriving from the ideals of toleration and religious liberty and the intellectual liberalism of the Enlightenment. In the first decades of the new century, as we have seen, there were beginning to appear institutional changes that laid the primitive basis for the development of academic freedom. The idea of freedom had won acceptance among at least a limited portion of the enlightened lay public, and it had also aroused enemies. Hence in the era of the old college we find something that had been absent before: a more or less continuous struggle, flaring up now in one place, now in another, for a freer atmosphere in education.

There can be found no better illustration of the extent to which the ideal of freedom had evolved among enlightened laymen than in the educational theory and practice of Thomas Jefferson; and no more helpful clues are available to its limitations, both in thought and in the American realities, than Jefferson's own compromises with the ideal and the difficulties he encountered in trying to realize that ideal at the University of Virginia.

Jefferson wanted to be remembered chiefly for three among his many achievements, each associated with the history of liberty: the Declaration of Independence, the Virginia Statute for Religious Freedom, and his work in the establishment of the University of Virginia. This institution,

[71] It should be noted also that stagnation and episodes of maladministration could bring about faculty rebellions. See, e.g., Samuel Eliot Morison, "The Great Rebellion in Harvard College, and the Resignation of President Kirkland," *Publications of the Colonial Society of Massachusetts*, XXVII (1932), 54–112; Theodore F. Jones, ed., *New York University* (New York, 1933), pp. 45–52; E. M. Coulter, *College Life in the Old South* (New York, 1928), pp. 254–63. For additional factors bearing on academic government see below, Chap. VI.

which he once referred to as "the hobby of my old age," [72] would be based, he said, "on the illimitable freedom of the human mind. For here we are not afraid to follow truth wherever it may lead, nor to tolerate any error so long as reason is left free to combat it." [73] This university, for which Jefferson worked so many years before it was finally opened in 1825, was to represent the realization of those reforms he had failed to effect at his own college, William and Mary, in 1779. It was to embody his faith in education, his taste in architecture, his love of science, his tolerant and unsectarian views, his political liberality. It was also to pioneer in the spread of the university idea in this land of colleges. Most of the changes which were to sweep over American education almost two generations after Jefferson's death were clearly foreshadowed in his plans for the university of his native state. There were to be eight schools altogether, including schools of law and medicine. The best available professors were to be secured, and they were to be sought abroad as well as at home, at whatever risk of criticism from provincials and chauvinists. They were to be paid ample salaries. They were to give lectures, not merely preside over recitations. The students, who (with a few exceptions) would not be allowed to enter until the age of sixteen, would be somewhat more mature than those at most American colleges, and they would not be bound by the prescribed curriculum: they were to choose among schools and select their own course of studies.[74] They would be governed by disciplinary rules more generous than those then in fashion, and they would exercise a distinct measure of self-government. Professors would have relatively secure, although not absolute, tenure. Moreover, there would be democracy within the faculty: an inoffensive rotating chairmanship would replace the customary university presidency, after the fashion of the rotation of the rectors in the German universities.[75]

[72] *Writings* (P. L. Ford, ed., New York, 1892–99), X, 174.

[73] *Writings* (H. A. Washington, ed., Washington, 1853–54), VII, 196. Cf. *Writings,* Ford, ed., X, 174: ". . . the illimitable freedom of the human mind to explore and to expose every subject susceptible of its contemplation."

[74] Although Jefferson was one of the curricular reformers who not only advocated an elective system but also encouraged a certain amount of utilitarianism in the curriculum, he did not belong to the barbarian wing of educational reform; he assigned to the classics a central role in a liberal education. Philip A. Bruce, *History of the University of Virginia* (New York, 1920), I, 54; see pp. 1–44 for Jefferson's views and their impress on the University. Cf. Roy Honeywell, *The Educational Work of Thomas Jefferson* (Cambridge, Mass., 1931), and Orie Long, *Thomas Jefferson and George Ticknor: A Chapter in American Scholarship* (Williamstown, Mass., 1933).

[75] Honeywell, *Educational Work of Thomas Jefferson,* pp. 99–100. Professors

Like William Livingston, Jefferson proposed above all to avoid the blighting influence of sectarianism by having no school or professorship of divinity, an omission which brought down upon him the expected accusations from sectarians and old political foes. To his mind the primary function of a university was not to engender piety but to foster knowledge in all its branches; and while knowledge of religion and theology, as knowledge in an historical and philosophical sphere of inquiry, was important, he hoped to escape the traps of sectarian antagonism by committing the university to no sect while respecting all. An early recruit to the faculty was advised that he and his colleagues would be expected to stay clear of sectarian doctrines.[76] Jefferson hoped to appease the sects by inviting them to establish their own separate little schools and professors in the vicinity of the university, offering their students the opportunity to attend its lectures and share its facilities. "And by bringing the sects together, and mixing them with the mass of other students, we shall soften their asperities, liberalize and neutralize their prejudices, and make the general religion a religion of peace, reason and morality." [77] The sects, however, were implacable. Not until the eve of the Civil War did one of them consider responding to this suggestion. In the interim they were often active in their hostility, and as Jefferson wrote in 1820, the serious enemies of the university were "the priests of the different religious sects, to whose spells on the human mind its improvement is ominous. . . . The Presbyterian clergy are the loudest; the most intolerant of all sects, the most tyrannical and ambitious. . . . They pant to reestablish by law the holy inquisition which they can now only infuse into public opinion." [78]

In one important respect Jefferson's philosophy of academic liberty was deficient and inconsistent: for all his fine and deeply felt rhetoric about

---

were to be removable only for cause and upon a vote of two thirds of the Visitors. Jefferson pointed out to one prospective appointee that the high character and liberal ideas of the Visitors amounted in effect to a guarantee of tenure. *Ibid.*, pp. 98–99.

[76] Francis Walker Gilmer, while searching for teachers abroad, told one: "Allay your fears . . . about religion. Far from requiring uniformity, we scrupulously avoid having clergymen of any sort connected with the University, not because we have no religion but because we have too many kinds. All that we shall require of each professor is that he shall say nothing about the doctrines which divide the sects." Bruce, *History of the University of Virginia*, I, 369.

[77] *Writings*, H. A. Washington, ed., VII, 267.

[78] Honeywell, *Educational Work of Thomas Jefferson*, p. 154. See Bruce, *History of the University of Virginia*, II, 361–80, for the post-Jeffersonian religious development of the university.

the illimitable freedom of the human mind he could not transcend the tendency, almost universal in his time, to subordinate intellectual freedom in some considerable measure to considerations of partisan politics. As early as 1800, observing with alarm "the general political disposition [i.e., Federalist] of those to whom is confided the education of the rising generation," he had consoled himself with the thought that the common sense of parents would remedy it and had doubted that any more drastic remedy was admissible.[79] This concern with the possible role of a higher education, monopolized by his political opponents, in indoctrinating students, grew with the years. By the time the University of Virginia was in the making he was actively concerned that Virginians were leaving their native state for schools like Princeton and Harvard where they might be expected, he thought, to imbibe the principles of Northerners on such issues as the Missouri question.[80] In the year of the university's opening he wrote to a fellow trustee that while they ought not to presume, like trustees elsewhere, to prescribe textbooks in the sciences, still there was one branch of knowledge "in which we are the best judges, in which heresies may be taught, of so interesting a character to our own State and to the United States, as to make it a duty in us to lay down the principles which are to be taught"—the field of government.[81] To James Madison he wrote in 1826 that "In the selection of our law professor we must be rigorously attentive to his political principles"; for he believed that while the Coke-Littleton tradition had made good Whigs, ardent for the liberties of Englishmen, the coming of Blackstone had made a generation of Tories. "If we are true and vigilant in our trust," he continued, "within a dozen or twenty years a majority of our own legislature will be from one school, and many disciples will have carried its doctrines home with them to their several states and will have leavened the whole mass." [82] Thus, in the sphere of politics in which his emotions were deeply engaged, Jefferson was as determined that the university should be an agent of ex parte indoctrination as his enemies, the Presbyterians, were in their sphere. Leaving all other subjects to the determination of the professors, he was bent on propagating principles of law and government that were consistent with the truth as it was understood by the enlightened Republican

[79] *Writings,* H. A. Washington, ed., VII, 455.
[80] *Ibid.,* VII, 202; cf. p. 204. Unlike many later Southerners, however, he would never have ruled out Northern professors. He was very eager to get Ticknor for literature and Bowditch for mathematics.
[81] *Ibid.,* VII, 397. [82] *Ibid.,* VII, 433.

Virginia gentry.[83] Had he been confronted with this inconsistency, he would doubtless have answered that his preference for Whig indoctrination was a preference for indoctrination in the principles of freedom itself, and hence not of a comparable order of stringency with the tenets of his foes. He might have said too—and correctly—that the fundamental bias of American collegiate education had long been so much in the hands of Federalists and sectarians that in tipping the balance the opposite way in one institution he was only redressing it. Nonetheless it is true that even Jefferson, the most enlightened lay educator of his time, had not thoroughly thought out the intensely perplexing problems of freedom in education; and that if he was remarkably libertarian in other areas he was in politics still an unwitting exponent of the kind of partisanship in education that, practiced by the Federalists, had impelled the Jeffersonian Meigs to leave both Yale and the University of Georgia.

To explain why so many of Jefferson's high hopes for his university were not fulfilled would be to explore at length the entire cultural milieu in which it was founded.[84] But there were three primary obstacles to a free and flourishing system of higher education in the ante-bellum era that revealed themselves in the early story of the University of Virginia. One, the incubus of slavery and sectional antagonism, which was vaguely foreshadowed by Jefferson's anxiety about the Northern education of Virginians, we will account for later. It remains here to explore the consequences of the other two, the sectarian animus, particularly with regard to the leading role of the Presbyterians, and the blighting effects of acts proceeding from civic and political motives of a far more urgent and demanding sort than the political partisanship Jefferson exhibited.[85]

In social terms the struggle over intellectual freedom during the early decades of the nineteenth century was one between the liberal gentry,

[83] Bruce, *History of the University of Virginia,* I, 327–29. See also Gordon E. Baker, "Thomas Jefferson on Academic Freedom," *Bulletin,* AAUP, XXXIX (Autumn, 1953), 377–87.

[84] The legislature never supported the university with the generosity which would have been necessary if many plans were to have been realized. Blighted by poverty only slightly less acute than many of its sisters', the university secured a faculty which was able, but not of that "first grade of science" Jefferson had hoped for. The rotating chairmanship proved onerous to many of the professors and had to be given up after twenty years. While control of students was perhaps a little more lenient than in many institutions, this did not eliminate the usual student disorders, and the university enjoyed the dubious distinction of having a faculty member murdered by an undergraduate during a riot.

[85] For further comment on the way in which denominational considerations entered into the college system, see below, Chap. VI.

generally representing in the South and West the principles of Jeffersonianism and the waning afterglow of the Enlightenment, and the ardently sectarian clergy, whose appeal reached wider but often less influential strata of the population. The hope of the liberals usually rested in institutions fostered by state legislatures and established upon a broad base of public responsibility, while the sectarians placed theirs in small denominational colleges.[86] In the South and Southwest, the liberals attempted to capitalize upon the fact that the state institutions were chartered before a system of private colleges had taken root. Such institutions as the University of Georgia (chartered 1785), the University of North Carolina (1789), the University of Tennessee (chartered as Blount College, 1794), and the South Carolina College (1801), later the University of South Carolina, were launched before the tide of Enlightenment thought had receded and in advance of the establishment of the denominational schools, while even Jefferson's University of Virginia, chartered in 1819, was not too late to benefit by the guidance of the declining generation of liberal aristocrats.

In promoting public institutions, most of the liberal educationalists seem to have been moved by no desire to promote an aggressive secularism or skepticism, but simply by a desire to advance the cause of higher education without getting ensnared in sectarian controversy. This was a goal easier to aim at than to achieve, and in the long run none of the state institutions maintained a secular atmosphere. Until the post-Civil War period not one of them grew to true university stature. While the sectarians were not strong enough to prevent such institutions from being founded and maintained, they did help to keep them from flourishing. Probably more important to the cause of freedom than all the individual cases of interference was the fact that sectarianism checked the growth of those internal institutional factors in the colleges that make for free and advanced scholarship.

It was a difficult path that the sponsors of nonsectarian education had to tread. To be neutral among the various sects was to keep clergymen of zealous denominational commitments out of professorships and presidencies, to forswear the teaching of divinity, and to avoid compulsory religious exercises with sectarian content—all of which left the institution

[86] For an excellent account of the state university idea see Curti and Carstensen, *The University of Wisconsin,* Vol. I, Chap. I; for the eighteenth-century background, Allen O. Hansen, *Liberalism and American Education in the Eighteenth Century* (New York, 1926).

vulnerable to charges of godlessness. To mollify one religious group by appointing clerical professors or a clerical president from its ranks was to heighten the competitive animosity of the others.[87]

Of all the churches, the Presbyterians were by far the most vigilant and censorious, as men like Jefferson, Thomas Cooper, Horace Holley, and Francis Lieber painfully learned. The history of collegiate education in the South and West is in a large measure the history of struggles in which that church played a central part.[88] This is not to say that there were no liberal Presbyterian educators in the Witherspoon tradition,[89] nor is it to say that the record of the Presbyterians was unambiguous, for they nourished education with one hand while throttling it with the other. But their vigorous role in sectarian controversies was a matter of common observation by contemporaries. The Episcopalians and Unitarians, who tended to be aristocratic and latitudinarian, drew fire from the Presbyterians on both counts. The Methodists and Baptists, although in most places far more numerous than the Presbyterians, were not nearly as interested or competent in the educational sphere.[90] The Presbyterians possessed an ardent concern for dogma, a rigorous spirit, a consistent interest in education, and a tight system of church organization. Their members were solid citizens of the middle and upper-middle classes whose place in the social structure enabled them to wield political influence far out of proportion to their numbers.[91] To staff a college in the South almost in-

[87] For the struggle between state universities and denominational colleges see Foerster, "The State University in the Old South," Chap. IV; Godbold, *Church College of the Old South,* Chap. V; Luther L. Gobbel, *Church-State Relationships in Education in North Carolina since 1776* (Durham, N.C., 1938).

[88] Jefferson concluded that the planners of his University of Virginia could get along with the Methodists, Baptists, and Anglicans of the Old Dominion, but that the Presbyterians were "violent, ambitious of power, intolerant in politics as in religion and want nothing but license from the laws to kindle again the fires of their leader John Knox." Foerster, "The State University in the Old South," pp. 221–22. C. Harve Geiger, *The Program of Higher Education of the Presbyterian Church in the United States of America* (Cedar Rapids, Iowa, 1940), treats informatively but indulgently of the Presbyterian record.

[89] For the effects of this tradition see Donald R. Come, "The Influence of Princeton on Higher Education in the South before 1825," *William and Mary Quarterly,* Second Series, Vol. II (October, 1945), pp. 359–96.

[90] The dogmatism of Presbyterians was hardly more imposing as an obstacle to educational development than the anti-intellectualism and educational indifference common among Baptists and Methodists in the ruder communities of the West. See Curti, *The Growth of American Thought,* pp. 268–70.

[91] On the social recruitment of the churches see H. Richard Niebuhr, *The Social Sources of Denominationalism* (New York, 1929). Such differences were embodied

evitably meant to turn to the Presbyterians for professors and presidents; but it was a fortunate institution that did not find them on occasion too vigilant in matters of doctrine or too provocative to the other sects.

A problem second only to the intrusions and failings of sectarianism was the rising spirit of political partisanship and the social hostilities that raged in the United States from about 1820 to the Civil War. The development of the democratic spirit in the years before and during the Jackson administration had complex results. It was attended by a vogue of humanitarianism and reform as well as an assertive mood of equalitarianism. One of its great contributions to American life was to make available to broader masses of people a free public education at the grammar-school level. In the field of collegiate education its consequences were far less favorable. One of the dominant popular motives was the passion for equalizing opportunity, which manifested itself in the political sphere by the cry for general suffrage, rotation in office, and the "democratization" of many political forms, and in economic life by the attempt to destroy all kinds of monopolies and privileges.[92] Whatever the benefits of this movement in such areas, its consequences for professional and higher education tended to be deleterious because the hostility to privilege and caste, the desire for opportunity, became in these fields a disdain for authority and excellence and *expertise* of all kinds. The public mood encouraged informal training of lawyers, doctors, and, in the popular denominations, ministers. It became far easier than it had been in the more stratified society of the eighteenth century for a young man who began life without money or family to apprentice himself to a lawyer and "read law" in his office; for a future physician to take a brief course in a commercial private medical school unconnected with university or hospital, or to serve an apprenticeship to a practitioner; for a pious lad to qualify without theological training for the ministry in an evangelical sect. Not only professional schools but colleges could thus be by-passed.[93] And if the well-to-do still preferred to employ conventional educational methods out of a sense of status or respect for knowledge, they were vulnerable to the

---

in an amusing piece of Protestant folklore: "A Methodist is a Baptist who wears shoes; a Presbyterian is a Methodist who has been to college; an Episcopalian is a Presbyterian who lives off his investments."

[92] For an interpretation of this aspect of Jacksonian democracy see Richard Hofstadter, *The American Political Tradition* (New York, 1948), Chap. IV.

[93] See Hofstadter and Hardy, *Development and Scope of Higher Education*, pp. 71–73, 82–84.

charge of aristocratic leanings. Even within the colleges, Francis Wayland noted, the old practice of assigning academic rank to students at commencement had often been "dropped like a polluted thing" because administrators were "awed by the hoarse growl of popular discontent." [94]

The most formidable manifestation of popular democratic sentiment was the widespread idea that the state universities were agencies for the rich that simply served to perpetuate and aggravate class distinctions. In fact, the early state universities, unlike those of today, did not offer free tuition, and generally they were patronized chiefly by the sons of the wealthy. Again and again their development and support were opposed before the public, to the great delight of promoters of sectarian colleges, on the ground that they required the taxing of the poor to educate the children of the rich. The situation of the state university of Georgia (then called Franklin College) is illustrative: it was forever under the accusation that it was an institution for the rich, but this very allegation was used to prevent placing at its disposal the funds necessary to create a system of scholarships that would have mitigated the charge.[95] This was an insoluble dilemma so long as the masses remained disdainful of education as an end in itself and so long as higher education was unnecessary to professional and vocational advancement.

The centers of aristocratic culture were far more generous in fostering higher education than were the regions in which popular democracy enjoyed a more unqualified reign. Thus such leading institutions as Harvard, the University of Virginia, and South Carolina were fostered by local aristocracies; and just as mercantile Boston sponsored a more liberal institution than the relatively democratic province of Connecticut, so the planters whose culture centered at Charleston produced a more liberal college than the more democratic states of Georgia and North Carolina. Likewise, as Howard Beale has pointed out in his *History of Freedom of*

[94] Wayland, *Thoughts on the Present Collegiate System,* p. 40; cf. pp. 92–93. Wayland compared this with the respectful evaluation of university distinctions in England. *Ibid.,* pp. 38–40. Not everywhere, however, did this dislike of academic rank win out. Many colleges kept it, and in elementary schools it persisted into the 1900s.

[95] See the excellent discussion in Coulter, *College Life in the Old South,* Chap. IX. For the popular hostility to the state institutions, see also pp. 130, 221–30. Cf. Daniel Walker Hollis, *University of South Carolina,* Vol. I: *South Carolina College* (Columbia, S.C., 1951), pp. 5, 6, 130; Foerster, "The State University in the Old South," pp. 61–62, 210 ff.; Kemp Battle, *History of the University of North Carolina, 1789–1868* (Raleigh, N.C., 1907), I, 132, 138, 142, 146–49, 332, ff.; Gobbel, *Church-State Relationships in Education . . . since 1776,* pp. 37n., 55.

Teaching in American Schools, Jeffersonian democracy (which was aristocratic in its leadership) was "anti-theological and liberal," while Jacksonian democracy, which was profoundly popular, was "pious and intolerant." [96] None of this should be taken to imply that those who stood in the democratic tradition were invariably hostile to freedom in higher education, while aristocrats were invariably tolerant. What does seem true is that the most enlightened aristocracies had a considerably better record than the most militantly democratic communities.

The principle had not been generally accepted on either side of the political fence—had not even been vigorously formulated and fought for by those most concerned—that the politics of a college president or professor ought to be considered irrelevant to his competence. To appoint a prominent professor or president whose politics were outspokenly opposed to the dominant politics of his own trustees was a rare thing and one that did not make for an easy tenure. To appoint one whose views, however congenial or acceptable to trustees, challenged those of the community, was to subject an entire institution to sniping. [97] It was a refreshing thing when the Jeffersonian trustees of South Carolina College elected a New Englander and a strong Federalist like Jonathan Maxcy to the presidency of that institution in 1804, and it was something of a landmark in American educational history when trustee Wade Hampton, urged to vote for a politically more congenial officer, retorted, "I know of no necessary connection between politics and literature." [98] The implications of this remark, made by a man considered to be perhaps the richest planter of his time, go as far beyond Jefferson as Jefferson himself would have gone beyond his predecessors. Hampton was expressing a rare attitude, but one still rarer where the populistic spirit was stronger.

The classic case in which the denominational spirit and popular level-

---

[96] Howard K. Beale, *A History of Freedom of Teaching in American Schools* (New York, 1941), p. 87; see Chap. III of that work for a discussion of the impact of evangelicalism and democracy on freedom.

[97] Foerster, "The State University in the Old South," Chap. VII, discusses in detail the relation of the political views of presidents and professors to the development of their institutions.

[98] *Ibid.*, p. 395; cf. Hollis, *South Carolina College*, p. 34. Foerster ("The State University in the Old South," pp. 104 ff.) concludes that the liberal attitude taken toward South Carolina College was attributable to the South Carolina aristocracy and its domination of the state legislature. North Carolina Federalists, however, were less tolerant. David Ker, the first presiding professor at Chapel Hill, felt it prudent to resign in 1796 because his religious liberalism and his Republicanism had made him unpopular. Battle, *University of North Carolina*, pp. 66, 100–101.

ing combined to destroy the work of a liberal educator may be found in the experience of Horace Holley at Transylvania University in Lexington, Kentucky.[99] Early Kentucky was, of course, largely under the influence of Virginians. The intellectual and political inheritance of the liberal Kentucky leadership was that of the Jeffersonians. Religious indifference was widespread among all classes in the state at the close of the eighteenth century, but indifference or skepticism was particularly common among the educated upper classes, who were known to have in their libraries works by such writers as Paine, Hume, Godwin, Condorcet, Voltaire, Rousseau, Volney, and Erasmus Darwin. The battle for the control of education in Kentucky in the early nineteenth century took the form of a fight between this liberal gentry and the Presbyterian clergy. Even before the establishment of Transylvania University in 1799, a seminary that preceded it had see-sawed between the control of the Presbyterians, who had been instrumental in founding it, and the liberals.[100] By 1805 the Presbyterians seemed to have gained control of the institution, but they lost ground in the state during the period of the War of 1812, partly because many prominent Presbyterians opposed the war in a region in which it was pre-eminently popular, and partly because their pretensions to power alarmed other denominations. Having only a small proportion of the state's total population, they were confronted with a serious problem in diplomacy, and the effects they were able to achieve in the educational sphere are a remarkable commentary on their cohesiveness and power. At the close of the war the liberals, inspired by a growing sense of the need for professional men educated at home and desirous of building a local institution to compensate for the economic decline of Lexington, made a concerted effort to recapture and revive the university, which had vegetated under Presbyterian domination. In 1817, by exerting legislative pressure, they forced the trustees to elect Horace Holley as president after a vigorous campaign to oust his predecessor.

At the time of his election Holley, the offspring of a well-to-do Con-

[99] The following account is based very closely on Niels H. Sonne's excellent study, *Liberal Kentucky, 1780–1828* (New York, 1939). See also Thomas D. Clark, *A History of Kentucky* (New York, 1937), and F. Garvin Davenport, *Ante-Bellum Kentucky* (Oxford, Ohio, 1943).

[100] An English-born Unitarian preacher, Harry Toulmin, armed with recommendations from Jefferson and Madison, had been chosen to preside over this institution in 1794, and had been impelled to resign by the hostility of Federalists and Presbyterians. A professor at the university had also been forced to resign by the pressure of opinion among liberal students. Sonne, *Liberal Kentucky,* Chap. II.

necticut family and a graduate of Timothy Dwight's Yale, was the minister of the Unitarian South End Church in Boston and a member of Harvard's Board of Overseers. He was also a convinced Federalist—a fact which did not disturb his Jeffersonian sponsors in Kentucky, as they were seeking, above all, a promising educator who was free of the limitations of provincial religion.

An able preacher, a man of the world, and a man of versatile mind, Holley brought to Lexington the precise qualities needed for the promotion of an institution of learning. "I aim," he promised, "to be liberal without indifference, moderate without coldness, rational without skepticism, evangelical without fanaticism, simple without crudeness, natural without licentiousness, and pious without the spirit of exclusion or intolerance." [101] Within a few years he took an institution which the trustees had reduced to a condition in which the entire course was offered in one year and fashioned it into a small but valuable university with an arts college, a creditable law school, and a medical college that was rapidly acquiring fame. The teaching staff included such men as Constantine Rafinesque, Judge Jesse Bledsoe, and the celebrated Dr. Daniel Drake. A traveler passing through Lexington in 1819 commented with approval on the fact that Transylvania's professors were "chosen purely for their talents, without an requirement of unanimity of religious opinion. . . . eminently calculated for their respective positions. . . . This institution promises to be in the moral world what the sun is in the natural world." [102] By 1823 Transylvania had achieved a national reputation and was drawing students from fourteen states.

When Holley arrived at Transylvania he was greeted cordially by members of all denominations except the Presbyterians, to whom no Unitarian would have been acceptable. The greeting accorded him was abundant testimony to the importance that was attached, quite realistically, to the leadership of a distinguished educator. Holley's very ability to fulfill the expectations of those who hoped to build a cultural center at Lexington increased the opposition of the Presbyterian clergy. Having begun to snipe at him even before his arrival, they continued to make intermittent criticisms throughout his early years there. In 1823 they opened a concerted campaign of criticism through pamphlets and the press, the goal of which was to discredit his work in the eyes of the public. Although they themselves were a tiny part of the state's total population, the Pres-

[101] Sonne, *Liberal Kentucky*, p. 168. [102] *Ibid.*, pp. 171–72.

byterians argued that since Holley was a member of a minority sect the popular will was being ignored at Transylvania. Thus they skillfully transmuted the issue from one of choice between a nonsectarian state university and a sectarian one to an issue of minority rule versus the popular majority.[103] Then they drummed up a barrage of ingenious charges against the person of Holley. He held Sunday parties, at which music was played. He encouraged students to study on the Sabbath. Because he had said that education might be an asset to a religious life, he was charged with having held that it was necessary to be educated to go to heaven. He was accused of denying human depravity and of asserting that the Devil is not a real personage. "Will you," asked one critic, "pay the President of a university to laugh and brow-beat your sons out of the little religion which they may possess?" [104] The graduates and the faculty rallied to Holley's defense, denied the false charges, and tried to convey a sense of Holley's distinction as a teacher and administrator,[105] but it soon became clear that the Presbyterian clergy had succeeded in making the control of the university a live political question once again by stigmatizing it as infidel and aristocratic.

On purely religious grounds the Presbyterian attack was formidable enough, but it was much heightened by current economic discontents. A depression, followed by a sharp political conflict over banking and currency policies, had split Kentucky between a conservative party and the party of debtors. Transylvania University was doubly affected: its income was sharply cut at the same time that criticisms of its "aristocratic" bias were heightened by social conflicts. It was forced to raise tuition at the very moment when the cries were loudest that it favored the rich. Holley's

[103] *Ibid.*, pp. 197–99. The early historians of Transylvania noted that the Presbyterians, "numbering but six tenths of one per cent of our [Kentucky] population in 1820, or being about one in every hundred and sixty, exerted a greater influence than all the other religious denominations on our educational institutions." Robert and Johanna Peter, *Transylvania University* (Louisville, 1896), p. 127n. The affiliated members of all sects, as recorded in the estimates, amounted to only a fraction of the state's population. Presbyterians were, however, outnumbered at least ten to one by Baptists and Methodists. See Robert H. Bishop, *An Outline of the History of the Church in the State of Kentucky* (Lexington, 1824), pp. 306–7.

[104] *Ibid.*, p. 205.

[105] The faculty proposed a scheme, designed to mollify the denominations, according to which the pastors of the Methodist, Presbyterian, Episcopalian, Baptist, and Roman Catholic churches should share in rotation the task of preaching in the college chapel. This plan was accepted by the trustees and endorsed by members of seven religious denominations, including the Presbyterian, but the intransigence of a few Presbyterian ministers and an indiscretion of Holley's blocked it. *Ibid.*, pp. 232–34.

past allegiance to Federalism was recalled, and he was charged with living luxuriously. The Jacksonian newspaper, the *Argus,* turned on the university, and finally the popular politician, Governor Joseph Desha of the Relief Party, attacked it as a hotbed of aristocracy that had ceased "to unite the confidence and affections of the people," and urged that more money be spent instead on the common schools. Actually there is more than a suspicion that the attack was motivated by the desire of many politicians to secure the accumulated literary fund, ordinarily earmarked for the university, for the construction of turnpikes.[106] Holley resigned in 1827, and before long the institution went into a decline from which it never recovered.[107] Thus the attempt to transplant into the hinterland the idea of the secular state university broke upon the rocks of popular hostility and the *odium theologicum.*

Sectarian considerations were less important and the democratic impulse considerably more so in the ousting of Henry P. Tappan from the presidency of the University of Michigan in 1863. Tappan was one of the outstanding educators in the country and one of the most advanced educational theorists. But he made no friends among the other denominations by his attendance at the Presbyterian church, while he lost the support of the Presbyterians themselves for not being a notably good churchman. He also offended the growing temperance movement by serving wine. But the dominant charge against him, the one that brought upon him attacks by the *Detroit Free Press* that were echoed by the Democratic press of Michigan, was the charge that he was "aristocratic," Eastern, foreign, and Prussian, that he espoused "the follies of a rotten aristocracy over the sea." His interest in adapting the Prussian university system to the State of Michigan, his affecting the title of Chancellor, his Eastern birth and accent, his cultivated manners, counted against him in many quarters and after a long press campaign brought into office a Board of Regents thoroughly hostile to him. In spite of his remarkable services he was unceremoniously ousted.[108]

[106] Thomas D. Clark, *A History of Kentucky,* pp. 315–16.
[107] For its subsequent history see James F. Hopkins, *The University of Kentucky* (Lexington, Ky., 1951), pp. 33–43.
[108] See Charles M. Perry, *Henry Philip Tappan* (Ann Arbor, 1933), pp. 195–211, Chaps. XII, XIII; for a full review by Tappan of his own connection with and achievements at the University of Michigan, see University of Michigan, *Regents Proceedings, 1837–1864* (Ann Arbor, 1915), pp. 1119–66. For a balanced comment on the situation, see Andrew D. White, *Autobiography,* I, 278–81. Cf. Wilfred Shaw, *The University of Michigan* (New York, 1920), pp. 45–55.

It is extremely doubtful that popular democracy was any more inclined than sectarian zeal to pay respect to the independence of the academic man or the academic institution. The case of Francis Bowen at Harvard in 1851 is evidence of the impatience of the popular side with an outspoken ultraconservative. Bowen, who was editor of the *North American Review* and who was destined to be one of the most able and productive academic scholars of his time, was chosen in 1850 by the Corporation to be McLean Professor of Ancient and Modern History. He had already taught for a term when his nomination came before the Overseers for confirmation. There it struck a snag. For two reasons Bowen was unpopular among the coalition of Democrats and Free-Soilers that had recently come into power: he had defended Daniel Webster's famous Seventh of March speech in favor of the Compromise of 1850, and he had attacked Louis Kossuth and the cause of Hungarian independence. Now at this time Harvard was under criticism in Massachusetts for all those reasons for which a good university might expect to suffer at the hands of an anti-intellectualistic democracy.[109] The Calvinists still disliked it for its religious liberalism, the Democrats for its Federalist-Whig traditions, the reformers for its alleged indifference to such issues as slavery (in spite of the fact that several of its professors were active Free-Soilers), and the popular editorialists because it was "aristocratic" and offered a rounded liberal education instead of courses that would help young men to become better farmers or merchants.[110]

Bowen, in defending the most unpopular act of Webster's political life, affronted one of the most profound strains of New England feeling. He was strategically far more vulnerable, however, for his sharp attack on Kossuth. At the time American jingoism had taken the form of a bumptious espousal of certain nationalist movements elsewhere, and Hungarian independence was all the rage among nationalistic Democrats. Bowen poured cold water over this enthusiasm by pointing out, in a well-documented if acidulous essay, that Hungarian independence involved the

[109] As Morison remarks, "What the New England democracy wanted in the period 1820–60, and even later, was not a liberal college, or a university, but a sectarian college, where sons would be reared in their fathers' beliefs, and obtain a Bachelor's degree in the shortest time, at the cheapest rate." *Three Centuries of Harvard,* p. 257.

[110] For the Bowen case and its background see Morison, *Three Centuries of Harvard,* pp. 286–93, and the same author's "Francis Bowen, an Early Test of Academic Freedom in Massachusetts," *Massachusetts Historical Society Proceedings,* LXV (February, 1936), 507–11.

persecution by the Magyars of millions of Slavs, Slovaks, Rumanians, and Germans. He further charged, in his characteristically cranky way, that American sympathy for the Hungarians had been drummed up by "a small *clique* of these infidel socialists, mostly refugees from Europe, who have obtained command of a few penny newspapers, and are endeavoring through their means to exercise the system of *terrorism* here which they practised on a large scale in the old world." [111] While the defense of Webster probably caused the greater animus against Bowen, his comments on Magyar independence were more easily used against him.[112] Although his professional competence was unquestioned, he was rejected by the preponderant ex-officio members of the Overseers, who were Free-Soilers and Democrats. However, the Board of Overseers was in the process of being reconstituted that very year. A legislative act of 1851 removed most of the ex-officio members, and in 1853 the new board made Bowen Alford Professor of Natural Religion, Moral Philosophy, and Civil Polity, a post in which he served until 1889. The case helped to persuade the friends of Harvard that the welfare of the university would be better served if power to elect the Overseers could be transferred from the Legislature, in whose hands it was left by the Act of 1851, to its alumni. This change was finally brought about in 1865.[113]

SLAVERY AND ABOLITION

The besetting moral problem of American political life from 1830 to the close of the Civil War, the issue which the colleges, for all their timidity, could not stay entirely clear of, was slavery. During these decades the slavery controversy caused more commotion and more proscriptions on college campuses than any other issue.

Open discussion of the slavery issue was all but impossible in the South after 1835 because that section had become almost of one mind on the subject, and it was exceedingly difficult in the North because that section

[111] [Francis Bowen], "The Rebellion of the Slavonic, Wallachian and German Hungarians against the Magyars," *North American Review*, LXXII (January, 1851), 240.

[112] "Every now and then," said Bowen, "a good-natured friend in the country sends me a copy of the *Worcester Spy*, or some other rural sheet, in which I am called a 'Russian Serf,' a 'college professor of despotism,' a 'hired slave of the Boston aristocracy,' or some other pleasant and high-sounding designation." Morison, "Francis Bowen," p. 509.

[113] Edward C. Elliott and M. M. Chambers, *Charters and Basic Laws of Selected American Universities and Colleges* (New York, 1934), pp. 218–21.

was so bitterly divided between friends, sympathizers, and descendants of the Southerners on one side and reformers stemming from the Puritan or evangelical traditions on the other. As a result, while there were many colleges so committed to proslavery views that nothing but a whole-hearted defense of slavery would be tolerated, and a few colleges committed entirely to abolitionism or free-soil beliefs, there seem to have been very few colleges in which all ranges of opinion could be found on the faculty.[114]

Berea College in Kentucky and Illinois College in Jacksonville, Illinois, offer rare examples of schools committed to antislavery existing in predominantly hostile territory. Berea was founded in 1855 in Berea, Kentucky, as an openly abolitionist institution by the Reverend John Gregg Fee, a graduate of Lane Seminary. In 1859, when Fee was in the East raising money for the college, a somewhat garbled report of one of his speeches in which he was said to have endorsed John Brown's activities (he had actually praised Brown's spiritual consecration) caused an uprising against the members of the college, who were forced to flee across the Ohio River. Fee returned to Kentucky in 1863 and restored the college, which he served until 1901.[115] The situation of Illinois College was somewhat easier. It was established in a territory settled heavily by migrants from the South and predominantly Southern in its social complexion. However, the school's trustees as well as its faculty stemmed from the New England Congregational tradition and its immediate locale, Jacksonville, was a New England outpost. Its faculty was always outspokenly antislavery, despite the fact that this attitude cost the college a great deal in both students and benefactions and stirred many press attacks in Illinois and Missouri. Although some members of the faculty were probably inspired to tone down their antislavery enthusiasm by concern for the position of the college, at least one was active in the underground

---

[114] Even Harvard, which had several organizers of the Free Soil party on its faculty, dropped Karl Follen, the refugee scholar, in 1835 after the appearance of his *Address to the People of the United States* on the subject of slavery; but in the light of Harvard's liberal policy toward professors it seems clear that Follen's abolitionism was far less vital in his dismissal than his inability to get along with the strong-minded President Josiah Quincy. On this point Morison (*Three Centuries of Harvard*, p. 254) is at odds with Kuno Francke's sketch of Follen in the *Dictionary of American Biography*. See also George W. Spindler, *Karl Follen* (Chicago, 1917); Eliza Cabot Follen, *The Works of Charles Follen* (Boston, 1842), I, 343 ff.

[115] On Fee see his *Autobiography* (Chicago, 1891); John A. R. Rogers, *Birth of Berea College* (Philadelphia, 1903), and Edwin R. Embree, "A Kentucky Crusader," *American Mercury*, Vol. XXIV (September, 1931).

railway system; and at one point the college refused to take disciplinary action against students who were involved in "stealing" Negroes from their masters.[116] That this college survived and even exerted a certain unmeasurable influence on the antislavery movement throughout Illinois was a testament to the determination of its trustees and faculty and an illustration of the possibilities of institutional resistance to community pressure. But to persist at all took courage. One of the faculty members received an anonymous letter warning that Missouri freeholders were planning to kidnap or assassinate him and destroy the college. "I would not consent," wrote President Julian Monson Sturtevant in 1844, "to suffer what I have suffered on that subject in the last seven years, and am still suffering, for any other consideration than the most imperious sense of duty." [117]

In the South the border states, notably Kentucky, showed the largest hospitality to dissent on the slavery issue, especially in the mountainous area, where slavery was unpopular. At Centre College in Danville President John C. Young, a Northerner by birth, wrote a pamphlet in 1836 advocating gradual emancipation, introduced a clause in the proposed state constitution of 1849–50 providing gradual emancipation, and twice emancipated groups of his own slaves. Perhaps because he was a slaveowner and a moderate who resisted the claims of extreme abolitionists, Young continued to preside, in spite of these deviations, over a successful institution, which was prospering at the time of his death in 1857. The more radical James G. Birney and another abolitionist professor, however, were dropped from the same institution.[118] Another Northern-born president, Howard Malcolm of Georgetown College in Kentucky, felt compelled to resign by the criticism aroused by his voting for an emancipation candidate to a constitutional convention.[119] In Tennessee a slaveowning professor, Nathan Greene of Cumberland University, managed as late as 1858 to express an old-fashioned Jeffersonian opposition to slavery without calling for immediate abolition. A professor of law with a distinguished career as a jurist, he was a widely respected figure, and was not removed from his post despite attacks in the press.[120]

[116] Rammelkamp, *Illinois College,* Chap. V; see the same author's "Illinois College and the Anti-Slavery Movement," *Transactions of the Illinois State Historical Society for the Year 1908* (Springfield, Ill., 1909), pp. 192–203.

[117] Rammelkamp, "Illinois College and the Anti-Slavery Movement," p. 202. Cf. J. M. Sturtevant, *An Autobiography* (New York, 1896), Chap. XV.

[118] Clement Eaton, *Freedom of Thought in the Old South* (Durham, N.C., 1940), p. 201; article on John Clarke Young in the *Dictionary of American Biography.*

[119] Eaton, *Freedom of Thought in the Old South,* p. 202.   [120] *Ibid.,* p. 207.

Up to about 1830 it was still possible to criticize the slave system in the South. The inheritance of the Jeffersonian generation, which had thought of slavery as an evil that must in good time somehow be eliminated, was still faintly alive, although the cotton empire had already reached such dimensions as to make it clear to a realistic observer that such an immense vested interest could not be unseated without social upheaval. During the 1830s, with the growth of the abolition movement and the increasing defensive commitment of the cotton-growing South to slavery, the mind of the South rapidly closed. The entire intellectual energies of the section, so far as public matters were concerned, were given to the moral justification of slavery and its defense in the political arena. Intellectual and spiritual considerations that interfered with this defense had somehow to be shoved out of view. Intolerance and repression with widespread ramifications in almost every area of thought developed on the base of the proslavery argument.[121] It was the tragedy of the South that while the blacks were enslaved by the whites, the whites were enslaved by slavery.

Such little glimmers of latitude in opinion as might be found were no more than tiny sparks glowing through the general darkness that descended upon the intellectual life of the South after 1835. As one of the University of Virginia professors wrote in a pamphlet published anonymously in Boston in 1857, "a funeral pall" had been drawn over rational discussion of the issue, anyone who held critical views, once openly expressed, now whispered them in confidence, and "No person can safely reside in the South who is suspected of liberal views on the subject of slavery." [122]

The history of Francis Lieber's residence at South Carolina College, the most liberal institution in the deeper South, offers a case in point. He had not been by any means a militant abolitionist, but even his theoretical repugnance to human bondage had to be kept under wraps to make possible his two decades in South Carolina. Lieber found himself in a dilemma: because he longed to get out of the Carolina milieu, which he found thoroughly uncongenial on several grounds, he had to avoid ap-

[121] On the fate of freedom in the old South see *ibid.*, esp. Chap. VIII, "Academic Freedom below the Potomac." An illuminating commentary on the Southern experience is that of W. J. Cash, *The Mind of the South* (New York, 1941); see also Virginius Dabney, *Liberalism in the South* (Chapel Hill, N.C., 1932), and Howard Beale, *History of Freedom of Teaching,* Chap. V.

[122] Eaton, *Freedom of Thought in the Old South,* p. 206.

pearing to some of his Northern friends as an apologist for slavery; but in Carolina his silence on the subject at a time when Southern academic men were expected to be outspoken on behalf of slavery, was taken as a sign of secret abolitionist sentiments. So the eminent Professor Lieber, who wrote big encyclopedic books on political ethics and civil liberty, remained uneasily silent about the great problem of political ethics in his own time. Even his nationalism was unpopular in the particularist environment of South Carolina, and his religious sentiments also had to be kept quiet. He was driven to emphasizing perhaps far more than he otherwise would have done the central point of agreement between his own and the Carolina philosophy—his belief in free trade. Essentially an opportunist,[123] aspiring to the presidency of the college, to which his scholarly eminence gave him a strong claim, he tempered his life and work to the prevailing winds, but when his chance finally came in 1855 he was defeated in favor of a mediocre Presbyterian professor of mathematics. Lieber resigned in anger, and although there was great protest among his friends and admirers, the trustees did not ask him to reconsider his action. He left, jobless, for New York, where in 1857 he accepted a more satisfactory professorship at Columbia College.[124]

During the 1850s the attempt to insulate the mind of the South quickened, Northern textbooks were on occasion proscribed, and the president of a Southern university might easily find himself under intense criticism for appointing a Northerner to a professorship. Chancellor F. A. P. Barnard of the University of Mississippi, a Northerner by birth who had spent more than twenty years laboring in the vineyards of Southern higher education, found himself unable to keep in step with Southern mores in 1859–60, when he accepted the testimony of a Negro slave girl who had charged assault against a student. Such testimony was not accepted in any Southern court, and for voting for the student's suspension, Barnard became vulnerable to the charge, originating in the faculty itself, that he was unsound on the slavery question. A slaveholder himself, without sympathy with any shade of antislavery sentiment, Barnard was investigated thoroughly by the Board of Trustees, who in the end pronounced their

[123] See, however, the eloquent and prophetic open letters that he planned to address to Calhoun but evidently never published. See *The Life and Letters of Francis Lieber,* Thomas Sergeant Perry, ed. (Boston, 1882), pp. 228–37, for selections, and the comments of Freidel, *Francis Lieber,* pp. 238–42.

[124] For Lieber's position at South Carolina see Freidel, *Francis Lieber,* esp. Chaps. VII, X, XI, XII, and Hollis, *South Carolina College,* Chap. X.

confidence in his ability, integrity, and fitness for his position "increased rather than diminished." [125]

Probably the most celebrated academic-freedom case arising out of the slavery issue was that of Professor Benjamin Sherwood Hedrick at the University of North Carolina. The prevailing level of Southern responses in the mid-fifties is illustrated by this case. Hedrick was a native of the state and had been educated at the university; but he came from a social class that commonly had reservations about slavery as the base of the aristocracy, and he had spent some time at Harvard. Following tradition, the young professor of chemistry had been a Democrat, but in 1856, when the Republican party first offered a national ticket, rumors got about that he favored it. The *North Carolina Standard,* a local Democratic paper of much influence, declared that the nascent Republican party was a subversive organization, "incompatible with our honor and safety as a people." [126] An outcry was directed against Hedrick, to which his only answer was a statement of his Jeffersonian reasons for opposing the extension of slavery and his support of Fremont, the Republican candidate. He denied that his students would be subjected to free-soil indoctrination. His candid statement of his ideas, however, aggravated the outcry against him. The faculty repudiated his views, the students burned him in effigy, and the press throughout the state demanded his resignation. Refusing to resign, he was soon dismissed by the trustees. The sole member of the faculty who had supported him, the subsequently famous scholar Henry Harrisse, also became unpopular among the faculty and left not long after because of disciplinary controversies.[127] The supreme irony in the Hedrick case was that there was no Fremont ticket in North Carolina, and the professor's support of him was purely a matter of sentiment.

No doubt there were very few native Southerners in academic posts in 1856 who would have cared to challenge the South's peculiar institution

---

[125] Fulton, *F. A. P. Barnard,* pp. 246–51.

[126] James G. de Roulhac Hamilton, "Benjamin Sherwood Hedrick," *James B. Sprunt Historical Publications,* Vol. X, No. 1 (1910), p. 8. This work provides a documentary history of the case.

[127] On Harrisse see Henry Vignaud, *Henry Harrisse* (Paris, 1912). "You may eliminate all suspicious men from your institutions of learning," Harrisse proclaimed at this time, ". . . . but as long as people study, and read, and think among you, the absurdity of your system will be discovered and there will always be found some courageous intelligence to protest against your hateful tyranny. Close your schools, suppress learning and thought, you have nothing else to do in order to be faithful to your principles, and it is the only means which remains to you of continuing the struggle with some chances of success." Eaton, *Freedom of Thought in the Old South,* p. 205.

or the mores connected with it. They would have sworn that to be unable with impunity to espouse "lunatic" notions like Hedrick's was no real deprivation of liberty.[128] They had, in short, subjective freedom on this issue. But there is no condition more dangerous to a community than subjective freedom of this kind without objective freedom. By the 1850s the South had lost its ability to take realistic stock of social issues. While the absence of freedom in its halls of learning was only one of the symptoms of this loss, it was a token of a severe general intellectual paralysis. The cost to the South, to the nation at large, from the incapacity of Southern leadership to take a more liberal and rational view of the immense problems arising out of slavery and the sectional conflict, was tremendous. The history of the ante-bellum South is a cogent illustration of the principle that the maintenance of intellectual freedom is not of concern to the intellectual classes alone, but is of central importance to all members of the community.

In the North the situation was better but far from ideal. Northern society was too pluralistic to be unified around one ideal and one code of thought on the slavery question. In many Northern institutions a philosophical exploration of the moral aspects of slavery appears to have been allowed so long as it did not lead to agitation. Northerners distinguished sharply between those who condemned slavery abstractly on moral grounds or proposed gradual or ultimate emancipation, and the "immediatist" abolitionists of the more radical school who engaged in politics outside the classroom. The latter were on occasion silenced,[129] although the tendency seems to have been toward a larger measure of freedom during the 1840s and after, when antislavery sentiment grew in strength, gained a modest amount of support from the respectable classes, and proved itself to be a political force to reckon with. Although a student abolitionist society was suppressed by the faculty of Amherst in the early 1830s, such organizations generally survived without difficulty in the colleges of the Northeast.[130] In the Northwest, where the streams of New

---

[128] Cf. the *Raleigh Register:* ". . . the Professor evinced more zeal than judgment on the subject, and . . . the Lunatic Asylum might become a fit receptacle for all such characters, if, upon examination, they should be found to be monomaniacs on the subject of the Presidency." Hamilton, "Benjamin Sherwood Hedrick," p. 34.

[129] For instance, a professor was discharged from the University of Michigan because he endorsed the "higher law" doctrine. Shaw, *The University of Michigan,* pp. 41–42; University of Michigan, *Regents Proceedings, 1837–1864,* p. 502.

[130] A brief general account of Northern college controversies may be found in Russel B. Nye, *Fettered Freedom: Civil Liberties and the Slavery Controversy, 1830–1860* (East Lansing, Mich., 1949), pp. 85–93.

England and Southern culture mingled, there were sharper controversies.[131] On those campuses where trustees as well as faculty members were of some variety of abolitionist persuasion, colleges could survive community pressures and a large measure of freedom of utterance and action was protected, although the preference of most colleges was for complete silence on the subject. Such institutions as Illinois College, Franklin College and Oberlin College in Ohio, and New York College were open centers of abolitionism. In a few cases, discriminations were actually practiced against men who were anti-abolitionist. At Franklin College President Joseph Smith lost his post because he was not an abolitionist, and Judge Edward Greely Loring was dismissed from a lectureship in Harvard Law School because in his capacity as a federal judge he had enforced the fugitive slave law in a famous case. In the midst of the tensions of the Civil War, President Nathan Lord of Dartmouth, who had long been an ardent and crusty defender of slavery as a divine institution, was driven to resign because, as the local Congregationalists put it, widespread criticism had aroused "a popular prejudice against [the college] arising from the publication and use of some of his peculiar views touching public affairs." [132]

In sum, while a number of Northern colleges were in a sense "aboli-

---

[131] For such controversies, in addition to the works cited by Nye and Beale, see Robert S. Fletcher, *A History of Oberlin College* (Oberlin, Ohio, 1943), Vol. I; Wilbur Greeley Burroughs, "Oberlin's Part in the Slavery Conflict," *Ohio Archeological and Historical Society Publications*, XX (1911), 269–334; Frederick Clayton Waite, *Western Reserve University: The Hudson Era* (Cleveland, 1943), pp. 94–103; Sydney Strong, "The Exodus of Students from Lane Seminary to Oberlin in 1834," *Papers of the Ohio Church History Society*, IV (1893), 1–16; James H. Rodabaugh, "Miami University, Calvinism, and the Anti-Slavery Movement," *Ohio State Archeological and Historical Quarterly*, XLVIII (January, 1939), 66–73; Charles H. Rammelkamp, "The Reverberations of the Slavery Conflict in a Pioneer College," *Mississippi Valley Historical Review*, XIV (March, 1928), 447–61; Shaw, *The University of Michigan*, pp. 41–42; University of Michigan, *Regents Proceedings, 1837–1864*, p. 502.

[132] Leon B. Richardson, *A History of Dartmouth College* (Hanover, N.H., 1932), II, 510, see also pp. 511–12. Although the trustees of Dartmouth had neglected to act upon the suggestion that Lord be removed, they had in effect censured him by dissociating themselves and the faculty from his views. He abandoned his office without hesitation, but not without a vigorous protest against the right of the trustees "to impose any religious, ethical or political test upon any member of their own body or any member of the College Faculty, beyond what is recognized by the Charter of the Institution or express Statutes or stipulations conformed to that instrument. . . . For my opinions and my expressions of opinion on such subjects [as Biblical ethics] I hold myself responsible only to God, and the constitutional tribunals of my country, inasmuch as they are not touched by the Charter of the College or any express Statutes or stipulations."

tionist colleges" and thus contributed much to the moral agitation over slavery, the academic culture of the Northern states did not make a striking contribution to a rational discussion and sober exchange of views on the possible solutions of the slavery question. In part this was a product of their traditional curricular practices and their neglect of advanced sociological inquiry. But in greater part it must be attributed to the absence of sufficient freedom and detachment. The Northern colleges were on the whole much freer than those of the South so far as this issue is concerned. But for the most part Northern academic freedom on the slavery issue seems not to have gone much beyond the possibility that a professor might discuss the moral question of slavery in an abstract way; or that a determined board of trustees and faculty could sustain an abolitionist school in a friendly, or at times even an unfriendly, social atmosphere. No doubt it was better to live in a society with both abolitionist and nonabolitionist colleges than in one in which only anti-abolitionist colleges were possible, and in this sense the North had the advantage. But to have institutions dedicated not merely to ideological and moral agitation but to research, discussion, and inquiry, in which faculty members were free to follow their minds to such ends as the search for truth would take them—to have, in short, institutions capable of making some contribution to the analysis and solution of the issues—this was a state of academic development that not even the North was able to achieve.

This is not to say that academic freedom on the slavery issue would in itself have educated a generation of leaders capable of avoiding secession and war, but simply that the state of the colleges was symptomatic of a more general state of mind that ultimately led to disaster. The suppression of academic discussion was a token of a more general and more important suppression of thought and criticism that in the end took the entire subject out of the sphere of discussion and into the realm of force. The breakup of the American union and the resort to war is perhaps the best instance in our history of the principle that societies that imagine themselves unable to meet the costs of free discussion are likely to be presented with a much more exorbitant bill.

THE IDEA OF ACADEMIC FREEDOM

The modern idea of academic freedom has been profoundly affected by the professional character of the scholar, by the research function and scientific conceptions of the search for truth, and by the manifold services, aside from teaching students, that are rendered to the community by the great university. These things were largely absent from the American colleges of the pre-Civil War era. The academic man was only beginning to be really professional. The university as it exists today, or as it then existed in Germany, had not yet appeared except in a very few places, and even in those on a very small scale. The intellectual life of the colleges was not profoundly affected by the sciences until the Darwinian era. And finally, the organic relation between university and community that so often gives the modern educator a talking point in appealing for funds or defending free inquiry was only vaguely foreshadowed by the time of the Civil War, for the early colleges had no more than a modest relation to the professional life of the country and hardly any relation at all to its science, technology, business, or agriculture.

This does not mean that an ideal of academic freedom was altogether lacking among educators and laymen of the ante-bellum period, or that there were no widely accepted sanctions that could be invoked. Indeed, the first major history of an American university, Josiah Quincy's history of Harvard, published in 1840, closed with an eloquent appeal for educational freedom.[133] The conceptions of religious toleration and religious liberty which had been so vigorously fought for during the seventeenth century and so widely accepted during the age of the Enlightenment, although weakened as a consequence of the Protestant Counter Reformation, were still ideals widely accepted in America. The English tradition of civil liberty, quickened in America by the Revolution and embodied in the Bill of Rights, was also a factor relevant in a broad way to academic life. The constitutions of the states, as well as the charters of the colleges, bore testimony to this dual inheritance of religious and civil freedom.

Of course neither civil liberty nor religious liberty is identical with academic freedom. Both of these are more inclusive rights than academic freedom, for they affect the lives of all citizens directly; academic freedom is an immediate concern chiefly of the teacher in his professional capacity. However, both of these more inclusive rights are at points broadly analogous to academic freedom, and together they pro-

[133] Quincy, *History of Harvard*, II, 444–46. See also Quincy's *Speech . . . before the Board of Overseers . . . February 6, 1845* (Boston, 1845). For a stirring appeal for intellectual freedom against "ecclesiastical prescription," see Henry P. Tappan, *University Education* (New York, 1851), pp. 36–43.

vided the historical matrix of the concept of academic liberties. Long before college presidents and professors used the phrase "academic freedom" they were invoking the spirit of tolerance, the right of conscience, freedom of speech or the press, the clauses in college charters against religious discrimination.

For the most part, the concept of academic freedom as it is usually expressed today had not received a clear formulation in the ante-bellum period. The usual strategy for the college president or professor who was subject to pressure because of his acknowledged opinions was to appeal to sanctions that had received their clearest expression in the fields of religion or politics. Most commonly it was religion. In fact academic freedom first appeared in the guise of religious liberty for professors. There was a rough analogy between the interdenominational college and the political state in which official religion had been disestablished, just as there was between the more easy-going denominational colleges and the state which had a religious establishment but practiced toleration. So long as most colleges had a denominational affiliation, it was all but impossible for any educator to assert with success his *right* to be judged on his competence alone without regard to his religious opinions; but he might manage to persuade many men that it would be *expedient* not to stand too firmly on doctrinal grounds. Most often this expedience consisted in the political or economic necessity to conciliate opposing sects; occasionally it involved the welfare of the educational institution. Where, however, an institution was to be formally free of denominational commitments, as with the state universities, a formidable case might be made on the grounds of constitutional rights alone. And where trustees were deeply concerned to develop an institution of real university stature, the consideration of institutional welfare alone could become an asset to emergent academic freedom. Where men of great talents were urgently wanted, their religious convictions would be overlooked.

The stage to which the idea of academic freedom had developed in the ante-bellum period may be analyzed by reference to two celebrated cases, the Cooper case at the College of South Carolina and the Gibbs case at Columbia. In the first of these, the most articulate and advanced rationale for academic freedom to be expressed by any American in that period was formulated by a college president in the face of community pressure and was sustained by the trustees. In the second, the victim himself was altogether silent; but the relationship of religious freedom to university development was given mature and impressive consideration by minority members of the Board of Trustees, whose views were destined, in the not too distant future, to become the predominant ones.

South Carolina College, at the time Thomas Cooper took over its presidency in 1820, was one of the best colleges in the United States. Cooper himself was one of the most distinguished men in American academic life.[134] Born in England in 1759 and educated at University College, Oxford, Cooper had come in 1794 to the United States, where he practiced law and medicine and engaged in polemics on behalf of the emerging Jeffersonian party. In many ways his life had been dedicated to the principle of freedom of discussion,[135] and he went to South Carolina with the history and temperament of an inveterate controversialist. He had been ineligible to take a degree at Oxford because of his unwillingness to sign the Thirty-nine Articles. He had left England because he felt that the reaction that followed the French Revolution was disastrous for freedom of expression, and had turned away from France itself because he was disgusted with the Revolutionary Terror. He thus came to America, which he considered a haven of freedom, as a self-exiled refugee. In 1800 he had been convicted in a celebrated case for violation of the Sedition Law—the result of his attacks on the Federalists—for which he had been fined and sentenced to six months in prison. Afterwards he served for seven years as a state judge in Pennsylvania, an office which came to him as a reward for his services to Republicanism and from which he was removed on charges of arbitrary conduct. Tired of politics, and alienated from the popular democracy to which he had long been devoted, Cooper turned to teaching and taught briefly at both Dickinson College and the University of Pennsylvania. Through Jefferson's friendship and patronage he had been elected to the faculty of the University of Virginia, but the Presbyterians made it impossible for him to occupy the position, and he went instead to South Carolina. Cooper had so often been at the center of some controversy in which freedom of expression was central that his choice as a professor, and im-

[134] For Cooper's life and relations with South Carolina College see Dumas Malone, *The Public Life of Thomas Cooper* (New Haven, 1926), and Hollis, *South Carolina College,* Chaps. V and VI.

[135] See for instance his essay, "The Right of Free Discussion," appended to the second and third editions of his *Lectures on the Elements of Political Economy* (Columbia, S.C., 1829 and London, 1831).

mediately afterward as president, was testimony to the spirit of liberalism in which the college at Columbia was then conducted.

In philosophy Cooper was a materialist, in religion a Deist, in church politics a militant anticleric, in civil politics a conservative and a patriotic South Carolina separatist. He defended slavery, taught a laissez-faire political economy that accorded with the interests of the South Carolina planters, espoused nullification in the famous constitutional controversy, and in general made himself so congenial to the ruling class of the state, which cared more about cotton than it did about the Trinity, that his religious views were long tolerated. Given a free hand by friendly trustees, he served the college well. "He enriched the curriculum, raised the entrance requirements and the academic standards, retained a competent faculty, handled disciplinary problems adequately, and enjoyed the continued financial support of the legislature." [136]

As a consequence of his outspoken opposition to Calvinism and his sharp attacks on the Presbyterian clergy, Cooper was under criticism from the beginning of his administration. As early as 1822 he triumphantly survived an investigation of the college. By 1830–31, however, the president, now past seventy, was more vulnerable than in his earlier years. To his clerical enemies were now added the forces of the South Carolina unionists, who resented his support of nullification. He had recently published two anonymous pamphlets, one of which attacked the principle of a hired clergy and the other the essential doctrines of Calvinism. In 1831 he published his translation of François J. V. Broussais' book on insanity, *De l'Irritation et de la folie* (1828), in which Cooper proclaimed his confidence in the triumph of materialism and even asserted that materialism was the doctrine of Christ and His apostles. The new provocations precipitated a pamphlet war which ended in one of the most important academic freedom cases of the period. The details of this case, which has been more than once carefully studied and retold, need not detain us here, but Cooper's self-defense deserves special attention as the most elaborate justification of academic freedom in the ante-bellum period.

The pamphlet war led to a movement in the legislature to unseat Cooper on the grounds that he had assailed the religious views of a large portion of the people and thus damaged the college, that he had interfered with the religious opinions of the students, taught them doctrines

---

[136] Hollis, *South Carolina College*, p. 97.

offensive to parents and guardians, and had sneered at the observance of the Sabbath, at public prayers, and at certain religious sects. A few of these charges, especially those bearing on his teaching, Cooper denied, but his essential argument was that the charges, being based upon his religious views, dealt with matters of which the legislature could not constitutionally take cognizance. Thus the greater part of Cooper's argument was a legal one. His chief sanction was a provision of the state constitution guaranteeing "the freedom of the press, and the freedom of religious belief and profession without discrimination or preference." [137]

Considerably more interesting to the modern student of academic freedom than Cooper's strictly legal argument are some of his broader historical observations linking academic freedom to religious freedom and freedom of the press, and some more specific observations bearing on the professional needs of the teacher. In the attempt to remove him Cooper thought he saw "a continuation of the warfare that has taken place from the very earliest period of letters to the present day." The friends of truth had always tried "to open wide the doors of free inquiry," knowing no other way to arrive at truth but through fair and free discussion, while there had always been civil and ecclesiastical rulers opposed to such freedom who had tried to curtail it by invoking positive law against heresy and sedition.[138] Cooper saw in the Constitution of the United States the first successful attempt to break down this coalition against freedom, and remarked that he had come here believing it a settled matter in the United States that "actions only and not opinions, were the proper objects of legal control." [139] Having had to wage one fight for freedom of the press against the Sedition Law, Cooper found himself now waging another against the power of the clergy. His opponents, he believed, wanted to interdict freedom of the press and discussion of all matters bearing on clerical interests, to es-

[137] *The Case of Thomas Cooper. . . . Submitted to the Legislature and the People of South Carolina, December 1831* (Columbia, S.C., 1831), p. 3. Elsewhere Cooper pointed out the inconsistency of withholding rights within the college that were supposed to prevail elsewhere in the state. "So, I may profess what I please in South-Carolina, but not in the South-Carolina College! Where is it laid down that the boundaries of South-Carolina do not include the College?" *Dr. Cooper's Defense before the Board of Trustees* (Columbia, S.C., 1832), p. 15. The logic of this argument is an excellent illustration of the influence of civil and religious freedom on the development of academic freedom.

[138] *The Case of Thomas Cooper,* Preface, pp. iii–iv.

[139] Cooper was mistaken on this point. The matter has not yet been settled.

tablish the right of the legislature to interfere in religious matters, to establish a religious test for the president of the college, and to broaden clerical influence in politics.[140] In truth neither the legislature nor the trustees, as its agents, had any right to inquire into the religious beliefs of any officers of the college. Not only did the constitution and their oaths forbid them, but the "interminable disputes and sectarian manouvrings" which such investigations would bring, not to speak of the hypocrisy that it would encourage among candidates for college offices, "ought to restrain them for attempting to do so." [141]

But, it had been argued, the unpopularity of the president's opinions had been doing harm to the college. What if they be so unpopular that many people would refuse to send their sons? To this Cooper gave an answer that went far beyond the usual legal considerations and anticipated in many ways modern sanctions for academic freedom. In part his case was purely factual: he was able to show that despite unfavorable economic conditions the reputation of the college had risen, and attendance had gone up.[142] But he also countered the charge by reference to other principles whose validity was borne out by the history of many denominational colleges and state institutions. The college was not a theological seminary. "Students are sent here to acquire useful knowledge, not sectarian theology." No religious denomination of students could be excluded. If a member of some particular sect were to be president, the prejudices of the other denominations might as easily be aroused against him as against a man committed to no denomination. If prejudice were rampant enough, it could thus harm the college under any president. In fact the good repute of the president as a scholar was more valuable to the development of the institution than any matters bearing on his opinions.[143]

Probably the most strikingly modern-sounding phrases uttered by Cooper came in connection with his attempt to say what might and might not reasonably be required by the trustees (and by implication the legislature) of the teacher. They ought not, he said, go beyond

requiring that he shall treat those questions only that are connected with the subject of his lecture, and that he shall treat them fairly and impartially.

[140] *Ibid.*, pp. 2–3.   [141] *Ibid.*, p. 11.   [142] *Ibid.*, pp. 19–21.
[143] *Ibid.*, pp. 14–15. To allow college policies to be governed by those parents who would not send their sons to the institution because of the opinions of its president, Cooper argued, would be to sacrifice the college to some of the more ignorant men in the community. *Ibid.*, p. 16.

If doubts bearing on the subject are concealed and not discussed, the students will have reason to complain of injustice. The difficulties which a professor is forbidden to approach will remain on their minds, and they will depart unsatisfied with half knowledge and doubts unsolved. They have a right to expect from their professor no concealment, no shrinking from unpopular difficulties, but a full and honest investigation, without suppression or disguise.

Whatever temporary advantage may result from a timid suppression of truth, or a compliance with unreasonable dictation, it is of great consequence to the permanent reputation of this College that students shall come here with the expectation of being taught fully, impartially, and honestly, whatever they are required to learn: and that they should leave this College with the impression that they have actually been thus honestly taught: any impression that their teachers are directed or inclined to avoid difficulties, because they are unpopular, or to suppress or conceal doubts that must arise hereafter, or any timid manouvring in the mode of teaching, may serve the purpose of a narrow minded caution, but it is not fair; and therefore it does not become the reputation of this College or its professors.[144]

Here was an argument derived squarely from the internal necessities of the teaching profession itself, from the relation between teacher and student, and not from such formal externals as contracts, charters, or constitutions. While it formed but a small portion of Cooper's whole argument it represents a distinct advance in the concept of academic freedom.

Although Cooper denied many of the charges concerning his indoctrination of the students, he did acknowledge that in the teaching of geology he had refused to accept the book of Genesis, and here again he stood firmly on professional and intellectual grounds. The whole subject of Mosaic geology, he asserted, was "so intertwined with the present state of the science, and so absolutely necessary to be settled, that the consideration of it is unavoidable." To this any competent man would agree, he said. Benjamin Silliman, who disagreed with Cooper on the religious issues involved, had used the Mosaic account: were his ideas not to be examined? "The book of Genesis," said Cooper firmly, "was not composed to teach either Astronomy or Geology; nor has it been directed as a College text book for these sciences." [145] Here, where treat-

---

[144] *Ibid.*, p. 16.

[145] *Ibid.*, pp. 19, 40. The essential arguments delivered to the legislature were repeated in *Dr. Cooper's Defense before the Board of Trustees,* but occasional appeals to the nullifying sentiments of the trustees were added, as were references to other victims of persecution for opinion, including Aristides, Socrates, Jesus, Servetus, Galileo, Locke, Buffon, and others. See esp. pp. 3, 6, 7, 12–13.

ment of the subject seemed necessary in the light of the internal needs of science, he would indeed persist in raising questions bearing upon Scripture, putting professional and scientific considerations above expediency.

It is perhaps significant that the boldest and most advanced argument for academic freedom to be made in the United States during the pre-Civil War period should have been made by a man in his seventies. While Cooper was, seen from our vantage point, ahead of his times, from the standpoint of his contemporaries he was behind them. For Cooper was a figure out of the Enlightenment bringing eighteenth-century ideals of civil, religious, and intellectual liberty to the support of academic freedom in the age of the great retrogression. Cooper deserves to be remembered for the link he tried to forge between the ideals of the Enlightenment and those of the university era. But in his own day he was hardly successful. Although his trustees, commissioned by the legislature to investigate Cooper, did so with the result that he was vindicated and retained, the publicity given to his views by the case hurt the college so badly that he was forced to resign a few years later, along with his entire faculty. The charges of his clerical enemies could be met with argument, but to the drastic shrinkage in the student body that followed the case there was no answer.

If the Cooper case belonged to the old conflict between Enlightenment ideals and sectarianism, the Gibbs case, which occurred more than twenty years later, anticipated, despite its unfavorable outcome, the future victory of the university idea over sectarian limitations. Indeed the fact that Columbia, as a great university, eventually emerged from the somnolent day school for New York boys that it was at the time of Gibbs' nomination for a professorship is in good part attributable to the repercussions of the Gibbs controversy. The Gibbs case shows how well some trustees were aware, as others were soon to become, of the fatal implications of sectarian narrowness for university development. Where Dr. Cooper had battled over broad religious and ideological principles, the progressive wing of the Columbia trustees was more concerned with the practical considerations involved in making a university out of a college. In both cases sectarian bigotry was the enemy, but the arguments were different.

At the time of the Gibbs case, Columbia, then about to observe its centennial, was still a small, nonresidential college, catering annually to about 140 students, chiefly from New York City, and governed by a tradition-minded body of trustees referred to by the great diarist, George Templeton Strong, who had recently joined it, as "the Board of Incurables." [146] The case probably would never have occurred, and certainly would have been of slight importance, had it not arisen from the urgent desire of a small group of trustees, notable among them Samuel B. Ruggles, an alumnus of Yale, a New York lawyer, real estate investor, and man of affairs, to make the modest little college a real university, "a broad, comprehensive seat of learning, science, and art." [147] When Professor James Renwick's retirement from the professorship of Natural and Experimental Philosophy and Chemistry in 1853 gave the reformers an opportunity for an opening move, they nominated as Renwick's successor Wolcott Gibbs, who was then teaching at the Free Academy which later became the College of the City of New York. Gibbs was an outstanding chemist who had studied with Liebig at Giessen and with other great European chemists. He was known and recommended by the most distinguished scientists in the United States.[148] But Gibbs was also by family inheritance a Unitarian, and a fierce prejudice still existed in many quarters against members of that denomination. The Columbia Board of Trustees, which was predominantly Episcopalian and included six clergymen of three denominations, reflected this prejudice with greater zeal than did the New York community at large.[149] After much maneuvering and discussion, Gibbs was rejected by a narrow vote in favor of another, far less promising candidate, Richard McCulloh. Although the Columbia charter forbade religious tests for trustees or officers, and some anti-Gibbs trustees publicly denied that their votes against him were decided by his Unitarianism, the *in camera*

---

[146] *The Diary of George Templeton Strong,* Allan Nevins and Milton Halsey Thomas, eds. (New York, 1952), II, 37. This work is a major source on the case, esp., II, 136–76, and *passim.* See also the searching analysis by Milton Halsey Thomas, "The Gibbs Affair at Columbia in 1854," unpublished M.A. thesis (Columbia University, 1942), and Daniel G. Brinton Thompson, *Ruggles of New York* (New York, 1946), Chaps. V, VI, and X.

[147] Samuel Ruggles, *The Duty of Columbia College to the Community, and Its Right to Exclude Unitarians from Its Professorships of Physical Science. . . .* (New York, 1854), p. 17.

[148] See the letters from such men as John W. Draper, Benjamin Silliman, James D. Dana, Joseph Henry, Louis Agassiz, and others, in *Report of the Select Committee Appointed to Examine into the Affairs of Columbia College* (Albany, 1855), State of New York, Senate Document No. 67, pp. 103–25.

[149] For an analysis of the Board of Trustees see Thomas, "The Gibbs Affair," pp. 36–58.

proceedings of the meetings made it clear that his religion was the real cause of his rejection.[150]

The case became a matter of public controversy, commanding the interest not only of the alumni but the local press as well. All the secular papers except the New York *Herald* took Gibbs' side, while the alumni by an overwhelming vote resolved to condemn the "spirit which would make a particular religious belief a test of fitness for a Professorship of Physical Science" as intolerant, unjust, inconsistent with the charter and the public character of the institution, and highly injurious to its best interests.[151] The most outstanding document of the Gibbs case was a powerful pamphlet written by Ruggles and Strong and published under Ruggles' name, which argued the case for university reform and religious liberalism in terms which at a few points go beyond the conventional arguments of the period. Ruggles linked the bigotry of the anti-Gibbs trustees with the backward character of the college in a manner which shows how intimately connected in his own mind were his fight for Gibbs and his idea for the development of a metropolitan university. He argued that the trustees had a duty to the community to meet its largest educational needs, and that their failure to give New York a university was the outcome not of insufficient means, but of insufficient imagination. He compared Columbia with Göttingen—which had also been founded under King George II in another of his dominions, but which had grown to a great university during the hundred years Columbia had slept—and with Yale, which by maintaining and encouraging Day and Silliman, at an annual cost of no more than four thousand dollars, had put Columbia to shame.[152] Gibbs, Ruggles maintained, was neither an infidel nor a proselytizing Unitarian, but a highly competent scholar and teacher, whose religious views had never been intruded into his teaching at the Free Academy. He was the victim of the "composite intolerance" of the Episcopalians, Presbyterians, and Dutch Reformed members of the board who, unable to agree among themselves in matters of dogma, had nevertheless established a factitious standard of heresy simply to exclude Gibbs.[153] It had been widely argued by the

[150] See *The Diary of George Templeton Strong,* Vol. II, esp. pp. 146–47.
[151] Thomas, "The Gibbs Affair," p. 104.
[152] Ruggles, *The Duty of Columbia College to the Community,* pp. 11–13.
[153] Ruggles was himself an observing Episcopalian, as was his ally, Strong, who considered Gibbs' religious views nonsensical. The real passion of these men was not religious libertarianism, liberal though they were, but the development of a university.

opposition that since exclusion from an office is not a punishment, it was therefore not punishing a man for heresy to decide him unfit on religious grounds. "This common-place of intolerance," said Ruggles in a significant passage, "has long been abandoned. Our criminal law recognizes exclusion from office as one of the penalties of crime." And here, by such exclusion, although we no longer impose legal punishment for heresy "we do in fact punish, quite as severely—in another mode— by professional, civil, and social degradation." [154] In these remarks Ruggles pierced the obscurantism of formal reasoning to assert the realities of social life. He was concerned about the possibility that if Gibbs were formally branded as heretical he might be stigmatized every- where and driven out of professional life, and after him a whole train of Unitarians who were eminent in science, letters, and politics.[155] (While this fear was not unreasonable, Ruggles did not reckon with the healthy pluralism of American society. Gibbs in fact went on to a distinguished career at Harvard as Dean of the Lawrence Scientific School, and in 1873 was awarded an LL.D. degree at Columbia by unanimous vote of the trustees.) [156] Like Cooper, Ruggles indicated that he placed the internal and professional demands of the teacher's posi- tion above sectarian interests when he declared that even if Columbia College were an organ of the Episcopal Church, pure and simple, it would still be the duty of the trustees to pick the best man of any faith as its professor of chemistry because the principles of chemistry were irrelevant to denominational theology.[157]

The immediate results of the Gibbs controversy were not of especial importance. The college lost the potential services of one of the coun- try's outstanding scientists, to receive instead those of a vastly inferior scholar and a sadistic teacher.[158] Such bitter feelings were aroused among trustees and alumni that Columbia's centenary observations had to be set aside. An investigation by the state Senate was procured by the pro-Gibbs faction, but the committee of inquiry was forced to conclude

[154] *Ibid.,* pp. 33–34.   [155] *Ibid.,* pp. 37–39.

[156] Ironically, McCulloh, who was elected in his stead, resigned from Columbia in 1863 and took a commission in the Confederate army—an action that so enraged the same trustees who had appointed him that they denounced him as a traitor and ingrate, and voted his expulsion from the faculty.

[157] *Ibid.,* pp. 34–35. Cf. Strong: "His duties will not carry him into contact with transcendental physics. And I cannot think that talking to boys about NO_3 and CHO_2 and Fer Cy Ka has any connection (for practical purposes) with theological truck. . . ." *Diary,* II, 141.

[158] On this point see Thomas, "The Gibbs Affair," p. 132.

that while individual trustees may have violated their trust, the corporation as a whole could not be found to have violated the antidiscriminatory terms of its charter.[159]

The long-run consequences of the affair were momentous for Columbia. As Ruggles' biographer remarks, it "acted as a powerful stimulus to the trustees," [160] and all through the next quarter of a century plans, discussions, and inquiries were afoot for university development. It is hardly an exaggeration to say that Columbia University arose out of the case. The progressive trustees and alumni were invigorated, and one may hazard the conjecture, in the light of the preponderance of pro-Gibbs sentiment in the community and among the alumni, that some of the more conservative trustees were sufficiently shamed to be thrown on the defensive. The reforming trustees now began to emphasize with more success what Jefferson had long ago understood when he proposed to acquire wholesale a faculty from one of the Scottish universities for the University of Virginia: that to develop a university one must begin by winning the battle for scholars of repute and meet their terms and needs, and that these include certain prerogatives and freedoms. "All that can be done in the first instance," suggested George Templeton Strong, when plans for expansion were under consideration in 1856, "is to employ professors of great repute and ability to teach, and to invite (if necessary to *hire*) students to learn: *confiding everything, at the outset, to the control of the teachers,* finding out, by degrees, what we want, and feeling our way towards a code of rules, step by step." [161] Strong's statement on the central importance of the professors is one of the most notable of the ante-bellum period:

It seems certain that we shall effect nothing lasting or important except by and through teachers of the first order and the highest repute. They are not merely necessary to the vigor of the Institution but conditions of its existence. Whether the experiment succeed or fail depends mainly on their presence or absence. With professors of respectable mediocrity or a little above it, a College will languish, but may subsist indefinitely. But a University cannot be planted and long sustained in life without professors of splendid name and

---

[159] *Report of the Select Committee* . . . , pp. 8–12.
[160] Thompson, *Ruggles of New York,* p. 90; cf. Thomas, "The Gibbs Affair," p. 140; note also Strong's remark, in a moment of discouragement: "Another Gibbs controversy must be got up, or the College will doze off for another hundred years . . ." *Diary,* II, 376.
[161] "Statement of George T. Strong, Esq.," in *Statements, Opinions, and Testimony Taken by the Committee of Inquiry Appointed by the Trustees of Columbia College* (New York, 1857), pp. 19–20. Italics added.

ability, especially in a community where such institutions are unknown and where general mediocrity of attainment and aspiration is the obstacle to be removed and the evil to be remedied. If they be obtained, the Academic system we establish for them, even if prematurely and unwisely settled, will do little harm. They must be diligently sought, and, like founders of Universities in all ages, we shall probably be obliged to seek them beyond (as well as within) the limits of our own country and language.[162]

In a statement like this, one sees intimations of the great university developments that lay not far in the future; and in the premium Strong placed on the able professor one sees a foreshadowing of those prerogatives that had to be given to the leaders of the teaching profession before great universities could be founded. Thus the soundest educational reformers of the period—those who proposed not to chop up or debase the existing curriculum so much as to supplement it by plans for systems of more advanced study—walked hand in hand with those who had a perception of the professor's need for dignity and freedom. The time was not far in the future when a college president could proclaim to the American community what the founders of the first European universities had understood from the beginning: "Professors are sometimes spoken of as working for the college. They are the college." [163]

[162] *Ibid.*, p. 20. For comparable statements on the need for professors of such caliber see Long, *Literary Pioneers*, p. 166; Sonne, *Liberal Kentucky*, p. 145; Morison, *Three Centuries of Harvard*, pp. 326–27.

[163] President Paul Ansel Chadbourne in his inaugural address at Williams College, 1873. Spring, *History of Williams College*, p. 234.